Florian Cord
J.G. Ballard's Politics

Buchreihe der ANGLIA/
ANGLIA Book Series

Edited by
Lucia Kornexl, Ursula Lenker, Martin Middeke,
Gabriele Rippl, Hubert Zapf

Advisory Board
Laurel Brinton, Philip Durkin, Olga Fischer, Susan Irvine,
Andrew James Johnston, Christopher A. Jones, Terttu Nevalainen,
Derek Attridge, Elisabeth Bronfen, Ursula K. Heise, Verena Lobsien,
Laura Marcus, J. Hillis Miller, Martin Puchner

Volume 54

Florian Cord

J.G. Ballard's Politics

Late Capitalism, Power,
and the Pataphysics of Resistance

DE GRUYTER

For an overview of all books published in this series, please see
http://www.degruyter.com/view/serial/36292

Zugl.: Würzburg, Univ., Diss., 2014

ISBN 978-3-11-063523-2
e-ISBN (PDF) 978-3-11-049071-8
e-ISBN (EPUB) 978-3-11-048830-2
ISSN 0340-5435

Library of Congress Cataloging-in-Publication Data
A CIP catalog record for this book has been applied for at the Library of Congress.

Bibliografische Information der Deutschen Nationalbibliothek
Die Deutsche Nationalbibliothek verzeichnet diese Publikation in der Deutschen Nationalbibliografie; detaillierte bibliografische Daten sind im Internet über http://dnb.dnb.de abrufbar.

© 2018 Walter de Gruyter GmbH, Berlin/Boston
This volume is text- and page-identical with the hardback published in 2017.
Druck und Bindung: CPI books GmbH, Leck

♾ Printed on acid-free paper
Printed in Germany

www.degruyter.com

Acknowledgements

I would like to sincerely thank Ralph Pordzik for supervising my dissertation. I am very grateful for his continuous enthusiasm, encouragement and support, his advice and criticism, and the countless stimulating conversations we have had over the years. One could not wish for a more inspiring teacher.

Special thanks are also due to Gerold Sedlmayr for his support and for many valuable discussions. Furthermore, I would like to thank Stephan Kohl for providing me with the opportunity to pursue my academic interests and for his unceasing support.

In addition, I am grateful to Jansen Harris for his thorough proof-reading and his helpful comments, as well as to Elke Demant, Pascal Fischer, Beatrix Hesse, Sabrina Hüttner, Daniel Schulze, and Angela Sedlmaier, with whom I have had the privilege of working during the past few years.

Finally, many thanks are due to my family, above all to my parents Heike and Uwe Niedlich, who have always encouraged and believed in me, and to Anna, for her love, constant support and understanding. Without them, this study would not have been possible.

Contents

Abbreviations —— IX

1 Introduction: Catastrophic Strategies —— 1

2 Celebration of Wounds: Excess, the Body, and Symbolic Exchange in *Crash* —— 18
2.1 Dystopian Vistas —— 20
2.2 Roads of Excess —— 33
2.3 Anarchic Bodies, or, Breughel and Bosch on the Freeway —— 42
2.4 Symbolic Violence —— 65

3 Becoming-Grass: De- and Reterritorialization in *Concrete Island* —— 81
3.1 Deterritorialization —— 82
3.2 Reterritorialization —— 101

4 Escaping the Subject: The Ballardian Theme of Abdication —— 108
4.1 Siding with the Object —— 111
4.2 Inverted Crusoes —— 114
4.3 Embrace the Fugues! —— 121

5 The Psychopath as Saint: *Cocaine Nights*, *Super-Cannes* and the Politics of Transgression after the End of History —— 134
5.1 The Violence of the Global and the Boredom of Paradise —— 136
5.2 The Spectral Reign of Global Capital —— 161

6 In Pursuit of the 21st Century: The Revolutionary Imagination and the Spectacle of Terrorism in *Millennium People* —— 193
6.1 Escaping the Soft-Regime Prison —— 195
6.2 Subversion, No End of Subversion – Only Not for Us —— 203
6.3 The Will to Spectacle —— 218

7 Conclusion: New Weapons —— 235

Works Cited —— 239

Index —— 257

Abbreviations

AE	*The Atrocity Exhibition*. 1970. London: Harper Perennial, 2006.
C	*Crash*. 1973. London: Harper Perennial, 2008.
CI	*Concrete Island*. 1974. London: Harper Perennial, 2008.
CN	*Cocaine Nights*. 1996. London: Harper Perennial, 2006.
CS1	*The Complete Short Stories*. Volume 1. 2001. London: Fourth Estate, 2011.
CS2	*The Complete Short Stories*. Volume 2. 2001. London: Harper Perennial, 2006.
CW	*The Crystal World*. 1966. London: Harper Perennial, 2008.
D	*The Drought*. 1965. London: Harper Perennial, 2008.
DW	*The Drowned World*. 1962. London: Harper Perennial, 2008.
KC	*Kingdom Come*. 2006. London: Harper Perennial, 2007.
KW	*The Kindness of Women*. 1991. London: Harper Perennial, 2008.
ML	*Miracles of Life: Shanghai to Shepperton. An Autobiography*. London: Harper Perennial, 2008.
MP	*Millennium People*. 2003. London: Harper Perennial, 2008.
RW	*Running Wild*. 1988. New York: Farrar, Straus and Giroux, 1998.
SC	*Super-Cannes*. 2000. London: Harper Perennial, 2006.
UD	*The Unlimited Dream Company*. 1979. London: Harper Perennial, 2008.

1 Introduction: Catastrophic Strategies

> Can we fight DNA?
> *Jean Baudrillard*

Without a doubt, J.G. Ballard must be considered one of the most important writers of the 20th and early 21st century, whose influence has always extended well beyond the sphere of literature and continues to make itself felt after his death in 2009. His substantial oeuvre has been praised by numerous leading contemporary authors, among them William Burroughs, Graham Greene, Kingsley and Martin Amis, Anthony Burgess, Angela Carter and William Boyd, as well as by key cultural theorists such as Jean Baudrillard, Fredric Jameson and Susan Sontag, and has been acknowledged as a source of inspiration by artists across the cultural landscape. Ballard's impact is distinguishable, for instance, in the work of writers like Will Self, Iain Sinclair and China Miéville, in the films of David Cronenberg, Michael Haneke, David Lynch and Brad Anderson,[1] the artwork of Damien Hirst, Tacita Dean or Dominique Gonzalez-Foerster, in the architectural imagination of Nigel Coates, Rem Koolhaas and Nic Clear, as well as in the work of a wide range of musicians and bands, most notably those associated with the Post-Punk and New Wave scenes of the late 70s and 80s such as Joy Division, The Comsat Angels, Cabaret Voltaire, Gary Numan and The Normal (Reynolds 2006), though connections can also be drawn to bands like Radiohead, Manic Street Preachers, Burial, Kode9, Klaxons and Django Django.[2] As Jeannette Baxter and Rowland Wymer point out, Ballard's unique imagination possesses an extraordinary "capacity to initiate a dialogue with other imaginations, creating a shared dream (or nightmare) universe" (2012: 2), a universe for which the *Collins English Dictionary* has introduced the term 'Ballardian'. The acceptance of this adjective into the English language certainly is a sure sign of the enduring significance of the English writer's work.

---

[1] Of course, Ballard's *Empire of the Sun*, *Crash*, *The Atrocity Exhibition* and, most recently, *High-Rise* have themselves been filmed (by Steven Spielberg in 1987, David Cronenberg in 1996, Jonathan Weiss in 2000 and Ben Wheatley in 2015 respectively) and a filmic adaptation of *Concrete Island* has been being planned for some time.
[2] Many of these lines of influence were first traced in an article published in the *Guardian* (Bradshaw et al. 2009). On Ballard's influence on pop music, cf. Sellars 2007; Dowling 2009; Myers 2009.

DOI 10.1515/9783110490718-001

This significance is also attested to by the respectable and, it seems, steadily growing[3] academic interest in Ballard's oeuvre.[4] The numerous essays and the handful of books devoted to his work investigate a wide variety of different aspects, many pieces of criticism reading his texts in the context of science fiction, utopian, dystopian, and apocalyptic traditions and discussing Ballard's idiosyncratic contribution to or re-working of these traditions.[5] Of the book-length studies, Gregory Stephenson's 1991 monograph *Out of the Night and Into the Dream: A Thematic Study of the Fiction of J. G. Ballard* combines elements of New Critical methodology and archetypal criticism in order to explore the themes of illusion and transcendence in Ballard's work, which he finds manifest in the content as well as in recurring motifs and imagery of the texts. Roger Luckhurst's *'The Angle Between Two Walls': The Fiction of J. G. Ballard* (1997) expertly explores how, especially generically, Ballard's writings time and again unsettle binary oppositions and received classifications, effectively inhabiting the place of the Derridean 'hinge' (*la brisure*) and thus both occupying and at the same time displacing established literary categories. Jeannette Baxter's instructive study *J. G. Ballard's Surrealist Imagination: Spectacular Authorship*, published in 2009, traces the visual as well as literary Surrealist contents, contexts and intertexts of Ballard's work and in this way establishes him as a radical Surrealist historiographer, who challenges official narratives of post-war history by accessing the historical unconscious and recovering suppressed or neglected realities. The most recent monograph, Samuel Francis' *The Psychological Fictions of J. G. Bal-*

---

[3] The last few years alone have seen the publication of two monographs (Baxter 2009; Francis 2011), two collections of essays (Baxter 2008; Baxter and Wymer 2012), one biography (Baxter 2011), and an edited volume of interviews (Sellars and O'Hara 2012). Another monograph, *The Empires of J. G. Ballard: An Imagined Geography* (2015) by David Ian Paddy, which addresses the theme of nation and empire in Ballard's work, was published when this study was already being prepared for publication and could thus unfortunately not further be taken into account.
[4] This interest has so far been centered in – though by no means restricted to – the UK. It is curious that especially English studies in Germany – the context from which the present volume emerges – have up to now paid very little attention to Ballard's texts. To my knowledge, apart from two essays dedicated to *Crash* (Pordzik 1999; Kutzbach 2007), to date no studies of Ballard's work have been produced in Germany. Astonishingly, in Ewald Standop and Edgar Mertner's *Englische Literaturgeschichte* (1992), one of the standard references for any German scholar of English literature, Ballard does not find mention at all, and similarly, in Hans Ulrich Seeber's edited book of the same title, another standard work, Ballard was only included in the most recent, fifth edition, published in 2012, and still appears only on the margins, solely under the aspect of 'ecology', and, in fact, as 'J.W. Ballard' (2012: 492). One goal of my study is also to remedy this neglect by hopefully fostering an increased interest in Ballard's fiction.
[5] Cf. e.g. Wagar 1982: 81–85, 194–205, 1991; Platzner 1983; Brigg 1985; Pordzik 1999; Sellars 2000.

lard (2011), focuses on the psychological dimension of Ballard's writing by investigating its pronounced concern with matters of the human mind and its creative dialogue with various psychological theories and discourses, above all with Freudian psychoanalysis. Along with the two introductory books by Michel Delville (1998) and Andrzej Gasiorek (2005), which lack a thematic focus, but of which especially the latter constitutes an extremely valuable response to Ballard's writing, these monographs, examining different facets of the Ballardian oeuvre, have all contributed to a better understanding of its complexities. However, what is still crucially lacking is a study of Ballard's *politics*. For Ballard is not only a science fiction writer, not only – and just to some extent, I would argue, thus dampening Stephenson's claim – a writer of transcendence and mysticism, not only a writer of the space of the between, and a Surrealist writer, but also, and fundamentally, a *political* writer.

For some time, critics – mainly of a Marxist orientation – have tended to see Ballard as a non-political, decadent, defeatist or quietist author, whose work, in one way or another, ultimately signals a passive acceptance of the status quo (cf. Fitting 1979; Franklin 1979; Finkelstein 1987). Stephenson, too, has asserted the a-political nature of Ballard's writing, though he recasts it in a more positive light. Ballard's work, he declares, "represents a sustained act of subversion", but "subversion of an ultimate character, directed against nothing so trivial as the governmental or economic systems"; instead, the central concern of Ballard's art lies "with the problem of exceeding or escaping the limitations of the material world, the space-time continuum, the body, the senses and ordinary ego consciousness, all of which are seen as illusory in nature" (1991: 1). Luckily, more recent analyses such as those of Luckhurst, Gasiorek and Baxter, to name only the most comprehensive ones, have rectified this distorted image and made it clear that Ballard's fiction is far more complex and ambivalent than such readings allow. In fact, as this study intends to show, the 'trivial' matter, as Stephenson absurdly puts it, of political resistance is of utmost importance to it.

The newer discussions of Ballard's oeuvre thus sharpen our awareness not just for its political dimension generally, but also for its resistant character, that is, the fact that, like that of Ballard's great hero Burroughs, it constitutes "an unmatched critique of the nature of modern society and the control and communication systems that shape our view of the world" (Ballard 1996e: 132). Yet, since the main thematic focus of these studies always lies elsewhere, this theme surfaces only occasionally and on the margins. A comprehensive analysis of the (subversive) politics of Ballard's work has not yet been conducted. Only Baxter's monograph explicitly politicizes Ballard, yet explores politics solely as a dimension of his Surrealism, which is the principal interest of her study. Thus, Baxter's focus is, overall, a very different one from mine, which also comes to different conclusions. On the whole, I do not see Ballard's work as determined "to recover that which the postmodern condition blocks – subjectivity, reality, time, memory and history" (Baxter 2009: 11). As I will argue, such a recovery is not an option anymore in Ballard's work.

I would claim that rather than as non-political or quietist, Ballard's writing should be considered as an unwavering exploration of the 'post-' or 'trans-political' (cf. e.g. Baudrillard 2008: 45 ff). When, in an interview, Ballard states: "I write out of what I feel to be a sense of great urgency and commitment. I'm certainly not a political writer, but I feel a great sense of urgency" (in Burns and Sugnet 1981: 19), it seems to me that it is precisely this shift from time-honored 'politics' to something else that is at stake. This new arrangement is a concern Ballard shares with numerous contemporary theorists. It is surely no coincidence that – again mostly by critics of Marxist persuasion – similar charges of political resignation and quietism as were directed against Ballard were also levelled against these theorists. Thus, for instance, Jürgen Habermas has famously spoken of a new generation of "young conservatives" (1993: 103) (explicitly mentioning Georges Bataille, Michel Foucault and Jacques Derrida) who, in his opinion, have effectively abandoned the emancipatory ideals of modernity, and likeminded critics such as Alex Callinicos (1989), Christopher Norris (1990) and Terry Eagleton have similarly lamented what they see as the essentially conservative tendencies of poststructuralist and/or postmodernist thinkers' "libertarian pessimism", which, they maintain, "rule[s] out the possibility of radical political programmes of an ambitious kind" and is hence "coupled with a political quietism or reformism" (Eagleton 2004: 51, 1991: 40 f, 40). The thought and writing of Ballard and the theorists criticized in this manner are a product of and reaction to the same cultural-socio-economic moment, one that can be broadly defined as the 'postmodern condition'.[6] As we will see, Ballard's work constitutes a sustained investigation of the postmodern,[7] examining it specifically as an expression of what Ernest Mandel (1999) has described as 'late capitalism', the third

---

[6] Particularly with thinkers such as Jean Baudrillard and Paul Virilio Ballard also shares a certain "apocalyptic and baroque" (Baudrillard 1994a: 111) imagery and rhetoric.

[7] It is only appropriate that Ballard's brilliant introduction to *Crash*, a short but dense reflection on postmodernity, has by now been included in the postmodernism section of a reader on European literature from Romanticism to the present (Travers 2001). It should be noted, though, that Ballard himself has repeatedly explicitly distanced himself from postmodernism (cf. e.g. 1991, in Di Filippo 1991: 71, in Frick 2012: 190 f). Needless to say, these comments do not, however, constitute evidence against readings that construe his fiction as postmodernist or that find postmodernist elements in it, and even less against an approach such as my own, which is more concerned with the relation of Ballard's work to *postmodernity* than to *postmodernism*. For an instructive discussion of Ballard and postmodernism, cf. Luckhurst 1997.

and, in fact, 'purest' stage in the evolution of capital. Ballard's literary career, from its beginning, with the publication of his first short story in 1956, during the 'golden age' of capitalism (cf. Hobsbawm 1996: 225–402), to its end in 2008, the year of the global financial crisis, unfolded contemporaneously with late capitalism and can be read as a continuous and developing meditation on it. At the heart of this meditation lies the question of resistance.

Not unlike the work of influential cultural theorists such as Fredric Jameson (1991) and David Harvey (1990), Ballard's fiction persistently maps the manifold (cultural, social, mental, emotional, spatial, etc.) transformations the new functional system entails. In doing so, it draws the picture of an airless world marked by an unprecedented expansion of capital, which ends up, in Jameson's words, "colonizing those very precapitalist enclaves (Nature and the Unconscious) which offered extraterritorial and Archimedean footholds for critical effectivity" (1991: 49). This system, in other words, has no 'outside' anymore. Its ever finer 'micro-physical' circuits of power pervade the entire social field and fully penetrate even the individual itself. Consistent with poststructuralist theories of 'subjectivation', Ballard portrays the subject as a social construction, whose formation takes place in a complex network of discourses and mechanisms of power that incessantly code and recode its mind and body. Beyond this, Ballard's work consistently implies what Baudrillard has described as the 'structural' revolution of the law of value, which "simultaneously puts an end to the regimes of production, political economy, representation and signs"; "[w]ith the code", Baudrillard avers, "all this collapses into simulation" (1993b: 8). As we will see, Ballard's texts time and again evoke this postmodern 'hyperreality', in which the 'reality principle' is cancelled, 'simulacra' of a new kind proliferate vertiginously and signs as well as money float freely, both value/the market and sign/communication having been wholly deregulated. Ballard's world thus emerges as one in which modernity's 'grand narratives' (Lyotard 1984) and central categories have been completely invalidated.

It seems to me that it is all these factors that account for the absence of 'politics' in his oeuvre. Certainly, critics have a point when they claim that "[p]raxis does not figure in Ballard's writing", that "[p]olitics is sidelined in Ballard's texts because it is seen to have little purchase on the economic, technological and social circuits that incessantly decode and recode twentieth-century life" (Gasiorek 2005: 206). However, such observations are correct only insofar as we understand the term 'politics' in its conventional conception. And it is precisely this conception that postmodernity has cancelled out. Class struggle, contradiction and opposition (dialectics), revolutionary movements, ideological critique, projects to 'liberate' use-value, the unconscious, and so on – these things indeed do not figure in Ballard's works. Yet, this omission – and this is what critics like

Bruce Franklin and Peter Fitting fail to see – does not signal Ballard's alleged political quietism, but his realization of the fundamental *ineffectiveness of received forms of resistance* in the age of late capitalism. This conviction also transpires in several interviews. For instance, Ballard argues that whereas in the past, the cultural and political events of the day "were all part of one *whole* – sort of *graspable* in a way", this is coming to an end in our "much more fragmented" time and surmises that "probably nobody will ever again be fully engaged with a sort of *central experience*" (in Vale 2012: 163), a statement that resonates with Jameson's observation that the subject under late capitalism lacks a 'cognitive map' or representation of that totality which is the ensemble of society's structures and of its own positioning in it (1991: 45–54). Elsewhere, in an interview conducted in 1983, Ballard explicitly contends that "[t]he world economic systems are so interlocked that no radical, revolutionary change can be born anymore, as it was in the past", an assertion he reaffirmed over 20 years later, when, in another interview, he declared that "social and political change of a radical kind are now virtually impossible" (in Revell 1984b: 52, in Baxter 2004: 33). As I will show, Ballard's fiction can be read as being predicated on this belief in the total exhaustion of established modes of political action.

A very similar belief fueled the work of many poststructuralist and/or postmodernist thinkers, for whom particularly the events of May 1968 in France represented a decisive moment of *dis-illusionment*, understood in both senses of the term: as frustration and despair, but also as an elimination of all illusions these intellectuals may still have held regarding the nature of power. As Peter Starr (1995) and others have pointed out, (French) critical theory in the wake of May '68 became unmistakably based on a 'logic of failed revolt'. In the face of late capitalism's apparently inexhaustible recuperative power – "[t]hat which is excluded completes, that which perturbs stabilizes, that which attacks reinforces[;] [...] [i]n the fully developed capitalist system, crisis is a state of normalcy" (qtd. in Starr 1995: 33), Régis Debray observed – resistance had to be fundamentally reconceived. Thus, Michel Foucault declared: "We are perhaps living the end of politics. For it's true that politics is a field which was opened by the existence of the revolution, and if the question of revolution can no longer be raised in these terms, then politics risks disappearing." (1996i: 223) This dilemma of the radical intelligentsia was, of course, further exacerbated by its increasing disenchantment with socialism, a process set into motion in 1956 by Nikita Khrushchev's 'secret speech' at the twentieth party congress of the Communist Party of the Soviet Union and by the invasion of Hungary and intensifying especially in the 1970s in response to the crisis of Mao Zedong's succession, the Khmer Rouge genocide, etc. In 1977, Foucault explained:

there is no longer anywhere a single point from which the light of hope shines. There is no longer an orientation. [...] I would say that we have returned to the year 1830, that is, we must start over again. Anyway, 1830 had the French Revolution and the whole European tradition of the Enlightenment behind it. We must begin from the beginning and ask ourselves, Starting from what is it possible to engage in a critique of our society in a situation where the thing we have implicitly and explicitly relied on for support to make this critique, namely, the important tradition of socialism, has been placed fundamentally in question (1994: 397f, trans. in Ransom 1997: 201fn6).

Faced with the uselessness of all the old revolutionary weapons and ideals, many of the 'children of May', as Sylvère Lotringer has called them, "revolutionaries bereft of a revolution", "resolved to sleep with the enemy", that is, "turned to capitalism, eager to extract its subversive energy they no longer found in traditional class struggles" (2007: 11), or saw "no alternative to the present form of rule except a blind anarchic other" and hence partook in what the Marxist philosophers Michael Hardt and Antonio Negri have – disapprovingly – termed "a mysticism of the limit" (2001: 387). To some extent, Ballard's engagement with the question of resistance revolves around similar responses.

A particular closeness can be ascertained between Ballard and Baudrillard. As Michel Delville notes, the latter's writings in fact "often appear as a theoretical counterpart to Ballard's fictional world" (1998: 2). This kinship has, to some degree, of course been acknowledged by both authors and been commented on by several critics. Yet, these commentaries rarely do more than observe and explicate the striking affinity between Baudrillard's notion of 'hyperreality' and the central role of mediation, simulacra and simulation in Ballard's fiction.[8] However, as will become evident in the chapters that follow, the correspondence between the two writers extends far beyond this and is particularly pronounced in relation to the political.

Perhaps more than any of his contemporaries, Baudrillard extensively concerned himself with the postmodern crisis of critique and resistance. Lotringer has rightly pointed out that the French philosopher "didn't disagree with them on the nature of the beast [i.e. capitalism], only on the extent of the damage" (2007: 11). As we will see, something similar could be said with regards to Ballard's texts, which also seem to concur in respect to the unrivalled power of the system, but which present different strategies of subversion and consequent-

---

[8] A notable exception is the essay by Bradley Butterfield (1999), whose reconsideration of the 'Baudrillard-Ballard connection' intersects with my own approach in numerous ways. Above all, he, too, emphasizes the a-moral and essentially pataphysical (though Butterfield does not use the term) nature of Ballard's fiction and indicates its political dimension.

ly do not create a coherent image of the 'extent of the damage'. This being said, their vision is, nevertheless, closest to Baudrillard's.

Similar to his fellow theorists, Baudrillard sees all the received forms of political critique and action as "outdated weapons" and urges us to discard all "liberal nostalgia" (1993b: 3, 2008: 61) we may still harbor. According to him, only a radically new perspective will be able to fathom and respond to the changed realities. What is needed is a fundamental transformation of theory that would reproduce the transformation of the system and hence yield a theoretical outlook that would be its equal. Baudrillard declares: "Since the world is on a delusional course, we must adopt a delusional standpoint towards the world." (1993c: 1) Thus, following the enemy, theory, too, "is moving into the hyperspace of simulation [...], a process whereby it loses all 'objective' validity but gains substantially in real affinity with the present system" (Baudrillard 1994f: 2f). "If the intellectuals of today seem to have run out of things to say", Baudrillard maintains, "this is because they have failed to assume this ironic function, confining themselves within the limits of their moral, political or philosophical consciousness despite the fact that the rules have changed, that [...] all radical criticism now belongs exclusively to the haphazard, the viral, the catastrophic" (1993c: 44). It was Alfred Jarry's proto-Surrealist anti-philosophy of 'pataphysics' – "*the science of imaginary solutions*" (Jarry 1996: 22) – that was to provide Baudrillard with a model for the kind of delusional stance he was calling for. He contends that postmodern reality, exceeding all limits, "corresponds to the pataphysical sphere" and that consequently, "[t]he only strategy against the hyperrealist system is some form of pataphysics" (2005: 45, 1993b: 4). Christian Bök has described pataphysics as "a philosophic alternative to rationalism", evoking and valorizing "cases of exceptional singularity", and as a radicalization of theory, devoted to "a spirit of permanent rebellion"; it is, he explains, a Nietzschean "'gay science,' whose joie de vivre thrives wherever the tyranny of truth has increased our esteem for the lie and wherever the tyranny of reason has increased our esteem for the mad" (2002: 3, 5, 9).

I would argue that Ballard's oeuvre embodies a very similar spirit, equally focused on the irrational, unlawful, counterintuitive and non-commonsensical. It seems to me that Ballard's oft-reiterated (by himself) comments on the changed role of the writer, whose role is no longer that of a moral arbiter but of a "scientist [...] faced with an unknown terrain", "devis[ing] various hypotheses" (*C* n.pag.), can be read in this context as well. Surely, if Ballard is to be a scientist, it can only be as a pataphysician.[9] When he describes his texts in

---

[9] In "The Assassination of John Fitzgerald Kennedy Considered as a Downhill Motor Race", one

terms of "imaginative alternatives" and "extreme metaphor[s] for an extreme situation" and as developing "a kit of desperate measures only for use in an extreme crisis" (*C* n.pag.), he distinctly echoes Baudrillard's sense of a need for new (thought) experiments, imaginary solutions and a new radicalness. And what else could the 'extreme crisis' he refers to be if not the unparalleled power of the current system and the concomitant cancellation of 'politics'? Ballard's "*extreme hypothes[e]s*" (in Revell 1984b: 42) on the one hand, Baudrillard's "radicalisation of hypotheses" (1993b: 5) on the other – both thinkers, convinced of this profound break, opt for a fundamentally different, unorthodox approach to the contemporary realities and the question of resistance.

Through this approach, new forms of resistance can be conceptualized. The pataphysical perspective yields pataphysical modes of resistance. Baudrillard asserts:

> from a certain critical density onward [...], rational behaviour no longer pays. [...] In our current situation, where we are everywhere on the verge of this critical density, if not indeed beyond it, the wise thing would be to act generally in irrational ways. Out of intolerance to the system itself. (2005: 195 f)

Today, Baudrillard proclaims, "the only strategy is *catastrophic*, and not dialectical at all" (1993b: 4). It seems to me that this very same conviction – which transpires, for instance, in Ballard's above-quoted comment on 'desperate measures' or in one of his characters' declaration that "[e]xtreme problems call for extreme solutions" (*SC* 365) – underlies the Ballardian oeuvre. The work of both Ballard as well as Baudrillard suggests that "at the same time as all dialectical resolution disappears, the extremes come to the fore", and hence emphasizes "the special status of such extreme phenomena – and of catastrophe in general" (Baudrillard 2005: 129, 1993c: 76). Ballard's fiction constitutes a veritable mapping of these extremes that materialize in response to an order from which virtually all negativity and singularity have been eliminated. Robert Scholes and Eric S. Rabkin have aptly described Ballard's writing as "a fiction of extremities" (1977: 89) – we are now in a position to recognize the reason for this centrality accorded to extreme phenomena: *their political significance*. The political perspective adopted here allows us to comprehend the catastrophe, "understood as an anomalous turn of events" (Baudrillard 1993c: 76), as a gen-

---

of the chapters or 'condensed novels' of *The Atrocity Exhibition*, Ballard explicitly makes reference to Jarry, effectively rewriting the latter's "The Crucifixion Considered as an Uphill Bicycle Race", and explains that "a less conventional view of the events of that grim day [i.e. November 22, 1963] may provide a more satisfactory explanation" (*AE* 171).

uine trans-political form of subversion. When the pataphysician Baudrillard proclaims man's (sic) "*right to catastrophe*" and asserts its quasi-anthropological relevance, he expresses an idea that similarly transpires in Ballard's oeuvre: "It is indeed your most fundamental and essential right – your right to accidents, to crime, to error, to Evil, to the worst as well as to the best – which, far more than your right to happiness, makes you a human being worthy of the name." (1993c: 99)

Catastrophe against catastrophe – this study makes use of the conceptual category of 'catastrophe' in order to show that Ballard's work can be read as developing a new discourse of resistance, one whose emergence is intimately linked with the passage towards late capitalism.[10] Borrowing Baudrillard's notion of the 'catastrophic strategy', I read the actions of Ballard's protagonists in terms of a new mode of subversion directed against a virtually all-powerful system. In doing so, I will not limit myself to a strictly Baudrillardian framework, for as was already pointed out, Ballard's texts present a variety of different forms of resistance which cannot be contained within a single theoretical schema. Instead, the notion of 'catastrophic strategies' will serve as an umbrella term and overriding concept to designate the common context and character of all these forms. The attribute 'catastrophic' is appropriate because a) its etymology (Greek, 'to overturn', 'turn against') suggests the resistant nature of these strategies and b) at the same time, it expresses their always calamitous character and implies their (individually and/or collectively) disastrous consequences (death, destruction, etc.). Through this combination of meanings, the adjective furthermore points to the trans-political horizon – the 'catastrophe' of late capitalism – in which these strategies must be located, the catastrophic form of resistance indicating its catastrophic condition – the *catastrophe of resistance*.

The extreme nature of the actions of Ballard's characters constitutes a serious challenge to readers, a challenge to which some have responded with revulsion and outright rejection, while others have believed to be able to discern in the texts a reassuring moral framework within which these actions are ultimately condemned. I believe both reactions to be wrong. Though in different ways, both basically sidestep the challenge thrown up by Ballard's writing by falling back on received ethical norms and values. Yet, it seems to me that it is precisely

---

[10] The significance of the category of 'catastrophe' as a tool to understand the present and to reconceive resistance has also been indicated by V. Vale, chronicler and explorer of counter- and subcultures, founder of RE/Search Publications and long-time champion of J.G. Ballard: "If our world seems headed toward catastrophe in every way", Vale suggests, "let us at least investigate the theories of catastrophism to see if some antidotes can be discovered or invented." (n.d.: n.pag.)

such conventional moral categories and the alleged verities of the common sense more generally that Ballard's fiction sets out to unsettle. We should take the author's repeated emphasis on the essentially a-moral nature of his fiction seriously. Again and again, Ballard has criticized the "Leavisite notion of the novel as a moral criticism of life" and "of the novelist as moral arbiter", arguing that such a notion may have belonged into "[a] world of static human values" but certainly "doesn't belong in the present world", and has suggested that in fact, "the job of the novel [...] is quite the opposite" (in Self 2006: 373, in Bresson 1982: 26) today. Evoking once again the notion of the writer as a scientist, Ballard declares: "My fiction really *is* investigative, exploratory, and comes to no moral conclusions whatever." (in Revell 1984b: 43) In this context, he has repeatedly asserted that "[t]he imagination is totally free of any moral constraints or overtones" (in Self 2006: 390), thus somewhat positioning himself in a Romantic/Surrealist tradition.[11] I would argue that Ballard's writing is deeply 'perverse', if by that we understand, following Roland Barthes and Michael Roes, the intellectual capacity to think the unthinkable, to boldly question the 'natural' and 'self-evident', and to refuse to censor one's own thought in any way (Roes 2007: 51f). As one character in *Millennium People* maintains: "We're trapped by categories, by walls that stop us from seeing around corners." (*MP* 248) Ballard's fiction demolishes these walls – 'writing with a hammer' (cf. Nietzsche 1998). In the case of Ballard's oeuvre, literature thus effectively becomes a medium for what Michel Foucault and Peter Sloterdijk would call a Nietzschean 'thinking otherwise' (*penser autrement*) or 'thinking dangerously' (*gefährliches Denken*). This thinking can only be analyzed if (conventional) morality is not falsely reintroduced into the texts.

The present study will investigate Ballard's 'dangerous' thought revolving around the notion of 'catastrophic strategies' by drawing on a wide range of concepts and ideas taken from the field of critical theory. It is the first analysis of Ballard's work that systematically examines it within the framework of this field. Of course, this methodological orientation is to some extent contingent upon my thematic focus: as was stated earlier, Ballard's writing will be read here as emerging from and reacting to the same, postmodern moment and as tackling similar questions concerning the fundamentally changed conditions of political action as numerous contemporary theorists. Thus, my study will also reveal and explore the often strikingly close affinity between Ballard's fiction and various theoretical approaches. Though never consistently investigated,

---

11 It has to be said, however, that Ballard's statements on the (a-)moral textures of his fiction are not always consistent (see below).

this affinity has, in fact, often been suggested, with critics arguing that Ballard's work "shares much in common with", "can be construed as a literary counterpart to" or even "anticipates" (Revell 1984a: 145; Delville 1998: 6; Bukatman 2005: 7) different theoretical lines of thought. And of course, Jean Baudrillard (1994a) and Fredric Jameson (1991: 154–180) have actually discussed Ballard's writing in reference to their own philosophical ideas. Some critics, for example Simon Sellars, Matteo Pasquinelli, Simon Reynolds and Steven Shaviro, have gone even further, claiming that Ballard, in fact, *was* a kind of philosopher or theorist, and one of the present's greatest ones at that. Pasquinelli, for instance, maintains that "[t]he novels of J.G. Ballard can describe the nature of technology and the contemporary mediascape better than any philosopher, media theorist or cultural studies academic" (2011: n.pag.), while Shaviro goes so far as to aver that "Ballard was a greater social theorist than Adorno, or than such contemporary sociological diagnostians of postmodernity as Bauman, Beck, Giddens, or Castells" (2009: n.pag.). Though I would not want to measure his 'greatness' in relation to that of other thinkers, I, too, see Ballard not just as an outstanding writer of fiction, but also as a brilliant theorist, whose work, in the words of Sebastian Groes, "speculates on current social and cultural trends by imaginatively projecting them into extreme situations" (2012: 123). Like philosophy for Baudrillard, literature for Ballard becomes a laboratory for pataphysical thought-experiments.

It seems to me that in the case of writers like these, the contingent boundary lines separating theory from literature are practically dissolved, a fact which I would interpret as itself a symptom of and/or reaction to the condition of postmodernity. In the age of hyperreality and in the pataphysical perspective responding to it, fact and fiction can no longer be clearly distinguished. Both Ballard and Baudrillard more or less consciously advocate this convergence of fiction and theory. Thus, the latter has frequently insisted that theory is not "in a position to 'reflect (on)' anything" anymore – a comment that echoes Ballard's observation that "the writer knows nothing any longer" (*C* n.pag.) – and hence "can only tear concepts from their critical zone of reference and force them beyond a point of no-return" (1994f: 2). It must, in other words, approach "science fiction" and turn into "theory-fiction" (Baudrillard 1993a: 82). Ballard, on the other hand, has since the 1960s persistently urged science fiction writers to abandon what he saw as the childish and irrelevant thematic and formal conventions of futuristic space fiction and to focus instead on the earth and the present (e.g. 1996t). Implementing this shift in his own work, Ballard's texts – more than most other works of literature – increasingly assumed an analytical-theoretical character, with a novel like *Crash*, for instance, occupying "an ambiguous space, somewhere between critical theory and cyberpunk sf" (Sellars 2000:

220). Particularly this latter genre, much of whose aesthetic and concerns, as Sellars points out, seems to have been anticipated or at least to be influenced by Ballard, may be considered a continuation or development of this Ballardian fiction-theory hybridity,[12] which can be seen as one of the dimensions of the 'in-betweenness' of Ballard's work analyzed by Roger Luckhurst (1997). Starting from opposite ends of the literature-philosophy spectrum, Ballard and Baudrillard meet in this 'angle between two walls' (*AE* passim), the interstitial zone in which pataphysical thought unfolds.[13]

In our exploration of this zone, we must also take into account the radically polysemic nature of Ballard's writing, which ultimately defies any attempt to produce conclusive readings of it. In the end, of course, Ballard's texts *are not* theory and hence cannot be contained within a single theoretical model. Luckhurst has argued that Ballard's work "constantly activates theoretical models", but that it is at the same time "awkward" and "overtheorized" (1997: xvii) and always escapes theoretical 'capture'. I would argue that this, and especially the impression of his fiction's 'overtheorized' nature, is largely – though by no means exclusively – due to what, extending the work of Luckhurst and Baxter, I would describe as a *clash of discourses* that characterizes virtually all of his texts. It seems to me that Ballard's works are best considered as 'sites' where numerous heterogeneous, sometimes even contradictory, discourses cross and collide, making them, in Julia Kristeva's (1986) terminology, highly 'dialogical'.[14] Because of this, every interpretation produced of them is ultimately to some extent displaced by a semantic excess that defies closure. Here, key elements (such as the crash in *Crash* or Richard Wilder's ascent of the apartment block in *High-Rise*) are coded in various different ways, events and the protagonists' behavior are overdetermined, the characters themselves frequently submit alternative readings of events, without one of them being privileged by the narrative, and so forth. In this way, diverse discourses constantly jostle with each other, activate competing meanings and invite a plurality of readings. Thus, this clash of discourses can help us account for the oft-noted paradoxical nature of Ballard's texts and for the multiplicity of different and often conflicting interpretations. In true poststructuralist fashion, the fundamental ambiguity resulting from the

---

[12] In this context, cf. also Jameson's (1991: 38) comments on the central role of cyberpunk as an attempt at 'cognitive mapping'.

[13] In this context, cf. also Brooks Landon's suggestion that it might be "fun to take almost any of the stories from Ballard's *War Fever* [...] and consider them as essays on Baudrillard" (1991: 326).

[14] In his discussion of *Crash*, Gasiorek similarly notes that "[t]wo antithetical orders of discourse meet in a head-on pile-up" (2005: 18) in the novel.

clash cannot even be contained by the author himself, as particularly Ballard's own incongruous statements about *Crash* make clear. While, on one occasion, he explains that "the ultimate role of *Crash* is cautionary", on another he denies the existence of a moral dimension in the text and designates the novel "a psychopathic hymn" (though, in yet another twist, adding that this hymn nevertheless "has a point") (*C* n.pag., in Self 2006: 372), in this way effectively making it apparent that the author is, indeed, 'dead' (Barthes 2007).

The Ballardian clash of discourses can itself be read against the background of this study's thematic focus. I would contend that the radical openness of meaning it entails[15] can significantly be linked to Jacques Derrida's (2001b) influential notion of the 'freeplay' of meaning and to Ernesto Laclau and Chantal Mouffe's (2001) adaptation of it in the field of political theory. If the social, just like language, is essentially an "infinite play of differences" and 'society' only a necessarily unstable 'hegemonization' of it, that is, a limiting of this play into a finite order, then I think the clash of discourses with its frustration of any attempt at closure can be considered as an affirmation of "the impossibility of any ultimate suture" and hence as a rejection of "the will to 'totality'" (1990: 90, 92) that Laclau, in his reformulation of the concept of 'ideology', identifies as the heart of the ideological. Against all totalizing and essentializing discourses, Ballard's work thus insists on the inevitably precarious and relative nature of meaning and social formations and on the infinitude of signification and of the social.

Of course, a discussion of Ballard's oeuvre that would in some way *not* constrain its polysemic nature is impossible (just like the fixation of meaning and the creation of order are necessary for us). The thematic orientation of this study inescapably ignores certain discourses and limits the range of meanings of Ballard's texts. Nevertheless, *within the imposed confines of this frame*, the following analyses will trace the different discourses that intersect in Ballard's works and in this way carefully explore all the complexities of the clash. In order to be able to do so, the texts will not be examined through the lens of one overriding theoretical approach, applied anew in every case, but instead each be addressed as a unique 'statement' (cf. Foucault 1972a) that must be studied in its very 'singularity' and not be forced into the homogenizing constraints of a 'master theory'. Consequently, in true postmodern spirit, this study will draw on a wide array of theoretical frameworks, some of which are not easily compat-

---

[15] This openness is certainly not as radical as in the work of highly experimental writers such as James Joyce, being somewhat diminished by the generally mimetic nature of Ballard's writing, yet I would argue that it is nevertheless distinctly present.

ible with each other. Yet, the tensions thus produced merely correspond to the tensions inherent in Ballard's work itself. Somewhat following the ideas of Michel Foucault and Gilles Deleuze (cf. Foucault 1996c), critical theory is treated here as a 'toolbox', from which different concepts and ideas are lifted in order to 'work on' Ballard's texts and 'produce' meaning. My approach is thus akin to what Gyan Prakash (2000: 133) – referring to Gayatri Chakravorty Spivak – has called a 'catachrestic' stance. It is a kind of 'interpretive *bricolage*' as described by Julie Kaomea, who declares:

> my theoretical framework and interpretive methods are intentionally eclectic, mingling, combining, and synthesizing theories and techniques from disparate disciplines and paradigms [...], moving within and between sometimes competing or seemingly incompatible interpretive perspectives and paradigms (2003: 16).

In the chapters that follow, this catachrestic approach will be used to investigate the representation of late-capitalist postmodernity, power and resistance in selected texts spanning Ballard's entire career. In the face of such an extensive oeuvre as Ballard's, selectivity is inevitable. I have chosen a spectrum of works that illustrate the range of Ballard's engagement with postmodernity and the (trans-)political and that, in my view, present the most interesting instances of his pataphysical thought experiments with what I have termed 'catastrophic strategies'. Though of course Ballard's numerous novels and short stories cannot by any means be reduced to one another, the texts under discussion in this study nevertheless arguably present the most direct, comprehensive and complex exploration of political topics and questions which can also be found in a more latent, embryonic or varied form elsewhere.

Proceeding chronologically, I begin with a detailed analysis of Ballard's best-known work *Crash* (1973). In the first step, I discuss the novel's dystopian portrayal of the alienating realities of life under late capitalism, which the text explores in relation to the transformations wrought in spheres such as space and place, 'dromology', the social, subjectivity, the body, and the media. I then argue that the protagonists' obsession with car crashes and wounds constitutes a form of resistance against these realities and go on to disclose and examine three different discourses through which it is coded. Whereas the first presents the crash as an extreme limit-experience shattering the experiential structures constructed by the dominant order, the second one links it to a 'desubjectivation' of the body and the emergence of a radically new sexuality (which, as we will see, is no 'sexuality' anymore), while the third one, finally, construes it in terms of what Baudrillard has called 'symbolic exchange' and hence clashes with the two former ones.

Chapter 3 presents a completely novel reading of Ballard's *Concrete Island* (1974), a work that has received considerably less critical attention than others. Principally using a Deleuzoguattarian theoretical framework, the chapter reads the eponymous traffic island as an emancipatory 'heterotopic' counter-site to the spaces of late capitalism, in which countless liberating 'deterritorializations' take place. These, however, are repeatedly countered by 'reterritorializations' as hegemonic discourses and ideologies tend to reassert themselves, so that the protagonist's escape to the island ultimately remains very ambivalent. The chapter carefully brings out this ambivalence, a task for which the flexible theoretical model of Gilles Deleuze and Félix Guattari is eminently suitable since it is highly sensitive to the complex relations that exist between power and its subversion.

The next chapter explores yet another facet of Ballard's pataphysics of resistance. It argues that what has often been interpreted as the death-wish, escapism, or passivity of the protagonists of certain texts actually is an expression of something else: a desire for abdication. Drawing on the work of Baudrillard, the chapter first develops this notion in terms of a wish for liberation from the constraints of socially produced identity and subjectivity. Not to be confused with postmodern conceptions of identity as protean and liquid, always to be created anew in a playful manner, abdication designates a dissolution of *subjecthood itself.* As such, it constitutes an act of subversion directed against a system that reproduces itself through specific forms of 'subjectivation'. The chapter then illustrates the concept and demonstrates its relevance through an overview-like discussion of various texts, including Ballard's first novel *The Drowned World* (1962). It is in tales of disaster like this one that the thought-experiment of abdication is acted out most clearly, and the chapter hence closes with an in-depth analysis of another catastrophe story, the so far almost completely neglected "News from the Sun" (1981). The analysis shows how, in a peculiar manner, posthumanist, Buddhist, Surrealist as well as Romantic discourses intersect in the story and code abdication in different ways.

Chapter 5 tackles the novels *Cocaine Nights* (1996) and *Super-Cannes* (2000), two texts that resemble each other in numerous ways and that are read here as addressing capitalism specifically in its *global* dimensions. The leisure and work enclaves that the novels respectively depict are realms of absolute stasis, paralysis and exhaustion. I argue that as such, they can be read as hyperbolic representations of what in philosophical discourse is frequently termed the 'end of history', that is, a state characterized by the practical disappearance of any 'other' or 'outside' to the capitalist system. Particularly *Super-Cannes*, the more multi-layered of the two narratives, focuses on the new, global structure of rule – what Michael Hardt and Antonio Negri have termed 'Empire' – which has established itself and explores the new forms of control as well as the 'biopoliticization' of the productive system that it entails. Both novels suggest that only a radical economy of transgression tied to a 'willed psychopathy' is able to overcome the acute social and psychological inertia that the end of history has bred, yet in both texts, even this catastrophic strategy ultimately fails, though for different reasons. The two novels thus end on a distinctly gloomy note, the vision of *Super-Cannes* being an especially bleak one: what initially appear to be acts of resistance here turn out to be deeply complicit with the system they purportedly attack, this making *Super-Cannes* easily the most unambiguously dystopian and pessimistic text in the Ballardian oeuvre.

My investigation into Ballardian politics concludes with an analysis of Ballard's late work *Millennium People* (2003), a text which brings the subject matter of this study once again into sharp focus. Indeed, as my reading shows, Ballard's penultimate novel is nothing but a profound inquiry into the possibilities of critical thought and dissident action in the 21st century. Unlike other critics, who have dismissed the middle-class revolt that is at the center of the narrative as inauthentic and superficial pseudo-politics, I argue that the novel's portrayal of the rebellion is, in fact, much more ambivalent and proceed to bring out its basic seriousness by analyzing its ideological thrust, its methods and goals. It will be shown that in the eventual failure of this revolution, the causes of which are closely examined here for the first time, Ballard overtly stages the futility of received modes of resistance which almost his entire oeuvre is a reaction to. Against this background, the violent terrorist attacks carried out by the character of Richard Gould are then read as a new, trans-political form of resistance which challenges power in entirely different ways. Yet, here too, the end of the novel, which the chapter analyzes in detail, casts an ambiguous light on these subversive acts, implying that even such radical practices may ultimately not match up to the ever more adaptable contemporary circuits of control. Finally, the study closes with a brief conclusion.

As the following pages will show, J.G. Ballard was not only a highly imaginative creator of intriguing fictional narratives, but at the same time also one of the most consistent mappers of our late-capitalist postmodernity, relentlessly investigating its changing realities and the pervasive, more and more protean networks of power in which all of us are caught, and a highly original explorer of the possibilities still open to us to subvert these networks. As such, his work is an invaluable contribution to both the literature and critical thought of the present.

2 Celebration of Wounds: Excess, the Body, and Symbolic Exchange in *Crash*

> Speed turns the point into a line!
> Gilles Deleuze & Félix Guattari

Crash is not only Ballard's most famous – or, according to some, most *infamous* – work, but also his most analyzed one, having provoked numerous and, in fact, often contradictory readings, not least concerning the presence or absence of a moral dimension in the text. As suggested in the introduction, this multiplicity of interpretations – including Ballard's own conflicting statements[1] – can be largely attributed to the overdetermined nature of the text, especially to what I have termed the 'clash of discourses'. It will be the goal of this chapter to extract, elucidate and analyze what are arguably the most important of the various discourses traversing the narrative. While I do not agree with those critics who discern in the novel a more or less straightforward morality manifest in what they perceive to be a decidedly negative judgment of the characters' lives, actions, etc. and who thus read the text as a quite distinct cautionary tale,[2] I also cannot fully endorse Jean Baudrillard's inverse argument of a total "resolution of all [...] critical negativity" (1994a: 119). Beyond these two poles, postulating a sweeping condemnation on the one hand and a complete absence of criticism on the other, I want to opt for a more differentiated perspective.[3] It seems to me that the novel does articulate a critique, though not a generalized and all-encompassing one, but one residing in its essentially dystopian presentation of the realities of late-capitalist postmodernity. My central thesis will be that the extreme behavior of the text's protagonists, far from being denounced, represents a radical form of

---

[1] Cf. *C* n.pag., in Bresson 1982: 24, in Revell 1984b: 43, and in Self 2006: 372.
[2] Cf. e.g. Hayles 1991; Sobchack 1991; Ruddick 1992; Pordzik 1999.
[3] More nuanced and, in my view, very insightful, readings have also been developed by Luckhurst (1997: 123 ff), Gasiorek (2005: 80–97) and Baxter (2009: 99–133), though their interpretations differ from my own reading in significant ways. Like the various critics who responded – some of them indignantly – to Baudrillard's *Crash*-essay in the journal *Science Fiction Studies* in 1991, especially Luckhurst and Baxter are intent on challenging the French philosopher's reading of the novel, but do so in what I see as a much more discerning way. Although my emphasis is a different one, I agree with these critics that Baudrillard's interpretation is a rather flattening one, since it ignores the actual complexity of Ballard's text. Yet, as I argue in this chapter, I do not think that his analysis can simply be *refuted*. Instead, it seems to me that the mentioned complexity of the narrative resides precisely in the fact that it is crisscrossed by a number of discourses – one of them being the one discussed by Baudrillard – which coexist uneasily and activate multiple, partly contradictory readings.

DOI 10.1515/9783110490718-002

2 Celebration of Wounds: Excess, the Body, and Symbolic Exchange in *Crash*

resistance – a catastrophic strategy – against these oppressive and alienating realities.[4]

This strategy is at the heart of the different discourses at work in *Crash*. As I intend to show, the novel suggests three main readings of it, not all of which are easily reconcilable with each other. The characters' crashing of cars and wounding of the body is at once presented as an 'event' in an emphatic sense,[5] that is, as something radical and transformative, connected with an absolute newness or alterity; as a means of 'desubjectivation'; and, finally, as a form of what Baudrillard has termed 'symbolic exchange'. In the first reading, two different though related discourses allow for an interpretation of the protagonists' actions as either forms of Bataillean 'expenditure' that, if only momentarily, shatter the 'discontinuous' and 'profane' existence enforced by bourgeois capitalism and reconnect the being with 'sacred continuity', or as a way to escape, equally fleetingly, from a society entirely given over to 'simulacra' and 'simulation' and marked by derealization on virtually every level through a return to the 'real' of the body. At this point, with the focus on the body, the first reading connects with the second one, which construes the incessant wounding of bodies that occurs throughout the text in terms of a desubjectivation of the body and of what Michel Foucault would call a 'desexualization' of pleasure and so of a subversion of the *dispositif* of sexuality. As will be shown, what thus emerges is a new type of subject that is 'posthuman' in all kinds of senses.

While these former discourses can roughly be labeled 'materialist', the third one I will discuss can perhaps be called 'semiotic' or 'symbolic' and hence stands in stark opposition to the other ones. This discourse is anchored in those elements of the text which suggest that crashing and wounding do not after all represent an actual break with the existing order. This is the discourse brought out and brilliantly elaborated upon by Baudrillard, according to whom the novel depicts a world in which "everything [...] is like a giant, synchronous, simulated machine" and where "[d]ysfunction is no longer possible" (1994d: 125, 1994a: 113). Yet, in contrast to this vision of an utterly airless, closed and integrated system, in which all types of radicality have lost their transgressive potential and into which, consequently, the accident, too, is fully incorporated, I still discern in the crash a form of resistance – only in this reading it is one that does not

---

4 In a gesture of self-reflexivity, let me point out that the novel's depiction of postmodernity is, in the end, not entirely unambiguous either. While, as I argue, the overall image is a dystopian one, the text repeatedly unsettles any such unequivocal presentation. Thus – though unavoidably – my reading, too, ultimately overrides the novel's radical indeterminacy to some extent.
5 Within the framework of his own philosophy, Alain Badiou (2007), for one, speaks of the event in this emphatic sense.

aspire to 'go beyond' the system in any way, seeking some kind of alternative (continuity, the real, a different economy of bodies and pleasures), but that fully remains on its terrain, attacking it with its own weapons, pushing its own logic to the extreme. This, of course, is precisely the kind of resistance Baudrillard has always championed. And indeed, in his discussion of Ballard's novel, he repeatedly refers to what are actually elements of his own theory of subversion, yet curiously fails to see the significance of this theory for an analysis of the text. Remedying this omission, I will draw on the Baudrillardian conceptualization of sacrifice, body marking, seduction, and photography in order to read the protagonists' actions as converging upon the restoration of a culture of symbolic exchange at the heart of a system that has virtually eradicated it.

Through the elaboration of these heterogeneous discourses, I hope to do justice to the dense texture of what I feel must be regarded as one of the most complex, ambiguous and fascinating English novels of the late 20th century.

2.1 Dystopian Vistas

As many of Ballard's texts do, *Crash* closely explores the idiosyncratic spatialities of late capitalism. In this, his work can be said to reflect the assertion made by numerous critics associated with the 'spatial turn' that, like time and history before, the category of 'space' needs to be denaturalized and subjected to critical investigation. More than that, reading novels such as *Crash*, *Concrete Island* and *High-Rise*, one senses a distinct affinity with the thought of Edward Soja (1989), David Harvey (1990), Fredric Jameson and others, who have argued that in contrast to modernity's preoccupation with temporality, the postmodern era is in fact dominated by spatiality, space having become "for us an existential and cultural dominant" (Jameson 1991: 365). Similar to the works of these theorists, Ballard's texts engage the "present phase of social and spatial restructuring" (Soja 1989: 183) and probe the new properties of space emerging concomitant with the more recent systemic modifications of capitalism. In line with the groundbreaking work of Henri Lefebvre (2003) and Michel Foucault (1979, 1986a) and the efforts of many sociologists and geographers since, there is a particular interest in his texts in what Soja has termed the 'socio-spatial dialectic' (1989: 76–93), meaning the ways in which society molds spaces according to its needs and – more importantly for Ballard – in which social life is in turn shaped by those spaces. As Ballard asserts in an interview: "the sort of architectural spaces we inhabit are enormously important – they are *powerful*" (in Revell 1984b: 44). Again and again, Ballard's oeuvre evinces a distinct awareness of and attentiveness to the 'politics of space', that is, the ways in which human geographies are always political and ideological, in which power relations are inscribed in and, indeed, reproduced and maintained through spatial organization, and in which space must thus be seen as a site of social and political struggle.

This also applies to *Crash*. The world of the novel, set as it is exclusively in the urban sprawl surrounding Heathrow airport – an "endless landscape of concrete and structural steel" (*C* 36) – must be read as a hyper-realist image of what Jameson has referred to as "the wholly built and constructed universe of late capitalism, from which nature has at last been effectively abolished" (1991: 121). Ballard's characters inhabit a radically mechanized and dehumanized universe, a "machine landscape" underneath a "metallized sky", filled with "metallized air" (*C* 40, 10, 59). There is, as David Pringle observes, a distinct atmosphere of claustrophobia to this world, "a continual sense of being hemmed in and enclosed by a universe of concrete" (1979: 26). In a sense, Ballard's suffocating vision of a world made of concrete – it is not for nothing that *Crash* and its two follow-ups are commonly referred to as the author's "'concrete' stories" (Pringle 1979: 26) – recalls Baudrillard's anecdote of the old cook who lived in the Ardennes and modeled everything in concrete – from furniture to an entire orchestra, trees and animals – and thus attempted to "eliminate all [the world's] organic spontaneity and replace it with a single polymorphous material: reinforced concrete" (1993b: 52). According to Baudrillard, this endeavor, though still belonging to an older order of simulacra,[6] already condenses the teleology of the later ones, including the contemporary one, in that it bears witness to the fantasy of a total and coherent system, to a "project of universal control and hegemony" over "a pacified society, cast in a synthetic substance which evades death, an indestructible artifact that will guarantee eternal power" (1993b: 52, 53). It would appear that in the claustrophobic universe of *Crash*, this project has largely become reality. Through its depiction of a fully "technological landscape" and its countless images of incessant and seamless traffic flows, "thousands of drivers sitting passively in their cars" (*C* 36, 40), the novel stages the realization of the technocratic vision of a perfect cybernetic realm of instrumentality and total control.

In fact, the text may be said to represent the contemporary as 'dromocracy'. Critics of the novel have often observed the numerous and meticulous accounts of crashes and wounds in the text (something I discuss below); what they have not noted is that there are about just as many and as detailed descriptions of the amount and direction of traffic, of motorways and access roads, of interchanges,

---

6 On Baudrillard's theory of the different orders of simulacra, see below.

slip roads and roundabouts, of over- and underpasses, flyovers and airport runways, the roads' various intersections and destinations. A veritable 'dromological' reason appears to dominate the depicted world of the text as well as the narrative voice relaying it. Coined by Paul Virilio, 'dromology', derived from the Greek word for race course (*dromos*), means both the government of movement and the study of its historical forms and transformations. According to Virilio, history, especially that of the last two hundred years, cannot be properly understood without the knowledge provided by such a 'science of speed', which demonstrates that there is not just a political economy of capital but also a "political economy of speed" and which therefore analyzes acceleration as a "major political phenomenon" and thus reveals that "speed is power" (in Armitage 2000: 35). In his materialist, military-historical rewriting of the history of modernity, the French thinker shows modernity to be profoundly, even essentially, *logistical:* "there was no 'industrial revolution,' but only a 'dromocratic revolution;' there is no democracy, only dromocracy; there is no strategy, only dromology." (2006: 69) From Virilio's perspective – one that may be read as extending the Foucauldian concept of 'biopower' (Foucault 1978: 133–159)[7] – modern governance is all about "moving-power", that is, the regulation of the circulation of people (as well as of goods, information, etc.) in order to harness and maximize their productive force and submit them to "techno-logistical oppression" (2006: 71, 164). For Virilio, power is exerted through – indeed, consists in – the organization of the mobility of the masses; it is the body-in-motion that is the principal locus for the exercise of political authority, and logistics consequently a crucial administrative horizon. According to the French theorist,

> political power [...] is only secondarily 'power organized by one class to oppress another.' More materially, *it is the polis, the police, in other words highway surveillance*, insofar as, since the dawn of the bourgeois revolution, the political discourse has been no more than a series of more or less conscious repetitions of the old communal poliorcetics, confusing social order with the control of traffic (of people, of goods), and revolution, revolt, with traffic jams, illegal parking, multiple crashes, collisions. (2006: 39)

This statement resonates powerfully with Ballard's novel, in which, on the one hand, images of uninterrupted circulation and the smooth flow of traffic abound and the characters are said to move through an "elaborately signalled landscape of traffic indicators and feeder roads", and in which on the other, "the vectors of speed, violence and aggression" (*C* 86, 33) keep on combining to produce ever more crashes. It is certainly no coincidence that one of the novel's central char-

---

7 On biopower, cf. chapter 5.

acters, Dr. Robert Vaughan, a one-time computer specialist and TV scientist now turned "nightmare angel of the expressways", used to work on "the application of computerized techniques to the control of all international traffic systems" (*C* 66, 48): here, we encounter once again the cybernetic dream of a technologically controlled and fully ordered and regulated system, on which Vaughan has now turned his back.

In a fascinating essay on the significance and the future of the car written two years before the publication of *Crash*, Ballard argues that "the future of the car will be the future of traffic" and declares that "[i]t seems inevitable that we will gradually surrender our present freedom" (1996n: 265). He predicts that "[t]raffic movements and densities will be increasingly watched and controlled by electronic devices, automatic signals and barriers" – controls, he avers, that "could even be used as an instrument of government policy" – until eventually, this "computer-controlled traffic flow" (1996n: 265) will be perfected with the elimination of the steering wheel and the introduction of the remote-controlled automobile.[8] Ballard conjures a bleak vision of "the remorseless spread of the regimented, electronic society",[9] in which traffic will be presided over by "the ever-watching computers of Central Traffic Control", whose "[i]nvisible eyes will guide [a] driver's car over every inch of his [sic] journey" (1996n: 266).

It seems to me that this essay, written at a time when Ballard was already working on *Crash* (cf. *ML* 241), explicates the implied dromological rationale governing the world of the novel. Read against this background, Vaughan and the other characters' intentional collisions may be taken to point towards an alternative, subversive use of speed, towards a political intervention in the dromocratic system's regulated circulation – on a literal as well as on a metaphorical level: the crashed car as the interruption of the smooth flows, the break in the circuit. In this context, the protagonists' suicidal commitment to *auto-destruction* can further be read as a provocation of biopower and, indeed, as an act of resistance against its pervasive mechanisms. For, as Foucault points out, once power becomes dedicated to the administration of life and to 'making life live', death turns out to be "power's limit, the moment that escapes it", and suicide hence becomes an act "at the borders and in the interstices of power" (1978: 138, 139). And is Vaughan, who "rehearse[s] his death in many crashes" (*C* 1), not heeding Foucault's declaration that "there is no conduct more beautiful, that

---

8 For a similar prediction, cf. Virilio 1997: 81f.
9 This society, anticipated in the essay and pointed towards in *Crash*, is fully developed and explored in Ballard's late novel *Super-Cannes* (cf. chapter 5 of this study).

merits more reflection with as much attention, than suicide" and that "[o]ne should work on one's suicide all one's life" (1996d: 318)?

From the dromological perspective developed here, the novel's obsessive staging of the car crash may finally also be read along the lines of what Virilio has termed the 'original accident', thus confronting today's ostensibly "benign" technologies with their repressed "sinister" (*C* 133, n.pag.) side. Alluding to Aristotle, Virilio has argued that "invention of the 'substance' is equally invention of the 'accident'" and that "the *visible speed* of the substance – that of the means of transport, of computing, of information – is only ever the tip of the iceberg of the *invisible speed* of the accident" (2007: 5, 13). "Every technology", Virilio explains, inevitably "produces, provokes, programs a specific accident" (Virilio and Lotringer 2008: 46): "To invent the train is *to invent the rail accident* of derailment. To invent the family automobile is to produce the *pile-up* on the highway." (Virilio 2007: 10) The exposition of this negative side of technology, which the French thinker sees as all too often censored by the "positivist ideology of Progress" (2007: 11), is, for Virilio, an urgent task in the struggle against potentially catastrophic (environmental, social, political, etc.) developments and the one-sided visions of technocratic reason. In light of this view, he has not only called for the establishment of an 'accidentology', but also for the foundation of a 'Museum of Accidents' (2007: 10, 4, 23–30). On one reading – and let me stress again that it is only one among several, so that, in the end, Ballard's text is much more ambivalent and cannot possibly be contained within the moralistic perspective set forth by Virilio – Ballard's efforts in *Crash* as well as in *The Atrocity Exhibition* – the title speaks for itself – and his 1970 exhibition of crashed cars at the New Arts Laboratory in London (cf. *KW* 213–234, *ML* 238–241) arguably aim in a similar direction. In this context, *Crash*'s images of "autogeddon" and cosmic standstill – traffic turning into an "immense motionless pause" or a "paralysed hurricane" (*C* 37, 124, 128) – bear a remarkable affinity with Virilio's "post-industrial *eschatology*" (2007: 6) and his (2007, 1999) notions of the 'integral accident' and of 'polar inertia'.

The dromological perspective brings us back to our discussion of space. Virilio has argued that accelerating technology increasingly decenters and fragments urban space, a development he sees as having become aggravated with the rise of electronic information and communication networks, which have created 'overexposed cities' (2012: 25–47). Certainly, Ballard's London is such a transformed city-space, dispersed and penetrated by media and advertising. In *Crash*, the city has effectively turned into something else, akin to what Baudrillard has described as the 'metro area', a change that "redistributes a whole region and population" and "concentrates and rationalizes time, trajectories, practices" (1994b: 75). The setting of Ballard's novel is just such an area, the result of a "new morphogenesis" which, Baudrillard – similar to Virilio – explains, "comes from the cybernetic kind [...], reproducing at the level of the territory, of the home, of transit, the scenarios of molecular control that are those of the genetic code" (1994b: 77). This new, hyperfunctional zone embodies "a whole lifestyle in which not only the country but the town as well have disappeared" and hence translates "the end of the city [...] as a determined, qualitative space, as an original synthesis of a society" (Baudrillard 1994b: 77, 78).[10]

More than that, it seems that in *Crash*, the very dialectic between public and private space that liberal political theory has generally considered characteristic of modern, democratic societies has become eroded, in the sense that, curiously, one does not really find *either* in the text. What used to be private space, the home, is not only – in a story mostly set on the motorway – largely absent from the narrative, but on the few occasions on which the reader *is* provided with glimpses of it, it appears strangely 'non-private', deprived of any sense of seclusion, protection and intimacy. Instead, the home here appears everywhere invaded by the omnipresent networks of the mass media and the all-powerful circuits of control (e. g. *C* 26), power having now perfected its "capillary functioning" so well analyzed by Foucault, bringing its effects "to the most minute and distant elements" through "an infinitesimal distribution of the power relations" (1979: 198, 216). The 'private' thus emerges as no longer 'set apart' (Latin, *privatus*) but as a mere extension of power. As Baudrillard observes in his analysis of the novel: "there is no longer a private and domestic universe, there are only incessant figures of circulation" (1994a: 113). On the other hand, the world of the text is devoid of 'public' spaces, the traditional place of modern liberal politics, too. In this, the novel may be said to mirror the development described by Michael Hardt and Antonio Negri: "In the process of postmodernization, [...] public spaces are increasingly becoming privatized. The urban landscape is shifting from the modern focus on the common square and the public encounter to the closed spaces of malls, freeways, and gated communities." (2001: 188) In *Crash*, all spaces appear similarly flattened, homogenized and emptied of meaning, all restructured and recoded by the forces of capital. No more *agora* here, no more *polis* – and no more 'citizen' either. For in fact, not only are there neither spaces of immunity and refuge nor open spaces for meeting, interaction and,

---

[10] Ballard's fullest exploration of the Baudrillardian metro area and its nucleus, the 'hypermarket', is to be found in his last novel, *Kingdom Come*, in which, appropriately enough, the gigantic shopping mall that is the setting of much of the story is called the Metro-Centre. The passage that introduces it to the reader echoes Baudrillard almost verbatim: "it fully justified its name, lying at the heart of a new metropolis that encircled London, a perimeter city that followed the path of the great motorways" (*KC* 15).

generally, *citizenship*, there are no actual 'subjects' to do the interacting either. As David Punter has pointed out in his instructive discussion of Ballard's work,

> [w]here character is concerned, Ballard is one of the few writers who can be sensibly termed post-structuralist: the long tradition of enclosed and unitary subjectivity comes to mean less and less to him as he explores the ways in which person is increasingly controlled by landscape and machine, increasingly becomes a point of intersection for overloaded scripts and processes which have effectively concealed their distant origins in human agency.[11] (1985: 9)

As Punter, in accord with numerous other theorists of postmodernity, indicates, this 'decentering' of the subject – more extensively discussed in chapter 4 – is, among other things, also due to the transformations of late-capitalist spatiality, which Ballard's texts so persistently map and explore. Already the very first page of *Crash* introduces us to it, inserting the reader into a realm made up of motorways, hotels, film studios, multi-story car parks, and Heathrow Airport, later complemented by supermarkets, all-night cafés, shopping malls, filling stations, and so forth. Ballard's characters live in a world in which what Marc Augé terms 'non-places' have displaced virtually all 'anthropological places' (Luckhurst 1997: 129–131). Whereas the latter, according to the French anthropologist, are "places of identity, of relations and of history", places that are meaningful, anchored in the local and that "create the organically social", non-places, in contrast, are purely functional

> spaces in which neither identity, nor relations, nor history really make any sense; spaces in which solitude is experienced as an overburdening or emptying of individuality, in which only the movement of the fleeting images enables the observer to hypothesize the existence of a past and glimpse the possibility of a future" (2008: 43, 76, 70 f).

Hotel chains and holiday clubs, leisure parks, supermarkets and commercial centers, airports, railway stations, and – significantly – motorways; Augé sees the proliferation of these and other transit places as having ushered in a world "surrendered to [...] the fleeting, the temporary and ephemeral" (2008: 63),[12] in which their attributes increasingly fall upon the people traversing them, thus creating more and more dehistoricized, rootless and uniform lives

---

[11] I will suggest an alternative interpretation of the 'flatness' of Ballard's characters below.
[12] In this vein, *Crash* explicitly mentions "transit hotels", a "transit and leisure complex" and the "anonymous bedrooms of the airport hotels" (*C* 46, 73, 90).

lived in anonymity and isolation. This, certainly, is an apt description of Ballard's protagonists.[13]

At one point, James Ballard, the suggestively named narrator of the novel,[14] inspects the concrete and steel landscape of freeways, housing units, gas stations, supermarkets, and London Airport surrounding his apartment house and muses:

> I realized that the human inhabitants of this technological landscape no longer provided its sharpest pointers, its keys to the borderzones of identity. [...] [A]ll the hopes and fancies of this placid suburban enclave [...] faltered before the solid reality of the motorway embankments, with their constant and unswerving geometry, and before the finite areas of the car-park aprons. (C 36)

"[T]he entire zone which defined the landscape of my life", James continues a little later, "was now bounded by a continuous artificial horizon, formed by the raised parapets and embankments of the motorways and their access roads and interchanges." (C 40) These passages evidently signal a "dehumanised world in which the human individual is a nugatory presence" (Gasiorek 2005: 86) and portend "late capitalism's brutal reshaping of the social and cognitive processes that determine everyday lives" (Groes 2012: 124). Postmodern spatiality here appears akin to what Fredric Jameson has referred to as 'hyperspace', that is, as an environment the human individual can no longer map, meaningfully relate to, shape and endow with meaning. In terms that distinctly resonate with Augé's analysis, Jameson diagnoses an

> evolutionary mutation of late capitalism toward 'something else' which is no longer family or neighborhood, city or state, nor even nation, but as abstract and nonsituated as the placelessness of a room in an international chain of motels or the anonymous space of airport terminals that all run together in your mind" (1991: 116).

According to the American theorist, the mutation in built space towards postmodern hyperspace reflects and, indeed, embodies these larger transformations. Jameson describes the experience of this new space as one of "bewilderment and loss of spatial orientation" and of a sense of "the messiness of an environment in which things and people no longer find their 'place'" (1991: 117 f). This, it seems to me, is also the experience articulated by Ballard's narrator, whose de-

---

13 In fact, the narrator even thinks of the apartment block in which he lives as a "glass coffin" (C 85).
14 In order to avoid confusion between character and author, the former will henceforth be referred to as 'James'.

scriptions – the traffic deck of the motorways below the veranda of his apartment "seem[ing] almost higher than the balcony rail", the embankments of the motorways "encircl[ing] the vehicles [...] like the walls of a crater several miles in diameter" (*C* 36, 40), etc. – repeatedly evoke a fully technologized landscape that continually threatens to overwhelm its human inhabitants. Here, postmodern space, in Jameson's words, "has finally succeeded in transcending the capacities of the individual human body to locate itself, to organize its immediate surroundings perceptually, and cognitively to map its position in a mappable external world" (1991: 44).[15]

As we have seen, along with this derealization of space, the novel posits a related derealization of experience, an "alienation of the older phenomenological body" (Jameson 1991: 116). This becomes perfectly clear when James – in what I would argue can be considered *the* key passage in the text – declares: "The crash was the only real experience I had been through for years. For the first time I was in physical confrontation with my own body" (*C* 28). In a novel that places such emphasis on movement and the acceleration of that movement, this displacement of the body can, following Virilio, furthermore be attributed to dromology. Drawing on the phenomenological work of, among others, Edmund Husserl, Martin Heidegger and Maurice Merleau-Ponty, especially on the latter's (1986) notion of the 'body-subject', Virilio has tirelessly analyzed and criticized the ways in which speed, as a structuring principle of the manner in which we have come to experience the world, has affected our bodily perception. According to Virilio, speed warps the original situatedness of the experiencing body, the familiar spatiality and temporality of its perception, and thus brings about a severe impoverishment of the subject's lived embodied experience. He writes:

> Each departure is a distancing that deprives us of contact, of direct experience; each instance of vehicular mediation is nothing other than a drawing and quartering, a torture of the locomotive body, a sensory privation of the passenger. Borne along, walled in by the violence of movement, we merely attain acceleration, that is to say, the loss of the immediate. Speed, by its violence, becomes a *destiny* at the same time as being a *destination*. We go nowhere, we have contented ourselves solely with leaving and abandoning the vivacious and vivid to the advantage of the void of speed. (2008: 40)

---

[15] It has to be said, however, that the narrator's depiction and experience of space is, like virtually everything else in the novel, ambivalent. Thus, James occasionally also perceives his environment as "reassuring", peaceful and even as an "enchanted domain" (*C* 36, 35).

Thus, for Ballard's protagonists, long-standing inhabitants as they are of the late-capitalist 'dromosphere', the violence of acceleration destroys the immediacy, fullness and density of sensible experience. With 'dromoscopy' – vision mediated by speed – the 'presence' of both their physical body and the world it perceives is hence profoundly undermined (cf. Virilio 2008: 101–114). As James' descriptions of his own life make clear, Virilio's bleak diagnosis of a wide-ranging derealization of being and of a general "decline in existence" (2009: 47) fully applies to the world of the novel.

With regard to *Crash*, it is interesting to note Virilio's declaration that "between the audiovisual media and the automobile (that is, the dromovisual), there is no difference; *speed machines*, they both give rise to mediation through the production of speed" (2008: 111). According to the French thinker, both the electronic media and modern means of transportation such as the car generate dromoscopy: "the trees that file past on the screen of the windshield, the images that rise up on the television... all substitutes for reality, these apparent movements are only simulacra." (2008: 110) It seems to me that a very similar logic is at work in Ballard's novel, which likewise insistently draws attention to the related processes of derealization triggered by both these 'speed machines'. *Crash* depicts a universe in which mediation has displaced any direct experience of the world, in which perception is determined by the omnipresence of the screen – whether that of television, billboards or the windshield – and in which 'simulacra' have taken the place of sensible reality. At this point, Virilio's argument, with its conclusion that today, "the image prevails over the object present, to say nothing of the being", so that virtuality now "dominat[es] actuality and turn[s] the very concept of reality on its head" (1994: 73, 63), noticeably overlaps with the thinking of Baudrillard, who, like Virilio or Jameson, has interpreted postmodernity with reference to the Platonic notion of the 'simulacrum', "the identical copy for which no original has ever existed" (Jameson 1991: 18). In Baudrillard's (1993b: 50–86) genealogical account of the historical development of the simulacrum, a development running parallel to that of capitalism and the successive transformations of the law of value, the emergence of this contemporary form, or 'order', of the simulacrum is only the latest mutation in a line that can be traced back at least as far as the Renaissance. According to Baudrillard, the dominant schema up until the Industrial Revolution was that of the 'counterfeit', where the image – for example in the shape of maps, the theater, stucco and Baroque art – finds its value as a copy or representation of 'nature'. While this first-order simulacrum never abolishes its dispute with the real, the difference between sign and being begins to get blurred with the appearance of the simulacrum of the second order during the industrial era. With the new possibilities of serial production and reproduction, a new generation of signs and objects arises, regarding which the question of the origin and of representational authenticity can no more be posed. No longer imitations of a unique original, signs are now *produced* on large scales and identically and infinitely reproduced, so that reference increasingly loses its value and, indeed, meaning.[16] This facilitates the general reign of the capitalist law of equivalences. As Baudrillard points out, throughout its history, capital has "fed on the destructuration of every referential, [...] shattered every ideal distinction between true and false, good and evil, in order to establish a radical law of equivalence and exchange, the iron law of its power" (1994g: 22). Following Baudrillard's model, this tendency reaches its climax in late capitalism, when the dominant schema is no longer that of production but of 'simulation'. With third-order simulacra, there is no more copying of an original as in the first order and no more pure series as in the second; instead, all forms are now derived from generative models and codes and conceived according to their very reproducibility. Here, particular importance attaches to the rise of the electronic mass media, which instate a new 'phase of the image' to the extent that it now has "no relation to any reality whatsoever: it is its own pure simulacrum" (1994g: 6). This absolute self-referentiality of signs finally completely dissolves the ties between sign and object and between signifier and signified: "the era of simulation is inaugurated by a liquidation of all referentials" (1994g: 2). According to Baudrillard, the new media-generated signs, the omnipresent models and the codes together generate a novel reality without origins, a 'hyperreality', in which the distinction between real and imaginary, true and false, authentic and fake can no longer be made. The French philosopher declares: "Today everyday, political, social, historical, economic, etc., reality has already incorporated the hyperrealist dimension of simulation so that we are now living entirely within the 'aesthetic' hallucination of reality." (1993b: 74) And: "Today the whole system is swamped by indeterminacy, and every reality is absorbed by the hyperreality of the code and simulation. The principle of simulation governs us now, rather than the outdated reality principle. [...] No more ideology, only simulacra." (Baudrillard 1993b: 2) As this last statement makes clear, the transition towards the age of simulation also entails a transformation of the schemata of social control, which now, Baudrillard avers, "reach a fantastic degree of perfection" (1993b: 60).

It is this evolution "[f]rom a capitalist productivist society to a neo-capitalist cybernetic order" and thus towards "absolute control" (Baudrillard 1993b: 60)

---

[16] As Baudrillard points out, Walter Benjamin's (1969a) influential essay on the changed status of the work of art in the industrial age – Benjamin considers the work's 'aura' as destroyed by the new technologies of reproduction – was one of the first texts to draw out these implications.

that, as we have seen, *Crash* dramatizes. As several critics, first and foremost Baudrillard himself, have already pointed out, the contemporary collapse of reality into hyperreality is likewise everywhere palpable in the novel.[17] We find it, for example, in the text's persistent emphasis on the ubiquity of mediation and simulation and the resulting derealization of the characters' experience of the world. This dimension is clearly present in the novel's stress on the mediated nature of virtually all relationships, even including their sexual side – mediated by technology in general, by the car, by television, by the camera, by fantasy (e. g. *C* 80, 26, 97, 21), etc.; in the narrator's sense that the wars, riots and disasters seen in television's "endless newscasts" constitute a "violence experienced at so many removes" (*C* 56, 26); in his intuition that major events of his life, including his death, have already been anticipated and simulated by the media (*C* 28); in the numerous simulations of accidents on television, at the stock-car racing stadium, where Vaughan assumes the role of a "film director" and stages and "choreograph[s]" reenactments of car crashes of celebrities as "spectacles" (*C* 67, 68), or at the Road Research Laboratory, where *already simulated* accidents are filmed and later replayed in slow motion and where, according to Vaughan, the technology of crash simulation is so advanced that accidents could be duplicated indefinitely (*C* 100), thus creating an endless line of copies of copies, that is, an uninterrupted loop of simulation; in Vaughan's sense that the lethal crash of his friend Seagrave, in which the latter was dressed up as Elizabeth Taylor, has "pre-empted" the real death with the actress that Vaughan had planned for himself, so that, "[i]n his mind, from that accident onwards, the film actress ha[s] already died" (*C* 154); or in James' visualizing of a 'real' accident as if it were filmed in slow motion, like the simulated collisions at the Road Research Laboratory (*C* 155).

Beyond these "potent confusions of fiction and reality" (*C* 89), the extent to which the world of the novel has already sunk into hyperreality is also evident in the way in which the protagonists' minds have been infiltrated, or rather, *constituted*, by the mass-medial sign-systems surrounding them. This, of course, means the end of any notion of an 'originary' subjectivity and of an 'authentic' perception of the world. It seems to me that it is with this in mind that Ballard, in his introduction to the text, speaks of "the pre-empting of any original response to experience by the television screen" (*C* n.pag.). When, for instance, James finds it difficult to focus on a discussion of business-related matters with Paul Waring, one of his colleagues, because his attention is fixed on a car waiting for him outside the offices, he asserts that "[e]verything else – Waring's irritation

---

[17] This aspect has been discussed in most detail by Aidan Day (2000).

with [him], the cramped perspectives of the offices, the noisiness of the staff – form[s] a vague penumbra, *unsatisfactory footage that [will] later be edited out*" (*C* 41, emphasis added). At the heart of the postmodern subject presented in *Crash*, there is no natural and essential 'core' of identity, but only a palimpsest of cultural 'texts' from which this identity is constructed and which are largely fabricated by the late-capitalist media machine. This is particularly evident in the case of Vaughan, who, of course, once was a TV personality. Vaughan is described as continually adopting different poses (e.g. *C* 70, 78) and as always "dramatizing himself", "holding his position […] as if waiting for invisible television cameras to frame him", and at one point, James reflects that Vaughan's features look as if they were "reassembled after [his] crash from a collection of faded publicity photographs" (*C* 69, 49). James, in turn, feels that this staging of the self preempts all of his responses to the other man (*C* 69), thus making clear that all relationships are here invaded by the logic of simulation. As Vaughan's obsession with photographic and filmic images (of wounds and accidents), the latter "endlessly repeated in slow-motion films" (*C* 2), and his countless imaginary and actual reenactments of car crashes, especially of those involving the famous, show, Vaughan engages the world exclusively at the level of the simulacrum. As Aidan Day points out: "Vaughan's imagination is externalised in and congruent with the second-hand order of 'reality' denoted by photographic or cinematic representation. […] Vaughan's mind does not connect with reality as conventionally understood but is in thrall to the artifice of the image" (2000: 280 f). This extends to his own sense of self, which likewise appears to depend on the mediation of the image: at Vaughan's apartment, the narrator observes the former's "attempt at tagging himself, to fix his identity by marking it upon some external event":

> the walls of the studio, bathroom and kitchen were covered with photographs of himself, stills from his television programmes, half-plate prints from newspaper photographers, polaroid snapshots of himself on location[.] […] Vaughan was self-consciously absorbed in these fading images, straightening their curling corners as if frightened that when they finally vanished his own identity would also cease to matter. (*C* 138)

In this way, Vaughan bears out Baudrillard's diagnosis that today, the "brain […] has itself become a screen" and that not only in the media, but "in our heads too", "the image-feedback dominates", that is, everything is confused with its own image, so that, strictly speaking, "human beings are no longer victims of images, but rather transform themselves into images" (2005: 78, 79, 94).

Finally, the hyperreality of Ballard's world is also intimated by the emphasis the text places on stylization. Whether cars, sexual acts, violence, empathy and affection, or even death (e.g. *C* 5, 8, 14, 26, 79, 115f, 178) – again and again, the novel stresses the stylized character of all events, things and actions, thus pointing to their derived, secondary nature. Here, nothing is original, authentic or spontaneous – instead, everything is always already reproduced, a simulacrum. In *Crash*, "reality is overexposed to the glare of models" (Baudrillard 1993b: 75), from which all the stylized objects and gestures descend. The world of the novel hence clearly emerges as that of 'semiocapitalism' (Berardi 2009) and hyperreal postmodernity, a world, as Ballard says in his introduction, in which "the balance between fiction and reality has changed significantly" and that is now "ruled by fictions of every kind" (*C* n.pag.). It is for this that Baudrillard has hailed *Crash* as a new kind of science fiction corresponding to the contemporary order of simulacra and as "the first great novel of the universe of simulation": "*Crash* is *our* world, nothing in it is 'invented': [...] In *Crash*, there is neither fiction nor reality anymore – hyperreality abolishes both." (1994a: 119, 1994d: 125)

How can the subject escape from this claustrophobic, derealized and depthless world and resist a system which has effectively penetrated all areas of existence and whose powers of control appear virtually unassailable? Certainly, only by means of the most extreme forms of behavior – through catastrophic strategies.

2.2 Roads of Excess

> The road of excess leads to the palace of wisdom.
> *William Blake*

The deliberate crashing of cars and wounding of the body of Ballard's main characters constitutes such a catastrophic strategy. As was already suggested, this strategy is highly polysemic, coded in several different ways which allow for different interpretations. In a first reading, the protagonists' actions can be construed in terms of Georges Bataille's theorization of excess. *Crash* clearly places itself in a long tradition of transgressive and pornographic fiction that can be traced back at least as far as to the Marquis de Sade, but the affinity with the work of Bataille is perhaps most pronounced. A few commentators have already drawn attention to the Bataillean legacy of the novel (cf. Bukatman 2005: 293; Baxter 2009: 101 ff, 111 ff) and the prominent English music critic Simon Reynolds has even referred to Ballard as "a British Bataille" (in Sellars 2007: n.pag.). What seems particularly relevant for a reading of *Crash*, obsessed as it is with excess, violence, death and sexuality, is the French thinker's key notion of 'expenditure'. Drawing on the influential work of the sociologist Marcel Mauss and his hypothesis that "[i]t is [only] our western societies who have recently made man [sic] an 'economic animal'" (1990: 76), Bataille (2007) challenges the dominant 'restricted economy', which recognizes only 'economic' exchange, based on the principle of equivalence, and which everywhere asserts the primacy of rationality, utility and necessity, production, accumulation and conservation, and opposes to it his formulation of a 'general economy', which not only focuses on those aspects excluded or denigrated by the former – recklessness, waste, luxury, squander, etc. – but, more than that, reveals these to belong to an *essential* dimension of human existence, in relation to which production and preservation are only secondary and which thus constitutes the true end of all economic activity – 'unproductive expenditure':

> Our only real pleasure is to squander our resources to no purpose, just as if a wound were bleeding away inside us; we always want to be sure of the uselessness or the ruinousness of our extravagance. We want to feel as remote from the world where thrift is the rule as we can. (1986: 170)

Games, spectacles and festivals, madness and drunkenness, eroticism, sacrifice, violence, destruction and death – contrary to the economic principle of balanced accounts, the diverse forms of unproductive expenditure, around which practically Bataille's entire oeuvre revolves, all adhere to the principle of loss, "a *loss* that must be as great as possible in order for that activity to take on its true meaning" (Bataille 1985c: 118). According to Bataille, once the individual or collective engages in processes of expenditure, they enter intense "*states of excitation*, which are comparable to toxic states" (1985c: 128). Importantly, for Bataille, these states are *ec-static* in the etymological sense of the word: through pure expenditure, the individual subject is 'beside itself', it spends and consumes itself, dissolves the boundaries of itself as well as everything around it and in this way leaves behind its 'discontinuous', isolated and, essentially, alienated existence to regain the fundamental 'continuity' of being: "We are discontinuous beings, individuals who perish in isolation in the midst of an incomprehensible adventure, but we yearn for our lost continuity." (1986: 15) Only excess causes "a rent in the seamless garment of the separate individuality", that is, produces what Bataille (1988) terms 'inner experience', which "calls into question within the subjective consciousness the feeling of self, the feeling of being and of the limits of the isolated being" and thus, if only fleetingly, allows us to perceive the "primal continuity linking us with everything that is" (1986: 102, 15). Following Bataille, such supreme moments of bliss, in which the subject squanders itself without reserve and the *principium individuationis* is temporarily annulled, are instants of 'sovereignty',[18] in which human beings realize their full potential, become truly free, and reach the "pinnacle of being" (1986: 276).

Are not Ballard's protagonists seeking just this sovereignty, described by Bataille as "the power to rise, indifferent to death, above the laws which ensure the maintenance of life" (2006: 182)? It is certainly striking that *Crash* contains almost all the many forms of expenditure discussed by Bataille: violence, destruction and death, mutilation of the body, eroticism – and, importantly, its connection with death[19] – madness, inebriation (cannabis, LSD), and the embrace of 'heterogeneity' (see below). The novel suggests that these forms of excess, to paraphrase William Blake – to whom Ballard and Bataille both seem to some degree indebted[20] (cf. esp. *UD*; Bataille 2006: 77–101) – offer a path to 'wisdom' (Blake 1973: 35), that is, to an alternative and, it appears, more authentic order of experience and mode of being. Again and again, the text emphasizes the "true significance of the automobile crash", its "excitements" and "quickening possibilities" (*C* 3, 145, 128), and stresses its transformative and invigorating nature – it is depicted as bringing about a complete "remaking of the commonplace" and characters are said to be "reborn" (*C* 39, 79) in it. Here, in Bataillean fashion, to crash is to experience "the *ecstasies* of head-on collisions" and "the erotic *delirium* of the car-crash" (*C* 3, 8f, emphases added). Accordingly, James is 'beside himself' in the wake of expenditure: "The ugly and violent impact of this […] crash, the rupture of metal and safety glass, and *the deliberate destruction of expensively engineered artefacts*, had left me lightheaded" (*C* 101, emphasis added). "Being", Bataille asserts, "is also the excess of being, the upward surge towards the impossible" (1986: 173), and it seems that it is just this surge that manifests itself in Vaughan's final and lethal crash, in which, travelling "at the car's maximum speed", his vehicle jumps the rails of a flyover, its driver "trying to launch himself into the sky" (*C* 182).

In both Ballard and Bataille there is something quasi-religious to excess. The latter, building on and modifying the thought of Émile Durkheim (2001), has argued that the realm of transgression and excess is, in fact, the domain of the true 'sacred', which he has opposed to the 'profane' world of laws and taboos, reason, order, and work. At the heart of the Bataillean sacred lie "horror, anguish, death" (Bataille

---

[18] However, Bataille argues that this sovereignty can only ever be approached asymptotically, but never fully reached (2006: 193f).
[19] Cf. e. g. James' sense of having "celebrated in [Helen Remington's] husband's death the unity of [their] injuries and [James'] orgasm" or Vaughan's plans for his and Elizabeth Taylor's joint "sex-death" (*C* 58, 151). In the same vein, the autogeddon anticipated by the narrator is depicted as a climactic conjunction of global death and universal orgasm (*C* 8).
[20] On the connection between Ballard and Blake, cf. Cormack 2012.

1991: 169). It is thus not to be confused with organized religion, which can give more or less room to the sacred; instead, it designates "something forbidden, which is violent and dangerous, mere contact with which presages destruction: it is Evil" (Bataille 2006: 182).[21] While the sacred was an integral part of 'primitive' societies, it has, according to Bataille (2007), been virtually eliminated in 'modern', capitalist ones, which are solely based on rationality and calculations of interest, the isolated individual, considerations of the future and the general will to survive, and wholly geared towards accumulation, productivity and profit. "The hatred of expenditure", Bataille declares, "is the *raison d'être* of and the justification for the bourgeoisie" (1985c: 124 f); "[a]t the origin of industrial society, based on the primacy and autonomy of commodities, of *things*, we find a contrary impulse to place what is essential – *what causes one to tremble with fear and delight* – outside the world of activity, the world of *things*." (2007: 129) All forms of the sacred, which allow man (sic) to lose him-/his self (sic) in continuity, are thus excluded from capitalist society, which hence "reduces what is human to the condition of a *thing* (of a commodity)" (Bataille 2007: 129).

It seems to me that the obsessive car-crashing of Ballard's protagonists can be read as an attempt to recreate a form of *sacrifice* – historically, one of the most important manifestations of expenditure – in the midst of the utterly 'profane' world of late capitalism and thus to reintroduce the sacred into it.[22] This includes the characters' passion for wounds and wounding, since automutilation, according to Bataille (1985b: 67), represents nothing other than an expression of the human spirit of sacrifice. As Bataille points out, "[i]n the etymological sense of the word, sacrifice is nothing other than the production of *sacred* things." (1985c: 119) It is, perhaps, in this sense that the narrator's remarkable description of the dead Seagrave – who has, in a way, rather *been* sacrificed by the manipulative Vaughan than sacrificed himself (*C* 74, 85) – must be read: "Seagrave's slim and exhausted face was covered with shattered safety glass, as if his body were already crystallizing, at last escaping out of this uneasy set of dimensions into a more beautiful universe."[23] (*C* 152) In this context, it is telling that the car in which Seagrave dies is at one point referred to as a "bloody altar" (*C* 154). Several times, the novel makes use of such quasi-religious imagery and rhetoric. For example, James, having visited the site of a fatal accident, has the impression that he and all the others among the large crowd of spectators are "members of a congregation leaving after a sermon" and "driving into the night to imi-

---

21 For a related, and contemporary, conception of the sacred, cf. Caillois 2001.
22 On the significance of sacrifice especially in Ballard's late work, cf. Tew 2008.
23 This passage distinctly echoes Ballard's *The Crystal World*.

tate the bloody eucharist [they have] observed" (*C* 129). Touching his own wounds in the wake of this, Ballard's protagonist feels "like a resurrected man basking in the healed injuries that [...] brought about his first death" (*C* 129). Similarly, he elsewhere notes his feeling that "Vaughan [can] never really die in a car-crash, but [will] in some way be re-born through [the] twisted radiator grilles and cascading windshield glass" (*C* 172). The most concentrated occurrence of such images can be found in the chapters detailing James' acid trip and its aftermath. These contain a striking imagery of light and ascension: in the narrator's ecstatic vision, the air, for instance, becomes "intense" and "golden", the concrete walls of sliproads turn into "luminous cliffs", oncoming cars emit a "fountain of light" (*C* 162, 161, 163), and the interior of the car in which he and Vaughan are having sex "glow[s] like a magician's bower", while the roads become "endless runways" from which cars are "soaring through the sunlight, ascending from the traffic jams that [...] locked them together" (*C* 164). More than that, the vehicles, their interior gleaming "like altarpieces", transform into "paradisial" and "angelic creatures" (*C* 164, 163, 164) celebrating a "metallized Elysium" and "laying down the blueprints of [James and his wife's] coming passage through heaven, the transits of a technology with wings" (*C* 163, 172). These and other passages strongly suggest that the crash is in fact an act of transcendence (Stephenson 1991: 68–74), that Dionysian expenditure constitutes a catalyst for the attainment of a kind of mystical rapture similar to the one described by Bataille. Indeed, as we will see below, *Crash* may be said to oscillate in its presentation of excess between the intimation of such transcendence on the one hand and a pure immanence on the other in an – in the end undecidable – way not unlike the French intellectual does, whose works seem to hover ambivalently between the modern and the postmodern, often – apparently following the Romantic philosophy of the early Nietzsche (1999) – proposing a quasi-metaphysical realm of ultimate reality, truth, harmony and unity through sublation, while at other times questioning the attainability of this realm or its very existence and actively deconstructing their own terms and concepts.[24]

---

[24] As a result of this ambiguity, numerous different interpretations of Bataille's oeuvre have been proposed. While, for instance, Jean-Paul Sartre (1947) has famously read Bataille as 'a new mystic' and Alice Owen Letvin has described him and other 'dissident Surrealists' as the "last of the romantics" (1990: 42), Jacques Derrida has drawn attention to the permanent slippage of terms in Bataille's texts – thus to some extent "interpret[ing] Bataille against Bataille" (Derrida 2001a: 348) – and in this way read them as instances of his (2001a) own concept of *écriture* and Steven Shaviro (1990) has likewise developed a fully non-metaphysical reading of Bataille's philosophy.

In an interview, Ballard himself has suggested a link between excess and the dissolution of the self that seems pertinent to my Bataillean reading of his novel:

> one cannot help one's imagination being touched by these people who, if at enormous price, have nonetheless broken through the skin of reality and convention around us... and who have in a sense achieved – become – mythological beings in a way that is only attainable through these brutal and violent acts. One can transcend the self, sadly, in ways which are in themselves rather to be avoided – say, extreme illnesses, car crashes, extreme states of being. [...] [One can] enjoy a sort of ultimate *blowing of the mind*. (in Revell 1984b: 47)

Here, Ballard noticeably echoes the ideas and rhetoric of the American cultural critic Susan Sontag in her important essay on 'the pornographic imagination'.[25] Sontag argues that at least certain 'literary' forms of pornography (de Sade, Bataille, Pauline Réage, etc.) must be read as speaking to one of the 'extreme forms of human consciousness' through their understanding of sexuality "as something beyond good and evil, beyond love, beyond sanity; as a resource for ordeal and for breaking through the limits of consciousness" (1983: 222). Ultimately, according to Sontag – who is evidently following Bataille – pornography is not about sex but transgression and death and thus about the transcendence of the self. This, Sontag suggests, explains the abundance of religious imagery in so much erotic literature: in her eyes, "[r]eligion is [...], after sex, the second oldest resource which human beings have available to them for blowing their minds." (1983: 222) All other vocabularies in which to address extreme experiences having become devalued, writers of pornography have frequently borrowed the prestige of the religious one. In the end, Sontag contends, what most pornography points to is

> the traumatic failure of modern capitalist society to provide authentic outlets for the perennial human flair for high-temperature visionary obsessions, to satisfy the appetite for exalted self-transcending modes of concentration and seriousness. The need of human beings to transcend 'the personal' is no less profound than the need to be a person, an individual. But this society serves that need poorly. (1983: 231)

As I have argued, the "desperate excitements" (*C* 139) of the protagonists of *Crash* can be read as symptomatic of and as a reaction against this very 'failure'.

---

[25] As a matter of fact, Ballard explicitly mentions and recommends this essay in his annotations to *The Atrocity Exhibition*, while declaring that he "would go much further in [his] claims" and argue that pornography represents "a powerful catalyst for social change" (*AE* 54). The connection between Sontag's text and *Crash* has previously been pointed out by Sam Francis (2008: 163–168).

Beyond that, the case could be made that the very form of Ballard's pornographic narrative may be understood in this context as well. As in de Sade's works, the list and especially repetition are essential structural elements in *Crash*, lists and detailed descriptions of car crashes, wounds and sexual acts recurring again and again throughout the text – a fact that has, of course, been sharply criticized by several reviewers, chief among them novelist Martin Amis, who complained about "the glazed monotony of its descriptions and the deadpan singlemindedness of its attitudes" (2001: 96). Yet, this repetitiveness appears to be intimately bound up with the pornographic tradition into which the novel consciously places itself. It seems to me that this tradition or (sub-)genre is the one discussed by Gilles Deleuze in his long essay on de Sade and Leopold Sacher-Masoch under the label of 'pornology'. The French philosopher describes this as a kind of literature in which the 'personal' function of language which dominates 'ordinary' pornographic writing transcends itself towards a higher, 'impersonal' function – hence, Deleuze explains, "the well-known *apathy* of the libertine, the self-control of the pornologist" – and which in this way aims "above all at confronting language with its own limits, with what is in a sense a 'nonlanguage' (violence that does not speak, eroticism that remains unspoken)" (1989: 29, 22). Viewed in this light, the obsessively iterative nature of Ballard's narrative, as well as the formal, technical language, might be interpreted as textual strategies to address the problem of *representation*, more specifically, the question of the (im-)possibility of a metaphysical presence or absolute outside a system of (differential) signs (cf. Derrida 1984a).[26] Read against this background, the narrator's remark that his wife's descriptions to him of her (real and imagined) sex acts with her female secretary seem to be "a language in search of objects" (*C* 24) assumes additional meaning as an instance of self-reflexivity signaling the constitutive rather than reflective relation of language to reality.

For now, let us briefly turn to another, though intimately related, discourse inscribed in the text. As we have already seen, for James, the accident that triggers his obsession with the car crash is "the only real experience [he has] been through for years" (*C* 28). The possibility for this 'return' to reality appears to be contingent upon the experience of radical physical pain: "For the first time I was in physical confrontation with my own body, an inexhaustible encyclopedia of pains and discharges" (*C* 28). It is this that Ballard's characters are seeking in the crash: "the extremes of pain and violence", "an exquisite and warming pain" (*C* 14, 129). In fact, the narrative as a whole is intensely preoccupied

---

[26] It seems to me that, on the whole, the precise nature and the implications of *Crash*'s pornography have not yet been fully explored and hence still require detailed discussion elsewhere.

with the materiality of the body and, above all, with the wound – hence the endless and detailed descriptions of bodily fluids and especially mutilations that fill the text. Ballard, as Mark Seltzer has aptly put it, is "one of the compulsive cartographers of wound culture" (1998: 264), his protagonists as well as his entire narrative being committed to a "celebration of wounds" (*C* 10). Again and again, the novel emphasizes the significance and, indeed, meaningfulness of the wound and attributes it with a liberating, quasi-redemptive potential (e.g. *C* 19, 129). Such a positive, even emancipatory, conception of the "wounded body" (*C* 80) or the 'body in pain' (Scarry 1985) can not only be found in various other works, Chuck Palahniuk's successful novel *Fight Club* and David Fincher's filmic adaptation of it being one prominent example, but can be linked to an important discourse in the field of critical theory. This discourse assumes an intimate connection between authenticity or reality and extreme somatic experiences and can be tracked in the works of diverse thinkers. Thus, for instance, in the domain of psychoanalytic theory, Jacques Lacan connected his concept of the undifferentiated and non-symbolizable 'real' with the notion of a material substrate underpinning the 'symbolic order' and hence with the pure physicality of the body. Drawing on this Lacanian model, Slavoj Žižek, adopting a term of Alain Badiou's, has diagnosed "a violent return to the passion for the Real" in the age of postmodernity, arising in response to "the virtualization of our environment" and "the basic sameness of global capitalism, the absence of an Event" (2002: 10, 7). Žižek argues that this passion manifests itself among other things in a deliberate injuring of the body, which, he explains, must be understood as "a desperate strategy to return to the Real of the body", "the Real in its extreme violence as the price to be paid for peeling off the deceptive layers of reality" (2002: 10, 5 f). Žižek's argument resonates strongly with Ballard's deliberations in the interview quoted above. Ballard declares: "One needs […] to dismantle that smothering set of conventions that we call everyday reality, and of course violent acts of various kinds, whether they're car crashes or serious illnesses or any sort of trauma, do have that sort of liberating effect." (in Revell 1984b: 47)

This discourse of extreme corporeality is further evident in the work of Bataille, who similarly emphasized that "the unity of being is revealed *through the intensity* of those experiences in which truth stands clear of life and of its objects" (1986: 275, emphasis added), and in the thought of Michel Foucault. The latter, of course, emphatically 'depresentified' (1972a: 47) things throughout most of his oeuvre, presenting the subject as an effect of discourse and power and asserting the inevitably mediated and derived, discursive nature of all perception, thought, feeling and action. Yet, at the same time, Foucault never entirely gave up the "effort to uncover and free […] 'prediscursive' experiences" (1972a: 47), and the realm in which he arguably most consistently sought to retrieve these was that of the body. It was the American Neo-Pragmatist philosopher Richard Shusterman (esp. 1997: 17–64, 2008: 15–48) who has most extensively elaborated on this dimension of Foucault's work, seeing in him "an exemplary but problematic pioneer" in the field Shusterman calls 'somaesthetics',[27] a discipline that is conceived as a corrective to what he considers as contemporary philosophy's fixation on language and neglect of the body in the wake of the 'linguistic turn' and that hence "puts the body's experience and artful refashioning back into the heart of philosophy as an art of living" (2008: 15). Shusterman points out that in Foucault, "preoccupation with language bears the glowing penumbra of a utopian nonlinguistic desire" and that, in the tradition of Bataille's "Dionysian aestheticism", nondiscursivity is usually linked with "rabid Dionysian excess", that is, with "the avant-garde ideology of radical transgression" (1997: 33, 123, 128). As Foucault asserts: "the essence of being radical is physical" (1996b: 262). For the French philosopher, it is only through intense, transgressive bodily experiences such as extreme states of pleasure or pain that one can escape, if only momentarily, from the "discursive cage" (Shusterman 1997: 33) that otherwise impenetrably encloses our existence on all sides. Strong drugs, 'deviant' sexual practices such as sadomasochism: these, among others, are areas for radical experiences and experimentation – two things which, according to Foucault (1987: 103f), in our days displace the utopia of earlier times – by means of which the immediacy of a nonlinguistic somatic dimension of life may be recovered. Foucault's thought thus aims at "using the body in emancipatory critique of the discursive order by pushing it toward extreme 'limit-experiences' which seem to defy or shatter the experiential structures of that order" (Shusterman 1997: 34).[28]

It seems to me that a very similar logic – denounced by Jürgen Habermas as an "aesthetically inspired anarchism" (1990: 5) – is at work in *Crash*. Ballard's protagonists, too, subscribe to a radical aesthetic of transgressive experimentation, using the car crash to test and transcend their limits in an extreme somatic experience and in this way uncover a nondiscursive, noncognitive dimension of life. Vaughan, James and the others are, in a sense, Foucault's disciples, heeding

---

[27] What makes Foucault's thinking 'problematic' in Shusterman's eyes, is his disregard for somatic experiences which are not of the transgressive and extreme kind.

[28] On another critical note, Shusterman points out that Foucault's transgressive aestheticism may, in the end, not mark a real break with the existing order after all: "Though Foucault's radical somaesthetic tastes will strike many as dreadfully deviant, his anhedonia and extremism clearly express a common trend of late-capitalist Western culture, whose unquestioned economic imperative of ever-increasing growth also promotes an unquestioned demand for constantly greater stimulation" (2008: 39).

his challenge "to make a discipline of the pursuit of undisciplined somatic dissolution, making oneself a radical artwork by submitting one's body to the programmatic demand for ever more risky and uncontrolled experimentation in anarchy" (Shusterman 1997: 36). Similar to Foucault, the novel ascribes a liberating potential to somatic limit-experiences, suggesting – as becomes evident when James stresses the reality of his crash experience – that they allow, in Elaine Scarry's words, a momentary "*reconnecting [of] the derealized and disembodied [subjects] with the force and power of the material world*" (1985: 128). In the world of the text, a world that is not only confined in 'the prison-house of language' (Jameson 1974) and discourse, but that has fully entered the age of simulation and is characterized by the omnipresence of simulacra and mediation and hence by a fundamental derealization of experience, it is only through the wounding of the body, through extreme pain, that a certain immediacy of experience – that is, an *unmediated* experience – can still be realized and the dungeon of sign-systems of the late-capitalist "semiocracy" (Baudrillard 1993b: 78) be escaped. The body is thus central to the novel's politics, and our exploration of its role in the text leads us directly to a second reading of the protagonists' catastrophic strategy beyond the one that construes it in terms of an 'event', though both readings are, as we will see, rather closely connected.

2.3 Anarchic Bodies, or, Breughel and Bosch on the Freeway

In the mid-1930s, Marcel Mauss, in what is now recognized as a pioneering text, first posited the thoroughly social nature of bodily actions. From movement to sex, every kind of action, Mauss (1973) asserts, carries the imprint of culture, so that there can be no such thing as 'natural' behavior. Many theorists have since followed, and radicalized, this line of thought, bringing out and analyzing the utterly constructed nature of the body and exposing the power mechanisms at work in its production. In this regard, the work of Pierre Bourdieu and Michel Foucault has proved particularly influential. Both, albeit in different ways, have convincingly argued that, even in its seemingly most natural, minute and personal dimensions, the body is fully invested with relations of power and domination and in numerous ways contributes to the reproduction of the existing social order. Thus, Bourdieu, in his work on the ways in which social values are literally *incorporated*, that is, "*made* body", by means of what he terms 'habitus' and 'field' – "arms and legs are full of numb imperatives", he asserts – declares that "the whole social order imposes itself at the deepest level of the bodily dispositions" (1992: 69, 75). Similarly, Foucault announces the existence of a "political technology of the body", principally manifested in what he calls the 'disciplinary' modality of power, through which "the body is reduced as a 'political' force [...] and maximized as a useful force" and which thus "assures the automatic functioning of power" (1979: 24, 221, 201). More recently, the American feminist Judith Butler has developed this Foucauldian direction of thought into a radical constructivist position, arguing that even the very 'materiality' of the body is culturally and, indeed, forcibly produced, in the sense that it is only through social constraints that bodies are 'materialized'. "[T]he matter of bodies", she explains, must be recast "as the effect of a dynamic of power, such that the matter of bodies [is] indissociable from the regulatory norms that govern their materialization and the signification of those material effects" (1993: 2).

A specific point of investigation for thinkers like Butler, Mary Douglas or Julia Kristeva has been the ways in which the boundaries of the body are culturally determined. What all of them have emphasized is that the limits of the body are never just material, but instituted and maintained through social taboos, separating the 'pure' from the 'impure' and punishing 'pollution' (Douglas 2002). It was Julia Kristeva who has arguably presented the most comprehensive exploration of this process of the social construction of bodily contours. Kristeva mainly draws on the work of Douglas, psychoanalytic theory, Bataille's 'heterology' – "[t]he science of what is completely other" (Bataille 1985e: 102n2) – and, especially, his (1985d, 1985e) thesis that the 'homogeneous' world of capitalist society is created and preserved through the exclusion of 'heterogeneous' elements, which, however, continually threaten to resurface and disturb this world. Following Bataille (1987), Kristeva terms this constitutive process of expulsion 'abjection' and relates it to the process of subject formation. Prior to the Freudo-Lacanian moments of the 'mirror-stage' and Oedipal triangulation and castration (*le non/nom du père*), Kristeva argues, the 'thetic phase', that is, the gradual process of the infant's separation from its primary unity with the mother necessary for its attainment of the position of a subject of the symbolic, is already inaugurated through other mechanisms, one of which is abjection. According to the Bulgarian-French theorist, it is through the child's violent rejection of the maternal body, or *chora*, that is, of that which forms an integral part of itself, that the most primal borders between self and other are rudimentarily established. The space of the 'proper' ('own'/'clean') subject is thus first demarcated through a process of expulsion that manifests itself in behavior tied to eating habits, toilet training and hygiene (spitting out food, discharging excrement, etc.). Hence, the abject is waste – but its status is far from unambiguous: it is, Kristeva explains, "*excluded* but in strange fashion: not radically enough to allow for a secure differentiation between subject and object, and yet clearly enough for a defensive *position* to be established" (1982: 7). Consequently, abjection signals both the constitution of the subject and its disruption, since the abject constantly challenges the tenuous borders of selfhood as something that is opposed to the 'I' but that is nevertheless not an object, "not my correlative, which, providing me with someone or something else as support, would allow me to be more or less detached and autonomous" (Kristeva 1982: 1).

In *Crash*, the abject assumes a central place, the narrative being littered with feces, urine, blood, semen, vomit, mucus, filth, wounded bodies and corpses. So far, critics have mostly read the novel's staging of the abject in terms of a critique of a commodified and only seemingly transparent socius as well as of its effects on the reader (Gasiorek 2005: 91ff; Baxter 2009: 103ff; Whiting 2012). Yet, it seems to me that at least equally important is the role it plays on the diegetic level. Importantly, for Ballard's protagonists, the abject has lost its horrifying character, which, as Kristeva has shown, is decidedly not a fact of nature but of social origin. Instead, it is accepted, even openly sought out and explored by them. One scene, for instance, has Vaughan, his hands covered with blood from his injured knee caps, "*examin*[*ing*] the vomit staining the lapels of his leather jacket, and *reach*[*ing*] *forward to touch* the globes of semen clinging to the instrument binnacle" (*C* 3, emphases added). Elsewhere, James, recovering in hospital from his first major crash, speculates on how long ago one of the nurses has last washed the "moist gulley" of her natal cleft, on the degree of cleanliness of the doctors and nurses' genitalia, if "small grains of faecal matter" still cling to their anuses, and whether there are still "traces of smegma and vaginal mucus" (*C* 19) on their hands. And the beginning of his sex act with Vaughan is narrated by James in the following manner: "I moved my mouth down his abdomen to his damp groin, marked with blood and semen, a faint odour of a woman's excrement clinging to the shaft of his penis. [...] I explored [his] scars with my lips, tasting the blood and urine." (*C* 166) These passages evidently signal a transgression of the social taboos that constitute the boundaries of the body, almost a reversal of the primal "ejection and transvaluation of something originally part of identity into a defiling otherness" (Butler 1999: 170). While in hospital, James, referring to the nurses, states: "I wondered why [...] all these women around me seemed to attend only to my most infantile zones. [...] [T]hese starched women in all their roles reminded me of those who attended my childhood, commissionaires guarding my orifices." (*C* 22) This statement – made just after Ballard's narrator, still under the lingering effects of anesthetics, has barely managed to control his sphincter – clearly points us to the boundary-instituting social interdictions and to what Kristeva has called the "primal mapping of the body", which,

> [t]hrough frustrations and prohibitions, [...] shapes the body into a *territory* having areas, orifices, points and lines, surfaces and hollows, where the archaic power of mastery and

2.3 Anarchic Bodies, or, Breughel and Bosch on the Freeway — 45

neglect, of the differentiation of proper-clean and improper-dirty, possible and impossible, is impressed and exerted (1982: 72; cf. Viney 2007: n.pag.).

According to Kristeva, this mapping is presided over by 'maternal authority', "an authority without guilt", which she opposes to 'paternal laws' – "the order of the phallus" – "where embarrassment, shame, guilt, desire, etc. come into play" and "within which [...] the destiny of man [sic] will take shape" (1982: 74, 72). I would argue that it is this 'territory' of the body beyond the law of the father that Ballard's characters attempt to recreate, an order in which "bodily wastes, while set apart from the body, [are] not seen as objects of embarrassment and shame" and hence "marked by an untrammelled pleasure in 'playing' with the body and its wastes" (Creed 1993: 13). If Vaughan and James seek the encounter with the abject, let their fascinated desire be seduced by it (Kristeva 1982: 1), embrace it and, in a sense, become, themselves, abject, it is because what is at stake in this is a subversion of the regulatory social practices through which the boundaries of the body and the contours of the subject are constructed. As Kristeva points out, what lies at the heart of the abject is not really lack of cleanliness or health, but "[w]hat does not respect borders, positions, rules", "what disturbs identity, system, order" (1982: 4). Such disturbance is precisely what Ballard's protagonists (and the novel as a whole) aim at. Thus, when, in a suggestive passage early on in the novel, James sees his own reflection in "a mirror of blood, semen and vomit" (*C* 9), this does obviously not indicate the specular constitution of subjectivity (Lacan 2004), but, on the contrary, its displacement through the abject. If this pool of bodily fluids "contains for [James] the essence of the [...] car-crash" (*C* 8 f), this is because it is just this renegotiation of the subject's ego and body that the protagonists' catastrophic strategy entails. Similar to Kristeva's 'stray', the main characters of the novel are 'non-subjects', wanderers in a fluid universe, who – to adopt a phrase of Kristeva's – the more they stray, the more they are saved (Kristeva 1982: 25, 8). *Crash* thus presents the encounter with the abject as a distinctly emancipatory process. Since, in the words of Judith Butler, "the body is not a 'being,' but a variable boundary, a surface whose permeability is politically regulated", the body's purity being "tenuously maintained for the purposes of social regulation and control", Vaughan and James' 'self-abjection' must be read as a political act, namely as a form of resistance against the social "border control that differentiates inner from outer, and so institutes the 'integrity' of the subject" (1999: 177, 170, 173).[29]

---

[29] In this context, cf. also the work of Pierre Bourdieu (1977, 1989) and Norbert Elias (1978), who

In *Crash*, 'integral' bodies are scarce. There are no unified subjects here, no wholeness or purity. Instead, *fragmentation* and *pollution* are the key elements of the novel's vision, maimed, porous, leaking and filthy bodies filling page after page of the text. What I read as the novel's exploration of an alternative corporeality is most consistently articulated through the character of Vaughan. The narrative not only presents Vaughan as obsessed with all kinds of bodily waste and deformation – for instance, "with the buboes of gas bacillus infections, by facial injuries and genital wounds" (*C* 3) – but moreover depicts his own body as the very epitome of this obsession: virtually his entire physique is "covered with scars", constituting a veritable "gallery of scars" (*C* 93, 122), which Vaughan, like the other characters, always displays openly. One of his nipples, severed after an accident, has been re-sectioned incorrectly and is now permanently erect, there are ulcers on his left index finger and his lower lip (*C* 122, 94, 120), his legs are uneven, an eye tooth is broken, his thumbnails are torn (*C* 99, 120, 94), and, especially towards the end of the text, he deliberately keeps on re-opening his many wounds and thus prevents them from healing (*C* 120, 157 f), turning his appearance into one marked by "leaking scars" (*C* 166). Beyond this, Vaughan's abject nature is further underlined by the fact that he is continually associated with a lack of hygiene and cleanliness: James describes Vaughan's "tacky navel and unsavoury armpits", "the minute nodes of dirt he pick[s] from his sharp nose and wipe[s] on the indented vinyl of the door panel [of his car]", the "dank odour" (*C* 172, 93 f, 121) that constantly rises from his body, the traces of various bodily fluids – his own as well as those of others – frequently visible on his clothes and body (e.g. *C* 137, 166), his "unsavoury skin and greasy pallor", as well as his always dirty car, which, with its "bloodsoaked instrument panels, seat-belts smeared with excrement, sun-visors lined with brain tissue" and so forth, is practically "marked with mucus from every orifice of the human body" (*C* 141, 5, 111).

As all of this makes clear, the image of the body that dominates the novel is akin to what Mikhail Bakhtin has called the 'grotesque' image of the body. Certainly, the body in *Crash* is not, strictly speaking, the one of the 'carnivalesque' tradition and the culture of folk humor that the Russian literary critic talks about, lacking as it does the latter's popular-festive and collective, universal, cosmic and utopian character. Nevertheless, like Bakhtin's, the novel's image of the body is obviously built around the 'material bodily principle', around what by dominant aesthetic standards is deemed ugly and monstrous, around excessive-

---

– though from a different perspective – likewise emphasize the political significance of the regulation of body functions and manners.

2.3 Anarchic Bodies, or, Breughel and Bosch on the Freeway

ness, disintegration, dismemberment and the transgression of bodily limits.[30] In short, it is an "unfinished and open body [...] not separated from the world by clearly defined boundaries; it is" – and here one need only think of the intimate connections between the protagonists and their cars – "blended with the world, with animals, with objects" (Bakhtin 1984: 26f). As Bakhtin explains, "the artistic logic of the grotesque image", which, I argue, is at work in *Crash*, too,[31] "ignores the closed, smooth, and impenetrable surface of the body and retains only its excrescences (sprouts, buds) and orifices, only that which leads beyond the body's limited space or into the body's depths" (1984: 317f). This concept of the body is radically opposed to "the bourgeois conception of the completed atomized being" as enshrined in the now dominant, 'classical' image of the body, which

> presents an entirely finished, completed, strictly limited body, which is shown from the outside as something individual. That which protrudes, bulges, sprouts, or branches off (when a body transgresses its limits and a new one begins) is eliminated, hidden, or moderated. All orifices of the body are closed. The basis of the image is the individual, strictly limited mass, the impenetrable façade. The opaque surface and the body's 'valleys' acquire an essential meaning as the border of a closed individuality that does not merge with other bodies and with the world. (Bakhtin 1984: 24, 320)

Ballard's novel repeatedly invokes this classical body as its counter-image, the bourgeois ideal it subverts, for example, through the narrator's allusion to the childhood 'commissionaires' guarding his orifices (see above) or through the character of Catherine Ballard, James' wife. The latter declares:

> What had first struck me about Catherine was her immaculate cleanliness, as if she had individually reamed out every square centimetre of her elegant body, separately ventilated every pore.[32] [...] During our first sex acts, [...] I would deliberately inspect every orifice I could find, running my fingers around her gums in the hope of seeing even one small knot of trapped veal, forcing my tongue into her ear in the hope of finding a trace of the taste of wax, inspecting her nostrils and naval, and lastly her vulva and anus. I would have to run my forefinger to its root before I could extract even a faint scent of faecal matter, a thin brown rim under my fingernail. (*C* 89f)

---

30 Appropriately, James at one point comments that "one almost expects to see Breughel and Hieronymus Bosch cruising the freeways in their rental-company cars" (*C* 38); references to the two Early Netherlandish artists are also made by Bakhtin (1984: 27) as well as Lacan (2004: 444), who consider the former's paintings as illustrations of the concepts of the 'grotesque body' and the 'fragmented body' respectively.
31 In fact, at one point the narrator explicitly describes Vaughan as "grotesque" (*C* 142).
32 The mechanistic vocabulary employed here ('ream', 'ventilate') suggests the objectified and machinic conception of the body of post-Cartesian modernity.

This, clearly, is the clean, finished and closed body of the 'proper' bourgeois subject, the – finally impossible – ideal of the dominant order whose regulatory practices establish and maintain the division between internal and external for the sake of the consolidation of hegemonic identities.[33] In Butler's words: "For inner and outer worlds to remain utterly distinct, the entire surface of the body would have to achieve an impossible impermeability. This sealing of its surfaces would constitute the seamless boundary of the subject" (1999: 170).

When James relates how his wife, visiting him at the hospital, absurdly worries about the little "cosmetic attention" given to patients and promises to bring some make-up in order to cover his wounds, when he states that her buttocks are "as immaculate as a doll's", or when he remarks on "the porcelain appearance of her face, an over-elaborate make-up like some demonstration model of a beautiful woman's face" (*C* 20, 92, 90), the novel, moreover, indicates the heightened significance that this ideal of the classical body has, on another level, assumed in the late 20th century in the shape of what has been called 'the tyranny of slenderness' (Chernin 1981), that is, the current "quest for firm bodily margins", for the prevalent "ideal […] of a body that is absolutely tight, contained, 'bolted down,' firm" (Bordo 1995: 191, 190). Jean Baudrillard has linked this ideal to the structures of global consumer capitalism. He, too, identifies a *"new ethics of the relation to the body"* which tends "to conjure away the 'organic' body and, in particular, the functions of excretion and secretion" and which "sanctifies it in its hygienic abstraction" (1998b: 132, 141, 142). Baudrillard, too, ascertains a new imperative requiring the body to be "as closed and as smooth as possible, faultless, without orifice and 'lacking' nothing" (1993b: 104), a 'vitrified' body, as he puts it, one that is fully functional. The postmodern subject, accord-

---

[33] Against the background of my reading of Catherine and Vaughan in terms of the classical and the grotesque body respectively, a detailed analysis of the powerful scene of their first sexual encounter – an episode, moreover, that takes place within Vaughan's car *while it is being cleaned in a car wash* – would surely be revealing. William Viney, in his instructive discussion of waste in Ballard's fiction, has pointed out the inconclusive (and morally ambiguous) nature of this scene, and argued that one possible reading of it would be to interpret Catherine and Vaughan's copulation in terms of the former's "being cleansed of her corporeal unreality" (2007: n.pag.). It seems to me that the fusion of the two different bodies in this episode and the repeated juxtaposition of abject and clean matter, of pollution and purification ("I sat quietly in the front seat as the white soap sluiced across the roof and doors like liquid lace. Behind me, Vaughan's semen glistened on my wife's breasts and abdomen." [*C* 134]), may also be taken to point to the fundamental – though disavowed at the level of official identity – connection between the two realms of the pure and high and the impure and low, i.e. to the basic hybridity produced at the level of the 'political unconscious' by the very attempt to demarcate insuperable boundaries (cf. Stallybrass and White 1986).

2.3 Anarchic Bodies, or, Breughel and Bosch on the Freeway — 49

ing to Baudrillard, is called upon to narcissistically 'invest' in its body – both psychically and economically – and 'realize' it – again, in two senses – as capital and as commodity. One of the modalities of this "functional imperative" is the "beauty imperative", which the last-quoted passages from *Crash* clearly point to, an obligation that entails "the reduction of all concrete values – the 'use-values' of the body (energetic, gestural, sexual) – to a single functional 'exchange value', which [...] in the end simply peters out into an exchange of signs" (Baudrillard 1998b: 132). "For", the French philosopher avers, "beauty is nothing more than sign material being exchanged. It *functions* as sign-value." (1998b: 132) For Baudrillard, the contemporary reappropriation of the body does hence ultimately not signal emancipation, since it "is not reappropriated for the autonomous ends of the subject, but [...] in terms of an enforced instrumentality that is indexed to the code and the norms of a society of production and managed consumption" (1998b: 131). Through the character of Catherine Ballard and her body, *Crash* suggests precisely this reappropriation for capitalist objectives in the form of the transformation of the body into a consumer object and sign, a labor that, Baudrillard contends, "doubtless represents a more profoundly alienated labour than the exploitation of the body as labour power" (1998b: 132). It seems to me that it is this alienation that Ballard's characters move beyond, the car crash constituting a catastrophic strategy to contest the late-capitalist involvement of the body "in the goals of production as (economic) support, as principle of the managed (psychological) integration of the individual, and as (political) strategy of social control" (Baudrillard 1998b: 136). The various "deviant anatom[ies]" (*C* 20) the novel fashions with its countless abject, fragmented and grotesque bodies effectively signal a subversion of the power mechanisms through which the body is produced and inscribed into the capitalist order and the elaboration of an alternative corporeality (and subjectivity) beyond the norms of social 'intelligibility'.

It is only logical that this refashioning of the body should be connected in the novel with a refashioning of sexuality – after all, as Foucault, Butler and numerous others have shown, sexual identities, desires, practices and beliefs are similarly far from natural but socially determined and always articulated within specific economic, political and social structures, which they are designed to uphold. Again and again, *Crash* emphasizes that the innumerable 'deviant' sexual acts the protagonists indulge in must be seen in the context of the emergence of a radically "new sexuality" (*C* 6). This sexuality is characterized by what we may call an uncompromising 'will to perversion', where 'perversion' is perhaps best defined along the lines suggested by Roland Barthes – one of the late 20th century's great champions of perversion[34] – as "the search for a pleasure that cannot be turned to the profit of social ends or the species" (1995: 206). As the novel progresses, the protagonists, having developed a strong "curiosity for the perverse in all its forms", "explore every byway of sex" and "all the deviant possibilities" it opens up, experiment with all kinds of "depraved acts" and "fascinating perversities", and in this way consciously aim at "becoming ever more perverse" (*C* 38, 141, 79, 184). This drive for transgression is a 'total' one; when, for instance, the narrator's wife – in a truly Sadeian spirit – declares that she "[will] never be satisfied until every conceivable act of copulation in the world ha[s] at last taken place" (*C* 86), or when James imagines a radically libertarian, indeed, an anarchist realm in which absolutely all taboos have been broken and abolished (*C* 148 f), it becomes clear that what is at stake is not just the infraction of binary structures, but a movement into an utterly negative space beyond the law and the structure of significance itself (cf. Stallybrass and White 1986: 18). The characters' unreserved dedication to transgression can thus be read as a quest for the uninhibited enjoyment of Lacanian *jouissance*,[35] in which 'one joys' violently and painfully (Kristeva 1982: 9), and which – appropriately, in light of my discussion of the novel – Lacan and Kristeva have linked with the fragmented body and the abject. As James remarks: "The endless highway systems along which we moved contained the formulas for *an infinity of sexual bliss*." (*C* 175, emphasis added)

Beyond this, it seems to me that the protagonists' fabrication of a "free and perverse sexuality" (*C* 79) must – despite its morally highly problematic nature – be accorded its full subversive potential. One way of reading their excesses is to see in them a liberation of the undifferentiated sexual pleasure of the Freudian infant, which, according to Freud, has to be largely repressed in the interests of socio-political organization. *Crash* repeatedly implies such a process of 'de-sublimation', as when the narrator talks about the "unconscious incest [of siblings] made explicit" in their crashes, about "the hidden faces of [one character's] psyche" coming to the fore, of the crash as "releasing" new sexual possibilities, or of his own "latent homosexual impulse" (*C* 6, 77, 79, 94) which he eventually acts out. Similarly, Ballard, in his introduction to the book, speaks of the "tapping [of] our own psychopathologies" and the "harnessing of our innate perversity", which, he argues, may "conceivably [be] of benefit to us" (*C* n.pag.). All of this,

---

[34] In his autobiography – if that is what this playful text can be called – Barthes declares: "perversion, quite simply, *makes happy*" (1994: 64).
[35] For an insightful psychoanalytic reading – albeit of David Cronenberg's filmic adaptation, not the novel itself – which uses the Lacanian model and focuses on the topic of *jouissance*, cf. Adams 1999.

clearly, is the language of psychoanalysis. It would seem that the 'perverse dynamic' that Jonathan Dollimore (1991), in his reading of Freud, has identified at the heart of Western constructions of sexuality, that is, the inevitable destabilization of the sexual norm due to the fundamental interconnectedness of civilization and perversion, runs wild in *Crash*, thus freeing a veritable 'polymorphous perversity'. However, in a novel that places such emphasis on the social constructedness of the subject and the colonization/production of its subjectivity by the mass media in particular as this one does, it remains, I think, ultimately an open question in how far we may actually speak of a 'regression' to pre-social libidinal instincts along the lines of the psychoanalytic model here – a process, moreover, of which classical psychoanalysis can only conceive in negative terms, while *Crash* portrays it as a distinctly emancipatory one.

A more appropriate way of understanding the protagonists' deviant acts therefore seems to be to view them in terms of the sexual experimentation and production suggested by Michel Foucault, Gilles Deleuze and Félix Guattari, and others. Foucault, for sure, can be considered the intellectual who has most extensively investigated the question of sexuality. For him, it is not just that sexual beliefs and behavior are always socially determined, but that it is in fact the law that *constitutes* desire – "[w]here there is desire, the power relation is already present" (1978: 81), he declares – and that the very notion of 'sexuality' and the conception of 'sex' as a fact of nature are, in truth, historical constructs. "Sexuality", Foucault explains, "must not be thought of as a kind of natural given which power tries to hold in check"; instead,

> [i]t is the name that can be given to a historical construct [*un dispositif historique*]: not a furtive reality that is difficult to grasp, but a great surface network in which the stimulation of bodies, the intensification of pleasures, the incitement to discourse, the formation of special knowledges, the strengthening of controls and resistances, are linked to one another, in accordance with a few major strategies of knowledge and power. (1978: 105 f)

According to Foucault, it was the operation of this *dispositif* that necessitated the establishment of the modern notion of 'sex', which "made it possible to group together, in an artificial unity, anatomical elements, biological functions, conducts, sensations, and pleasures" and "to make use of this fictitious unity as a causal principle" (1978: 154). In this way, crucially, 'sex' "made it possible to invert the representation of the relationships of power to sexuality, causing the latter to appear, not in its essential and positive relation to power, but as being rooted in a specific and irreducible urgency which power tries as best it can to dominate" (Foucault 1978: 155) – with the result that power is conceived of only in terms of repression and prohibition. For this reason, Foucault urges us not to believe that freedom lies along the path of a 'liberation' of sex, but to recognize that sex is only the "most internal element in a deployment of sexuality [*un dispositif de sexualité*] organized by power in its grip on bodies and their materiality, their forces, energies, sensations, and pleasures" (1978: 155). To speak, as psychoanalysis does, of a 'polymorphous sexual perversity' thus only means coloring infancy "with the monotonous monochrome" (Foucault 1996i: 219) of adult sexuality. In Foucault's eyes, "the liberty of not being an adult consist[s] exactly in not being enslaved to the law of sexuality", the child having "a flow of pleasure for which the 'sex' grid is a veritable prison" (1996i: 219). It is, according to the French theorist, such a flow that we need to (re-)create. He declares: "The rallying point for the counterattack against the deployment of sexuality [*le dispositif de sexualité*] ought not to be sex-desire, but bodies and pleasures." (1978: 157)

I want to argue that the protagonists' exploration of "the possibilities of an entirely new sexuality" (*C* 81) in Ballard's *Crash* must be read in terms of such an elaboration of "a different economy of bodies and pleasures", that is, in terms of a "counter[ing of] the grips of power with the claims of bodies, pleasures, and knowledges, in their multiplicity and their possibility of resistance" (Foucault 1978: 159, 157). Certainly, a commitment to the multiplicity of bodies and pleasures lies at the heart of *Crash*. As James observes, he himself, Vaughan and the others are driven by an "obsession with the sexual possibilities of everything around [them]" (*C* 19). Crashes, cars, wounds, violence, pain, dejecta, bodies, especially non-normative, transgressive ones – all of these become sources of pleasure for Ballard's protagonists, and in this proliferation of possible sources, (genital) sex is only one among myriads of others. The narrative thus to some extent stages what Foucault has called the 'desexualization of pleasure' (1996e: 212, 1996g: 384): it dissolves the established conflation of bodily pleasure and sex and points towards "a general economy of pleasure that would not be sexually normed" (Foucault 1996e: 212). The narrator is therefore exactly right when he notes that his and the others' sexual acts are "devoid of ordinary sexuality" (*C* 132). The characters' endless 'perversions' mark an experimental and *creative* enterprise in the Foucauldian sense, inventing numerous new possibilities and forms of pleasure, attachments and intensities, and hence signal the end of the "austere monarchy of sex" and the inauguration of a more liberal, "non-disciplinary eroticism" (Foucault 1978: 159, 1996f: 189), which allows, as Foucault puts it, to "have polymorphic relationships with things, people and bodies" and to "produce pleasure with very odd things, very strange parts of our bodies, in very unusual situations, and so on" (1996i: 219, 1996g: 384). These words, surely, are an apt characterization of the novel's protagonists.

Aside from the countless passages that depict the car as the locus or object of pleasure, one part in which this logic of a post-sexual innovation of pleasure

2.3 Anarchic Bodies, or, Breughel and Bosch on the Freeway — 53

becomes fully manifest is the one relating James' erotic encounters with Gabrielle, a severely disabled young woman, in the latter's invalid car. Appropriately, the narrator refers to their sexual acts as "exploratory ordeals" (*C* 145). As James quickly discovers, "the nominal junction points of the sexual act – breast and penis, anus and vulva, nipple and clitoris – fai[l] to provide any excitement for [them]" (*C* 147), which leads them to shift the focus of their caresses from these conventional points to other regions, in particular to their scars and wound areas. Subsequently, James' orgasms take place "within the deep wound on her thigh", "within the scars below her breast and within her left armpit", and "in the wounds on her neck and shoulder" (*C* 148). For James and Gabrielle, these wounds become exciting "sexual apertures", to be used in "extraordinary sexual acts", and the former consequently dreams of "dozens of auxiliary orifices" "that might enlarge this repertoire of orifices" (*C* 148, 149, 148). Like the grooves and markings left on the woman's skin by her various braces, the narrator comes to consider these orifices as "invagination[s] of [...] sexual organ[s] still in the embryonic stages of [their] evolution", as "templates for new genital organs" and "moulds of sexual possibilities yet to be created in a hundred experimental car-crashes" (*C* 146). In such passages, Ballard appears to be working under the influence of his great hero William Burroughs,[36] in whose novel *Naked Lunch* one finds the following segment:

> The physical changes were slow at first, then jumped forward in black klunks, falling through his slack tissue, washing away the human lines... [...] no organ is constant as regards either function or position... sex organs sprout anywhere... rectums open, defecate and close... the entire organism changes color and consistency in split-second adjustments... (2010: 9)

It seems to me that, in their different ways, both Ballard's and Burroughs' texts aim at a representation of what Foucault has termed the "great pleasure of the body in explosion" (1996f: 188). Foucault explains: "It's a question of multiplying and burgeoning of the body, an exaltation [...] of its least parts, of the least possibilities of a body fragment. There is an anarchizing of the body, in which hierarchies, localizations and designations, organicity if you like, is being undone." (1996f: 186f) A very similar logic of "making the body escape itself" is at work in *Crash*; a scene like the one just discussed presents a volatile and diffused body, one "made entirely malleable by pleasure: something that opens it-

---

[36] For Ballard's discussions of Burroughs' work, cf. e.g. 1996e, 1996k, 1996m.

self, tightens, palpitates, beats, gapes" (Foucault 1996f: 187).[37] The incessant fragmentation and 'anarchization' of the body performed by the narrative – turning the body into a veritable "fretwork of scars" (*C* 121) – can thus be read in terms of Deleuze and Guattari's concept of the 'body without organs' (BwO). Like Foucault, the two French thinkers counter the Lacanian narrative of a necessary transition from fragmentation to (the illusion of) corporeal (and psychical) unity and autonomy and instead celebrate bodily (and psychical) dis-organization. Opposed not to the organs as such but to their organization in the totality of the organism, the BwO is a body in a state of continuous 'becoming', "populated by multiplicities" and "alive and teeming" (Deleuze and Guattari 1987: 30). When, at the beginning of the novel, James compares "the perverse eroticism of the car-crash" to "the drawing of an exposed organ through the aperture of a surgical wound" (*C* 9), does this, at first sight puzzling, image not suggest precisely this unmaking of the organism that Deleuze and Guattari propose? The 'essence' of the BwO, they maintain, consists in the "connection of desires, conjunction of flows, continuum of intensities" – indeed, "[t]he BwO *is* desire; it is that which one desires and by which one desires" (Deleuze and Guattari 1987: 161, 165, emphasis added).[38] As in the work of the two theorists, in *Crash*, too, desire appears not to originate in lack, as the Lacanian model has it, but to be fundamentally *productive*, creating ever new possibilities. Desire here emerges as something fluid, protean and unconstrained that exceeds all determinations and has no fixed aim or object. James, Vaughan, Gabrielle and the novel's other main characters effectively become (part of) what Deleuze and Guattari (1983) term 'desiring-machines' which ceaselessly 'produce', making desire flow, expand and enter into always fresh and as yet unheard-of conjunctions. With this 'rhizomatic' and proliferating desire and its continuously changing linkages and connections, Ballard's protagonists have successfully dismantled not only the "castration machine" (Hocquenghem 1995: 262) of 'sexuality' but also all the received and falsely naturalized distinctions and catego-

---

[37] In this context, cf. also Alphonso Lingis' instructive discussion of 'primitive' incisions and body markings, which, he argues, function as "new intensive points, pain-pleasure points" that "exten[d] the erotogenic surface" (1983: 38) of the body (cf. also Grosz 1994: 138ff). It seems to me that Lingis' deliberations constitute another fruitful framework – though one related to the one adopted here – for the reading of the violent restructuring of the body surface in *Crash*.

[38] For a more detailed discussion of the notion of the 'BwO' and the thought of Deleuze and Guattari generally, cf. chapter 3.

ries such as 'man' and 'woman' or 'hetero-' and 'homosexual'.[39] What the novel outlines is, in fact, a world beyond 'sexuality' and 'gender'.[40] It seems to me, for example, that when James, towards the end of the text, has sexual intercourse with Vaughan, this is not, strictly speaking, a 'homosexual act', but just another of the multiplicity of nomadic conjunctions fashioned by desire for the creation of pleasure, for which the old, binary classifications simply do not hold anymore. As a matter of fact, Ballard himself has suggested such a reading in an interview conducted in 1984, in which he remarks that "[t]he few homosexual elements in *Crash* [...] are there for reasons other than sexual – in fact, to show a world beyond sexuality, or, at least, beyond clear sexual gender" (in Frick 2012: 189). In this way, the novel effectively subverts what Deleuze and Guattari call the "anthropomorphic representation" of sexuality, sex and gender and replaces it with a "nonhuman" conception, consisting, in the words of the two philosophers, in a "microscopic transsexuality, resulting in the woman containing as many men as the man, and the man as many women, all capable of entering [...] into relations of production of desire that overturn the statistical order of the sexes" (1983: 294, 295f). *Crash*'s desiring-machines are "not one or even two sexes, but *n* sexes" and thus realize the slogan of the Deleuzoguattarian "desiring-revolution": "to each its own sexes" (Deleuze and Guattari 1983: 296). Hence, it is only appropriate that Vaughan, who is at one point compared to a "deranged drag queen", is said to "us[e]" his sex "casually as if he might discard it for ever at any moment" (*C* 166, 2);[41] here, virtually all determinism – including the kind our culture renders as 'natural' or 'biological' – has been extinguished. *Crash* thus depicts a world in which the "whole scouring of the unconscious" called

---

39 Nevertheless, it might be argued that despite all of this, desire in the novel still remains rather phallic (Luckhurst 1997: 112f) and orgasm-centered. This, however, seems to be somewhat undercut at least on the formal level: while *Crash*, strictly speaking, consists of a linear narrative, I would argue that this linearity has almost nothing in common with that of the traditional, realist novel, since it is, structurally speaking, severely weakened by the obsessive repetitiveness and 'plot-lessness' and the lack of closure of the text (in this context, cf. Ballard in Louit 2012: 74). If we accept the connection between narrative design and sexual trajectories posited by Roland Barthes (1975), Peter Brooks (1992) and others, then this undermining of linearity can, I think, be read as a deflation of the teleology of the male orgasm. For another reading that complicates a straightforward identification of the novel with phallocentrism, cf. Beckman 2010: 162ff.
40 In a somewhat related reading, Konstanze Kutzbach (2007) discusses the novel with reference to Thomas Laqueur's work on the 'one-' and the 'two-sex model' and argues that *Crash* culminates in a 'none-sex model'.
41 The repeated cross-dressing of the character Seagrave – whose name, beyond his destructiveness, already implies a certain proteanness – can be read in this context as well. The fact that it is recurrently designated as a form of 'parody' (*C* 83, 88) moreover evokes Judith Butler's (1999: 163ff) interpretation of drag as gender parody or pastiche.

for by Deleuze and Guattari – "[d]estroy Oedipus, the illusion of the ego, the puppet of the superego, guilt, the law, castration" (1983: 311), they demand – has been achieved and in which the flows of desire consequently travel entirely freely.⁴²

One important element in this desexualization of pleasure and the concomitant desubjectivation of the body is violence. New forms of pleasure always involve or are based on some kind of violence, bodies have to be 'remade' in ever more brutal ways – at the heart of the novel's notion of liberation lies the car-crash wound. In *Crash*, the excitements of a new sexuality necessarily mean "the excitements of a new violence", too, the protagonists' alternative eroticism is an "eroticism of wounds", and the "infinite futures" the narrator envisages will "flower from the marriage of violence and desire" (*C* 145, 5, 128). With this, the novel once again places itself in the (masculinist) tradition of transgressive erotics that also includes Bataille and Foucault. The latter, too, argues that "[a] pleasure must be something incredibly intense" and consequently advocates experimentation with, among other things, forms of "pleasure-pain" (1996a: 378, 1996d: 313) such as homosexual sadomasochism in order to attack the normalized self. In both *Crash* and certain writings of Foucault, emancipatory pleasure is thus identified with violent transgression, a logic that leads both to adopt a celebratory view of death: just like Ballard's characters continuously fine-tune the plans for their own "sex-death" (*C* 151), so Foucault, too, declares that "complete total pleasure" is "related to death" (1996a: 378).⁴³

Just as crucial as violence in the resistance to "somatic-power" (Foucault 1996e: 209) and its construction of bodies and their desire is technology, here mainly represented by the car. After all, it is principally through the violence

---

42 At this point, perhaps, another possible reading of the oft-observed (and oft-criticized) 'flatness' of the novel's characters presents itself. Instead of considering their lack of psychological depth as an indication of the late-capitalist decentering of the subject as was suggested above, it may also – more positively – be construed in terms of a conscious break with what the German film director Werner Schroeter, in conversation with Foucault, referred to as "the system of psychological terror" (in Foucault 1996d: 317) in the arts, and consequently be taken to signal the 'de-personalization' of desiring-production, that is, the liberation of the individual from its bourgeois personhood (Deleuze and Guattari 1983: 55). As Foucault, in line with Deleuze and Guattari, declares: "The art of living is to eliminate psychology, to create, with oneself and others, individualities, beings, relations, unnameable qualities." (1996d: 317)

43 Here, as elsewhere, another revealing reference text for a reading of *Crash* is François Peraldi's (1995a, 1995b) essay on 'polysexuality' (and, indeed, the entire collection of that name of which it is a part), in which the subjects discussed here – power, the body and its desubjectivation, official and polymorphous sexuality, *jouissance*, death, and language – all come up for discussion.

2.3 Anarchic Bodies, or, Breughel and Bosch on the Freeway — 57

of the car that bodies are transformed in the text, and it is likewise the automobile that opens up new pathways of desire and new forms of pleasure. At this point, the novel thus indicates a positive, liberatory side to technology. *Crash* presents the motor-car as "the sexual act's greatest and only true locus", a "small museum of excitement and possibility" (*C* 141, 53), and as an object of desire itself (e.g. *C* 65), establishes an "equation [...] between sex and the kinaesthetics of the highway" (*C* 141), so that driving and intercourse turn into models for one another (*C* 24, 116f.), incessantly emphasizes that "invisible eroticisms" and "undiscovered sexual acts" "[lie] waiting" in the automobile, its "instrument binnacles provid[ing] a readily accessible anthology of depraved acts" (*C* 29, 79), and thus suggests that it is the car, especially in collision, that is "the key to a new sexuality" (*C* 96). The new economy of pleasure created by the novel's protagonists is hence one that is "born from a perverse technology" (*C* 6). In this economy, the boundary line between the animate and the inanimate is increasingly hard to draw. For one thing, the characters enter into ever more intimate relationships with their machines, their bodies effectively "marry[ing]" with parts of their cars, so that, for instance, the treadles of Gabrielle's car come to appear as "extensions of her clitoris" (*C* 110, 79), a phrase that recalls Marshall McLuhan's (1994) famous notion of technologies as 'extensions of man' (sic). Similarly, James notes his "growing sense of a new junction between [his] own body and the automobile" – and countless variations of this junction are observed by all the characters throughout the text – and at one point even refers to his vehicle as "[his] own metal body" (*C* 41, 90). Aside from this, the novel also continuously establishes correspondences between man (sic) and machine and in this way destabilizes any clear-cut distinction. Thus, on the one hand, technology is frequently depicted in terms of a living organism – "dying chromium" and "injured transmission[s]", "machine fellatio" (*C* 2, 70, 5), air vents "beckon[ing] as invitingly as the warmest organic orifice", styling details of cars "contain[ing] an organic life as meaningful as the limbs and sense organs of [...] human beings" (*C* 30, 140) – while on the other, human beings are regularly portrayed as inanimate and machine-like – "the soft technology of Catherine's breasts", eyes "flicking like windshield wipers", moisture on the skin appearing "like the bloom on a morning windshield" (*C* 23, 46, 63), the "metallic sheen" of Vaughan's body, "like the worn vinyl of the car interior", and the "metallic grimace" of his smile, Catherine and Vaughan's bodies during their lovemaking in the car wash looking "like two semi-metallic human beings" (*C* 71, 75, 133) in the refracted light, and the numerous passages in which men and women are compared to mannequins and dolls (e.g. *C* 38, 98, 131) are all compelling examples of this.

What all of this signals, is, I think, the crucial collapse of the distinction between human and machine that theorists like Donna Haraway have identified with regards to the late twentieth century.[44] According to the latter, contemporary machines have fully undermined the certainty of what counts as 'nature'. In a passage that resonates with the imagery of *Crash*, she observes: "Our machines are disturbingly lively, and we ourselves frighteningly inert." (2010: 2193) For Haraway, the breakdown of this boundary – along with the one between human and animal and the one between physical and non-physical – is, however, nothing to be lamented. Instead, it offers the opportunity to leave behind the "border war" which the relation between the human and his/her 'others' has so long been in the West, and hence to create a new, non-essentialist politics: a "cyborg politics" (Haraway 2010: 2191). It seems to me that Ballard's protagonists, for whom "machines can be prosthetic devices, intimate components, friendly selves" (Haraway 2010: 2218), as well as the novel as a whole, subscribe to just such a politics. Having realized that the cyborg – a hybrid of machine and organism – "is our ontology", they set about constructing a "cyborg world" that, as in Haraway's vision, is "about lived social and bodily realities in which people are not afraid of their joint kinship with animals and machines, not afraid of permanently partial identities and contradictory standpoints" (2010: 2191, 2196).[45] The character of Gabrielle can be read as an embodiment of this cyborg logic infusing the text. Having been severely injured during a car crash, her deformed body is now reinforced with metal, supported by leg braces, a spinal harness, straps, and a metal cane. In fact, the text consistently portrays her as a veritable *(re-)assembled* creature, whose ontology is undefined and unfixed: thus, James describes the "unmatching planes" of her face – which, he notes, seem "to mimic the deformed panels of [her crushed] car" – the "angular contours" and "unexpected junctions" (*C* 79, 145) of her body, and the "causeways driven through her flesh" by the instruments of the car in which she crashed, and recounts how, during their sex acts, "the unfamiliar planes of her hips and legs stee[r] [him] into unique culs-de-sac, strange declensions of skin and musculature", the "bizarre geometry" (*C* 147, 145) of her invalid car effectively mirroring that of her own physique. In fact, when James undresses Gabrielle, he observes that the "exposed portions of her body [are] *joined together* [only] by the loosened braces and straps" (*C* 147, emphasis added), and comes to expect

---

[44] For another, though very different, reading of the novel that makes reference to Haraway's "Cyborg Manifesto", cf. Roden 2003.

[45] As I try to show, the last part of this quotation is a very apt characterization not just of the protagonists of the text, but of the novel as a whole, and, indeed, of Ballard's entire oeuvre. We may, therefore, perhaps speak of a veritable 'cyborg novel' and a 'cyborg oeuvre' here.

that her breast, too, will be "a detachable latex structure, fitted on each morning along with her spinal brace and leg supports" (*C* 147). In view of this cyborg ontology – which, with varying degrees, defines the other characters as well – it is only appropriate that the narrator identifies Gabrielle as the "queen of [the] overactive technarchy" (*C* 144) of which they all are a part.

Similar to Haraway, Ballard's novel celebrates the cyborg as the one who uncompromisingly constructs the body without organs, who "has no truck with [...] seductions to organic wholeness", to identification with nature or unitary identity, and who – happily – exists as "a kind of disassembled and reassembled post-modern [...] self" (Haraway 2010: 2191, 2205). Gabrielle's aberrant physique is consequently presented not so much in terms of 'disability' and impairment, but of a powerful transformation, indeed, of a rebirth (*C* 78f) that awakens a "sense of the real possibilities of her body" and produces "new parameters" for it which allow for the development of a radically new "sexual expertise" (*C* 79). James remarks: "I felt no trace of pity for this crippled woman, but celebrated with her the excitements of [the] abstract vents let into her body by sections of her own automobile" (*C* 148). Similarly, when Gabrielle caresses him, James feels like she is "searching for [his] own missing armatures of bright chromium" (*C* 146). Here, the alteration of the body through the fusion with the machine is clearly nothing to be lamented, on account of its alleged distortion of some kind of 'nature', but something avidly desired for its radical sexual potential. Scars, deformations, braces, harnesses, and prostheses are hence not handicaps, but an arsenal of sexual possibilities. The protagonists' deliberate crashes, as well as, for instance, Helen Remington's conscious mimicking of Gabrielle's postures (*C* 97f) or Vaughan's miming of the "equations between the styling of a motor-car and the organic elements of his body" (*C* 140) in his own behavior, can thus be read in terms of what Deleuze and Guattari (1987: 232–309) would call 'becoming-machine'. It is this metamorphosis that brings about the libidinal freeplay beyond 'sex' and 'gender' discussed above. As the narrator observes: "The deformed body of the crippled young woman [...] revealed the possibilities of an entirely new sexuality." (*C* 81) In this way, *Crash* seems to anticipate arguments concerning the 'erotics of disability' more recently made in the field of Disability Studies, in which critics such as Margrit Shildrick have not just underlined the striking compatibility of their discipline with Queer Theory generally and Deleuzian thought in particular, but even claimed that "the Deleuzian project will be realised at least in part through the medium of rethinking disability" (Shildrick 2009: 127). Highlighting this project's shift of emphasis from unified and integrated bodies and reproductive heterosexual desire to 'becoming' and the only ever temporary coming together of disparate parts, to connections across received boundaries such as the one between man (sic) and machine, and the unmapped circulation of desire, Shildrick maintains that people with disabilities by necessity oftentimes already materialize the rhizomatic conjunctions and libidinal possibilities envisaged by Deleuze and Guattari, which, though in principle open to all of us, are for the most part kept in check by the rigid structures of normative sexuality and corporeality. The disabled body, she argues, "is a material site of possibility where de-formations, 'missing' parts and prostheses are enablers of new channels of desiring-production unconstrained by predetermined – or at least normative – organisation", so that "the anomalous nature of disability holds out the promise of an immanent desire that embraces the strange and opens up to new linkages and provisional incorporations" (2009: 122). It seems to me that these remarks perfectly encapsulate the essence of *Crash*, in which, similarly, "a reliance on prosthetic devices – the linkages between human and machine – [...] figure[s] not as limitations [sic] but as transformative possibilities [sic] of becoming other along multiple lines of flight" (Shildrick 2009: 126) beyond what Lennard J. Davis has called the "somatic judicial system" (1997: 68).[46] This, as we have seen, entails the shattering of received gender positionalities. As Haraway – whose theoretical approach evidently has much in common with Deleuze and Guattari as well as Shildrick – explains, "[c]yborgs might consider more seriously the partial, fluid, sometimes aspect of sex and sexual embodiment" and thus, perhaps, realize the utopian dream of "a monstrous world without gender" (2010: 2219, 2220).

It is certainly no coincidence that the harbinger of this monstrous world should be called Gabrielle, a name that recalls a much more ancient herald. While Jeannette Baxter sees in the disfigured woman only "a prosthetic parody of the archangel Gabriel" (2009: 112), I propose to read her as, in a sense, the latter's postmodern equivalent. Whereas the Bible's messenger was a (male) angel, the epitome of purity and benevolence, and foretold a (heterosexual) immaculate conception and the eternal kingdom of good, Ballard's contemporary version is a (female/post-gender) cyborg, the archetype of impurity and hybridity, and prefigures a new anarchy of excess and radical pollution, of "disturbingly and pleasurably tight coupling" (Haraway 2010: 2193) with anything and anyone. In this coming era, as Haraway remarks, "[b]estiality has a new status" (2010: 2193). Hence, what the reader can glimpse very clearly on the horizon of the novel's world is, in Foucault's well-known words, "that man [sic] [will] be erased, like a face drawn in sand at the edge of the sea" (2002: 422). The new realm heralded by Gabrielle is a distinctly posthuman one, since all the boundaries that

---

[46] With such an argument, there is, of course, always the danger of romanticizing disability (of which Shildrick is fully aware). Nevertheless, I think that her case is a compelling one.

have defined 'man' (sic) in the Western tradition are here transgressed and thus revealed in their fictitiousness: human and machine (and animal), culture and nature, mind and body, male and female, self and other, and so on. The characters' bodies are posthuman bodies, their corporeal mutations constituting what Michael Hardt and Antonio Negri have called an "anthropological exodus" (2001: 215), something they identify as an extraordinarily important element of contemporary political struggle. Despite the novel's emphasis on technology and the seamless articulation of human being with the machine, Ballard's world is posthumanist in a much more comprehensive and fundamental way than a mere vision of a technologically enhanced humanity – a vision that, as N. Katherine Hayles has observed, frequently consists in nothing more than a "grafting of the posthuman onto a liberal humanist view of the self" (1999: 286f). *Crash*, instead, largely undermines this view. It seems to me that the essence of the novel's posthumanism resides in what I would characterize as its uncompromising subversion of humanist modernity's 'will to purity' (Kroker and Kroker 1993: 12–14). As various scholars have argued, human identity – a tenuous discursive construct rather than an ontological absolute – is existentially dependent on what Bruno Latour (1993) has termed 'the work of purification', that is, the positing of pure essences and insuperable boundaries, the absolutization and hierarchization of differences both within the human and between the human and the non-human. At the same time, it remains haunted by its excluded others, by 'translation' (Latour 1993), pollution and hybridity, a threat that constantly and obsessively has to be warded off through what Elaine L. Graham (2002: 33–37) calls 'ontological hygiene'. As Arthur and Marilouise Kroker point out, humanism's will to purity must therefore be seen as a "form of cultural fascism, with its nostalgic defense of pure referents that never existed and its panic fear about a dirty world" (1993: 14). Dirt, of course, is what *Crash* is all about. "Recognition of a posthuman agenda", Judith Halberstam and Ira Livingston aver, "requires new protocols for reading the positivity of horror and abjection, not as representational (as pedagogical object-lessons: don't try this at home) but as functional dysfunctions that make other things happen" (1995: 14) – as we have already seen, Ballard's novel invites just such a protocol. I would argue that *Crash* is one of the late 20th century's great 'pollution-narratives', a text in which nothing is ever 'pure'. Man (sic) fuses with the machine, bodies are sullied and deformed, pleasures are multiple, sex as well as gender are unfixed and protean,[47] sexual acts generate "an homunculus of blood,

---

[47] Referring to the Krokers, we may think of the novel's characters as members of 'the last sex', practicing 'recombinant sex', which the Krokers describe as "[s]ex without origin, localizing gen-

semen and engine coolant", odors are "an amalgam of rectal mucus and engine coolant" or "a blend of [...] mucus and some [...] pharmaceutical compound" (*C* 63, 121, 146), and so forth. This notion of a general hybridity also finds expression in the emphasis the text places on the 'marriage' of different realms: "marriage of sex and technology", "marriage of violence and desire", "marriage of [...] bodies with [...] technology" (*C* 116, 128, 133), etc. It is in this fundamental embrace of a radical impurity that the novel's posthumanism consists (cf. Halberstam and Livingston 1995: 13). Like Haraway's, *Crash*'s cyborg politics "insist on noise and advocate pollution, rejoicing in the illegitimate fusions of animal and machine" and suggesting that all the "transgressed boundaries, potent fusions, and dangerous possibilities" the text depicts are ones "which progressive people might explore as one part of needed political work" (Haraway 2010: 2216, 2195). If Ballard's protagonists cease being men and women and cease being human, it is not so much because they have evolved (or devolved) into something else, but because difference and identity are profoundly redistributed (Halberstam and Livingston 1995: 10). In this way, the novel effectively subverts what Judith Butler has referred to as "the fictions of an imperialist humanism" and disorganizes "that field of discourse and power that orchestrates, delimits, and sustains that which qualifies as 'the human'" (1993: 79, xvii).

It is perhaps against this background that an as yet unnoticed part of the novel's imagery can be read, too. Scholars of Ballard's work have frequently observed that *Crash* develops a veritable aesthetics of destruction and the abject, for instance comparing crushed bodies to "a haemorrhage of the sun" and fragments of broken glass covering crash victims to "jewels" (*C* 1, 4), likening clots of blood to "liquid rubies", a semi-circular bruise to "a marbled rainbow", armpits to "mysterious universes" (*C* 8, 18, 149), concrete highways to a "serene motion sculpture" and a crushed car to "a tableau sculpture" (*C* 4, 78), and repeatedly presenting wounds as "flowering" and as constituting "real beauty" (*C* 6, 136). These striking similes and metaphors on the one hand signal the characters' transformation – specifically that of James, with him being the narrator – and on the other mark Ballard's avant-garde legacy.⁴⁸ What has so far gone unnoted

---

der, or referential signifier[,] [...] a transgendered sex for an age of transsexuality where sex, most of all, has fled its roots in the consaguinity [sic] of nature, refused its imprisonment in the phallocentric orbit of gender, abandoned the metaphorical sublimations of discursive sexuality, finally finding its home in a virtual sex" (1993: 15). Though virtual reality is, of course, absent from the novel's world, with regards to the last observation, cf. James' anticipation of "a new sexuality divorced from any possible physical expression" (*C* 24).

48 Passages such as the numerous ones that mention 'sculptures', another one that equates scars with "the gouges of a chisel", or yet another one which relates James' spectatorship of

is the fact that this imagery also includes numerous images referring to the *human* abject: the characters are compared, for example, to an "injured cripple", a "mentally defective girl", a "demented madonna" (*C* 9, 14, 15), a "paraplegic", a drunk "elderly transvestite", a "distraught witch" (*C* 70, 88), a "suburban voyeur", a "dead matador", and a "deranged drag queen" (*C* 100, 153, 166). In light of my discussion of the novel's multifaceted disruption of hegemonic constructions of normalcy, these similes, which recur throughout the text, may perhaps be read in terms of an attempt to write these 'abnormal' and discarded subjects – note the frequent augmentation of deviance through the combination of noun and adjective – back into the field of visibility and thus amplify the novel's challenge to the matrix of cultural 'intelligibility' – a challenge epitomized by the character of Gabrielle, who, to take up an argument developed by Lennard J. Davis (1997: 55 ff) in the context of Disability Studies, can be read as a kind of 'posthuman' or 'cyborg Venus', which, of course, effectively collapses the binarism enshrined in the two artistic traditions of Venus (the beautiful, whole, normal) on the one hand and Medusa (the ugly, fragmented, abnormal) on the other.

We have unearthed this important challenge by way of an investigation of the novel's body politics. In this, my second reading of the protagonists' catastrophic strategy, I have read their intentional wounding and mutilating of their own bodies in terms of what Guy Hocquenghem has described as the necessity "to direct the revolutionary struggle against capitalist oppression there where it is most deeply rooted – in the living flesh of our own body" (1995: 260 f). Thus, analogous to what Richard Shusterman maintains with regards to Foucault, I have suggested that the actions of the novel's main characters should not be considered as "a selfish withdrawal from politics, but [as] the pursuit of transformational politics by other means" (1997: 57). Vaughan and his followers effectively "open up the body's space to subversion", that is, they desubjectivate their bodies and construct what Hocquenghem calls "a revolutionary body" (1995: 261). As we have seen, this involves the undoing of abjection and Oedipalization and the liberation from the constraints of 'sex', 'sexuality' and 'gender'. Car crashes figure in the novel as veritable "laboratories of sexual experimentation" (Foucault 1996h: 330) allowing the characters to produce ever new and ever more intense pleasures (cf. Foucault 1996h: 331). The text presents this unmapped, rhizomatic desire as dialectically linked with the fusion it stages between

---

a sexual act between Vaughan and a prostitute, an act he observes "[i]n a triptych of images reflected in the speedometer, the clock and revolution counter" (*C* 71, 116), all explicitly make reference to the realm of the arts and thus throw the novel's implied challenge to received ideas about art into relief.

man (sic) and machine. What Sylvère Lotringer terms "technophilic intensity" is at the heart of the novel: "What is truly erotic", he asserts, "is to be one with the machine, one with the beast – flying at high speed away from this domestication of our body and our senses that we call humanity." (1995: 274) As for Lotringer, so for the protagonists of Ballard's novel, "[b]ecoming unhuman" means "an access to non-exclusive connections" (1995: 288).

With this strong focus on the body and on sexuality, *Crash* is clearly to some extent indebted to the spirit of the 1960s' counter-culture and the Freudo-Marxian liberationist thinking of Wilhelm Reich (1972), Herbert Marcuse (1998), Norman O. Brown (1985), and others. Yet – possibly under the impression of the failure of May '68 – their notion of revolutionary desire is being reworked in the novel in a non-essentialist, posthumanist way. As I have argued, polymorphous pleasures are here not so much *liberated* as – following Foucault, Deleuze and Guattari – *produced*. There is, here, no beach to be discovered under the cobblestones, but the novel suggests that a new kind of beach may be built from those very stones. To refer once more to Donna Haraway (2010: 2220), what is at stake in the protagonists' remaking of the body and of sexuality is not 'rebirth', but 'regeneration', not a recovery of some previously repressed nature, but a subversive experimentation that attacks power from within.

In conclusion, a final point about this reshaping may be made. Mary Douglas has famously argued that "[t]he physical body is a microcosm of society" and that consequently, "[i]nterest in its apertures depends on the preoccupation with social exits and entrances, escape routes and invasions" (2003: 80, 78). Hence, bodily "pollutions are used as analogies for expressing a general view of the social order" and "the social experience of disorder is expressed by powerfully efficacious symbols of impurity and danger" (Douglas 2002: 4, 2003: 90). Read against this background, the transgressions of bodily boundaries in *Crash* may be taken to signal corresponding transgressions of social boundaries, the polluted, leaky, fragmented and hybrid (post-)human bodies to signal an equally porous, unbounded and heterogeneous social body.[49] In this way, the novel seems to refute conservative calls for a more or less closed, ordered and tidy socius – one may think, for instance, of contemporary politicians such as Enoch Powell or Keith Joseph here – and instead appears to champion a continuation of the process of increasing the 'permissiveness' of English society begun by the vari-

---

[49] Kutzbach, too, draws on Douglas in her reading of the novel, but does not develop a clear argument as to the implications which the transgressions of bodily boundaries have on the macrocosmic, social level. As her pronouncements on a "decadent and dehumanized 'society'" and a "sick community, where taboos and boundaries have vanished" (2007: 189), indicate, she – unlike myself – seems to tend towards negative implications.

ous new social movements in the 1960s. *Crash* seems to suggest that the 'body politic' itself needs to be dismantled – here, too, a body without organs instead of a Leviathan (Hobbes 2008).

2.4 Symbolic Violence

And yet, in the end, the discourses that have been the subject of the former two sections never entirely convince us. This is because they continuously clash with another discourse, one which suggests that, ultimately, there is no flight from capitalist hyperreality to some kind of Bataillean 'continuity' or pre-discursive 'presence' and likewise no escape from the system's coding of the body and desire, its programming of subjectivity, and its immense powers of containment. In the end, any reading focusing on the excessive and ec-static nature of the experience of the car crash, on its unmediated directness, and on the polymorphous pleasures connected with it is immediately contradicted by the protagonists' calculated, cerebral and affectless behavior and responses[50] – as James himself realizes, their sexual acts are, in fact, "divorced from all feeling" (*C* 132) – something that is further underlined by the sober tone and clinical language of the narrative, as well as by the implied omnipresence of mediation and simulation in the novel's world, that is, by the fact that the alleged 'referents' that such readings have recourse to (continuity, somatic limit-experiences, the body, desire, pleasures, etc.) themselves continue to exist only as simulacra. This, of course, was exactly the critique that Baudrillard leveled against Foucault, Lyotard, Deleuze and Guattari. According to Baudrillard, use value, this time in sex rather than in production, remains "the ultimate alibi" in the work of these thinkers, their pleasures (Foucault), 'intensities' (Lyotard 2004) and desire (Deleuze and Guattari) still being "opposed to the 'exchange value of the body' [...] insofar as they constitute the use value of the body" (2007a: 45n). For Baudrillard, this use value is only an illusion. What philosophers like Foucault fail to realize is "a new peripeteia of power" which entails "the end of the strategy of the real" (Baudrillard 2007a: 45). Foucault, Baudrillard maintains, "spoke so well of sexuality only because its form, this great *production* (that too) of our culture, was, like that of power, in the process of disappearing"; "sex's reality effect [...] [has] started to fade away radically, giving way to other simulacra and dragging down

---

[50] Parveen Adams, writing about Cronenberg's movie, captures the peculiar nature of the characters' crash experience quite well when she asserts that "*Crash* deals with trauma that doesn't traumatise" (1999: 65).

with it the great referents of desire, the body, and the unconscious" (2007a: 32). "[S]exuality as we hear about it and as it 'is spoken,' even as the 'id speaks,'" Baudrillard declares, "is only a simulacrum" (2007a: 43). For the French theorist, it is one of the prime ruses of power to wind 'the body', 'desire', 'the unconscious', etc. into a "new spiral of [...] simulation" (2007a: 33) and thus generate them as simulacra of another order, that is, to keep simulating these illusory referents *as referents*. It is this ruse that, according to Baudrillard, Foucault and his fellow intellectuals cannot see, and for this reason, they remain caught inside power's traps. By contrast, *Crash*, for its part, draws attention to "the frenzied semiurgy that has taken hold of the simulacrum" (Baudrillard 2007a: 33) under late capitalism. When James, for instance, designates the car crash as "the only real experience" in his life, emphasizing the fact of being "in physical confrontation with [his] own body" and the experience of bodily pain, he continues:

> After being bombarded endlessly by road-safety propaganda it was almost a relief to find myself in an actual accident. Like everyone else bludgeoned by these billboard harangues and television films of imaginary accidents, I had felt a vague sense of unease that the gruesome climax of my life was being rehearsed years in advance, and would take place on some highway or road junction known only to the makers of these films. (*C* 28)

These lines effectively destabilize James' earlier statement and the entire discourse connected with it and introduce a fundamental ambivalence into the text, suggesting as they do that that the real that is being recovered here is only a simulacrum (Luckhurst 1997: 125). Here, there is no 'outside' to the system of simulation; even the most extreme of experiences and even the individual's relation to his/her own body has been anticipated and pre-programmed and become inseparable from the culture's incessant circulation of images and models.

It was, of course, Baudrillard himself who first elucidated this 'non-presentistic' discourse. *Crash*, he argues, presents a "universe [...] without secrets": "No affect behind all that, no psychology, no flux or desire, no libido or death drive", "[n]o repressed unconscious", "no perversion" (1994a: 117, 112, 113). In this hyperreal universe, sex "is not a question of orgasm, but of pure and simple discharge", "the coitus and sperm that traverse the book hav[ing] no [...] sensual value", and even "[t]he Accident, like death, is no longer of the order of the neurotic, the repressed, the residual or the transgressive", that is, "no longer the exception to a triumphal rationality" nor "even the 'accursed share'", but merely "the instigator of a new mode of *nonperverse* pleasure" (Baudrillard 1994a:

116, 113).⁵¹ Baudrillard's reading of Ballard's novel has been the subject of a lively and, at times, fierce debate. I myself find his analysis to be an illuminating one, yet would criticize it for two reasons: first, his interpretation is a partial, one-sided one; Baudrillard neglects the other discourses which, as we have seen, are distinctly manifest in the text and absolutizes the one discourse that more or less corresponds with his own theoretical ideas; secondly, as far as this last discourse is concerned, it seems to me that Baudrillard's essay does not sufficiently accommodate the complexities and subtleties of the text and therefore overlooks the crucial moment of resistance that is, in effect, part of this discourse. My goal in this last section of the chapter will be to disclose just this moment. For while the novel can indeed be read as depicting a world that has become, as Ballard puts it in his introduction, "a complete fiction" (*C* n.pag.), that is, a world given over entirely to simulation and having no more outside, this does nevertheless not automatically entail the "resolution of all finality or critical negativity" (1994a: 119), as Baudrillard claims. Instead, I would argue that it is once again possible to read the protagonists' actions as a form of subversion of (simulative) power – a form that, ironically, can only be adequately described with reference to Baudrillard's own thinking of resistance. This form he labels 'symbolic exchange', and it is manifest in the novel in relation to the crash, the scar, 'sex', and photography.

Interestingly, Baudrillard's *Crash*-essay already contains the seeds of such a reading, though it fails to develop them. Towards the end of his text, Baudrillard declares: "In *Crash*, everything is hyperfunctional [...]. But at the same time, the functionalism of *Crash* devours its own rationality, because it does not know dysfunction. It is a radical functionalism that reaches its paradoxical limits and burns them." (1994a: 118) This passage points us to what Baudrillard has elsewhere termed 'the principle of evil' or 'the rule of reversibility'. He explains: "In every compulsion to resemblance, every extradition of difference, in all contiguity of things and their own image, all conflation of beings and their own code, lies the threat of [...] a diabolical otherness boding the breakdown of all this humming machinery." (1993c: 73) It would appear that just such a reversal lies at the heart of Ballard's novel – here, indeed, the "crash looms over [...] excrescence" (Baudrillard 2005: 194). The novel's cybernetic world of perfect functionality, regulation, instrumentality and control clearly betokens an 'integral reality' as envisioned by Baudrillard, that is, one which "leaves behind it all kinds of useless functions: the body, sex, [...] language, death" (2005: 197). These, as

---

51 For a somewhat similar argument made with regards to the film version, cf. Botting and Wilson 2003.

the French philosopher (esp. 1993b) conceives them, are all manifestations of 'symbolic exchange', the gift without a counter-gift, or with a counter-gift beyond the principle of equivalence. Symbolic exchange – a concept Baudrillard develops building on the work of Marcel Mauss (1990) – is, in fact, "the opposite of exchange" (2007a: 85), since it is subject to no system of value. Modeled on social exchange among 'primitive' tribes, it is a form of (agonistic) reciprocity beyond the laws of 'the economy', based solely on generosity. For Baudrillard, this non-commercial form of exchange, having all but disappeared in the productivist societies of the West (and elsewhere), is something radically alien to the system of (late) capitalism, a principle of absolute subversion, capable of destroying universal simulation. Baudrillard identifies symbolic exchange in its purest form in death: "Life given over to death: the very operation of the symbolic." (1993b: 131) This communication between life and death has been lost in modern, capitalist societies, which categorically exclude death and the dead and conceive of life only as one great process of accumulation. Today, "[t]o be dead is an unthinkable anomaly; nothing else is as offensive as this." (Baudrillard 1993b: 126) Yet, here, too, the principle of reversibility applies. In a passage that aptly captures the portrayal of the metropolis in *Crash* – recall that James compares the apartment block in which he lives to "an up-ended glass coffin" (*C* 85) – Baudrillard writes:

> The cemetery no longer exists because modern cities have entirely taken over their function: they are ghost towns, cities of death. If the great operational metropolis is the final form of an entire culture, then, quite simply, ours is a culture of death.[52] [...] In survival, death is repressed; life itself [...] [is] nothing more than a survival determined by death. (1993b: 127)

As one principal way to eliminate the threat of symbolic exchange, the exclusion of death must, according to Baudrillard, ultimately be seen as one of the foundations of power: "Shattering the union of the living and the dead, and slapping a prohibition on death and the dead: the primary source of social control. Power is possible only if death is no longer free" (1993b: 130).

Against this background, I think it is possible to read the crash in Ballard's novel in terms of the fundamental reversals that Baudrillard talks about, that is, as "a violent abreaction to [the] captive life, to [the] protected existence, to [the] saturation of existence" under late capitalism, and as an attempt to (re-)introduce

---

52 In this context, Baudrillard speaks of the modern "necropolis" (1993b: 187n3).

the symbolic exchange of death into a culture[53] in which the individual is forced into "the relentless situation of receiving" from "a technical system of generalized exchange and general gratification" and in which "the counter-gift is impossible, since all the paths of sacrifice have been neutralized and defused" (Baudrillard 2003: 103, 102). Baudrillard has noted the immense fascination that catastrophes, accidents and terrorist violence as sudden, inexplicable and uncontrollable intrusions of death into life exert today and has linked it with a secret desire of the masses to see power destroyed. People, he argues, increasingly harbor a "sacrificial passion": "we are all dreaming, instead of dying stupidly working oneself to the ground, of *receiving* death and of *giving* death. Giving and receiving constitute one symbolic act (the symbolic act *par excellence*), which rids death of all the indifferent negativity it holds for us in the 'natural' order of capital."[54] (1993b: 165, 166) This passion is thus at the same time also a *"passion for the artificial"* (Baudrillard 1993b: 165), rejecting our culture's reduction of death to what it constructs as private, individual 'natural death', which effectively removes it from the cycle of symbolic exchange and fully neutralizes it. Tellingly, the automobile accident is one of Baudrillard's prime examples of the contemporary passion for sacrifice. He writes:

> We, for our part, no longer have an effective rite for reabsorbing death and its rupturing energies; there remains the phantasm of sacrifice, the violent artifice of death. Hence the intense and profoundly *collective* satisfaction of the automobile death. In the fatal accident, the artificiality of death fascinates us. Technical, non-natural and therefore *willed* (ultimately by the victim him- or herself), death becomes interesting once again since *willed* death has a meaning. This artificiality of death facilitates, on a par with the sacrifice, its *aesthetic* doubling in the imagination, and the enjoyment that follows from it. [...] Only the automobile accident re-establishes some kind of sacrificial equilibrium. (1993b: 165f)

The doubling in the imagination and the collective dimension of the crash mentioned by Baudrillard are fully borne out in Ballard's novel, in which the crashes have something ceremonial about them and every crash attracts a large crowd of spectators, who are always depicted as enthralled and stirred by the accident and for whom it each time appears to carry a special meaning which they all

---

53 Scott Durham (1993: 164–168) and Bradley Butterfield (1999: 72f) have pointed into a similar direction, with the former, however, being ultimately somewhat skeptical of such a reading, while the latter, who argues that Ballard and Baudrillard should be seen as representatives of a radical, postmodern aestheticism, spends only very little time with an actual discussion of the novel itself.
54 It will already have become clear by now that Baudrillard's theory owes much to the thought of Bataille discussed earlier – a fact that Baudrillard (esp. 1993b: 154–158) has repeatedly acknowledged.

share. Thus, for instance in the case of the accident in which Vaughan kills himself and which Elizabeth Taylor narrowly survives, James recounts how, standing "three deep", "at least five hundred people ha[ve] gathered on every verge and parapet", how he "seem[s] to recognize them all", and how still more "spectators mov[e] towards this huge stage" – a term that recalls the ceremonial stages of sacrificial rites – "drawn there by the logic and beauty of Vaughan's death" (*C* 182, 183). In another case, he notes the marked calm of the "enormous crowd", "[n]one of the spectators show[ing] any signs of alarm", "[t]heir relaxed postures impl[ying] a shared understanding of the most subtle points" (*C* 127). Here, death once again becomes social and public, a meaningful event inscribed into a ritual of symbolic exchange – an 'event' in a world full of simulations, simulacra and 'non-events' (cf. esp. Baudrillard 2005) or "pseudo-events" (*C* n.pag.).

No wonder, then, that in one scene which I would read as highly symbolic,[55] a policeman "scatter[s] lime on the blood-smeared concrete" of the road after a crash and, using a broom, "[w]ith careful strokes, as if frightened of working out the complex human arithmetic of these injuries, [...] [sweeps] the darkening clots against the verge of the central reservation" (*C* 127 f). In light of Baudrillard's reflections, power has every reason to be afraid of this anti-natural violence and to want to conceal its existence. The crash as sacrifice represents a challenge to the system's unilateral exercise of the gift, effectively "turn[ing] the principle of its power back against the system itself: the impossibility of responding or retorting" (Baudrillard 1993b: 36 f). According to Baudrillard, the *giving* of one's life places an unavoidable "symbolic obligation" on the system, "and it is in this trap that the only chance of a catastrophe for capital remains" (1993b: 37). "[O]nly the scrupulous reversion of death", he declares, "corresponds to the code's indeterminacy and the structural law of value", indeed, belongs to a higher order than the code, and thus "is the only symbolic violence equivalent to and triumphant over the structural violence of the code" (1993b: 5), which, as we have seen, is everywhere apparent in the novel's world. The crash, then – as an attack against the hyperreal system located on the plane of the symbolic, not that of the real – "*[defies] the system with a gift to which it cannot respond save by its own collapse and death*" (Baudrillard 1993b: 37), namely with the gift of death. This gift lies at the heart of and frames the entire narrative, which opens with the declaration of Vaughan's death and ends – the epilogue-like last two sentences aside – with a premonition of the narrator's death (*C* 1, 185) – a veritable 'thanato-narrative'.

---

[55] A similar reading has been suggested by Jeanette Baxter (2009: 103).

2.4 Symbolic Violence — 71

Beyond sacrificial death, there are yet other ways through which the protagonists of the novel restore symbolic exchange to the society in which they live. One of them is linked to the characters' wounding of their bodies discussed above. We have already seen how, especially through the character of Catherine Ballard, *Crash* points to the late-capitalist commodification of the body, which is shown to entail its 'vitrification' as a closed, whole, smooth body without orifices, a body "[a]s functional as a cellophane wrapper" (Baudrillard 1993b: 105). In this way, the novel bears out Baudrillard's observation that

> [t]he entire contemporary history of the body is the history of its demarcation, the network of marks and signs that have since covered it, divided it up, annihilated its difference and its radical ambivalence in order to organise it into a structural material for sign-exchange, equal to the sphere of objects, to resolve its playful virtuality and its symbolic exchange [...] into sexuality taken as a determining agency (1993b: 101).

The aforementioned emphasis the text places on the stylized nature of the characters' postures, gestures and movements and the repeated comparison of characters to mannequins (e.g. *C* 25, 96, 131) can be read in this context as well. As Baudrillard points out, while the reference model of the body for the system of political economy was the robot, the embodiment of absolute productivity, the ideal type of the body for the current system of the political economy of the sign is the mannequin, which "also represents a totally functionalised body under the law of value, but this time as the site of the production of the *value-sign*. It is no longer labour power, but models of signification that are produced – not only sexual models of fulfilment, but *sexuality itself as a model*." (1993b: 114) And yet, Baudrillard avers, at the same time as it is enclosed by a web of signs and models, the body has also never stopped being "their radical alternative, the irreducible difference that denies them": the body "as anti-object", "as material of symbolic exchange", for which "*there is no model*, no code, no ideal type, no controlling phantasm" (1993b: 114). It seems to me that it is this body that Ballard's protagonists recreate.

Once again, Baudrillard himself has laid the groundwork for such a reading in his *Crash*-essay, in which he speaks of "a semiurgy of contusions, scars, mutilations, wounds" and of "a body delivered to 'symbolic wounds'" (1994a: 112, 111). What has so far gone unmentioned in my reading of the novel is the peculiar status that the multiplying cuts and scars have for the protagonists. This status can be deduced from the imagery and vocabulary the narrator uses in connection with them: here, wounds and scars are 'translated', 'read' and 'meaningful' (*C* 17, 18, 32, 19), they 'mark' and 'describe' things (*C* 32, 63, 71), and are referred to as "raw symbols", "signatures" "inscribed" on the body, and as "codes" to be "decipher[ed]" (*C* 137, 147, 148). Of course, the isotopy here is that of a 'language', and indeed, the scars on Vaughan's body are once likened to "an exact language of pain and sensation, eroticism and desire" (*C* 71). It would seem that this language, too, is something like "a language in search of objects", that is, one whose signs are essentially meaningless – signifiers without a (definite) signified – but which, precisely *because of* this "apparently meaningless" nature, become "meaningful" (*C* 24, 71, 19).[56] In this context, it is telling that James at one point speaks of "a cuneiform of the flesh" (*C* 71). This reference to one of the earliest known systems of writing not only renders the body as a clay-like medium engraved by a stylus, but, more importantly, relates this 'engraving' to a writing that began as a system of picto- and ideographs. Significantly, poststructuralist philosophers such as Jacques Derrida, Julia Kristeva and Roland Barthes have repeatedly noted the subversive potential of picto- and ideogrammatic languages (such as Chinese or Japanese), emphasizing their power to undermine the representational language and the phallogocentric discourse of the West. It seems to me that, through their scars, Ballard's protagonists fashion – just as in Barthes' (1982) Japan – a system of empty signs that never disclose an (ultimate) signified.

In his reading of *Crash*, Baudrillard, too, speaks of "the pure inscription of the empty signs of [the] body" and notes that "as in primitive initiation tortures, which are not ours [...], the whole body becomes a sign to offer itself to the exchange of bodily signs" (1994a: 112). This exchange, of course, has nothing to do with the exchange of signs (of beauty, the erotic, health, happiness, etc.) that the objectification of the body by late capitalism entails. It is, instead, a symbolic exchange, a form of exchange that subverts the former and the entire code. As Baudrillard (1993b: 106f) points out, archaic practices of body marking are radically distinct from and hence not to be confused with something such as make-up. While Catherine, the novel's embodiment of capitalism's classical, functional body, attempts to conceal scars with make-up (*C* 20), Vaughan and James seek and celebrate the wound and thus turn their bodies into material for symbolic exchange. In Ballard's novel, bodies constantly "gaze at each other and exchange all their signs", yet not "*under the regime of the general equivalent*, where they have an exchange-value", but in a kind of gift-exchange, in which they are "consumed in an incessant relaying and refer neither to a transcendental law of value, nor to a private appropriation of the subject" (Baudrillard 1993b: 107). Thus, for instance, Vaughan "lay[s] each scar in turn against [Catherine's] mouth", while she "explor[es] the patterns of scars on his skin", James "explore[s] [his wife's] body and bruises, feeling them gently with [his] lips

---

[56] This Baudrillardian figure of thought will be further explored in chapter 6.

and cheeks" and "trac[ing] the raw symbols" (*C* 132, 136, 137) with his penis, and, during his sex act with Gabrielle, who "revolv[es] her body around [him]" to show him her various wounds, he similarly "explore[s] the scars on her thighs and arms [...], as she in turn explore[s] [his]", "running the tip of her tongue into each one" and, "one by one, [...] endors[ing] each of these signatures" (*C* 148, 147). Elsewhere, Vaughan "parad[es] his scarred face *as if these wounds were a sympathetic response* to Gabrielle's crippled legs" (*C* 144, emphasis added). In *Crash*, then, mutilations constitute "a new currency of pain and desire" (*C* 109), a non-economic currency, in an exchange based solely on the generosity of the gift and the counter-gift. As the quotations make clear, along with the body, sexuality, too, is here reinstated as symbolic exchange. Like the body, it is torn away from political economy, the law of value and general equivalence, no longer neutralized through individualization, naturalization and functionalization and no longer collapsed into the use-value/exchange-value dualism (cf. Baudrillard 1998b: 149f). Baudrillard himself has brought out this aspect of the text very clearly, and I therefore quote at length:

> 'sexual desire' is never anything but the possibility bodies have of combining and exchanging their signs. Now, the few natural orifices to which one usually attaches sex and sexual activities are nothing next to all the possible wounds [...] through which the body is reversibilized [...]. Sex as we know it is nothing but a minute and specialized definition of all the symbolic and sacrificial practices to which a body can open itself, no longer though [sic] nature, but through artifice, through the simulacrum, through the accident. [...] [Sex] is largely overtaken by the fan of symbolic wounds, which is in some sense the anagrammatization of sex on the whole length of the body – but now precisely, it is no longer sex, it is something else (1994a: 114f).

Despite the brilliance of his analysis, and even though his very own theoretical model should lead him to it, Baudrillard fails to see the subversive impetus of this 'anagrammatization' of sex and the body. He opposes the "dispersion of the body as anagram in the order of mutilation" to the "gathering [of] the body as labor in the order of production" (1994a: 112), but ignores the fact that it is also, and more fundamentally, opposed to the production and consumption of the body as commodity-sign in the order of simulation. Like the graffiti in New York, which Baudrillard (1993b: 82) so ingeniously analyzes and links with 'primitive' body-marking in *Symbolic Exchange and Death* and to which he actually alludes in his *Crash*-essay (1994a: 112) – though again without drawing the necessary conclusions – the scars on the characters' bodies in the novel are "*empty signifiers*" that challenge the "*functional*" and "*full signs*" (Baudrillard 1993b: 79) of the existing order. Turning the hyperreal system's indeterminacy against itself, the reference- and meaningless 'names' sprayed onto New York's walls, subways, buses, elevators, and monuments in 1972 and the violent inscription of the body both mark a "reversion of the code according to its own logic, [...] gaining victory over it because it exceeds semiocracy's own non-referentiality" (Baudrillard 1993b: 78). Both are forms of symbolic exchange that subvert power.[57]

The wounding of the body in the crash can thus be read, not as its recovery from the realm of simulation through the immediacy of the experience of physical pain, but as a way to transform the body and sexuality from systems of signs arranged by models into material for symbolic exchange. The body in symbolic exchange, particularly in the case of Vaughan, furthermore seems to be engaged in the rituals and games of what Baudrillard has elsewhere called 'seduction' – understood in its radical, not its 'soft' sense (1990: 156). Ballard's characters may be said to turn sex into a medium of seduction by "push[ing] sexual pleasure to its limits and beyond" or, more correctly, by giving the sex act "a discontinuous form that cuts short every emotion, pleasure and relation in order to reaffirm the superior character of seduction" (Baudrillard 1990: 18, 86). We have already noted the striking emotionlessness and the very calculated and stylized nature of the sexual acts in the novel. As much as these qualities cast doubt on a reading that construes the protagonists' behavior in terms of an emancipatory experimentation with new pleasures and an uninhibited desiring-production, they at the same time move it closer to Baudrillard's conception of seduction.[58] The immorality of seduction, Baudrillard explains, "does not come from abandoning oneself to the joys of sex in opposition to all morality; it results from something

---

[57] Perhaps, as Baudrillard suggests with regards to the graffiti, there is also something tribal, a sense of group initiation and affiliation, about the marking of the body in *Crash*. A related line of thought has been pursued by scholars in the field of sociology – in which body marking or modification has for some time now been a subject of investigation – who speak of 'modern primitivism' (e.g. Klesse 2000; Sweetman 2000; Turner 2000). In this context, a reading of Ballard's novel within the fascinating theoretical framework developed by Michel Maffesoli appears to me to be particularly promising. Maffesoli (1993, 1996), who can be seen as continuing a vitalist, 'Dionysian' tradition of thought and whose work seems to be especially influenced by Bataille, identifies a distinctly postmodern 'neo-tribalism' based on 'orgiasm'. One of the ambiguities of the postmodern tribes that is significant with regards to *Crash* is that they do "not disdai[n] the most sophisticated technology" but "remain nonetheless somewhat barbaric" (Maffesoli 1996: 28).

[58] For Baudrillard, the Deleuzoguattarian model of an unconstrained, rhizomatic desire is, in any case, far from liberatory, the whole sexual model being nothing but value's "mode of appearance at the level of the body" (1990: 38). He writes: "This pressure towards liquidity, flux and the accelerated articulation of the sexual, psychic and physical body is an exact replica of that which regulates exchange value: capital must circulate, there must no longer be any fixed point, investments must be ceaselessly renewed, value must radiate without respite" (1990: 38).

more serious and subtle, the abandonment of sex itself as a referent and a morality, even in its 'joys.'" (1990: 125) What is at stake is not the pleasure of the transgression of the 'law', but the passion of the observance of 'rules' (Baudrillard 1990: 131ff). Like the pervert (as Baudrillard reads him/her), the seducer or seduced "is cold when it comes to sex" and "transmutes sex and sexuality into a ritual carrier, a ritual and ceremonial abstraction" (Baudrillard 1990: 125). This seems to me to be a rather accurate characterization of what is happening in *Crash*. Without exception, the sex acts in the novel are presented as "stylized and abstracted", as "conceptualized acts abstracted from all feeling" (*C* 82, 104), and there is undoubtedly something formalized and ritualistic about these acts. Indeed, the narrator at one point describes his wife and Vaughan's sex as "a ritual devoid of ordinary sexuality" (*C* 132). Here, sex is torn away from psychology, desire and 'truth' (cf. Foucault 1978), "*transsubstantiat[ed]* [...] *into signs*" and "transposed into a stake" (Baudrillard 1990: 13, 140). *Crash*'s universe is one that "can no longer be interpreted in terms of psychic or psychological relations, nor those of repression and the unconscious, but must be interpreted in the terms of play, challenges, duels, the strategy of appearances – that is, the terms of seduction" (Baudrillard 1990: 7). Vaughan's inscribed body is no longer 'natural' – nature itself being nothing but a simulation – but entirely artificial, pure sign or surface, and it continuously exchanges its signs with those of other bodies in "an uninterrupted ritual exchange where seducer and seduced constantly raise the stakes" (Baudrillard 1990: 22). It is in this light, I would argue, that Vaughan's persecution and 'harassment' of Catherine must be read. When he waits for her and continuously follows her with her car, this is, indeed, as James maintains, an "exquisitely prolonged mating ritual", when he besets her on the road, this represents a "form of compliment", and when he hits her car with his, this is a "gesture of courtship" (*C* 176, 91, 173), a challenge in a duelistic game. Similarly, Helen Remington's husband, who dies in an accident caused by James, becomes "an anonymous opponent killed in a pointless duel" (*C* 22) in this logic of seduction, for, as Baudrillard maintains, seduction is always "an escalation of violence and grace" and hence need not manifest itself in sex but "can just as easily exhaust itself in the process of defiance and death" (1990: 81).[59]

Ballard's protagonists thus (re-)create a culture of ritualistic interchange, of gifts and counter-gifts, opposed to generalized exchange, and "a pactual, ritual, and contingent sociality" (Baudrillard 1990: 152) – a 'rituality' – defying the so-

---

[59] Significantly, with regards to *Crash*, Baudrillard (1990: 127) declares that, just like violence, the odious and the abject, too, possess the power to seduce.

cial contract and the whole edifice of the social. At the same time, this culture based on reversibility undermines hyperreality. As a pure play of appearances and signs, seduction signals a "will to power by the simulacrum" that turns the logic of the system against itself, displacing the simulacra of 'the real', 'meaning', etc. produced by the latter by means of a "hypersimulation" (Baudrillard 1990: 87, 63). Seduction thus emerges as a highly ironic form (Baudrillard 1990: 21), since its playfulness cannot be anchored in any fixed foundation. James' suspicion that "everything around [him] [...] [is] part of some ironic intention of Vaughan's" hence seems fully justified, and the answer to his question "Were there any limits to Vaughan's irony?" (*C* 161, 113) can evidently only be 'no'.[60] Of course, Vaughan – the chief seducer of the text – is himself seduced, too – by the other characters, but also, and above all, by (the image of) Elizabeth Taylor. Baudrillard has argued that seduction – though a 'cold' one as opposed to the 'hot' one of earlier times – lies at the heart of the cinema and that "the only important constellation of collective seduction produced by modern times" (1990: 94) is that of film stars. Viewed in this light, is Vaughan's attempted crash with the actress not an instance of outbidding and reversal, wholly located on the level of the simulacrum, a try to take up the challenge and surpass the gift through the counter-gift?

If the media-image seduces, this is, of course, the result of reversibility, since generally, the mass media function as part of the system and the order of production/simulation, not seduction. It seems to me that this kind of reversibility is also at work on the formal level of Ballard's narrative. "*Crash*", Ballard has claimed, "is the first pornographic novel based on technology" (*C* n.pag.), a characterization that, in view of the text's explicit portrayal of sexual subject matter, one can safely endorse. Now, pornography as such, according to Baudrillard, is very much opposed to seduction. As in science – and several scholars have considered *Crash* and *The Atrocity Exhibition* as works that point to just this convergence of science and pornography, explicitly proclaimed by one character of the latter novel (*AE* 49) – there is an "excess of reality" in pornography, an "orgy of realism", which consists "in having everything pass into the absolute

---

[60] Perhaps, what the narrator characterizes as Vaughan's constant deliberate side-stepping into self-parody as well as Seagrave's cross-dressing, which is likewise explicitly described as parodic (*C* 151, 88), can be read in this context as well. Cf. Baudrillard's (1990: 12ff) (somewhat proto-Butlerian) discussion of transvestism as a form of seduction. He reads it as a theatrical game of signs, whose "surface hypersimulation of [the] in-depth simulation" of 'sex' effectively "puts an end to every insoluble biology or metaphysics of the sexes" – "a triumphant parody" (1990: 15).

evidence of the real" (Baudrillard 1990: 29, 32, 29).⁶¹ This obsession with the 'truth' of sex, pornography's tendency to leave no secret intact and to drag everything, down to the smallest detail, into the realm of visibility, to "hun[t] down seduction by means of visibility" (Baudrillard 1990: 29f), results in the hyperreality/-realism of pornographic representations. For Baudrillard (1990: 34f, 2008: 73ff), however, these are only the purest epitome of a culture that has become pornographic and 'obscene' in its entirety. And yet, the French philosopher avers, "sexual discourse [...] is continually threatened with saying something other than what it says"; since "a cessation of signs at some zero point of the real or the neutral" is impossible – the fever of exposure leading only to an escalating accumulation of signs – there is "always a reversion of the neutral itself into a new spiral of stakes, seduction and death" (1990: 42, 44). In this way, by "mov[ing] beyond their truth into a reversible configuration", "[e]ven the most anti-seductive figures can become figures of seduction" – in the end, "seduction is inescapable" (Baudrillard 1990: 45, 42). I would argue that this applies as well to the obscenity of *Crash*. What Baudrillard observes with regards to one of Philip K. Dick's texts, to an unspecified American film and the French-Japanese movie *In the Realm of the Senses* holds true for Ballard's novel, too: its obscenity is "too brutal to be true", enticement lies just beneath the surface of its cold objectivity and detachment, and the sex act, "by its very persistence, comes to be possessed by the logic of another order" (1990: 43, 44), the order of seduction. The very clinical, non-sensual nature of the novel's representations would hence signal the passage from a logic of pleasure and desire, that is, of the simulacrum of the sexual, to a logic of challenge and death, in which the sexual act appears as a ritual act. Thus, on the formal level, too, *Crash* follows the Baudrillardian strategy of resistance, the tactics of escalation that consist in always going further than the system itself, of "push[ing] [things] to the limit, where quite naturally they collapse and are inverted" (1993b: 4). The very excessiveness of the narrative, the extreme, exaggerated nature of the exactitude of its pornographic representations, can consequently be read in terms of a deconstruction of all discourses that believe in transparency, their claims to the truth being effectively turned against themselves and thus undermined.

After the sacrifice, the marking of the body, and seduction, a final manifestation of symbolic exchange in the novel remains: Vaughan's photography. It is to Jeannette Baxter's credit to have shown that its role in the text is finally more

---

61 A recent, fascinating pop-cultural parody of this 'orgy' is Vaughan Arnell's music video for Robbie Williams' song "Rock DJ". In fact, it almost appears as if Arnell's script for the clip was directly lifted from the pages of Baudrillard's *Seduction* (cf. esp. 1990: 32).

ambivalent than most readings allow. Whereas critics have tended to discuss Vaughan's photographic projects in terms of voyeurism or the omnipresence of mediation and simulacra (cf. e.g. Baudrillard 1994a: 116 f; Day 2000: 280 ff; Gasiorek 2005: 84), Baxter sees them as Surrealist experiments that disturb habitual perception and open up new trajectories of meaning, thus inviting historical and critical reflection. In her fascinating reading, Vaughan emerges as a quasi-Surrealist artist whose pictures, through defamiliarization and montage, "illuminate [...] repressed narratives of historical trauma" and construct a "critique of violence and technology" (2009: 125, 128). While I subscribe to her argument that Vaughan's photographic work is far more complex than previously acknowledged and contains a strong subversive or at least critical element, it seems to me that the nature of this element is a very different one from that posited by Baxter. I am not convinced by her claim that the main role of photography in the novel is a historiographic one, at least not on the diegetic level; it may be that *the reader* is sensitized to the dangers of technology and the long history of violence by Vaughan's photographs, but they certainly do not fulfill such a function for James and the other characters (Baxter 2009: 127), and Vaughan himself can hardly be said to feel "pain and disgust" (Baxter 2009: 132) at the sight of mutilation and violence. Vaughan's snapshots do not contain the critical messages that Baxter ascribes to them. Indeed, they appear to hold hardly any meaning at all, and this, I would argue, is the true source of their subversive potential – a potential entirely located at the level of the signifier, not, as Baxter maintains, of the signified. As such, they bear a certain similarity to Baudrillard's conception of the photograph as 'pure image'.

Vaughan, as James observes, is a photographer "[o]f a special kind" (*C* 67), most of whose pictures show details of sexual acts, cars, particularly crashed ones, and bodies, mainly injured ones. One set, for instance, consists entirely of "magnified details of [Elizabeth Taylor's] knees and hands, of the inner surface of her thighs and the left apex of her mouth", others display "sections of automobile radiator grilles and instrument panels" (*C* 1, 85). Here, each object is "illuminated in detail under its fractal aspect" – the photo as "the image of a fractal world" (Baudrillard 1993c: 175, 176). James notes that "no recognizable human figures" appear in many of Vaughan's photographs – a curious way of putting it, yet one which implies that they may simply not be discernible as such – and that, similarly, in the pictures Vaughan took of James' accident and recovery, the photographer's interest in the narrator is "clearly minimal" (*C* 77, 80). Instead, Vaughan's interest lies with the object. Even when taking pictures of human beings, as in the case of James, what concerns him are things like "the interaction between an anonymous individual and his car, the transits of his body across the polished cellulose panels and vinyl seating, his face silhouetted

2.4 Symbolic Violence — 79

against the instrument dials" (*C* 80), that is, the interaction *between objects*, man (sic) being only one object among many. "Only the non-human is photogenic" (1993c: 173), Baudrillard declares, and Vaughan seems to follow this maxim – which, as we have seen, does not *per se* exclude the photographing of human beings; only they have to be shown in their otherness, in their 'radical exoticism' as objects, free(d) of psychology and introspection (Baudrillard 1993c: 173). It appears that the peculiar simile – also discussed by Baxter (2009: 125 f) – according to which some of the prostitutes photographed "in the postures of uneasy sex acts", their faces and thighs lit by the camera flash, look "like startled survivors of a submarine disaster" (*C* 3) can be read in this light as well. According to Baudrillard, "[t]he only genuinely photographic subjects are those which are violated, taken by surprise, discovered or exposed despite themselves, those which should never have been represented because they have neither self-image nor self-consciousness." (1993c: 173) This, certainly, applies to these women who, caught by Vaughan's camera lens, cease being 'subjects' and are endowed with (or given back) an aura of mystery and strangeness. Vaughan thus creates 'pure images' as defined by Baudrillard, images, that is, which have the "quality of a universe from which the subject has withdrawn", which do not seek to represent anything but instead "rupture with the real" (1993c: 175, 2005: 97), denying truth and meaning, and which do not aspire to the realm of art (Baudrillard 1998a: 89 ff). They capture a "non-representability, the otherness of that which is foreign to itself (to desire, to self-consciousness), the radical exoticism of the object" (Baudrillard 1993c: 173). Vaughan's pictures – at least many of them – are not 'critical', not even testimonial, documentary or informational; there is no morality to them. And it is precisely this escape from signification that makes them 'images' in the Baudrillardian sense – "we kill images with meaning" (2005: 92), the French theorist avers – and that accounts for their subversiveness. Like seduction[62] and the marking of the body, Vaughan's photography effectively ruptures the code and defies the order of visibility, meaning and truth. Its role is "not to illustrate the event, but to constitute an event in itself" (Baudrillard 2005: 99). When, in one of his pictures of James' sex acts in the latter's car, the window sill of the automobile and the strap of the woman's brassiere "[b]y some freak of photography" "for[m] a sling of metal and nylon from which the distorted nipple [of the woman's breast] seem[s] to extrude itself into [James'] mouth" (*C* 81), it becomes evident that the image here constitutes "a singular event", that is to say, "an absolute surprise", affecting the viewer "directly, below the level of rep-

---

[62] In fact, for Baudrillard, photography in this sense *is* a form of seduction, the photographer being seduced by the object.

resentation: at the level of intuition, of perception" (Baudrillard 2005: 95, 91). These images, created through "unusual camera angle[s]" (*C* 81), affect the viewer not so much in terms of what Roland Barthes (1981) has called the 'studium' of the photograph, but of its 'punctum', an acute and intense affect that *punctuates* any meaning the image may be said to have (the studium) and – purely on the level of the signifier – *punctures*, stings or pierces the viewer. "A photograph's *punctum*", Barthes explains, "is that accident which pricks me (but also bruises me, is poignant to me)." (1981: 27) The accident of photography corresponding to that of the automobile – everywhere a 'fall' (Latin, *cadere*) from order, a breakdown of the system.

Thus, regarding the role of photography, but also the novel as a whole, *Crash* turns out to be much more ambivalent than Baudrillard's reading allows. Not only does his discussion of Ballard's text overlook the other discourses woven into the texture of the narrative, discourses, as we have seen, which construct the protagonists' actions in terms related to Bataillean expenditure, the irreducibility of the body recovered in the immediacy of somatic limit-experiences, and to the desubjectivation of the body and the desexualization of pleasure as described by Foucault, Deleuze and Guattari and others – all discourses which continuously conflict with the one Baudrillard is concerned with, yet which are not eclipsed by it. More than that, the French philosopher also fails to see the relevance of his very own conceptualization of resistance to the interpretation of the novel. He does not recognize that far from being fully integrated into the hyperreal universe, the actions of the protagonists, Vaughan in particular, actually constitute acts of resistance against just this universe. Not unlike Baudrillard's own 'theory-fictions', *Crash* in fact develops a pataphysics of resistance based on the idea of symbolic exchange. Catastrophic strategies are thus at the heart of this discourse as of the other ones, so that what Baudrillard has identified as "the first great novel of the universe of simulation" (1994a: 119) may at the same time already be the first great one of its subversion.

3 Becoming-Grass:
De- and Reterritorialization in *Concrete Island*

> It's not easy to see the grass in things.
> Gilles Deleuze & Félix Guattari

With regards to *Concrete Island*, the second book after *Crash* in Ballard's 'urban disaster trilogy', most critics have indeed not paid much attention to the 'grass in things'. While Punter (1985: 15–19), Stephenson (1991: 74–80), Luckhurst (1997: 134–137), and Gasiorek (2005: 107–120) have all skillfully shed light on various facets of the novel, none of them has developed a reading of the text that would place the events of the plot in the context of late capitalism and, above all, consistently disclose the subversive momentum of protagonist Robert Maitland's stay on the traffic island. This omission seems to be due to the fact that this momentum once again derives from what we must term a 'catastrophic strategy' and not from anything akin to received forms of political praxis. While there are some passages in Gasiorek's discussion of the novel which touch upon these topics, it is, to my knowledge, only Laura Colombino who, in her illuminating essay on the imagining of London's cityscape and architecture in the fiction of Ballard and Geoff Ryman, thoroughly deals with the space(s) of capitalism and the forms of resistance to it in Ballard's work. Her analysis of the spatial politics in the text focuses on its representation of a "rift in the network of cultural codes, a yielding or crack in the solidity of the system": she shows how, in the fictional worlds of *Concrete Island* and the other novels she discusses, "there exist pockets of opacity and partial inaccessibility; folds which destabilise perfect transparency by opening up chances of transgression and real experience" (2006: 617). Colombino describes the rupture suggested by these novels in terms that resonate with my characterization of the Ballardian forms of resistance: "This rupture does not appear in the form of the artist's itinerant and diffuse regeneration of the capitalist space [as in the fiction of writers drawing on Situationist strategies] but in terms of a difficult, sometimes tragic, negotiation with its ensnaring frames." (2006: 617)

The following analysis of this negotiation in *Concrete Island* will recast the debate within the theoretical framework developed by Gilles Deleuze and Félix Guattari. This will allow us not only to arrive at a better understanding of the nature as well as the different dimensions of resistance beyond the spatial one discussed by Colombino, but also to take into account and investigate the crucial presence of a 'reterritorializing' impulse, which Colombino, unfortunately, neglects.

3.1 Deterritorialization

At its beginning, *Concrete Island* follows the logic of *Crash*. As the title of the novel's first chapter indicates, the plot begins with the protagonist's car bursting 'through the crash barrier' of a motorway due to a tire blowout, an accident that maroons him on the eponymous traffic island. As several commentators have remarked, space is an important concept for an analysis of the text. While this is usually stated above all with regards to said island, it seems to me that the study of the politics of space in the novel has to be extended to include this very first scene as well. Considering the representation of the motorway, one is struck by the persistent recurrence throughout the text of very closely related images: again and again, the traffic is described as "unbroken", "unceasing", "relentless" (*CI* 29, 48, 57), "endles[s]", "steady" (*CI* 83, 129), and, repeatedly, as a "stream" (*CI* 21, 129, 144), one that is constantly "lunging" or "surg[ing]" (*CI* 20) forward. Through the frequent use of such imagery, the motorway effectively ceases to be a mere road and turns into a metaphor for the abstract 'space of flows' (Castells 1989) of global capitalism.[1] The unending circulation of traffic and the networks of the motorway thus come to represent the interminable circulation of capital, people, information, commodities, and images on the global marketplace and the intricate capitalist networks of power. Read against this background, Maitland's crash takes on new, metaphoric meaning, too: when his car bursts through the barrier along the edge of the road, thus breaking out of the ordered and regulated forward stream of traffic, he enacts an escape from the totalizing system, 'deterritorializing' its coded flows. 'Deterritorialization', a key term in the thought of Deleuze and Guattari, "is the movement by which 'one' leaves the territory. It is the operation of the line of flight."[2] (Deleuze and Guattari 1987: 508) In this first scene of the novel, Maitland indeed 'leaves the territory'. By breaching the palisade, he transgresses the limits of the abstract space of capitalism and plots a 'line of flight': "The shredding tyre laid a black diagonal stroke across the white marker lines" (*CI* 7). Here, the 'rigid' or 'segmented line' of 'overcoding' is crossed by a line of flight, a "mutant flow [which] always implies something tending to elude or escape the codes" (Deleuze and Guattari 1987: 219). As Deleuze and Guattari point out, "[t]here is always something that flows or flees, that escapes the binary organizations, the resonance apparatus, and the overcoding machine" (1987: 216).

---

[1] Ballard's comments in his introduction to *Crash* on the car as "a total metaphor for man's [sic] life in today's society" (*C* n.pag.) give additional support to such a reading.
[2] The quotation marks around the word 'one' already point us towards the dissolution of the subject occurring in this process. This aspect will be discussed below.

Maitland's escape lands him on the traffic island, a forgotten "waste ground" (*CI* 11) between three converging motorways, filled with all kinds of debris, from which he is unable, and increasingly *unwilling*, to get away. Andrzej Gasiorek has linked the island with Marc Augé's notion of the 'non-place', which was already referred to in the preceding chapter. He describes it as "a symbol of the waste and destruction modernity leaves in its wake", as an "alienated terrain, characterised by an absence of meaning and social relations" (2005: 108, 110). Yet, what might initially appear as a space "in which neither identity, nor relations, nor history really make any sense" (Augé 2008: 70) soon turns out to be something else and takes on new meaning for the protagonist. As Maitland roams the island, he gradually discovers traces of its former history: foundations of Edwardian houses, half-buried World War II air-raid shelters, the ruins of a Victorian mansion, former street patterns, an abandoned churchyard including a cemetery, remnants of a printing shop, the remains of a Civil Defense post, and a derelict cinema (*CI* 38, 40f, 65, 68f). Unlike Augé's non-places, which "do not integrate the earlier places" (Augé 2008: 63), the island thus emerges as a kind of "physical palimpsest" (Gasiorek 2005: 113).[3] Moreover, Maitland develops an intense relation to the space in which he is trapped, one that, in view of his rambling, may be linked to the thought of Michel de Certeau (1988: 91–130) concerning the possibilities for the reappropriation of 'places' as 'spaces' through 'spatial practices' such as 'walking in the city'. The label 'non-place' therefore only has a very limited validity in connection with Ballard's island and may in fact – as in *Crash* – be more suitably applied to the cityscape surrounding it. But perhaps the unusual spaces of *Concrete Island* can be understood best by situating them in an altogether different theoretical model.

Deleuze and Guattari have introduced the useful conceptual distinction between 'striated space' and 'smooth space', and it seems that the novel's opposition between city and island functions along similar lines. London's cityscape manifests itself in Ballard's text in the shape of the concrete motorways, the television studios in White City, a shopping center, office towers, and high-rise apartment blocks (*CI* 11, 13, 16, 23). Not only do all of these, to varying degrees, lean towards Augéian non-places, they also constitute the homogeneous space of the state apparatus that Deleuze and Guattari term 'striated space'. According to the two philosophers, "the city is the striated space par excellence" (1987: 481), and

---

[3] With regards to the fact that the island is furthermore portrayed as a space of waste and debris, one may perhaps also read it as a product or embodiment of the process Marxists refer to as 'creative destruction', i.e. the continual transformation of cityscapes effected by the cycles of capitalist investment (cf. Harvey 1990).

the London of Ballard's novel clearly confirms this declaration by appearing as a functional, rigid, sterile, and profoundly "alienating" (*CI* 130) space, based on architectural planning and fully subordinated to, indeed itself expressive of, the logics of late capitalism.[4] It is telling that Ballard renders the city through precisely those sites which Deleuze and Guattari identify as being vital to contemporary capitalism: "capitalism operates [...] by a complex qualitative process bringing into play modes of transportation, urban models, the media, the entertainment industries, ways of perceiving and feeling – every semiotic system" (1987: 492). The fact that "the elaborately signalled landscape" of the city's motorways, another structure of signification, "seems to anticipate every possible hazard" (*CI* 4) is symptomatic of the system as a whole: everywhere, deviation/deviance must be thwarted in order to guarantee the complete insertion of the individual into the subject-positions (as producer and consumer) constructed for him/her; everywhere, any threat of destabilization must be predicted and contained in order to ensure the smooth functioning of the capitalist machine. In the striated space of the city, then, "the subject is perceived as mainly integrated into the system and compliant with its requirements of functionality, planning, and readability" (Colombino 2006: 617).

While some commentators have criticized Deleuze and Guattari's thought for its apparently binary logic (e.g. Žižek 2004: 28), it has to be emphasized that they constantly insist on the non-dichotomous nature of the numerous oppositions they introduce in their work.[5] This also applies to the distinction between smooth and striated space: the former is in constant danger of being striated and the latter frequently re-imparts a smooth space, so that "the simple opposition 'smooth-striated' gives rise to far more difficult complications, alternations, and superpositions" (Deleuze and Guattari 1987: 481). In this way, not only does the contemporary perfection of striation produce a global capitalist smooth space of multinational organizations and endlessly circulating capital (Deleuze and Guattari 1987: 492) which I have shown to be metaphorized in Ballard's

---

4 As Sebastian Groes points out with regards to Ballard's early novels, "London function[s] as an anonymous signifier of power" (2008: 93).
5 Cf. e.g.: "No, this is not a new or different dualism. [...] We invoke one dualism only in order to challenge another. We employ a dualism of models only in order to arrive at a process that challenges all models. Each time, mental correctives are necessary to undo the dualisms we had no wish to construct but through which we pass." (Deleuze and Guattari 1987: 20) In spite of this, I would argue that Deleuze and Guattari cannot, in the final analysis, entirely eradicate the traces of binarism underlying their work.

novel in the image of the incessant flow of traffic.[6] The striated space of the city also yields new, oppositional smooth spaces in its very midst: "The smooth spaces arising from the city are not only those of world-wide organization, but also of a counterattack [...] turning back against the town" (Deleuze and Guattari 1987: 481). The traffic island on which Maitland finds himself is such a space.

Ballard's representation of London through the waste ground of the concrete island on the one hand and the 'proper' city ('actual' as well as 'clean', the two meanings being closely connected in the dominant conceptualization of the contemporary metropolis) on the other is reminiscent of the analyses of the postmodern city carried out by political geographers and urban theorists such as Edward Soja (1989), David Harvey (1990), and Mike Davis (2006). Often taking Los Angeles as a paradigmatic example, they show how today's permutations of capital create an increasingly contradictory urban scene with glass skyscrapers, shopping malls, grand plazas, museums, high-technology industrial complexes, and advertising on the one hand and decrepit landscapes of post-industrial decline, dirt, and decaying neighborhoods on the other – what Davis (2006: 15ff) refers to as 'Sunshine' versus 'Noir'. While the shopping centers, TV studios and high-rises which Maitland sees when looking back at the city center from his island are clearly manifestations of the power of capital, the island itself is one of its geographical by-products[7] – albeit one of a special kind – one of the numerous smooth spaces in the postmodern metropolis "to which the striations of money, work, or housing are no longer even relevant" (Deleuze and Guattari 1987: 481). With his crash on this patch of waste ground Maitland leaves behind the economic relationships of work, production and consumption that to a large degree shape life in the late 20th and early 21st century. Accordingly, he feels as if "he ha[s] suddenly exited from reality" (*CI* 24). This, of course, is only reality as defined by hegemonic discourses. What kind of reality, then, is it that he *enters*?

As the novel progresses, the reader becomes increasingly aware of the unusual nature of the traffic island on which Maitland is stranded. It has already been pointed out how, in contrast to the striated space of the city, it is a

---

6 Of course, this space, while largely independent of the classical striations at the state pole of capitalism, is nevertheless subject to new striations on the global level which are bound up with the requirements, necessities and restraints of capital. Cf. Michael Hardt and Antonio Negri's observation that the smooth space of 'imperial sovereignty' "might appear to be free of the binary divisions or striation of modern boundaries, but really [...] is crisscrossed by so many fault lines that it only appears as a continuous, uniform space" (2001: 190). On the subject of the smooth space of global capitalism, cf. chapter 5.
7 Similarly, Sebastian Groes reads the island as an example of 'junkspace' as defined by Rem Koolhaas, as the "spatial fallout" (2012: 130) of modernization.

space characterized by a radical heterogeneity (cf. Deleuze and Guattari 1987: 488), where various architectural styles are overlaid as traces of different historical epochs.[8] Besides this, it is also a liminal space:[9] not only is the island situated "*between* three converging motorway routes" (*CI* 11, emphasis added), its liminality is above all due to its status in the city, to whose territory it officially belongs, yet of which – as the city's 'accursed' or 'abject' other – it does not effectively form a part. Similar to a Foucauldian 'heterotopia', it is a place that is "outside of all places", even though it has a "location in reality" (Foucault 1986a: 24). Furthermore, as a "concrete wilderness" (*CI* 149), dominated by grass, the island has an ambiguous character (organic/artificial), as it does an indefinite shape: Maitland observes that it is characterized by a "peculiar topography" of "dips and hollows, rises and hillocks", "markedly uneven" (*CI* 43, 13, 140), and compares it to a "labyrinth" (*CI* 102). The island appears to change form continually and especially its borders are difficult to discern: not only are some of its boundaries made up of heaps of garbage and thus explicitly porous (Viney 2007: n.pag.), but there is also a constant "yellow haze [...] blurring the perimeter walls" (*CI* 38). Twice, Maitland has the impression that the island has actually grown (*CI* 102, 122). Unlike the "limited and limiting [...] striated space", the island is thus "an *amorphous*, nonformal space" (Deleuze and Guattari 1987: 382, 477). This is further underlined by the unusual nature of its vegetation. One of the most curious traits of the island is certainly the ubiquitous waist-high grass – despite its designation as a 'concrete island'. Remarkably, this grass cover is frequently associated with water: it is compared to an "ocean" and "a calm and peaceful sea" (*CI* 127, 75, cf. also 40, 44), Maitland "wade[s]" and "paddle[s]" through it, emerges from it like a "swimme[r] coming ashore" (*CI* 10, 15, 127), and fears that it might "inundate" (*CI* 48) him.[10] Such metaphors are truly telling in light of the reading of the island space I have advanced, since, according to Deleuze and Guattari, "the sea is a smooth space par excellence, [...] the archetype of all smooth spaces" (1987: 479f). At the same time, the water imagery underscores the unstable, mutable quality of the island – what, particularly in consideration of its abject character, we may designate as its Bataillean 'formlessness' (Bataille 1985a; Bois/Krauss 1999).

---

[8] This quality, as well as some of those discussed in the following, also allows us to link Ballard's island with such postmodern spatial concepts as Michel Foucault's (1986a) 'heterotopia', Edward Soja's (1998) 'thirdspace' or Bernard Tschumi's (1994) 'cross-programming'.
[9] Of course, there is a long cultural tradition of seeing islands, and especially beaches, as liminal spaces.
[10] With regards to its liminal and heterotopic character, it is interesting to note that the island thus contains *within itself* the opposed realms of water and land.

Yet, the grass is not just an ocean: it is also variously figured as a "forest" and a "wilderness" (*CI* 121, 63), a "bower" and an "underground cavern" (*CI* 31, 74), and even as an "immense green creature" and an "affectionate dog" (*CI* 68, 102). Moreover, it is repeatedly personified: the grass is said to be "whispering", "speaking", and "dancing" (*CI* 8, 63, 29), "eager to protect and guide" Maitland, its blades once inclining forwards "like the members of an eager audience" (*CI* 68, 53). If, in addition, we take into account that the grass is portrayed as being almost always in motion, incessantly seething, swirling and swerving around Maitland, moving in "circular waves" and "spirals", and constantly "opening a dozen pathways" for him, "[i]ts corridors open[ing] and clos[ing]" (*CI* 68, 74, 42), it becomes clear that the grass here constitutes a complex, protean system akin to what Deleuze and Guattari have called a 'rhizome'. Radically different from systems modeled on the ideal of the tree or the root, the rhizome defies the notion of a center, hierarchies and binary logic, fixity and order, homogeneity and purity, unity and stable, clear-cut structures (Deleuze and Guattari 1987: 3–25). Like the "deep underworld of grass" (*CI* 160) in Ballard's novel, it is a "subterranean" (non-)structure with "multiple entryways and exits", "has neither beginning nor end, but always a middle (*milieu*) from which it grows and which it overspills", and "operates by variation, expansion, [...] offshoots" (Deleuze and Guattari 1987: 6, 21). In this context, it is revealing that Deleuze and Guattari at one point lament that in the contemporary West, "[w]e have lost the rhizome, *or the grass*" (1987: 18, emphasis added).[11] On Ballard's island, one such rhizome reconstitutes itself and, as in the model of the two French philosophers, resists the hegemony of the signifier: all of Maitland's attempts to *signify*, to create and inscribe the waste ground with meaning – whether by setting his car on fire, scrawling messages on the concrete, or signaling with a burning blanket – are ultimately deflected by the island (Colombino 2006: 619 f; Viney 2007: n.pag.). The island does not allow itself to be overcoded and hence functions as an "asignifying rupture" (Deleuze and Guattari 1987: 9) of all codes of signification. The broken remains of the printing shop which Maitland discovers in an, appropriately, "*weed-grown* basement" (*CI* 65, emphasis added) can be read as a metaphor for this. The island thus proves to be "meaningless soil" (*CI* 32) indeed.

The trans-political dimension of the novel emerges most clearly in its suggestion that such a rhizomatic smooth space allows for a refashioning of subjectivity and the development of alternative modes of being. Drawing on the work of

---

[11] Cf. here also the interesting comments on weed by Henry Miller, which Deleuze and Guattari (1987: 18 f) quote.

Deleuze and Guattari, Canadian social theorist Brian Massumi argues that it is precisely in the derelict spaces of the postmodern metropolis that new emancipatory practices begin to take shape. As in the case of Ballard's island, these 'autonomous zones' are "perceived by good/common sense as a simple negative: a lack of functioning, a wasteland" (Massumi 1992: 104), yet actually constitute powerful breaches in the existing order. In a passage that superbly encapsulates the nature of the concrete island, Massumi writes:

> Even though autonomous zones are derelict spaces that become sites of escape, they should not be thought of as 'outside' the existing structures in any straightforward sense. Escape always takes place *in* the World As We Know It. Autonomous zones are interstitial, they inhabit the in-between of socially significant constellations, they are where bodies in the world but between identities go: liminal sites of syncretic unorthodoxy. (1992: 105)

Maitland's patch of waste ground is just such a site, a zone, as all smooth spaces, of 'free action' and 'becoming' (cf. Deleuze and Guattari 1987: 490, 486). In this context, it is significant that Ballard, in his introduction to the novel, refers to the island as a place that is "out of sight of the surveillance cameras" (*CI* 4). This, I would argue, refers us not only to traffic monitoring and public control systems in general – today's 'CCTV Britain' comes immediately to mind – but, beyond that, to a whole paradigm of power which Michel Foucault (1979: 195–228) famously termed 'panopticism'. According to Foucault, contemporary 'disciplinary societies', whose emergence he dates back to the 18th century, are characterized by a state of "generalized surveillance" (1979: 209), in which, however, control is *internalized* so that the exercise of actual, external observation is rendered unnecessary. Instead, the citizens are "caught up in a power situation of which they are themselves the bearers", the individual policing himself (sic) and hence, in Foucault's words, "becom[ing] the principle of his [sic] own subjection" (1979: 201, 203). By assuring that individuals adjust themselves to social norms and conformize their behavior of their own accord, the disciplinary modality of power is able to fabricate bodies and subjectivities amenable to the smooth functioning of the capitalist economy. Maitland's line of flight away from the surveillance cameras thus removes him from disciplinary society and its "micro-physics of power" (Foucault 1979: 26). From the moment he enters the smooth space of the island, a process of 'desubjectivaton' is set in motion, in which, to adopt the terminology of Deleuze, Guattari and Massumi, the 'segments' or layers that make up his socially produced, 'molar' individual subjectiv-

3.1 Deterritorialization — 89

ity are gradually 'destratified' (Deleuze and Guattari 1987: 208 ff; Massumi 1992: 47–92).[12]

Initially, however, being confronted with the deterritorializing possibilities of the island, Maitland still tries to reassert his sense of selfhood. This is why, in the first two chapters of the novel, the narrative so insistently focuses on his briefcase, hat and raincoat (*CI* 14–22); by repeatedly drawing attention to their presence, always emphasizing that Maitland is still in possession of them, the narrative endows these items with additional meaning, turning them into tokens of his bourgeois lifestyle, into signifiers of a unified, stable and coherent personal identity. "He put on his raincoat and buttoned it neatly, straightened his hat and waved calmly at the passing vehicles" (*CI* 19); buttoning, straightening, neatly, calmly – are these not symptoms of a fear of chaos and of an attempt to restore wholeness, order and solidity, that is, to preserve an identity that is already beginning to fracture? This wish to uphold a sense of subjecthood essentially fashioned to serve the purposes of the capitalist system also manifests itself in Maitland's efforts "to rally all his powers of self-control" and to "maste[r] himself", as well as in his initial attempts to create an "inventory of his body" and to "[take] stock of himself" (*CI* 21, 8, 43). Here, the choice of words alone is suggestive of the disciplinary imperative to make oneself a socially adapted and useful 'docile body' (Foucault 1979: 135–169).

Yet, as he spends more time on the island, Maitland is increasingly able to free himself from bourgeois individuality and thus pass from the 'molar' to the 'molecular'. Accordingly, he soon takes off his hat and "tosse[s] it under the massive rear wheels" of a passing fuel tanker, while his briefcase and raincoat end up lying "at his feet in a grimy bundle like the luggage of a tramp" (*CI* 20, 16). From an architect of late-capitalist non-place (cf. Maitland's admiration for the French resort complex La Grande Motte [*CI* 65]) to a tramp at home on a waste ground – this trans-political transition encapsulates Maitland's passage from striated to smooth space, from subjection to becoming.

From early on, the novel repeatedly implies that its protagonist is progressively moving towards insanity: thus, Maitland is compared to a "madman" (*CI* 13, 46) and he himself feels "like visiting an insane asylum and seeing [himself] sitting on a bench" (*CI* 117). Instead of construing such passages as evidence

---

[12] With regards to the fact that the traffic island has repeatedly been read as a Ballardian 'inner space', i.e. as partially a reflection and/or projection of Maitland's psyche (Stephenson 1991: 74–80; Gasiorek 2005: 108, 113 ff), Deleuze and Guattari's geological imagery seems particularly appropriate, given that Maitland steadily uncovers more topographical sediments of the island's history.

of "a disordered mind slipping into delirium" (Gasiorek 2005: 113) or of an "inner metamorphosis" leading to "psychic integration" (Stephenson 1991: 76, 75), I propose to read them as signs of Maitland's growing deterritorialization of flows and the concomitant corrosion of the socially sanctioned ideal of personhood. In this way, I would argue, Ballard's protagonist accomplishes the "destructive task" of 'schizoanalysis': "disintegrating the normal ego" (Deleuze and Guattari 1983: 362).[13] What is here called 'madness' signals his transition from what Deleuze and Guattari term the 'paranoiac-reactionary' pole of social desire to the 'schizoid-revolutionary' one. It is therefore fitting that images of doubling and splitting recur in the novel: Maitland frequently talks to himself (e.g. *CI* 8, 14, 37),[14] realizes that "*half his mind* [is] revelling in [his] drunken tantrum" (*CI* 21, emphasis added), and once has the impression that "a psychotic twin brother" (*CI* 9) is staring back at him from the rearview mirror of his car. The schizophrenia that Maitland embraces is not a pathological condition and not a state, but a process, marked by "lines of escape that follow the decoded and deterritorialized flows" (Deleuze and Guattari 1983: 367). As Massumi explains: "Schizophrenia as a positive process is inventive connection, expansion rather than withdrawal. Its twoness is a relay to a multiplicity." (1992: 1) This process not only challenges the regulatory discourses that produce 'intelligible' subjects, but subverts "the illusion of the ego" (Deleuze and Guattari 1983: 311) itself. The subject, the self, the ego – for Deleuze and Guattari, these are effects of power, blocking and territorializing the flows of desire, overcoding the multiplicities. While (re-)territorialization and deterritorialization continually vie with each other, Maitland nevertheless more and more escapes from the molar aggregate of identity: even though he intermittently feels a need to "tr[y] to identify himself", for example through speaking aloud to himself "as a self-identification signal" (*CI* 64, 30), such endeavors prove increasingly futile and superfluous. When he feels as if the crash has "jolted his brain loose from its moorings" or as if "[p]arts of his mind [...] [are] detaching themselves from the centre of his consciousness" (*CI* 37, 63), what is at stake is precisely the (re-)constitution of a decentralized, rhizomatic multiplicity; what these images of dissolution and centrifugal motion convey is the crumbling of the stable ego, the fragmentation of the unified subject – "everyone is a little group (*un groupuscule*) and must live as such" (Dele-

---

[13] Here, Deleuze and Guattari echo R.D. Laing, who likewise claimed that "[t]rue sanity entails in one way or another the dissolution of the normal ego" (1967: 144). On this subject, cf. also chapter 5.
[14] Cf. also Jane's comment "you talk to yourself all the time" (*CI* 84).

uze and Guattari 1983: 362).[15] Accordingly, Maitland begins to feel as if he has "forgotten who he was" (*CI* 63). Ballard's protagonist does not, then, as Stephenson (1991: 76, 78) claims, overcome self-dividedness and achieve a new sense of identity, but, on the contrary, welcomes division and 'depersonalization', is thus liberated from the "minidespotism" (Massumi 1992: 126) of the self, and opens himself up to the multiplicities pervading him.

In this context, the fact that the grass that covers the traffic island is constantly depicted as a sea or an ocean becomes relevant once again. Such imagery has traditionally been used to suggest the unconscious (Stephenson 1991: 77), so that we are entitled to ascribe additional meaning to the grass and construe it as a metaphor for the unconscious. Such a reading is substantiated by the fact that Deleuze and Guattari (e.g. 1987: 14, 18) depict the unconscious and desire as equally rhizomatic as the grass in Ballard's novel and actually themselves use the metaphor of grass to describe them. The two philosophers vehemently attack psychoanalysis for making the Oedipus complex into a universal law, for personalizing and structuralizing the unconscious, subjecting it to the hegemony of the signifier and the logic of representation, and for defining desire as an unfulfillable lack. Radically opposed to this, their schizoanalysis sees the Oedipal family structure as in effect a social overcoding mechanism restricting the flow of desire and consequently seeks to "de-oedipalize" (Deleuze and Guattari 1983: 81) the unconscious. According to Deleuze and Guattari, desire must be understood as essentially productive – hence their machinic terminology – and as independent of personal identities and of signification (expression or interpretation). It is a kind of primary force, not a desire for an object, a pleasure, or a drive in the Freudian sense. If the grass on the concrete island also functions as a metaphoric representation of Maitland's desire, it is a desire that has been freed from its blockages and territorializations and become a rhizome (again), an unbridled multi-directional flow effecting ever new syntheses and connections. Maitland, similar to the protagonists of *Crash*, has (re-)become a 'desiring-machine'. He ceases to be a 'monad' and changes into a 'nomad' (Deleuze and Guattari 1987: 493, 573fn27), whose "primary determination [...] is to occupy and hold a smooth space" (Deleuze and Guattari 1987: 410). As a nomad, continually traversing the smooth space of the island – a *nomos* opposed to the striated *polis* (Deleuze and Guattari 1987: 380f) – he travels in the "rhizomatic direction", which means "to move between things, establish a logic of the AND, overthrow

---

15 Even though Deleuze and Guattari are, of course, highly critical of Lacanian psychoanalysis, the repeated instances of distorted reflections in the text (*CI* 9, 13, 30, 37) might perhaps nevertheless be related to Lacan's (2004) notion of the 'mirror-stage' and thus read as metaphors of the disintegration of identity.

ontology, do away with foundations, nullify endings and beginnings" (Deleuze and Guattari 1987: 25).

Like that of the island itself, his existence turns into a liminal one, into a mode of being not characterized by a stable subjectivity and a fixed and unified identity, but by an unceasing *becoming* without arrival. I would contend that the narrative's countless references to childhood and Maitland's animal-like behavior towards the end of text can be understood with reference to this central Deleuzian concept as well. Andrzej Gasiorek (2005: 114 ff) has related these to the notion of 'regression', arguing that Maitland undergoes a psychological regression back to childhood and an evolutionary one to primordiality. Yet, it is a case of regression only from the traditional points of view of psychoanalysis and evolutionary anthropology. Schizoanalysis, on the other hand, provides us with alternative terms with which to interpret Maitland's transformation. Instead of regression or (de-)evolution, we might speak of an 'involution' then, of a development remaining entirely within the in-between of fixed terms (Deleuze and Guattari 1987: 238 f), instead of a reversion to an infantile and primal state, of a 'becoming-child' and a 'becoming-animal'. A becoming is not a progress or a regress, but neither is it an imitation, an identification or a correspondence (even though elements of these may well be part of it). It is the process in which the power of an 'affect' "throws the self into upheaval and makes it reel", a relation that uproots both its terms, disrupting their boundaries, "a *proximity, an indiscernibility*" (Deleuze and Guattari 1987: 240, 279).[16] The effect of becoming is that it "unfolds potentials enveloped in a singular individual at a crossroads of mutation" (Massumi 1992: 98). Maitland is placed at just such a crossroads, one with a number of arms: "He massaged his bruised chest, realizing that his body was more and more beginning to resemble that of his younger self" (*CI* 91 f) – becoming-child; "[m]oving like a crab on his feet and forearms, he climbed the more shallow soil", "forcing himself across the crumbling surface like a wounded snake" (*CI* 16, 25) – becoming-animal; "[i]dentifying the island with himself, he gazed at the cars in the breaker's yard, at the wire-mesh fence, and the concrete caisson behind him. These places of pain and ordeal were now confused with pieces of his body. [...] He spoke aloud [...]. 'I am the island.'" (*CI* 70 f) – becoming-island; "he crawled through the grass, feeling his way with his outstretched hands, sensing the stronger vibrations of the tall grass" (*CI* 175) – becoming-Proctor/-beast; "[t]he warm air moved across the is-

---

[16] As Brian Massumi points out, becoming "cannot be exhaustively described. If it could, it would already be what it is becoming, in which case it wouldn't be becoming at all, being instead the same." (1992: 103)

land, soothing both the grass and his own skin, as if these were elements of the same body" (*CI* 156) – becoming-grass. There is a zone of proximity and co-presence between Maitland and all these 'others', in which a perpetual exchange of elements and particles takes place and which consequently obscures all boundaries and forms new multiplicities. A particular closeness seems to exist between Maitland and the grass,[17] which is constantly speaking to him and leading him, "transfer[ring] some of its warmth to him" (*CI* 40), etc. It is a kind of permanent exchange back and forth: "Laughing at the grass, Maitland patted it reassuringly [...], *stroking* the seething stems that *caressed* his waist" (*CI* 68, emphasis added) – these are unusual participations, "unnatural nuptials" (Deleuze and Guattari 1987: 273) indeed. As was already indicated, the grass, for its part, is itself engaged in various becomings: becoming-ocean, becoming-human, becoming-animal, and so forth. Thus, the smooth space of the island appears as a zone of indeterminacy, in which everything is in flux, the social grid of permissible identities is ruptured, and the formed subject swept away by fluctuating flows of desire, in which all seemingly steady entities are destabilized, and new trajectories for the vagabond subject continuously opened up.

Maitland's becomings, his transgressions of "the programmed body" by way of "*an inhumanity immediately experienced in the body as such*" (Deleuze and Guattari 1987: 273),[18] also entail an expansion of his body's range of perceptions and responses beyond those pre-programmed for it by social codes and discourses. His perceptive coordinates of space and time are fundamentally altered as he enters "a universe of microperceptions" (Deleuze and Guattari 1987: 248). Gregory Stephenson has called attention to the fact that Maitland gradually forsakes "quantitative time" and "becomes responsive to the immediate stimuli of the diurnal cycle: the morning and the evening dew, the movement of shadows across the terrain, the quality of light, the warmth or coolness of the air" (1991: 78). Already early on, Maitland is once presented as "too drunk to be able to focus on his wrist-watch" and hence as "[giving] up all sense of time" (*CI* 26f). Later, towards the end of the narrative, he has finally completely "forgotten what day it [is]" (*CI* 157). The time of the wrist watch versus that of the diurnal cycle: these are the two modes of temporality referred to by Deleuze and Guattari (1987: 261f) as 'chronos' and 'aeon', that is, measured time developing stable forms and firmly situating things and persons as opposed to an indefinite, floating and dynam-

---

17 Perhaps, we could say that, for Maitland, the grass fulfills the function of what Deleuze and Guattari (1987: 243ff) call the 'anomalous', a kind of borderline phenomenon with which it is necessary to enter into alliance in order to become-other.
18 Deleuze and Guattari here quote the French thinkers Guy Hocquenghem and René Schérer.

ic time keeping things in a state of becoming.[19] An analogous change can be identified in Maitland's perception of and relation to space. More and more, he takes in his environment, orients himself in it and moves through it by simply "follow[ing] the swirling motions" of the grass, sensing its "patterns" (*CI* 68). Maitland increasingly discards entrenched habits and resembles Proctor, who finds his way across the island by "steer[ing] himself with his scarred hand, his thick sensitive fingers feeling the density, moisture and inclination of the stems [of grass], rejecting one and selecting another of the well-used corridors" (*CI* 144). This is a radically different, non-/posthuman experience of space, in large part derived from new, tactile circuits of response. As Maitland observes with regards to Proctor, he rejects making use of his sight and instead "prefer[s] to rely on his scarred fingers and his sense of touch" (*CI* 150). It is, in the words of Deleuze and Guattari, "*haptic* rather than optical perception" (1987: 479).[20] Unlike striated space, the smooth space through which Maitland moves is filled with intensities and affects, with what Deleuze and Guattari variously call 'singularities', 'events' or 'haecceities',[21] that is, unformed, unorganized, non-quantified elements. "Perception in it is based on symptoms and evaluations rather than measures and properties." (Deleuze and Guattari 1987: 479)

At this point, we can, for a moment, extend our analysis to the formal level of the text in order to draw attention to an interesting correspondence between content and narrative perspective. Deleuze and Guattari (1987: 492ff) expand on their conception of the smooth and the striated as the difference between, among other things, haptic space and close-range vision on the one hand and optical space and long-distance vision on the other. Against this background, it is instructive to compare the very beginning of the novel with any one of its later passages. This is how the novel opens:

---

19 This opposition is reminiscent of Henri Bergson's (2001) differentiation between the spatialized and quantitative conception of time of the natural sciences on the one hand and what he calls 'duration', the creative, indivisible flow of time underlying the 'élan vital', on the other, something that, elsewhere, Deleuze and Guattari (1987: 483f) actually refer to. In general, there seems to be a rather close affinity between the thought of the two theorists and what has come to be known as *Lebensphilosophie*.
20 Deleuze and Guattari (1987: 492ff) point out that this differentiation cannot be reduced to the opposition between two sense organs, but must rather be understood as different modes of relating to one's environment.
21 Deleuze and Guattari adopt this latter term from the medieval philosopher John Duns Scotus. They write: "There is a mode of individuation very different from that of a person, subject, thing, or substance. We reserve the name *haecceity* for it." (1987: 261, cf. also 260–265)

3.1 Deterritorialization — 95

> Soon after three o'clock on the afternoon of April 22nd 1973, a 35-year-old architect named Robert Maitland was driving down the high-speed exit lane of the Westway interchange in central London. Six hundred yards from the junction with the newly built spur of the M4 motorway, when the Jaguar had already passed the 70 m.p.h. speed limit, a blow-out collapsed the front near-side tyre. The exploding air reflected from the concrete parapet seemed to detonate inside Robert Maitland's skull. (*CI* 7)

The narrative situation is clearly an authorial one; or, using Gérard Genette's model, we can speak of a zero focalization. The amount and exactitude of the information that is given – the precise time and date, age and profession of the protagonist, the place and specific location, the car brand, exact speed, and position of the tire – are so unusually high that the reader gets the impression of perusing a police report. This, I would argue, is only appropriate. For what does the bird's-eye view intimate if not the controlling gaze of the surveillance cameras mentioned in the introduction; what does the sheer density of detail conveyed by the apparently all-seeing eye of an anonymous, invisible and untouchable observer suggest but the distant vision of striation Deleuze and Guattari speak of? To see everything without being seen – at this point, Maitland is still inside the "panoptic machine" (Foucault 1979: 217), subjected to its gaze and invested by its power. In this way, the initial authorial/authoritarian perspective brilliantly reflects Maitland's subjection. It is only the last sentence of the excerpt that, with its suggestion of a Ballardian 'inner space', signals a change of perspective – aptly at just that moment when the tire explodes and Maitland draws his line of flight. The sentence thus anticipates the figural narrative situation, or internal focalization, that dominates most of the rest of the text. Contrast the opening of the novel with any passage from the later parts: Maitland in 'delirium' (as the title of chapter 21 has it), Maitland crawling through the high grass, sensing the currents of the stems – this is close vision and continuous variation, without any constant orientations or elevated and unifying perspective. Even though all of this is presented from Maitland's point of view, his perspective nevertheless does not provide a stable center, since it is swept up in a process of becoming – it is a nomadological, not a monadological point of view. Through this change of the narrative situation, then, the novel formally reenacts the liberation from the controlling grasp of the system that it depicts on the level of the content.[22]

---

[22] Perhaps, we could even go so far as to assume another correspondence between form and content with regards to the proliferation of metaphors and similes in the text, especially relating to the grass and to Proctor – the grass as an ocean, a cavern, a dog, a forest, a person, etc.; Proctor as a clown, a bull, a mole, a bird; a dog, a crab, and so forth. Could this excess of images be

Maitland is freed from 'signifiance' and from subjectivation, but also from the last of the "three great strata" (Deleuze and Guattari 1987: 159) that bind us, the organism. There are numerous images of bodily fragmentation in the text and several passages depicting Maitland's (unconsciously) willful damaging of his own body (e.g. *CI* 45, 47). In an oft-quoted section of the novel, he sees himself as casting off parts of his body:

> As he tottered about, Maitland found himself losing interest in his own body, and in the pain that inflamed his leg. He began to shuck off sections of his body, forgetting first his injured hip, then both his legs, erasing all awareness of his bruised chest and diaphragm. [...] He would leave his right leg at the point of his crash, his bruised hands impaled upon the steel fence. He would place his chest where he had sat against the concrete wall. (*CI* 70 f)

Surely, this episode can be read as part of a process of self-healing, in which Maitland gradually frees himself from all kinds of pain, including, towards the end of the text (*CI* 156), the psychological one, through an act of 'splitting' (Gasiorek 2005: 115). Yet, if we abide by the anti-psychiatric approach delineated by Deleuze and Guattari, we may consider this process of discarding not so much as a 'phantasy' in need of interpretation, but rather as a 'program' of experimentation (Deleuze and Guattari 1987: 151). The goal of such experimentation is the (re-)constitution of what Deleuze and Guattari term a 'body without organs' (BwO). As we already saw in the preceding chapter, the BwO is opposed not to the organs as such but to the organization of the organs called the 'organism'. The organism, the two French thinkers explain, "is a stratum on the BwO, in other words, a phenomenon of accumulation, coagulation, and sedimentation that, in order to extract useful labor from the BwO, imposes upon it forms, functions, bonds, dominant and hierarchized organizations" (1987: 159). It is precisely this body as organism that Maitland dismantles. In this way, he replaces a unified body tied to the self and defined by its functioning within the capitalist economy with a 'self-less' BwO that is continuously causing flows to pass, producing and circulating intensities. The semi-intentional harming and overexerting of his body, which transform it into an "atlas of wounds" and make it "blosso[m] into a garden of bruises" (*CI* 27, 47),[23] can be read as Maitland's attempt to "invent self-destructions that have nothing to do with the death drive" (Deleuze and Guattari 1987: 160) and that serve the purpose of taking

---

read as a sign of a writing that is itself becoming rhizomatic, branching out into various semantic directions, establishing ever new connections and associations?

23 Such imagery continues the aestheticization and valorization of injuries that we have observed in *Crash*.

apart the organism. Such destratification is diametrically opposed to Maitland's initial attempt to create an "inventory of his body" (*CI* 8) immediately after the crash. The more he escapes the social imperative to be a subject (subjectivation) and an interpreter (signifiance), the more he also rejects the command to be a coherent, determinate and productive body (organism) and instead devises a dynamic body, a body in becoming, one defined by its full potential and the entire repertory of states and connections.

In view of this, it is fitting that the traffic island is once compared to a "festering [...] wound" and that, with regards to sleeping Europe, Maitland is on one occasion described as "the nightmare of this slumbering continent" (*CI* 14, 25) – the rhizomatic smooth space of the island constitutes a wound in the symbolic order indeed, a challenge to all the striations of power; and of course, the nomadic schizo-subject is capitalism's nightmare, subverting every dictate underpinning its social order: "You will be organized, you will be an organism, you will articulate your body – otherwise you're just depraved. You will be signifier and signified, interpreter and interpreted – otherwise you're just a deviant. You will be a subject, nailed down as one [...] – otherwise you're just a tramp." (Deleuze and Guattari 1987: 159) Depraved, tramp, deviant – in connection with Ballard's novel, the choice of words is telling, for the patch of waste ground that Maitland makes his home is a space of deviance and depravity par excellence. Not only are both Maitland and Proctor repeatedly referred to as 'tramps' (e.g. *CI* 16, 88), but Proctor and Jane, the island's two other inhabitants, are social rejects, "two outcasts", the one a "subnorma[l]" and "mental defective" (*CI* 114, 98, 86), the other a drug-using motorway prostitute and "dropout" (*CI* 95).

It seems that the escape from social systems of control and the creation of a BwO are in the novel rather closely tied to the notions of 'waste' and 'destitution', both understood in a wider sense.[24] Firstly, the island itself is introduced to us as an unintended and unwanted byproduct of road building, lying as it does "in the *waste ground* between three converging motorway routes" (*CI* 11, emphasis added). What is more, Maitland soon discovers that it also *consists* of not much else besides waste; it is "a forgotten island of rubble and weeds" (*CI* 4). On the one hand, there are the derelict and decaying remnants of former architectural structures, on the other, all kinds of garbage pile up on the island, especially at its eastern end, where the area beyond the fence has been turned

---

24 In a related manner, Jean Baudrillard has argued that "cemeteries, waste ground and 'accursed' spaces" increasingly become the only sites "where living is tolerable [...] in the modern necropolis" (1993b: 187n3). On the role of waste in *Concrete Island* and other Ballard texts, cf. the instructive analyses in Viney 2007.

into an "unofficial municipal dump" (*CI* 13). There, at the only side of the triangle where there is no motorway embankment keeping Maitland in, it is the piles of trash, a veritable "jungle of refuse" (*CI* 39), that form an insurmountable barrier precluding his escape. Ballard's island is thus essentially a realm of waste and loss, of the Bataillean 'accursed share' (Bataille 2007). This includes, thirdly, the individuals that live on it, who are 'waste products' as well, those that do not conform, that are redundant and cast out of the social order, forced to live on its margins. They are the victims of this order, in particular of patriarchy in the case of Jane[25] and of the 'repressive state apparatus' (Althusser 1971) of the police in the case of Proctor.[26] Both are 'minoritarian' – understood in a qualitative, not a quantitative sense (Deleuze and Guattari 1987: 291) – and Maitland, too, initially a representative of the white-male-middle-class 'majoritarian' standard, is deterritorialized and torn from his major identity on the island and thrown into a becoming-minoritarian.

This process is connected with his transposition into a state of destitution as well. Discussing the emergence of smooth spaces re-imparted by the striations of the city, Deleuze and Guattari speak of an "explosive misery secreted by the city" and refer to "temporary, shifting shantytowns of nomads and cave-dwellers, scrap metal and fabric, patchwork" (1987: 481). Although there are, of course, no shantytowns on the island, I would argue that the smooth space of this derelict land with its socially discarded occupants is nevertheless clearly linked to such kind of misery. After all, Jane and Proctor are in fact urban 'cave-dwellers', living as they do in the basement of a ruined cinema and a half-buried air-raid shelter, made out by Maitland as a "beggar's hovel" (*CI* 76). And is not the shack that Proctor builds for Maitland out of various discarded car parts an actual patchwork shanty?[27] In fact, just like Proctor's (and, to a lesser degree, Jane's), Maitland's life on the island is one of radical penury: deprived of all that was previously taken for granted, he is forced to sleep in the open or within the ruins, to continue wearing his torn and filthy clothes, to make do without medical treatment, to quench his thirst with water from the windshield reservoir of his car, to hunt for food that has been thrown away, etc. His destitute state is further underlined by numerous descriptions, similes and metaphors: Maitland is

---

[25] The details of Jane's personal history are largely open to conjecture, as the novel provides only sparse information about her background.

[26] Proctor's abjectness is already implied in the scatological allusion of his very name (Colombino 2007: 623).

[27] It may be added that in light of the deliberations of Deleuze and Guattari, it is telling that Maitland's as well as Proctor's shelters are furnished with quilts, given that the two philosophers (1987: 474, 476f) cite the quilt with its patchwork formula as a paradigmatic smooth space.

variously portrayed as a "derelict figure" and a "haggard figure" (*CI* 29, 31), a "drifter", a "scarecrow" and a "cripple" (*CI* 35, 48, 147), as "grimy", "gaunt and ragged" (*CI* 37, 124). Yet, the longer he stays on the island, the more he accepts his "newly stripped and unhoused condition" (Connor 2000: n.pag.). For instance, Maitland comes to "[feel] no sense of revulsion" at the "amorphous mass of gleaming mucilage" (*CI* 128) – an image that seems deliberately crass – formed by the kitchen waste he and Proctor have to subsist on. Likewise, his attitude towards his shabby clothes and unkempt appearance changes: "A thick beard covered his face – he looked down at the grimy dress-shirt, the blackened trousers slit from the right knee to the waistband. Yet this collection of tatters less and less resembled an eccentric costume." (*CI* 92) By the end of the text, it has become clear to the reader that Maitland now cherishes his new life and will most likely never leave the island – despite his resolution, in the final lines of the novel, to make plans for his escape. This inversion of values is also evident in Maitland's admiration for what he sees as the island's "unique guile and persistence", which, he believes, will allow it to "continue to survive [...] long after the motorways [have] collapsed into dust" (*CI* 69).

Through its protagonist's reappraisal of waste, including the derelict space of the island, and of his own abject condition the novel seems to point us towards their unseen value and potential. To a certain degree, Ballard's work can therefore be read as an attempt to 'think, or write, destitutively' (Connor 2000: n.pag.). In a brave and illuminating essay, British cultural theorist Steven Connor has outlined a philosophical reassessment of the phenomenon of 'destitution' and suggested that we understand it not only, perhaps not even primarily, as a state defined by a profound lack – although this lack is no doubt real – but instead as a form of life in its own right, whose meaning is not exhausted by its negativity.[28] As Connor explains: "Everything is full of itself. There are no forms of life that are exhausted by the minus sign that hovers over them: every kind of deficit [...] has a reality in excess of that of which it is deficient [...]; it is an utterly new condition" (2000: n.pag.). Destitution, according to Connor, should thus be regarded as "a loss which loses the dimension of loss itself", as "an other life in [its] less than life" (2000: n.pag.). Maitland's island existence is such an 'other life'. As we have seen, Ballard's protagonist increasingly subscribes to a "will-to-destitution" and opts for "a form of life which declines to belong to our ways of belonging" (Connor 2000: n.pag.). The novel hence not only suggests that the concrete island might be a viable space to live in, but also that an expe-

---

28 Connor acknowledges the influence that, among others, Bataille as well as Deleuze and Guattari have had on his deliberations.

rience of radical loss and depletion could possibly yield valid alternative forms of being. In view of the ambivalent, liminal position of the island discussed earlier, its being part of the city yet lying without, it is furthermore telling that Connor interprets destitution as "a principle opposed to economy which nevertheless works on the inside of economy", a principle that opens economies "to their outside on their inside" (2000: n.pag.). Ballard's island and his protagonist's deliberate 'doing without' thus represent a powerful rift in the late-capitalist system. *Concrete Island*, it seems, is in part dominated by a radical logic of paring away, aimed at the unfolding of a way of "*being degree zero*" (Bukatman 2005: 325). Interestingly, the legal definition of destitution that Connor takes as a starting point for his deliberations describes it as "a condition [...] in which the individual can no longer be assumed to have self-ownership, or economic responsibility for himself or herself *at all*" (2000: n.pag.). At times, it appears that it is precisely such responsibility, indeed, *any* kind of responsibility, and just this ownership of a self, the very status as a subject, that Maitland wants to divest himself of. To a certain extent, the will to be without thus transforms itself into a desire for abdication. This desire is evident in the "mounting urge to sleep all the time" that Maitland experiences or in his being "tempted to stand [in one place] forever, [...] only reluctantly push[ing] himself forward" (*CI* 44, 63). It is also discernible in the "transfer of obligation from himself to the island" he performs in his mind as well as in his eventual movement "beyond exhaustion and hunger to a state where the laws of physiology, the body's economy of needs and responses, ha[ve] been suspended" (*CI* 71, 163). This – almost Buddhist – wish for a liberation from subjecthood itself is manifest in several other of Ballard's works, too, and will be the subject of the next chapter. Indeed, it is much more pronounced in those other texts, so that with regards to *Concrete Island*, Maitland's willed depletion is better understood as part of what Deleuze and Guattari term 'becoming-imperceptible', that is, the elimination of "everything that roots each of us (everybody) in ourselves, in our molarity" (1987: 279). It is in Maitland's becoming-imperceptible that his other becomings – becoming-animal, becoming-child, becoming-minoritarian, etc. – converge and that the "(anorganic)" BwO is linked up with the "(asignifying) indiscernible" and the "(asubjective) impersonal" (Deleuze and Guattari 1987: 279). Having freed his body and desire from the apparatus of overcoding, Maitland is finally "no longer anything more than an abstract line" (Deleuze and Guattari 1987: 280). An escape from all stratifications – "[o]ne is then like grass" (Deleuze and Guattari 1987: 280).

3.2 Reterritorialization

Lines of flight, smooth space, rhizome, nomadism, becoming, BwO – as we have seen, Ballard's novel presents us with a radical transgression of capitalist society's circuits of control. Maitland's island life challenges the dominant 'representations of space' (Lefebvre 2003), that is, capitalist forms of spatial organization, defies panopticism and disciplinary power, and contests subjectivation and the docility of the body. And yet, Maitland cannot unreservedly be considered a figure of subversion and emancipation. Indeed, his existence on the traffic island is finally an ambivalent one, marked by a continuous friction, alternation and superposition of de- and reterritorializations. As Deleuze and Guattari repeatedly point out, their numerous conceptual opposites of molar line and line of flight, striated space and smooth space, root and rhizome, tracing and map, and so forth must not be understood as simple dualisms, but rather coexist in complicated ways, constantly undermining, replacing and crossing over into one another. In a similar vein, Maitland is never entirely able to free himself from the codes and strata that bind him, because the social scripts and discourses that have in fact produced him time and again reassert themselves.

Ballard underscores the determining power of these scripts by effectively incorporating them into his narrative, which is clearly modeled on the 'master narratives' of William Shakespeare's *The Tempest* and Daniel Defoe's *Robinson Crusoe*, the latter of which the novel even explicitly refers to (*CI* 3, 32). Not only does the presence of these pre-texts allegorize Maitland's entrapment in discourses and meaning-systems beyond his control, the choice of texts is highly significant as well, for it is precisely the ideological codes enshrined in them that Maitland to a certain degree reproduces. This is particularly true of *Robinson Crusoe*, a work that bears witness to and reflects, among other things, the rise of European capitalism, including the ascendancy of the bourgeoisie, as well as imperialism.[29] Again and again, Maitland emulates his literary forebear. His line of flight gets blocked, his deterritorialization overlaid by reterritorializations of money and property, thus reconstituting a pared-down version of the capitalist relations he actually sought to escape; the smooth space is to some extent striated again, measured, ordered and organized, submitted to the striations of work and housing; the trajectory is re-subordinated to the points, the nomadic journey partially replaced by the dwelling; roots once again take hold and the rhizome gets arborified, allowing itself to be overcoded and folded back into a binary, dialectical

---

[29] For a more detailed account of the role of Defoe's novel in Ballard's fiction, cf. the next chapter.

and hierarchical logic of self and other; being substitutes itself for becoming, with the multiplicities re-comprehended and re-unified in the stable individual self; and the BwO gets locked back into the strata, becoming 'cancerous' (Deleuze and Guattari 1987: 163–166).

Similar to Defoe's Crusoe, Maitland's approach to his environment and to human relationships seems strictly instrumental, based on a utilitarian, means-end type of rationality (Gasiorek 2005: 120). Thus, he seeks to "harness [the island's] limited resources" (*CI* 65) and exploits both Jane and especially Proctor. By making Proctor work for him – including the construction of his "summer house" (*CI* 163) assembled out of car parts, something that recalls Crusoe's island replica of the bourgeois comforts of coast and country retreats – effectively *buying* his labor power with capital and goods, he essentially reestablishes all the dependencies and inequalities that characterize the capitalist economy. It is therefore only appropriate that Jane at one point accuses him of showing "real capitalist gratitude" (*CI* 113). Time after time, Maitland fashions and exploits asymmetries of power in order to create unequal hierarchies on the island. Indeed, his growing need to dominate the island as well as its other inhabitants is obsessively reiterated throughout the narrative. He even begins to take pleasure in his own cruelty and comes to believe that the subjugation of the others is "[a]ll that matter[s]" (*CI* 139). In this way, Maitland bit by bit reproduces the ideological codes and social power structures that mark the striated spaces beyond the island. When he subdues Jane, orders her about, and feels satisfied with his new "domestic retreat" (*CI* 140), he clearly replicates those patriarchal arrangements that Jane wanted to get away from. Similarly, his humiliation of Proctor repeats the same action – urinating on him – to which Proctor was once subjected by a police sergeant. And when he turns the abandoned churchyard into his "observation post", turning "his gaze" here and there, watching over the territory "with the sharp eyes of a gamekeeper on the lookout for an escaping poacher" (*CI* 144, 169), does this surveillance not in fact mimic the panoptic modality of power he originally sought to escape?

Certainly, Maitland's 'will to power' finds its fullest expression in his relationship with Proctor, and it is here, too, that the novel's intertextual parallels with *Robinson Crusoe* and *The Tempest* are most evident. In fact, Ballard's novel self-consciously employs and adapts the (post-)colonial discourses inscribed in these earlier texts. Like Friday and Caliban by their respective masters, Proctor is effectively transformed by Maitland into a colonial subject. Re-rooted in the bourgeois ideology of the Cartesian subject-object split and the sovereign individual, Maitland reenacts numerous of his literary forebears' strategies for dominating the other: he physically and verbally abuses him, provides him with alcohol, and "change[s] the whole economy of [his] life" (*CI* 149) by teaching him 'manners' and how to read and write (including curses, as in the case of Shakespeare's Prospero). Furthermore, just like Caliban, who is always interpellated by the other characters as some kind of beast, Proctor, too, is continuously portrayed as an animal.[30] There is, however, yet another correspondence with the work of Defoe and especially of Shakespeare, one that almost all critics have tended to ignore, namely that the relationship between Maitland and Proctor is finally more ambivalent than it initially seems. While the former clearly dominates the latter, he is nonetheless not in total control: for one thing, as in the Hegelian dialectic of master and slave, Maitland is actually dependent on Proctor, on whose back he rides across the island and without whom, getting weaker, he would not be able to move around the patch of ground at all (*CI* 145).[31] For another, Proctor habitually disobeys Maitland when it comes to the choice of their routes, to which Maitland submits "without argument" (*CI* 144). On the whole, the relationship between the two men seems to bear out Homi Bhabha's (2006) theory, according to which the colonial situation and discourse are characterized by a profound 'ambivalence', authority and domination never being as complete and the identities of colonizer and colonized never as distinct and stable as it appears. In this vein, Bhabha has convincingly argued that "post-Enlightenment man [sic] [is] tethered to, *not* confronted by, his dark reflection, the shadow of colonized man [sic], that splits his presence, distorts his outline, breaches his boundaries, repeats his action at a distance, disturbs and divides the very time of his being" (2006: 62).

A similar breakdown of the ostensibly clear-cut binary opposition between self and other occurs towards the end of Ballard's narrative. As Bhabha (2006: 121–131) has shown, colonial 'mimicry', by requiring at once similarity and difference ('almost the same, but not quite'), always entails a slippage leading to a destabilization of identities, which are thus revealed as 'partial presences'. Bhabha has pointed out the role of the 'scopic drive' and of the subversive "gaze of otherness" (2006: 126) in this process, and perhaps we may read the novel's repeated reference to Proctor's eyes in this context: when Proctor "alert[ly]"

---

30 Even though Maitland is not the narrator of the text, this animal imagery can nevertheless be ascribed to him, since he functions as the focalizer for most of the text, which entails, in the words of Shlomith Rimmon-Kenan (2008: 84), the 'coloring' of its language in such a way that it appears as a transposition of his perceptions.

31 Cf. also the fact that Proctor's influence endures beyond the grave: even after the tramp's death, Maitland leaves "token portion[s]" (*CI* 176) of food beside his tomb. This act might also be read as a kind of offering and thus be taken to signal Maitland's movement towards some kind of religion. Another intertextual reference point for Maitland and Proctor, especially with regards to the Hegelian dialectic, seems to be Samuel Beckett's pair of Pozzo and Lucky from his famous play *Waiting for Godot*.

watches Maitland, "gaz[ing] at him with his crafty, expectant eyes", and Maitland, for his part, "avoid[s] Proctor's eyes, composing his face so that it [will] show no trace of any expression" (*CI* 146, 147, 146), is this not a moment in which "the look of surveillance returns as the displacing gaze of the disciplined, where the observer becomes the observed and 'partial' representation rearticulates the whole notion of *identity* and alienates it from essence" (Bhabha 2006: 127)? Moreover, a curious reversal takes place in Ballard's novel: at the end of the text, it is Maitland who mimics Proctor, having effectively adopted the latter's way of life and identity. With this hybridization of identities the simple dichotomy of self and other is powerfully undermined. Beyond this, a further instance of ambivalence can be observed in the discrepancy between Maitland's certainty to have "tamed the old tramp" and, like Crusoe, to reign as unchallenged chief "over his barren kingdom" on the one hand and his simultaneous obsessive fear that "[o]nce he relaxe[s] he [will] be destroyed by Proctor" (*CI* 144, 163, 146) on the other. In the words of Bhabha, Maitland is "caught in the ambivalence of paranoic identification, alternating between fantasies of megalomania and persecution", so that his identity "is predicated as much on mastery and pleasure as it is on anxiety and defence" (2006: 88, 107). Such 'contradictory belief', a continuous wavering between narcissism and aggressivity, is a clear case of colonial ambivalence.

Finally, another interesting moment of resistance[32] to Maitland's domination occurs in the process of Proctor's schooling. Still looking for a way to leave the island (while subconsciously obviously wanting to stay), Maitland pretends to be teaching Proctor how to write his own name, but really makes him write Maitland's name and the word 'help'. Symbolically, this scene spells out the 'epistemic violence' (Spivak 2003) involved in colonial 'education', the close connection, in the colonization process, between language, culture and knowledge on the one hand and power on the other, as well as what many have seen as the dilemma faced by the subaltern subject of desiring to create an oppositional discourse and to articulate a self-determined sense of identity and nevertheless having to speak from a position in which the very medium of this subject's discourse is a sign of its oppression. In Ballard's novel, however, Proctor – albeit unconsciously – undermines Maitland's authority. Not only does he, in another act of refusal, reject to write the swearwords Maitland teaches him (or pretends to teach him, since they are once again really different words), he also distorts

---

32 With regards to the question of resistance, Bhabha has repeatedly been criticized for neglecting the actual political contest involved in colonial antagonism, including forms of active anticolonial struggle, and for dissolving individual and collective agency by locating subversion solely in textual and psychoanalytic processes of ambivalence (e.g. Parry 2004: 55–74).

the words he does write, "garbling the letters together into an indecipherable mass" (*CI* 152). As when he wipes away the messages Maitland scrawls on the concrete or when he declines the pound note with the rescue message in the margin, Proctor here effectively disrupts the process of signification.

Interestingly, to Maitland, Proctor's jumbled letters appear to be "cryptic anagrams" (*CI* 156). If we take into account Julia Kristeva's thought on language and the anagram, this seems appropriate; drawing on Ferdinand de Saussure's groundbreaking work, Kristeva argues that the anagram, or 'paragram', as she calls it, "extends from *zero* to *two:* the unit 'one' (definition, 'truth') does not exist in this field. Consequently, the notions of definition, determination, the sign '=' and the very concept of sign, which presupposes a vertical (hierarchical) division between signifier and signified, cannot be applied" (1986: 40). According to Kristeva, ana-/paragrams like Proctor's, by "break[ing] up the linearity of the signifying chain" (1984: 152) that constitutes the 'symbolic', point beyond language as a conveyor of messages to the underlying 'geno-text' of the 'semiotic', that is, to the material base of language, its sounds, rhythms, etc.[33] In light of Kristeva's theory, it is telling that it is Maitland's name that Proctor anagrammatizes: Kristeva posits an immediate connection between signifiance and subjectivity and contends that fixed meaning and the unitary and stable 'thetic' subject must both be considered as temporary fixings of an essentially endless process.[34] Accordingly, a distortion of the structure of signification such as the anagram, understood as "a resumption of the functioning characteristic of the semiotic *chora* within the signifying device of language" (Kristeva 1984: 50), necessarily entails a destabilization of the thetic subject – "the multiplying fragments of [Maitland's] name" (*CI* 162).

Beyond that, the identification of Proctor's garbled writing as 'anagrams' is notable for another reason: strictly speaking, these words *are not* anagrams. We speak of an 'anagram' when the letters of the original word or phrase are rearranged in such a way as to produce a new meaning. However, for all we know, the illiterate Proctor just haphazardly jumbles the letters up, apparently without any conscious meaning-creating agenda. Yet, the term 'anagram' clearly indicates that some new meaning has in fact been produced. Is this, then, a kind of meaning that is radically other? Do these words, while remaining indecipherable and enigmatic to Maitland, actually signify for Proctor? It would certainly seem so, for whereas Maitland feels "taunt[ed] and confuse[d]" by Proctor's writing, to the tramp, it holds his "serene message to himself" (*CI* 162, 156). Perhaps,

---

[33] For a different reading of Saussure's work on anagrams, cf. Baudrillard 1993b: 195–213.
[34] Kristeva therefore speaks of the 'signifying process' and the 'subject-in-process'.

we may therefore read his disordered letters not just as a manifestation of the Kristevan semiotic within the symbolic, but as a veritable counter-discourse (Kristeva's 'unit' two) challenging the law enshrined in Maitland's master-discourse (unit one). Proctor ignores all linguistic rules of grammar and orthography and starts every word "in its centre, moving outwards to left and right" (*CI* 152); instead of proceeding in a grammatical, 'linear' fashion, connecting the required clause elements according to the obligatory sentence patterns, thus generating meaning, he uses language in a radically different, non-normative way and disperses or 'disseminates' (Derrida 1988) meaning. Here, nurture does indeed not stick. Not unlike Shakespeare's Caliban, who turns the colonizers' language into a medium of native articulation through his resistant use of curses, Proctor abrogates Maitland's prerogative to determine the usage of language, his categories and meanings and appropriates his language – albeit in a radical way, which undermines its very structure – to create alternative (non-)meanings.[35] Similar to Caliban's poetic "The isle is full of noises"-speech, Proctor's linguistic fragments, which soon cover large parts of the island, are a counter-representation of the island, challenging Maitland's "I am the island" (*CI* 71), that is, the image he creates of it in language as well as his claim for possession of it. And in view of the rhizomatic, amorphous, a-signifying character of the island space, Proctor's (non-)representation – as Caliban's in comparison with the numerous other ones in Shakespeare's play – is arguably the more adequate one. His writing would then indeed perform, as the title of the respective chapter suggests, 'the naming of the island'. This struggle over/in language and representation and the general ambivalence that marks the balance of power in the relationship between Maitland and Proctor last until the end of the text. For although Proctor eventually gets killed and Maitland remains alone on the island, the latter is now "surrounded [...] everywhere" (*CI* 156) by Proctor's inscrutable signs, which even follow him into his very home, where "[f]ragments of the tramp's finger-writing cove[r] several of the door-panels" (*CI* 162) that make up his shelter. In this way, Maitland effectively remains trapped in Proctor's system of signs.

As has been shown, Ballard's *Concrete Island* portrays the eponymous traffic island as an emancipatory heterotopic counter-site to the space(s) of late capitalism. It is a space in which numerous deterritorializations take place, in which lines of flight are drawn that liberate the protagonist from the grip of power exercised by the system. Yet, Maitland's deterritorializations are partly overlaid by compensatory reterritorializations that block and divert his lines of flight. Be-

---

[35] On abrogation and appropriation, cf. Ashcroft, Griffiths and Tiffin 2005: 37f.

cause of this, not only does the collective dimension of emancipation that Deleuze and Guattari emphasize fail to materialize on the island, but more than that, the lines of flight, "due to their eventual divergence, reproduce the very formations their function it was to dismantle or outflank" (Deleuze and Guattari 1987: 13). As hegemonic discourses and ideologies reassert themselves, Maitland himself to some extent turns into an agent of power, trying to (re-)establish social hierarchies and inequalities. On another level, it is now Proctor who plots lines of flight, to a certain degree resisting Maitland's new order.

Thus, de- and reterritorialization coexist and alternate throughout the text, so that Maitland's existence on the island as well as the novel as a whole remain essentially, and unresolvably, ambivalent.[36] Referring back to the quotation from Deleuze and Guattari that forms the epigraph of this chapter, we might say that there is indeed a lot of grass on Maitland's island, but that this grass is simultaneously in constant danger of being paved over again.

---

[36] Colombino (2006: 620) likewise emphasizes that the reading of the novel must necessarily be open-ended.

4 Escaping the Subject: The Ballardian Theme of Abdication

> The liberating practices respond to the constant ultimatum to make of ourselves pure objects, but they don't respond at all to the other demand, which is to constitute ourselves as subjects, to liberate ourselves, to express ourselves at any price, to vote, produce, decide, speak, participate, play the game – a form of blackmail and ultimatum just as serious as the other, probably even more serious today.
> Jean Baudrillard

Andrzej Gasiorek has argued that two predominant responses to late capitalism and its pervasive circuits of power can be discerned in Ballard's writing:

> On the one hand a powerful redemptive strain of almost mystical proportions characterises some of his work, envisaging the transfiguration of both the world and the humans who desecrate it. On the other hand, a strong urge to escape from and even to destroy a world seen as irredeemable is also manifested in his writing (2005: 204).

While it is true that both, the theme of metamorphosis and that of escape, are unmistakably present in much of Ballard's fiction, it nevertheless seems hasty to me to derive two clearly separate trends from this and to allocate different texts to each of them. For very often, in texts like *The Crystal World*, "The Enormous Space", "The Overloaded Man", or "News from the Sun", both themes appear together and are in fact closely connected. When, for example, in *The Crystal World*, the protagonist Dr. Sanders comments on the crystallizing forest and states that "[t]here the transfiguration of all living and inanimate forms occurs before our eyes, the gift of immortality a direct consequence of the surrender by each of us of our own physical and temporal identities" (*CW* 169), it is not only a transformation and re-enchantment of the world that is at stake, but at the same time an acute desire to escape, which can be fulfilled in the forest. Thus, instead of assuming two more or less distinct imaginative tendencies at work in Ballard's texts, of which – as Gasiorek suggests – one is to be read as 'redemptive' and the other as "pessimistic" (2005: 205), I want to argue that both themes are derived from and expressions of a more profound impulse that traverses much of Ballard's work: that towards abdication. Any notion of a death-wish, of transfiguration, regression, solipsism, etc. that his fiction might be construed as representing is frequently only secondary to this radical longing for a release from the confines of identity, a release exemplarily articulated by Dr. Sanders in the passage quoted above.

The term 'abdication' is adopted here from David Punter. In his instructive discussion of Ballard's novels, he describes Robert Maitland, the protagonist of *Concrete Island*, as an "advance guard of passivity", who "experiences no real opposition, only a continuous adjustment and scaling down of his needs", so that the traffic island on which he is stranded comes to symbolize "a renunciation of the impulse towards the ideal society, and replaces it with a wish for abdication" (1985: 16, 17). Surprisingly, subsequent scholars have not commented on these remarks or picked up on the topic of abdication. Yet, it seems central to many of Ballard's works, especially his disaster tales. The desire for abdication, that is, for liberation from socially produced and accepted forms of subjectivity and identity, appears to be born from a realization of the problematic status of the 'subject' under late capitalism. Like many (post-)structuralist and postmodernist thinkers, Ballard seems to have come to the conclusion that the autonomous and unified subject of the liberal-humanist tradition, conceived as possessing an originary, coherent and stable identity, is nothing but a fiction – albeit one that is indispensable for the smooth functioning of the system. As Jacques Lacan, Louis Althusser, Jacques Derrida, Michel Foucault and others have shown, the individual's identity is always 'imaginary', 'deferred', displaced, and, above all, constructed in and through a vast anonymous network of power relations and discourses. As particularly Foucault has repeatedly emphasized, power has to be understood not just, or even primarily, as prohibitive and repressive, but as productive – productive, above all, of subjectivity. The term 'subjectification' or 'subjectivation' designates this simultaneity and inseparability of the processes of becoming-subject and becoming subjugated:

> Subjection is, literally, the *making* of a subject, the principle of regulation according to which a subject is formulated or produced. Such subjection is a kind of power that not only unilaterally *acts on* a given individual as a form of domination, but also *activates* or forms the subject. Hence, subjection is neither simply the domination of a subject nor its production, but designates a certain kind of restriction *in* production, a restriction without which the production of the subject cannot take place, a restriction through which that production takes place. (Butler 1997: 84)

If the status of the sovereign subject has always been precarious, late capitalism dissolves this subject entirely. It is in this context that theorists of postmodernity like Fredric Jameson have spoken of the "*decentering*" or even of the "'death' of the subject [...] – the end of the autonomous bourgeois monad or ego or individual" (Jameson 1991: 15). To postmodern thinkers and authors like Ballard, the site of the speaking and acting subject is now more than ever always already colonized and scripted, the individual a mere node in the web of power, its subjectivity traversed by numerous discourses and forces which continually code and recode it. At the same time, of course, the existence of the originary, unified and self-directed subject is being continuously reaffirmed in public discourse; as Judith Butler has persistently shown, this view remains a potent ideological fantasy allowing power to hide its own effects, "preclud[ing] an analysis of the political constitution of the [...] subject and its fabricated notions about the ineffable interiority [...] of its true identity" (1999: 174). It thus obscures the fact that actually, as Butler succinctly puts it, "the subject as a self-identical entity is no more" (1993: 230). Once this is accepted, all conventional calls for a 'liberation' of the subject are revealed to be futile: if, in the prominent words of Foucault, the subject "described for us, whom we are invited to free, is already in himself [sic] the effect of a subjection much more profound than himself [sic]" (1979: 30), then the idea of a possible freedom from domination in an 'outside' of power must necessarily be an illusion. It is against this background that the theme of abdication in Ballard's texts has to be read.

A parallel could be drawn here to the work of George Orwell, particularly to his novel *1984*, about which more recent re-readings have suggested that it is expressive of a profound disillusionment with the humanist belief in individual freedom, conscience and responsibility (e.g. Sandison 1986; Pordzik 2006, 2009). Thus, Ralph Pordzik contends that Winston Smith, the novel's protagonist, rather than representing the last heroic defender of individualism against the terrors of totalitarian rule, actually

> seeks to escape the realm of communal and ethical responsibility in order to hand himself over to some kind of authoritative faith denouncing the individual's presence [...] – in this almost complete self-effacement of the individual [...] lies the true, if only implicitly argued, utopian dimension of *Nineteen Eighty-Four.*" (2009: 112)

It could be argued that Ballard's works in a similar vein render "the dystopian as utopian" by turning "political disenfranchisement into cultural empowerment" (Pordzik 2009: 123). The longing for abdication felt by Ballard's protagonists might then be considered as symptomatic of a general disenchantment with the humanist subject and its agency and of a pervasive loss of hope concerning the possibility of resistant, politically effective action, resulting in utter resignation and a concomitant desire to see the subject liberated from the 'burden' of personal judgment, responsibility and sense-making. David Punter's discussion of *Concrete Island* follows such a track: according to Punter, Maitland's actions are ultimately signs "not of opposition and escape but of capitulation" (1985: 17).

The novel as a whole presents itself to him as "the fiction of a (British) society which has already, through the abortive 'special relationship', abandoned its right to protest, and whose only role now can be as the less than conscious harbinger of the terminal tedium of the over-consuming West" (1985: 19).

This is a perceptive and convincing analysis. Yet, it seems to me that Ballard's fiction of abdication is, on the whole, more ambivalent and thus allows for alternative readings. While Punter is right to see in a figure like *Concrete Island*'s Robert Maitland an agent of passivity, it seems to me that this passivity does not automatically denote acceptance and surrender. What Punter fails to realize is that the protagonist's "free[dom] [...] from any location in discourse" (Punter 1985: 17) is not something to be lamented, but *precisely what he aspires to* – a sign of the radicality of his wish for abdication. Thus, I want to argue that where Punter sees only hopeless acquiescence and defeat, subjects "realis[ing] their places on the web, retreat[ing] into the spaces left for them in the all-powerful lines of communication" (1985: 16), Ballard actually stages another catastrophic strategy, another form of defiance of the system's controlling grasp. In accordance with this defiance, abdication has to be re-conceptualized along much more radical lines.

4.1 Siding with the Object

If the Western concept of the autonomous individual first began to take shape in the early modern period (aided, among other things, by Renaissance humanist thought, the Reformation, and the philosophy of René Descartes), it was not until the 18th century and the concomitant rise of capitalism and the bourgeoisie as well as Kantian transcendental philosophy that individualism truly came into its own. From the first, this conception was linked to bondage. According to Michel Foucault, the individual emerging in the 'classical' age is purely a product of what he calls 'disciplinary power' – it is always already a "disciplinary individual" (1979: 227). Similarly, Jean Baudrillard points out that "only over the last two centuries [...] did we find ourselves forcibly inducted into this individual existence" (2005: 55f). Foucault, more than anyone else, dedicated himself to the struggle against this form of subjectivation. Thus, he passionately proclaims that

> the target nowadays is not to discover what we are, but to refuse what we are. We have to imagine and to build up what we could be [...] to liberate us both from the state and from the type of individualization which is linked to the state. We have to promote new forms of subjectivity through the refusal of this kind of individuality which has been imposed on us for several centuries. (1982: 216)

Especially in his late work, Foucault (1985, 1986b) analyzed how new types of subjectivity and identity could be fashioned through an active 'aesthetics of the self' based on ancient 'technologies of the self'.

Postmodern thinkers, too, have repeatedly stressed the need for the construction of alternative and resistant identities. With their emphasis on the fundamental lack of essences and the open-ended freeplay of the signifier, they have, in fact, frequently been much more optimistic and assertive than Foucault, confidently celebrating fragmentation, heterogeneity and plurality, and seeing identity as "a freely chosen game, a theatrical presentation of the self" (Kellner 1995: 246). Here, identity is regarded as multiple and always in flux, a performance in which one's self can be perpetually changed at will through the self-conscious play with signs and which, consequently, holds an immense emancipatory potential.

Others, however, have been less sanguine. Brian Massumi, for instance, has called attention to the fact that "[t]he expansion of potential in 'postmodernity' goes hand in hand with the real subsumption by capital not only of society, but of all of existence" (1992: 136). According to Massumi, the postmodern constitution of the self cannot be considered "in any way revolutionary. If it is a becoming, it is fundamentally a becoming-consumer." (1992: 136) Indeed, the postmodern notion of a continuous shifting between various identities can, in the final analysis, be considered as not *subversive of* but rather perfectly *suited to* the dynamics of late-capitalist commodity flows. Not only can every oppositional practice and identity today be easily commodified and thus incorporated into the all-embracing market, the market itself even *depends* upon such permanent production of difference and deviance. As Michael Hardt and Antonio Negri (2001: 137–159), who see in postmodernist and postcolonialist thought mere symptoms of the epochal passage from modern to postmodern sovereignty, point out, "[d]espite the best intentions, [...] the postmodernist politics of difference not only is ineffective against but can even coincide with and support the functions and practices of imperial rule" (2001: 142).[1]

Baudrillard, too, has argued that forms of resistance based on the logic of identity, even if this means the construction of ever new identities for a 'protean self' (Lifton 1999), present no serious challenge to power: "Multiplying identities never produces anything more than all the illusory strategies for decentralizing power: it is pure illusion, pure stratagem." (2005: 59) The French philosopher diagnoses an "identity syndrome" (1994f: 109) from which Western societies suffer: "It is as though liberty and individuality [...] had become [...] a kind of moral im-

---

[1] On Hardt and Negri's notion of 'Empire', cf. chapter 5.

perative, whose implacable decree makes us hostages to our identities and our own wills." (Baudrillard 2005: 56) How, then, can the system and what we might call its 'identitary imperative' be resisted? Only by refusing the very status of 'subject':

> The resistance-as-subject is today unilaterally valorized and held as positive – just as in the political sphere only the practices of liberation, emancipation, expression, and constitution as a political subject are taken to be valuable and subversive. But this is to ignore the equal or perhaps even superior impact, [sic] of all the practices-as-object – the renunciation of the position of subject and of meaning [...] which we bury and forget under the contemptuous terms of alienation and passivity. (Baudrillard 2007b: 107)

According to Baudrillard, every opposition that relies on the categories of the 'subject' and of 'identity' must necessarily fail because it still abides by modalities dictated by the system, based as it is on meaning and difference. Instead, "[w]e must live without reference to a model of identity or a general equivalent." (Baudrillard 2005: 58) Baudrillard's advice to us is to follow the example of the 'silent majorities' and to opt for a practice of "non-participation" (2007b: 66), whose extreme form is the hyperconformity of the masses. We must "side with the object" and thus offer a "challenge to all that was asked of the subject by philosophy and morals, that is, a challenge to any exercise of will, knowledge, or liberty" (Baudrillard 2008: 229, 125f). By thus replacing revolution with "*devolution*", with "*de-volition* and withdrawal of the will" (Baudrillard 2008: 126), we pass beyond the field of the political, which is always defined by power, to Baudrillard's 'trans-political'. This quasi-Bartlebian strategy, adopted by Ballard's protagonists, refuting as it does the ideas of liberation and emancipation (and, indeed, that of a 'strategy' itself), must not be read as a sign of alienation, submission or defeat, but as part of an anti-metaphysical or pataphysical "philosophy of the involuntary, of the 'un-will'" (Baudrillard 2008: 126).[2]

---

[2] Alluding to Herman Melville's story "Bartleby, the Scrivener", Baudrillard explains that such behavior, not to be confused with passive resistance, "is not exactly a choice, nor is it a rejection: there is no longer sufficient energy for that. It is a behaviour based on an uncertain negative preference." (2005: 90) The reference to Melville's text is significant; after all, it is, as the subtitle has it, 'a story of Wall Street'. It would be interesting to investigate whether the desire for abdication actually emerged with the rise of industrial capitalism and is now slowly becoming something like a late 20th- and early 21st-century literary motif, repeatedly employed by writers in the face of apparently unassailable systems (be they economic, political, cultural, or something else). In this context, it might prove instructive to analyze works such as J.M. Coetzee's *Life & Times of Michael K*, Tim Crouch's *My Arm*, or John Burnside's *The Devil's Footprints*, even though the contexts and functions of abdication in texts like these are, of course, radically different.

For Baudrillard, then, just as for Foucault, frontal resistance and movements aimed at a deliverance of the subject from repression will always be futile, because "greater autonomy" only means "a more complete introjection of all forms of control and constraint under the banner of freedom" (Baudrillard 1993c: 191). Equally, however, Baudrillard holds no hope for the emancipatory possibilities of a modern 'care of the self' (Foucault) or of 'nomadic', plural identities (Deleuze and Guattari), since he sees such postmodern subjectivities as increasingly "becoming isomorphic to capital" (Massumi 1992: 135).[3] The only way out therefore seems to be *to cease occupying the position of the subject* and "to slough off identity in every possible way" (Baudrillard 2005: 56). In this manner, we arrive at "[a] minimal definition of freedom [...], and one which more resembles a relinquishment" (Baudrillard 2005: 90). As will now be shown, it is precisely such a posthumanist logic of abdication that many of Ballard's works subscribe to. In the following, I will first illustrate the relevance of this logic for Ballard's oeuvre through an overview-like discussion of various texts and then embark upon an in-depth analysis of the representative short story "News from the Sun".

4.2 Inverted Crusoes

Much of Ballard's work, particularly that of the 60s and 70s, belongs to the genre of science fiction. As Ballard has repeatedly declared, science fiction represented for him "the most important fiction that has been written for the last hundred years" and "the true literature of the twentieth century" (1996d: 205, 1996f: 14). More than any other genre – certainly the much despised English social or 'bourgeois' novel (cf. esp. Ballard 1996d, 1996i) – he saw its chief concerns as the contemporary, everyday life under global consumer capitalism, change in all its dimensions, as well as science, technology and the media (all this linking it with Pop Art; cf. 1996d: 207). At the same time, it was equipped with a "hot line to the unconscious" (Ballard 1996b: 193) (this being its connection to Surrealism;

---

3 As was already noted in chapter 2, Baudrillard has repeatedly polemicized against the thought of Deleuze and Guattari – according to him, a "molecular hodge-podge of desire-breaching minorities" (2007b: 66) – arguing that what he sees as a "compulsion toward liquidity, flow, and an accelerated circulation of what is psychic, sexual, or pertaining to the body is the exact replica of the force which rules market value: capital must circulate; gravity and any fixed point must disappear; the chain of investments and reinvestments must never stop; value must radiate endlessly and in every direction" (2007a: 39f).

cf. Ballard 1996s: 200).[4] Of course, Ballard's variant of science fiction – which became influential in the context of what is now known as the British 'New Wave' – differs markedly from its more traditional manifestations: in keeping with his belief that "[t]he only truly alien planet is Earth" (1996t: 197), Ballard's 'speculative fiction' rejects the conventional futuristic space stories in favor of a concern with the terrestrial present or the immediate future grown out of it and with what Ballard termed 'inner space'. In addition to this substitution of inner for outer space, Ballard also moved away from what he saw as the often overly optimistic outlook of the genre and replaced its faith in progress and technological achievement with representations of entropic and exhausted worlds and visions of "a failed future, now consigned to history" (Gasiorek 2005: 7). Finally, his science fiction became – as he claimed the whole genre should – "abstract and 'cool'" (1996t: 198), marked by a much higher degree of experimentalism in terms of theme, narrative, character and imagery than was usually the case.

All of this also applies to Ballard's first novel *The Drowned World*.[5] The desire for abdication that characterizes many of his texts is already evident in this early work. At first sight, this text, set in a post-apocalyptic future, in which solar radiation has caused the climate, flora and fauna of Europe to become tropical and the polar icecaps to melt and inundate the continent, seems unconcerned with late capitalism and the contemporary structures of power. However, a closer look reveals that this is not the case. It is through the characters of the military officer Riggs and the pirate Strangman that these thematic dimensions are implied. Focalized through the perspective of the biologist Robert Kerans, the protagonist of the book, the narrative describes Colonel Riggs as "obeying reason and logic, buzzing around his diminished, unimportant world with his little parcels of instructions like a worker bee about to return to the home nest" (*DW* 75). In spite of the enormous transformations taking place around him, Riggs, who is also compared to "a district commissioner", exhibiting "[a]ll that stiff upper lip stuff and dressing for dinner in the jungle" (*DW* 160f, 80), tries to uphold a rigorous ethic of work and discipline and a conception of the subject as a self-determined and responsible individual – tenets upon which capitalism is effectively built. This is already enshrined in his name, which, like that of his colleague Macready or of humanity's last resort Camp Byrd – a reference to the American explorer Richard E. Byrd – suggests a pragmatic and rational military individu-

---

[4] Both Pop Art and Surrealism were important influences on Ballard's work. Cf. e.g. Gasiorek 2005: 8–16 and Baxter 2009.
[5] As a matter of fact, Ballard's first novel was *The Wind from Nowhere*, yet he later distanced himself from this text and it is now not even mentioned in the publisher Harper Perennial's listings of his works.

alism. Similarly, the mobile scientific testing station, whose purpose it is to chart and describe the changing ecosystem and to "polic[e] the movements of individuals" (Gasiorek 2005: 34), also represents order and control.

Even though the ruthless criminal Strangman appears as Riggs' antagonist, Gasiorek rightly points out that both "are bound by the same law, the same system" and "merely represent its opposed poles" (2005: 39). This system is Western capitalism. The pirate and scavenger on the one hand and the soldier, worker bee and district commissioner on the other are only two sides of the same capitalist coin. Thus, Strangman's pillaging and violence constitute nothing but the dark underside to Riggs and the United Nations' order, salvaging of goods and reclaiming of land. Consequently, Riggs, despite his general dislike of Strangman, praises the latter's pumping out the lagoon as an act of urban reclamation, for which he "deserves a medal" (*DW* 157). Similarly, while looting is officially "highly penalised, [...] in fact the authorities [are] only too eager to pay a generous price for any salvage" (*DW* 89) (thus even perpetuating the reign of exchange value and keeping a basic money flow intact). In light of these parallels, it is certainly no coincidence that when Kerans first sees Strangman's craft, he is immediately reminded of Colonel Riggs' cutter (*DW* 86).

Like most of Ballard's catastrophe stories, *The Drowned World* is a fantasy of abdication, in which the transformations that are taking place entail the falling apart of systems of power and control and the emergence of new modes of life.[6] These modes differ from text to text. In *The Drowned World*, abdication is coupled with a discourse of regression, which finds expression in the idea of a reversed evolution as well as in the implied death-wish of the protagonist. In the aptly titled chapter "The Pool of Thanatos", Kerans nearly drowns himself during a dive. The tempting pull of the ocean that the scientist feels is consistently rendered in imagery that strongly suggests a return to uterine *jouissance* (*DW* 104–110). Drifting through the water in an almost unconscious state, Kerans is "only aware of the faint glimmer of identity within the deepest recesses of his mind", a glimmer that is rapidly "receding" (*DW* 110). Finally, before he is rescued, he floats "from one pool to another, in the limbos of eternity, a thousand

---

[6] Thus, in light of the thematic concern of this study, Ballard's idiosyncratic transformation of the catastrophe genre takes on new, political significance. The fact that the texts (narrative voice, imagery, etc.), just like their protagonists, celebrate the destruction can be read as a manifestation of what Baudrillard has identified as an "ever increasing fascination with the catastrophe", which, he argues, must be understood as an expression of a growing desire to see the system in ruins, of the fact that an ever more totalitarian "reason itself is pursued by the hope of a universal revolt against its own norms and privileges" (1993b: 162).

images of himself reflected in the inverted mirrors of the surface" (*DW* 110). What is at stake here, as in the novel as a whole, is not, as Gasiorek maintains, a Jungian 'individuation', that is, "a process of self-discovery and self-realisation" (2005: 55), but a dissolution of the self, not a remaking of identity (Gasiorek 2005: 34, 208), but an escape from the very logic of identity.[7] With reference to the Lacanian concept of the 'mirror-stage' (Lacan 2004), the splintering of Kerans' unified image into a thousand broken and shifting reflections can be taken to signify this disintegration of identity. Unlike Strangman and Riggs, who remain subjectivated and tied to the imperatives of the system whose representatives they are, Kerans adapts to the changed circumstances and "enter[s] a new zone, where the usual obligations and allegiances ceas[e] to operate" and "where old categories of thought [are] merely [...] an encumbrance" (*DW* 81, 14). On a symbolic level, it is thus only appropriate that Kerans first sinks the testing station, later re-floods the lagoon, and finally sets off on a journey into the jungles of the South, in the exact opposite direction of his birthplace Camp Byrd in Northern Greenland. These acts all clearly mark his growing defiance of the system and his increasing casting off of "the straitjacket of our individual being" (Baudrillard 2005: 211).

Re-read in this light, the last page of the book presents us with a momentous scene: "At last he tied the crutch to his leg again, and with the butt of the empty .45 scratched on the wall below the window, sure that no-one would ever read the message: *27th day. Have rested and am moving south. All is well. Kerans.*" (*DW* 175) Considering all that has gone before, the reader might pause in bewilderment with regards to this passage, which one may be tempted to read as representing a reassertion of the sovereignty of the "self-authoring subject" (Colebrook 2005: 236), once again affirming its presence through its voice. Yet, what initially seems to be incongruous with Kerans' movement towards abdication on closer inspection turns out to be an ironic deconstruction of the bourgeois subject, very much in line with the general impetus of the text I have discussed. Here, the position of the subject is subverted, so to speak, 'from within': Kerans does not write with chalk or a pen, but with the butt of a gun, which points to the violence inherent in the process of subjectivation, that is, to the fact that "violence is embedded within the constitution of the subject from the start" (Mills 2007: 148), since, as Kristeva (1982), Butler (1993, 1999) and others have shown, the condition of its 'intelligibility' is a violent process of normalization and 'abjection'. The fact that the

---

[7] In his essay "Time, Memory and Inner Space", Ballard states that the uterine sea in his novel "is as much the graveyard of their [i.e. the principal characters'] own individuality as it is the source of their lives" (1996s: 199).

gun is empty, of course, makes clear how untenable the status as subject, at least for Kerans, has become. Just as 'empty' is the gesture of the writing itself, since Kerans' words fail to actually form a 'message', as no one will ever read them. Without an addressee, there can be no communication, without the validating presence of an other, meaning evaporates. This ironic corrosion of the site of the speaking subject is topped off with the final statement 'All is well'. With his last words, Kerans quotes, of all people, Immanuel Kant, in whose subject-centered epistemology Foucault (2002) saw the true beginning of the modern philosophy of the subject – and not just any, but his *dying words* (cf. Geier 2004: 9). If, in addition, we take into account the metaphoric significance of the crutch and of the ending of the novel, which has Kerans entering the jungle again and, before long, becoming utterly lost, then this entire scene must certainly be read as a swansong of the subject. At the very end of his first novel, Ballard thus momentarily re-invokes the liberal-humanist subject with all its autonomy and willpower – the position that his protagonist has so persistently sought to relinquish – only to effect more fully its complete erasure.

A similar wish for abdication underlies the plot of Ballard's next novel, *The Drought*, which, as Gasiorek aptly puts it, depicts "a process of wearing away" (2005: 46) to which the main characters willingly submit. The post-apocalyptic desert landscape in which the story is set signals the formation of a posthumanist order (Gasiorek 2005: 42), in which people abdicate their will and responsibilities and thus defy a form of power which "categorizes the individual, marks him [sic] by his own individuality, attaches him to his own identity, imposes a law of truth on him which he must recognize and which others have to recognize in him" (Foucault 1982: 212). With the transformation of their environment, the characters continuously feel that "everything is being drained away", "the endless stretches of wet salt [during their stay on the beach, from which the water is increasingly receding] sucking away from them all but the hardest core of themselves" (*D* 16, 146). These "tiny nodes of identity" (*D* 146) must not, however, be mistaken for the individual's originary, natural and essential self, but should rather be understood in terms of the Foucauldian 'soul', that is, as an incorporated "normative and normalizing ideal" (Butler 1997: 90), "the effect and instrument of a political anatomy" (Foucault 1979: 30). Eventually, even these tiny nodes will be dispersed in "the zone of nothingness that wait[s] for them to dissolve and deliquesce like the crystals dried by the sun" (*D* 146). Towards the end of the novel, the protagonist Dr. Ransom comes to feel that even "[t]he succession of humps" formed by cars submerged in the sand, "the barest residue of identity, interrup[t] the smooth flow of the dunes" (*D* 188). Inner space metaphors like these abound in the text: there is a recurrent imagery of 'smoothing out' and 'wearing away' that is used to express the increasing dissolution of identity. One of the finest metaphors for this is given at the very end of the text when Ransom notices "that he no longer cast[s] any shadow" (*D* 233).

Presiding over the trajectory of the protagonist as a kind of guiding metaphor stands the painting *Jours de Lenteur* by the Surrealist artist Yves Tanguy. The work is first introduced at the beginning of the novel as one of two photographs on Ransom's desk, the other one being a snapshot of himself at the age of four together with his parents (*D* 11). If the latter hints at the process of identity-formation through the 'ideological state apparatus' (Althusser 1971) or 'disciplinary' space (Foucault 1979: 215f) of the nuclear family as a major agent of subjectivation, the other, "[w]ith its smooth, pebble-like objects, drained of all associations, suspended on a washed tidal floor" (*D* 11), signifies both Ransom's and the novel's dream of abdication. It is thus only fitting that the last chapter, which has Ransom, in Baudrillardian terminology, fully passing on the side of the object, is named after Tanguy's work. As Ransom himself realizes, "this painting ha[s] helped to free him" (*D* 11).

Critics have called attention to the fact that *The Drought* is also a complex reworking of Shakespeare's *The Tempest*, and Gasiorek (2005: 46) has argued that the intertextual connections between the two works are most salient in the context of the novel's critique of domination. In connection with the Ballardian theme of abdication, such critique has, however, been most forcefully articulated through the repeated rewriting of another text from the English canon. It is, arguably, one of the literary master texts of Western capitalism and imperialism, Enlightenment thought, and bourgeois individualism: Daniel Defoe's *Robinson Crusoe*. Thus, the narrator of *The Drowned World*, for instance, speaks of an "inverted Crusoeism" (*DW* 48) with regards to Kerans, and the protagonist of the short story "Deep End" is said to be "a Robinson Crusoe in reverse" (*CS1* 321). By having his protagonists refute precisely those modes of perceiving, thinking, valuing and behaving embodied by Defoe's eponymous hero, Ballard effectively undermines the discourses and the entire ideology from which these modes are derived.

Another such inversion of the 'Crusoe myth' (Watt 1996) can be found in the short story "The Enormous Space". Ballantyne, the narrator and protagonist of the text, decides to cut himself off from the world by never leaving his house again: "In every way I am marooned, but a reductive Crusoe paring away exactly those elements of bourgeois life which the original Robinson so dutifully reconstituted. Crusoe wished to bring the Croydons of his own day to life again on his island. I want to expel them" (*CS2* 700). Here, with expressions like 'reductive' and 'paring away', we are once again confronted with the same semantic fields we encountered in *The Drought*. As the story progresses, Ballantyne increasingly discards his old habits and sense of self, moving towards "a vivid tabula rasa", in which "[n]othing matters any more" (*CS2* 701, 699). Unlike Crusoe, who is driven by the desire to increase his wealth as well as his power and who is obsessively concerned with warding off the threat of otherness and with stabilizing his fragile sense of self, Ballard's protagonist welcomes his new-found freedom from the confines of identity:

> Without doubt, I am very much better. [...] Above all, I am no longer dependent on myself. I feel no obligation to that person who fed and groomed me, who provided me with expensive clothes, who drove me about in his motor-car, who furnished my mind with intelligent books and exposed me to interesting films and art exhibitions. Wanting none of these, I owe that person, myself, no debts. I am free at last to think only of the essential elements of existence – the visual continuum around me, and the play of air and light. (*CS2* 701)

When Ballantyne burns his "passport; birth, degree and share certificates" (*CS2* 700), he symbolically erases not only the insignia of a successful bourgeois existence, but also, on a more abstract level, all the ideological essentials – embodied by Defoe's hero – the system is built on. In this context, it is, of course, hardly a coincidence that Ballard's protagonist is named Ballantyne. In his numerous adventure novels such as *The Coral Island* (rewritten by William Golding in *Lord of the Flies*), the 19th-century Scottish writer R.M. Ballantyne advocated a kind of entrepreneurial individualism that can be compared to the one found in *Robinson Crusoe*. The name is thus another ironic reversal through which Ballard deconstructs the ideological script of the pre-text and overwrites it with his counter-discourse of abdication. From the first, Ballantyne himself is aware of the disruptive potential of his action, stating that "it runs counter to every social value" and "subvert[s]" (*CS2* 697, 702) conventional behavior.

At the same time, his new state of indolence and passive drifting enables him to experience an alternate reality and to move into "a far richer realm formed from the elements of light, time and space" (*CS2* 700). Liberated from "the submission of subjectivity" (Foucault 1982: 213), Ballantyne's senses are now "tuned to all the wave-lengths of the invisible", his eyes "see[ing] everything as it is, uncluttered by the paraphernalia of conventional life" (*CS2* 704, 705). Consequently, reality presents itself to him as nothing but an "over-worked hologram", a "small illusory world" that prevents us from perceiving "another larger and more real one" (*CS2* 702, 706).

Nevertheless, the process of abdication presented in this story remains problematic. On the one hand, the end of the text suggests that all of what has happened might merely have been a figment of Ballantyne's solipsistic mind as it slowly descends into psychosis. On the other hand, the story makes clear that his abdication is only an imperfect one, that in the end, his freedom can only be sustained at the cost of murder and even anthropophagy. Thus, his seeming liberation from identity and subjecthood is ultimately predicated on a violent negation and introjection of the other. With this, we are reapproaching Robinson Crusoe.[8] Indeed, if, as Dean MacCannell avers, late capitalism must be understood as "an only partly sublimated form of cannibalism", a "*metaphoric* cannibalism" producing "social totalities by the [...] *incorporation* of otherness" (1992: 20, 66), then Ballantyne's anthropophagy represents merely a literalization of this tendency to consume alterity characteristic of the socio-economic formation as a whole. From this point of view, Ballard's protagonist ends up reproducing the very system he seeks to challenge.

Yet, in spite of this, the fantasy of abdication remains. As we have seen, it lies at the heart of various Ballard texts, only a few of which have been discussed here. In some of these, as in "The Enormous Space", it appears in connection with the theme of an entrance into new domains. It is to one of the stories in which this theme is fully realized that we will now turn.

4.3 Embrace the Fugues!

"News from the Sun" is a story still widely neglected by scholars, yet typical of Ballard's unique brand of science fiction. In this text, we once again encounter the characteristic Ballardian rewriting of the disaster tale. As in his early story "The Voices of Time", as well as in "Memories of the Space Age" and "Myths of the Near Future", with which "News" forms a kind of triptych, the cataclysm here is a disease: the "time-sickness", which was set off by man's (sic) "evolutionary crime" (*CS2* 540, 544) of transgressing his natural boundaries by traveling into outer space and which causes a continuously increasing number of people to uncontrollably slide into incrementally lengthening 'fugues' of unconsciousness. In the vein of his other catastrophe stories, and contrary to more conventional manifestations of the genre, the focus of "News" is not so much on the calamity itself – how it emerged, how it works, etc. – nor on the struggle against it, but on its psychological dimension. The story is another inner space fiction, in which external reality and the characters' inner mindscapes overlay each other and the derelict and depleted landscapes exteriorize the realm of their psyches. Most significantly, the protagonists of Ballard's story eventually embrace the transformations brought about by the disease in-

---

8 Ballantyne's eating of human flesh might be considered as another link to Defoe's hero: not only is cannibalism, as an alleged practice of the natives of the Caribbean, a recurring topic in the novel, Crusoe is also concerned with food conspicuously often and, in addition, obsessively afraid of being engulfed.

stead of fighting against them. Like Dr. Kerans in *The Drowned World*, they learn to accept and to adapt to the changes taking place and come to see them as merely a new step in evolution. Towards the end of the text, as their daily time of wakefulness approaches zero, Franklin and Ursula, two of the main characters, find a way to stay conscious during the fugues, which allows them to ensure their own subsistence (eat, wash, etc.). Finally, Franklin welcomes the onset of a new way of being, liberated from time: "Happy now to be free of time, he embraced the great fugue." (*CS2* 567)

A passive drifting through the days, in which there is just enough awareness to keep oneself from starving; a happy sort of vegetative state; a kind of blissful waking or lucid dream – what better image for the strange Ballardian topos of abdication? The desire for freedom from the identitary imperative that underlies the text is presented here in the terms of an evolutionary discourse, as "some great biological step forward" (*CS2* 552) that is taking place. Yet, I want to argue that, as in *The Drowned World*, what stands behind this discourse is a radical reaction against socially constructed forms of individual identity and against the capitalist system these forms underpin. Thus, I somewhat disagree with Brian Baker when he states that "[t]he Ballardian escape from contemporary conditions" in stories like "News from the Sun" "is less bound to an economic critique of the social [...] than a willed transformation out of consciousness, the conditions of subjectivity" (2008: 20). I believe, instead, that it is precisely *through* this transformation or escape that such a critique is formulated.

The object of this critique is inscribed in the text through the name of the main character: Franklin. At this point, we must take seriously the structuralist insight that meaning only ever derives from the differential relations between signs, as well as the related Derridean concepts of 'différance' and 'iterability' (Derrida 1984a, 1984b). If the author is 'dead' (Barthes 2007) and the text consequently opened up to an 'unlimited semiosis' (Eco 1979), an endless 'freeplay' of meaning (Derrida 2001b), then we are surely justified – in the characteristic deconstructive manner – in singling out the seemingly incidental detail of the protagonist's name in Ballard's story and considering it as a 'specter' or 'trace' that points us to non-present remainders. If repetition is always tied to alterity (Derrida 1984b: 315), then I believe we can make out (at least) one distinct web of discourses that this name refers us to, a web which thus, so to speak, forms the sub- or unconscious dimension of the text and allows us to unlock another meaning. What the sign 'Franklin' points to is, of course, the historical figure of Benjamin Franklin and the various discourses associated with that name. More than anything else, Franklin can be seen as an embodiment of Western Enlightenment thought and the 'spirit of capitalism' (Weber 1958), as well as their convergence. The works and biography of the American Founding Father are indicative of the rise of both individualism and capitalism during the 18th century. Thus, notions of self-reliance and -fulfillment, a profound humanistic belief in individual agency and perfectibility, progress and the power of reason, as well as eulogies on capitalist aspiration permeate his writings: passages like "*God helps them that help themselves*" or "*Sloth makes all things difficult, but industry all easy, [...] early to bed, and early to rise, makes a man healthy, wealthy, and wise*" (Franklin 2003c: 517, 518) abound. Franklin's works read like an inventory of Puritan virtues: there is an incessant praise of "industry, and frugality, and prudence" – what Richard Weiss has called "the great trinity of the Protestant ethic" (1988: 28) – and a concomitant persistent warning of the dangers inherent in "sloth, [...] idle employments, or amusements, that amount to nothing" (2003c: 522, 517), so that the Protestant ethic that is at work here – in almost fully secularized form – stands out quite clearly.[9] In the context of Ballard's "News from the Sun", one of Franklin's pronouncements is of particular importance, namely his famous declaration that "Time is Money" (2003a: 51). With regards to a story that ends with an abdicational escape from time, this assertion is obviously highly resonant. Baudrillard has pointed out that it was only with the dominance of bourgeois reason, capitalism and the science of political economy that "the infinite accumulation of time as value under the sign of general equivalence" (1993b: 147) began to take hold. The movement out of time of Ballard's characters is thus also a movement away from capitalism.

The connection to Benjamin Franklin and, through him, to capitalism and the liberal-humanist concept of the autonomous and unified self is established not only through the protagonist's name, but also through his diary: "Calming himself, he looked at the last pages of his diary. June 19 – fugues: 8–30 to 9–11 am; 11–45 to 12–27 am; 5–15 to 6–08 pm; 11–30 to 12–14 pm. Total: 3 hours. The totals were gaining on him. June 20–3 hours 14 mins; June 21–3 hours 30 mins; June 22–3 hours 46 mins." (*CS2* 542f) Ballard's and the historical Franklin, in whose autobiography "daily Examination" and a "Scheme of Employment for the Twenty-four Hours of a natural Day" (2003b: 594, 595) play an important role, at first share a propensity for timekeeping and introspection. Such introspection, significantly furthered in post-Reformation times by the Protestant emphasis on personal responsibility and self-examination, is, of course, a central element of Western individualism. Read against this background, the passage in the story in which the diary entries cease takes on a new meaning. Franklin's writing comes to an abrupt end as he enters yet another fugue and "the pen snap[s] in [his] hand" (*CS2* 555).

---

9 On the close connection between the mentality of Protestantism and the genesis of capitalism cf. Max Weber's classic study *The Protestant Ethic and the Spirit of Capitalism*. Weber also refers to Franklin, observing that "[t]he earning of money within the modern economic order is [...] the real Alpha and Omega of Franklin's ethic" (1958: 53f).

In light of what has so far been said, this breaking of the pen can be read as a powerful metaphor for the end of the humanist "self-authoring subject" (Colebrook 2005: 236). As the story progresses and Franklin comes to embrace the fugues, he increasingly vacates the position of the sovereign individual subject. "I'm losing all sense of urgency"; "[e]verything is slowing down, I have to force myself to remember to eat and shower. It's all rather pleasant" (*CS2* 552, 552f) – sentences like these indicate that Franklin is progressively escaping from what Baudrillard has called the "truly unheard-of servitude" of being "a slave to his identity, his will, his responsibilities, his desire" (1993c: 189, 188). By abdicating one by one all these pillars of the subject, Ballard's protagonist rejects all that his namesake Benjamin Franklin represents. This is also underlined by his relationship with the director of the clinic at which he used to work, Dr. Rachel Vaisey, who epitomizes the Franklinian way of life. While she is "baffled by [his] calm appearance, despite [his] beard and coffee-stained trousers", Franklin, in turn, feels gradually more ill at ease in her company, unable to relate to "her closed mind and closed world" and "her discrete existence, her prissy point-to-point consciousness" (*CS2* 554, 542, 554). The text presents this ethic as superseded and inadequate to the new realities. Like the other works discussed in this chapter, "News from the Sun" subscribes to abdication, to a state of radical passivity in which the human being is liberated not only from some particular form of subjectivity and identity, but from the very status of individual subjecthood, through which power continuously reproduces itself. Franklin defies this subject-producing type of power and the capitalist system built on it by what Baudrillard terms "inertial strength" (2007b: 36).

In an essay on science fiction cinema, Ballard has rejected the view that the science fiction film is nothing but a medium of escapist entertainment and instead commended it as "a sensitive barometer of the cultural and political climate of the day" (1996a: 17). Surely, this is true of other science fiction media besides film as well. What historical climate might it then be, we may ask, that Ballard's "News from the Sun" is measuring? If, as the New Historicists maintain, the literary – and, indeed, any other – text is not a closed and unified whole but rather a focal point of various 'social energies' and discourses (Greenblatt 1988, esp. 1–20), a site always traversed by a range of "half-hidden cultural transactions" (Greenblatt 1988: 4), then it seems possible to establish a more specific context for the short story's rejection of Franklinian individualism and capitalist ambition. For at the time that Ballard's story was published – 1981 – many of the discursive/ ideological elements that are inscribed in the text through the 'spectral' sign of the protagonist's name were being effectively reactivated (after and against the permissive society of the 1960s and 70s) and, to borrow Ernesto Laclau and Chantal Mouffe's (2001) term, 'rearticulated' into a new hegemonic consensus. This hegemonic formation which came to dominance in Britain during the late 70s and early

80s was, of course, Thatcherism. In its interconnection of the conservative discourse of the Tories with the discourse of neo-liberalism, so competently analyzed by Stuart Hall (1988), Thatcherism propagated, among other things, a fierce individualism (self-reliance, personal interest and responsibility, competition, etc.)[10] combined with capitalist aspiration and the striving for material success. The ideological tenets of Thatcherism and those of Benjamin Franklin's writings thus coincide to a considerable degree. Placed in historical context, the abdication depicted in Ballard's story can therefore be specifically read as a reaction against Thatcherism. Such a reading is further supported by the fact that the place where Franklin and Ursula eventually learn to stay conscious during the fugues and begin to welcome their impending total escape from time and the new existence connected with it is the imaginary city Soleri II. It is named after the Italian-American architect Paolo Soleri and apparently modeled on his plans for the experimental settlement in Arcosanti, Arizona, which began construction in 1970 and which is supposed to provide a model of what Soleri calls 'arcology', meaning a connection of architecture and ecology. Arcosanti's purpose is to become a prototype of Soleri's ideal of a high-tech self-sufficient, communal town that is at the same time harmoniously integrated with its natural environment. It is not hard to see that such a vision is strongly indebted to the collectivist and ecological thought of the counter-culture of the 1960s and 70s.[11] Hence, it is only fitting that the city in Ballard's story is once referred to as a "hippy commune" (*CS2* 531). What Soleri II represents is thus the 'antagonistic' (Laclau and Mouffe 2001) other of the hegemonic formation of Thatcherism, that is, the permissive society that Thatcher wanted to overcome through the restoration of essentially Victorian values and 'vigorous virtues' (Letwin 1993: 33ff). At the end of the text, Soleri II becomes a space of abdication, an "empty city of a future without time", and so a place where Rachel Vaisey's capitalist "'[c]lock time'" (*CS2* 561, 552) no longer exists.

While "News from the Sun", analyzed from a broadly New Historicist point of view as a force field of warring cultural discourses, can be read as a repudiation of

---

10 In this context, cf. Thatcher's famous remarks made in an interview with *Woman's Own* magazine, published in 1987: "who is society? There is no such thing! There are individual men and women and there are families and no government can do anything except through people and people look to themselves first." (n.d.: n.pag.) In his study on Thatcherism, Eric J. Evans refers to this as "the cultural essence of Thatcherism: make people stand on their own feet and replace a dependency with an enterprise culture." (1997: 122)
11 In his history of American architecture, Mark Gelernter refers to the designs of Soleri and the English Archigram group as "sci-fi technology placed in the service of the tune in, turn on, and drop out generation" (1999: 289).

Thatcherism, it is nevertheless at the same time not an endorsement of communitarian forms of sociality as propagated by the counter-culture movement. Instead, the text subscribes to a radically posthumanist logic: the desire for abdication. It should be noted that here as elsewhere, there is something akin to Buddhism in this.[12] In Buddhist thought, the human condition is essentially one of suffering. This suffering arises not only out of physical pain and emotional or psychological misery, but also, and more fundamentally, from the very fact of our individual existence and from what is seen as an endless cycle of craving and gratification. Only when this cycle is broken does suffering cease and is nirvana attained. *Nirvana* literally means 'blowing out'; it is a state in which desire as well as individual consciousness are extinguished. It is this striving for a sphere of nothingness that Ballard's fiction is reminiscent of. In Buddhist philosophy as in Ballard's works of abdication, the individual subject is seen as possessing no essence[13] and as finding relief only once it is freed from identity itself. In both cases, this can be achieved through a process of 'paring down'; in texts like "The Enormous Space" and "News from the Sun", the main characters one by one relinquish all their activities, increasingly just drifting through the days, until eventually even bodily self-subsistence is reduced to a minimum. In due course, Franklin has to make an effort to remind himself to eat and shower (*CS2* 552f), his body by now consisting of not much more than "sticklike arms and legs, a collection of bones" (*CS2* 564). While this is certainly not a Buddhist ideal, there is in the Asian religion nonetheless a related tendency for increasing reduction, for example in Buddhist meditational practices, which can aim at a stage of trance known as the 'attainment of cessation', in which all mental operations and even heartbeat and respiration are diminished to the point of stopping. By thus giving up all the elements of his personality, Franklin is "[l]ess and less the subject of desire – closer and closer to the nothingness of the object" (Baudrillard 1993c: 195). Baudrillard asserts: "When I speak of the object and its fatal strategies, I'm speaking also of people and their inhuman strategies", "I speak of all of us and our political and social order" (2008: 222, 220) – Ballard's "News from the Sun" presents abdication as just such an in- or posthuman strategy, as a way to free oneself from the con-

---

[12] There are strikingly numerous correspondences between poststructuralism, especially deconstruction, on the one hand and Buddhism and 'Asian thought' more generally on the other. On this fascinating topic, cf. e.g. Magliola 1984; Coward 1990; Wang 2001; Park 2006; and Davies 2011.
[13] This is one way of interpreting the Buddhist notion of the 'not-self'. It goes without saying that in their particulars, the postmodern/poststructuralist and the Buddhist conception of the subject are by no means identical. The relevance of the concept of the 'not-self' for Ballard's fiction, especially for "The Voices of Time", has also been pointed out by Rowland Wymer (2012).

straints of subjectivity through which power is continuously exercised and reproduced by passing on the side of the object.

Some of the Surrealist elements that Ballard embeds in his story can be read in this light as well. Franklin and especially the wayward Slade may be considered as quasi-Surrealist artists, who, through their work, attempt to anticipate the new reality they are about to enter. The photographs both take with the perimeter camera in Franklin's office as well as Slade's eccentric psychosexual shrines, which juxtapose radically disparate elements, represent efforts to decipher the underlying logic of the transformations that are taking place by employing what Ballard has called "transformational grammars" (*AE* 62) which de-/encode reality in terms of an alternative 'language'. As Roger Luckhurst (1997: 92f) points out in his discussion of Ballard's *The Atrocity Exhibition*, such a practice is reminiscent of Salvador Dalí's 'paranoiac-critical' method, which sought to interpret reality according to a consciously delusional pattern in order to discover/create alternative structures of meaning. In a similar manner, Franklin and Slade's photographic experiments provide insights into an other reality, namely the realm without time experienced during the fugues: "Standing or reclining on the rotating platform, the volunteer patients had been photographed in a continuous scan that transformed them into a landscape of undulating hills and valleys, not unlike the desert outside." (*CS2* 543) Through such Surrealist procedures, which are clearly inspired by Etienne-Jules Marey's and Eadweard Muybridge's experimental 'chronophotography', the characters are able to experience time and space in as yet unknown ways. There is a constant interchange of codes here, the human and the geological worlds being persistently overlaid in a manner that recalls the artistic technique of 'decalcomania' as practiced by Oscar Domínguez or Max Ernst. In true Surrealist fashion, then, Franklin and Slade depart from received accounts of reality and experiment with new ways of thinking and perceiving the world, which reveal to them different modes of being.

Yet, these Surrealist elements can also be understood in another way, as metaphors for the protagonists' Baudrillardian strategy of abdication. We have, as Baudrillard says, arrived "at this paradox, at this conjuncture where the position of the subject has become untenable, and where the only possible position is that of the object" (2008: 143). When Franklin thinks about his wife's body drained of time during the fugues and assumes that "the contours of her breasts and thighs [will] migrate to the polished walls, calm as the dunes and valleys of the perimeter photographs", or when he feels "sections of his [own] mind [...] migrating towards the peaceful geometry of the bathroom walls" (*CS2* 548, 555), it is the passage from the position as subject to the position as object as called for by Baudrillard that this imagery suggests. For what does the 'peaceful geometry' of the walls, where the subject dissolves, signify but the Baudrillardian notion of the object seducing the subject, the object as "strange attractor", as the subject's "vanishing point" (Baudrillard 1993c: 197), in short, the dream of abdication?[14] In light of Baudrillard's opposition of the "universe of chance, luck and play" to the "integral universe" of the system and of his assertion that "[a]mong all the possibilities for shattering the mirror of identity, [...] there is the option of surrendering oneself to chance, to the dice" (2005: 202, 58), it is furthermore telling that Ballard's story is set in and around the city of Las Vegas and that it is described as a "city of empty mirrors" (*CS2* 549). In Ballard's texts, the Lacanian mirrors, through which the self imagines itself as a unified and coherent whole (Lacan 2004), are empty and shattered, the subject dissolved.

By way of this dissolution, Franklin gains access to a new order of being – somewhat like the Surrealists hoped to do in their pursuit of a synthesizing *surrealité*. Through his portrayal of this timeless realm, Ballard provokes yet another clash of discourses, for what emerges from the story's descriptions of it is a decidedly Romantic discourse. The process of Franklin's gradual realization of the beneficial nature of the changes occurring in and around him, for instance, is repeatedly portrayed in terms of the development of an exceptional aesthetic awareness. Thus, towards the end of the text, Ursula asks Franklin when he "learn[ed] to see", tells him that it was the steel mirrors of the solar farms that "helped [her] open [her] eyes", and declares that "there are so many doors" (*CS2* 562). Phrases like these recall Romantic conceptions of the imagination as a visionary faculty, as expressed in Wordsworth's image of "an eye made quiet by the power / Of harmony" (1973b: 147) or Blake's notion that the "doors of perception" need to be "cleansed" (1973: 40), an expression that Ursula evidently echoes.[15] In the fugues, "serial time [gives] way to simultaneity":

> Like a camera with its shutter left open indefinitely, the eye perceived a moving object as a series of separate images. Ursula's walking figure as she searched for Franklin had left a hundred replicas of herself behind her, seeded the air with a host of identical twins. Seen from the speeding car, the few frayed palm trees along the road had multiplied themselves [...]. The lakes had been the multiplied images of the water in that tepid motel pool, and the blue streams were the engine coolant running from the radiator of his overturned car. (*CS2* 563)

---

14 To a certain degree, this dream may itself be part of Ballard's Surrealist legacy: as André Breton pointed out in his preface to the 1920 exhibition of Max Ernst: "Who knows if we are not somehow preparing ourselves to escape the principle of identity?" (qtd. in Hebdige 1979: 165n7)
15 The trope of the 'doors' can also be found in "The Enormous Space" (*CS2* 703).

In this process of what we may describe, referring to Max Weber (2004), as a 're-enchantment' of the "iron cage" (1958: 181) of an overly rationalized and functionalized capitalist world, the mind is presented as creative and at least partially constituting its own experiences: "*Our eyes are filling* the whole state with blossom. One flower makes the desert bloom." (*CS2* 562, emphasis added) As M.H. Abrams explains, this is a distinctly Romantic idea: poets like Wordsworth and Coleridge "usually agree in picturing the mind in perception as active rather than inertly receptive, and as contributing to the world in the very process of perceiving the world" (1971: 58). This "lucidity of the timeless" allows Franklin and Ursula to see through the physical world to a different, more profound reality behind it: "Each fugue [...] gave him a glimpse of that real world"; "[the] last fugue [...] would free them from the world of appearances" (*CS2* 563, 562, 563). This, too, is clearly reminiscent of Romantic thought. Thus, in the passage previously quoted, the speaker of Wordsworth's "Tintern Abbey", for instance, holds that once our sensitivity is rightly attuned, "We see into the life of things" and feel "a sense sublime / Of something far more deeply interfused" (1973b: 147, 149). In similar fashion, Blake claims that if our perception were pure, "every thing would appear to man as it is, infinite" (1973: 40) – which, of course, is precisely what Franklin discovers. Blake adds: "For man has closed himself up, till he sees all things thro' narrow chinks of his cavern." (1973: 40) The related opposition in Ballard's story between a world of appearances and a real one points us not only to poets like Wordsworth and Blake, but also to the Romantic philosophy of Arthur Schopenhauer (1966a, 1966b) and the early Friedrich Nietzsche (1999), who, following Kant, proclaimed an analogous division between the 'appearances' on the one hand, that is, being subjected to the *principium individuationis* as well as to time and space, and the 'will', the metaphysical truth of being behind all phenomena, on the other. It also directs us, especially when we take into account Blake's metaphor of the cavern, to Plato and his theory of Ideas. As numerous scholars have shown, Platonic and Neo-Platonic philosophy infuses a great deal of Romantic thought. This is also evident in Romantic conceptions of childhood, which often seem to be inspired by the Platonic notion of the immortality and the pre- and post-existence of the soul. "News from the Sun" alludes to such conceptions when the beautiful timeless realm the protagonists enter is said to be "beyond all the fantasies of Franklin's childhood" and when the new language Ursula begins to speak during the fugues is compared to "a baby's burble": "the babbling infant, and this young woman, spoke with the lucidity of the timeless [...]. The babbling new-born were telling their mothers of that realm of wonder from which they had just been expelled." (*CS2* 564, 563) Here, Ballard's text unmistakably resonates with the poems by Blake, Wordsworth, Coleridge and others which portray the child as a yet uncorrupted, perfect being still partaking in the harmony and unity of the realm of the divine. As Wordsworth's "Ode: Intimations of Immortality" has it:

> Our birth is but a sleep and a forgetting:
> The Soul that rises with us, our life's Star,
>   Hath had elsewhere its setting,
>   And cometh from afar:
>   Not in entire forgetfulness,
>   And not in utter nakedness,
> But trailing clouds of glory do we come
>   From God, who is our home:
> Heaven lies about us in our infancy!
> Shades of the prison-house begin to close
>   Upon the growing Boy,
>   But He
> Beholds the light, and whence it flows,
>   He sees it in his joy;
> The Youth, who daily farther from the east
>   Must travel, still is Nature's Priest,
>   And by the vision splendid
>   Is on his way attended;
> At length the Man perceives it die away,
> And fade into the light of common day.[16] (1973a: 178)

Ballard's story subscribes to a very similar discourse on childhood.[17] Indeed, even the imagery of light and the sun ('rises', 'setting', 'the light', 'the east', 'the light of common day') is the same: opposed to the "realm of harsh light and rigid perspectives" (*CS2* 565) of ordinary reality stands the powerful light of the fugues: "Free from time, the light had become richer"; "[t]he air was engorged with light"; "[a]ll the light in the universe had come here to greet him, an immense congregation of particles." (*CS2* 564, 560, 567) This imagery (cf. also Wordsworth's 'shades of the prison-house') once again refers us back to Plato as well as to Plotinus' Neo-Platonism: both use the metaphor of the sun, which gives Ballard's story its title, to describe the origin of all being – 'the

---

[16] In his study on Platonism and English Romantic thought, David Newsome says about this poem that "it contains the finest Romantic exposition of the Platonic doctrine of *anamnesis*, as an explanation of the visionary powers of the child" (1974: 26).

[17] Perhaps, the mention that is made in the text of Dalí's famous painting *The Persistence of Memory* – the shrine that Slade creates for Franklin contains a reproduction of it – can be placed in this context as well: in an essay on Dalí, Ballard has connected this work with "[t]he trauma of birth, [...] the irreconcilable melancholy of the exposed embryo. This world of fused beaches and overheated light is that perceived by the isolated child." (1996p: 95f)

Idea of the Good' and 'the One' respectively – and Plotinus in particular draws on images of light to explain his theorem of 'emanation'. This (Neo-)Platonic discourse that informs the text is manifest in Franklin's increasing denigration of the body, too. When he finally manages to stay conscious during the fugues, "his mind [...] scramble[s] free inside his skull" while "[h]is body ha[s] given up", so that he feels like "the driver of a slow-witted automaton" (*CS2* 560). Likewise, the more he comes to accept the fugues, the more he feels "embarrassed by the continued presence of his body" (*CS2* 564). Such passages recall not only the Platonic equation of *sōma* and *sēma*, but also the debasing of the body in certain Buddhist traditions.

In "News from the Sun", Ballard draws on discourses like these in order to develop the transcendental character of abdication. Thus, a posthumanist/poststructuralist discourse is welded to a Romantic/(Neo-)Platonic one. It would seem that this has to be attributed to Ballard's (1996b: 193f) conviction that one of science fiction's tasks is to fuse together science and myth and "to place some kind of metaphysical and philosophical framework around man's [sic] place in the universe" (1996o: 204). As he states programmatically:

> I believe that the catastrophe story [...] represents a constructive and positive act by the imagination rather than a negative one, an attempt to confront a patently meaningless universe by challenging it at its own game.[18] [...] Each one of these fantasies represents an arraignment of the finite, an attempt to dismantle the formal structure of time and space which the universe wraps around us at the moment we first achieve consciousness. It is the inflexibility of this huge reductive machine we call reality that provokes infant and madman alike, and in the cataclysm story the science fiction writer joins company with them, using his imagination to describe the infinite alternatives to reality which nature itself has proved incapable of inventing. (1996c: 208f)

These deliberations resonate strongly with "News from the Sun" – not least in the story's identification of Franklin and Ursula's lucidity with that of "the babbling infant" and that which "others tr[y] to achieve in delirium and brain-damage" (*CS2* 563). In true Surrealist form, reality – or, more specifically, our received idea of time – is in the story revealed as an artificial construct (*CS2* 552) that obstructs the path to alternate perceptions and ways of being. Abdication is presented here – as, to some extent, in "The Enormous Space" – not only as a way to defy power through the liberation from the forms of identity it imposes, but simultaneously also as a means to discover just this path. By embracing the fugue-state and thus abdicating their subjectivity, the characters escape from linear time and con-

---

18 This statement distinctly resonates with Ballard's late novel *Millennium People* as well as with Baudrillard's philosophy (cf. chapter 6).

ventional reality and enter an ecstatic realm of simultaneity,[19] which, through the imagery of oases, light and angels (*CS2* 564, 567), comparisons with "a wonderful garden" and "a paradise" (*CS2* 562), as well as the implication that there is no death without time (*CS2* 564), is clearly rendered as Edenic.[20]

Similar to several Romantic poets, especially those of the second generation like Shelley and Keats, who intensely concerned themselves with the possibilities of a representation of sublime experiences of transcendence, Ballard's story, too, subscribes to a view of language as constitutive, not reflective, of social reality and experience. Accordingly, Franklin and Ursula's entry into the paradisal world beyond the clock is connected to a loss of language and the emergence of a new form of communication that is somehow not subject to the endless movement of 'différance' and therefore allows for an unmediated experience of 'presence':

> There was a new language to learn, sentences whose nouns and verbs were separated by days, syllables whose vowels were marked by the phases of the sun and moon. This was a language outside time, whose grammar was shaped by the contours of Ursula's breasts in his hands, by the geometry of the apartment. [...] He and Ursula lisped at each other, lovers talking between the transits of the moon, in the language of birds, wolves and whales. (*CS2* 565)

The lisp, as speech impediment, metaphorically marks a rift in the symbolic order. Though still a mode of signification, this new language is nevertheless paradoxically depicted as granting an animal-like, unmediated relation to the world, that is, an experience of the Lacanian 'real', in which things present themselves in their "dumb reality", in the form of what Lacan, referring to Kant, has termed *das Ding*, "the beyond-of-the-signified" (2008: 65).

---

19 However, it should be noted that there are also cues in the story which permit a questioning of this escape. For one thing, the text indicates that, in the end, there can be no flight from this world, that the *materiality* of existence will always reassert itself. This is implied not only by the fact that profane things like tepid pool water and engine coolant remain the indispensable basis of the new, enchanted realm (cf. the above-quoted passage, *CS2* 563), but also by the repeated intrusion of the mundane world into it: "clouds of dust blew into the apartment, a gritty reminder of a different world"; "the noise and violence of the engine were tearing apart the new world he had constructed so carefully" (*CS2* 562, 565). For another, the fact that the whole plot is presented in the form of an elaborate analepsis, with Franklin "remember[ing]" the narrated events, and the very end of the story, which has the protagonist "waiting for his wife to [...] bring him news from the sun" (*CS2* 531, 568), are curiously at odds with the idea of simultaneity, involving as they do the notion of a past and of a future. In view of this, Franklin's escape from time seems somewhat incomplete and the alternate reality rather fragile.

20 The notion of a regained Eden can be found in several other works by Ballard as well.

Thus, "News from the Sun" is characterized by a striking discursive heterogeneity. As the analysis has shown, abdication is here placed in a network of posthumanist, Buddhist, Surrealist as well as Romantic discourses, which are overlaid and collide and which code abdication as political as well as transcendental: as a form of resistance against the system which defies the identitary imperative on which its power is built, and as a way to access a kind of ontological absolute.[21]

In line with postmodernist thought, Ballard's works expose the liberal-humanist subject as an ideological illusion necessary for the smooth functioning of the system and replace it with the radical passivity of abdication through which his protagonists are liberated from power's "blackmail by identity" (Baudrillard 2008: 62). In texts like *The Drowned World*, "The Enormous Space" and "News from the Sun", Ballard thus presents us with a form of resistance which can be subsumed under what Slavoj Žižek has adequately called "Bartlebian politics" (2009: 180). Žižek explains:

> Better to do nothing than to engage in localised acts the ultimate function of which is to make the system run more smoothly (acts such as providing space for the multitude of new subjectivities). The threat today is not passivity, but pseudo-activity, the urge to 'be active', to 'participate' [...]. The truly difficult thing is to step back, to withdraw. (2009: 183)

By resisting the very status as subject, Franklin and Ballard's other protagonists perform a most radical form of such withdrawal, a trans-political challenge to the system that represents an affirmative answer to Baudrillard's rhetorical question:

> Today, now that all critical radicality has become useless, now that all negativity seems resolved in a world that pretends to realize itself, and now that the critical spirit has found its summer home in socialism, and the effects of desire are largely depleted – what remains but to bring things back to their enigmatic ground zero?[22] (2008: 229 f)

---

21 In light of the connection between literary form and ideology posited particularly by Marxist critics (cf. Eagleton 1992: 20–31), especially of the link between a realist epistemology and the emergence of the humanist 'episteme' (Foucault 2002) and the interconnection between the rise of the realist novel and the development of individualism, the growing power of the bourgeoisie and the unfolding of capitalism (Watt 1987), this discursive syncretism, and the self-conscious departure from realism that it entails – Ballardian texts like "News from the Sun" are possibly best characterized as 'slipstream' or 'transrealist' fiction (Broderick 2000) – can perhaps itself be considered a reaction against bourgeois hegemony and the liberal-humanist notion of the sovereign individual subject associated with it.
22 The symbol of 'zero' can similarly be seen throughout Ballard's fiction of abdication (cf. Wymer 2012: 29 f).

5 The Psychopath as Saint: *Cocaine Nights*, *Super-Cannes* and the Politics of Transgression after the End of History

> To the insane. I owe them everything.
> J.G. Ballard

Ballard's *Cocaine Nights* and *Super-Cannes* read like companion pieces to each other. Besides the various conceptual, structural and thematic resemblances, both novels are clearly fueled by the utopian imagination, a fact that is already evident in the names of their settings: while the Costa del Sol and the fictitious resort of Estrella de Mar in *Cocaine Nights* trigger associations with Plato's Republic (cf. his use of the sun as a symbol for the 'Idea of the Good', the philosopher-kings' ultimate object of desire), his (or Francis Bacon's) Atlantis, or Tommaso Campanella's City of the Sun, the utopian dimension is immediately apparent in the double allusion of *Super-Cannes*' business park Eden-Olympia. Moreover, both places are repeatedly referred to as 'paradises' (e.g. *CN* 90; *SC* 96) and Eden-Olympia is variously described as a "beautiful garden city, everything town-planners have been working towards for centuries", a place in which, as in Ebenezer Howard's schemes alluded to here, "[a]ll the old urban nightmares ha[ve] been dispelled", and as a place of fulfillment and abundance: "Everything is here at Eden-Olympia." (*SC* 254, 54) Thus, both locales to a certain degree emerge as heterotopic textual spaces where diverse utopian discourses are overlaid. These discourses revolve around the notion of the leisure society in *Cocaine Nights* and the idea of a working and living environment perfectly geared to its residents' needs, so that work becomes the context in which the individual finds happiness, in *Super-Cannes*. The reader quickly realizes that the novels' divergent speculations about the future are extrapolated from the same system and are really two sides of the same coin. That coin is global capitalism.

Pointing to the increased interest in international settings and global politics in Ballard's writing since *Empire of the Sun*, David Ian Paddy has identified an "internationalist turn" (2012: 190) in Ballard's oeuvre. It is, perhaps, no coincidence that this turn roughly coincides with what sociologists have described as a new phase or novel acceleration of globalization, brought about by a range of economic, political, information-technological and cultural changes (cf. e.g. Castells 1996: 5ff, 1998: 355ff; Rosa 2005: 335f). It seems to me that it is in *Cocaine Nights* and *Super-Cannes* that we find Ballard's most ambitious engagement with the new global realities of the late 20th and early 21st century. The picture he paints of them is a bleak one.¹ As Paddy rightly points out, globalization here appears "as a new form of international imperialism" (2012: 191). Thus, what initially appear as utopian spaces quickly turn out to be far from perfect. The reader soon becomes aware that the societies of both novels are profoundly anomic, marked as they are by anonymity, isolation and alienation, by apathy and a generalized 'death of affect' (*AE* 116). Whereas in *Cocaine Nights*, the very realization of the utopian ideal is revealed to be the central predicament – a fact that places the text within the anti-utopian genre – the world of *Super-Cannes* increasingly emerges as a downright dystopian one.²

In both novels, the overall image is one of absolute stasis, paralysis and exhaustion. I want to argue that in this, they are the products of a specific historical moment, whose significance for the evolution of globalization cannot be overestimated: the revolutions of 1989, most notably the fall of the Berlin Wall, and the subsequent dissolution of the Soviet Union. Written in the changed world after these events, *Cocaine Nights* and *Super-Cannes* portray realms of the 'post': though the societies they depict are very different, both texts are deeply concerned with the related phenomena that have come to be known as the 'end of history' and the 'end of ideology' and/or 'of utopia'. Andrzej Gasiorek, as always an astute critic of Ballard's work, who, however, here omits joining a more complete analysis to his insightful observations, has written that "[the] sense of an ending, a historic ending, haunts these books. [...] This is postmodernity as end-game and terminal zone, the site of a late capitalist colonisation so complete that temporality has been evacuated from it" (2005: 20). Both novels are set in a world in which, almost unchallenged, the capitalist market spreads across the globe, re-shaping – indeed, homogenizing – local economies, cultures and spaces and thus creating a capitalist 'world system' (Wallerstein 1979)³ without any 'outside' or 'negativity' (Hardt and Negri 2001: 186–90). Whereas this world system is only the implied – though nonetheless clearly palpable – horizon for the events of *Cocaine Nights*, it moves center stage in *Super-Cannes*, whose business enclave can be read as a microcosmic representation of what Mi-

---

1 The pessimistic view of globalization that transpires in the two novels is already evident in some of the earlier short stories such as "Having a Wonderful Time" and "The Largest Theme Park in the World" (cf. Baxter 2008).
2 This inversion or folding into each other of the utopian and the dystopian in the two novels has led Jeannette Baxter (2008: 96) to speak of 'nightmare utopias'. For a discussion of the terms 'utopian', 'anti-utopian' and 'dystopian', cf. Sargent 1994.
3 According to Wallerstein, the inner logic of capitalism makes it necessarily global and "from the beginning an affair of the world-economy" (1979: 19). While this may be true, I believe that Hardt and Negri (2001: 8f) are nevertheless right in arguing for the novelty of the contemporary capitalist order.

chael Hardt and Antonio Negri term 'Empire'. Similar to the two theorists, Ballard's novel emphasizes the importance of the shift towards the Deleuzian 'society of control' as well as the central role of 'biopower' in the new world order.

In the depicted post-political realms, the novels seem to maintain, only a radical economy of transgression tied to a 'willed psychopathy' is able to overcome the acute social and psychological inertia that the end of history has bred. This catastrophic strategy, however, finally fails. Whereas, in *Cocaine Nights*, while successful in the recreation of a sense of community, it nevertheless fails because of its inability to produce a new type of collectivity – one that would be politically subversive and not ultimately tied to received forms of subjectivity – and because, in the end, it turns out to be recuperated by the powers that be, the outlook in *Super-Cannes* is even bleaker as what appear to be acts of resistance are here revealed to be always already deeply complicit with the system they purportedly attack.

5.1 The Violence of the Global and the Boredom of Paradise

Too bad. We're in paradise.
Jean Baudrillard

Like *Super-Cannes*, *Cocaine Nights* draws not only on the tradition of utopian but also on that of detective fiction. Charles Prentice, the novel's narrator and protagonist, travels to the Costa del Sol because his younger brother Frank has pleaded guilty to an arson attack that killed five people. Finding that like himself, almost everyone, including the local police, is convinced of Frank's innocence, Prentice embarks upon a "detective investigation" in order to dissolve "the larg[e] question mark that preside[s] over the gutted mansion" (*CN* 64, 55). His "amateur sleuthing" (*CN* 76) is clearly inscribed in the conventions of crime fiction: Prentice, as it were, goes 'undercover' in the subculture of Estrella de Mar, questions its members, gathers evidence, attempts to trace and recreate the events of the night of the murders (esp. in chapter 9), develops and discards different theories to explain what happened, combines the use of an analytical intellect with creative imagination in a manner reminiscent of the 'ratiocination' of Edgar Allan Poe's Dupin, is forced to find his way through numerous contradictions, loose ends and wrong tracks, is repeatedly hindered and attacked during his investigations, and has an uneasy relationship with the police. In addition, the novel employs the familiar cliffhanger technique at the end of several chapters and contains some of the staple imagery of detective fiction (Estrella de Mar is continuously described in terms of "a cabinet of mysteries", "Chinese boxes", "a huge riddle", "*trompe-l'œil*" [*CN* 121, 147, 151] effects, "secret spaces", "a maze" [*CN* 161, 189], etc.) as well as intertextual references to Franz Kafka's *The Trial* (*CN* 71, 72), Alfred Hitchcock's *Psycho* (*CN* 71), Lewis Carroll's *Alice*-books (*CN* 150), as well as the artworks of Giovanni Battista Piranesi (*CN* 173, 202) and M.C. Escher (*CN* 151), which all serve to strengthen the reader's impression of the resort as a labyrinth in which nothing is what it seems to be and to amplify the classical atmosphere of mystery and confusion.[4]

Yet, appearances are deceiving not only in Estrella de Mar, but also in generic terms. For while Ballard clearly draws on the conventions of crime fiction, he also departs from and, indeed, subverts them. As Michel Delville accurately observes, "[t]he plot of Ballard's novel superficially resembles that of a classic murder mystery – but one which follows the lurid associational and intertextual logic of a David Lynch movie" (1998: 83).[5] For one thing, as Gasiorek (2005: 171) and Baxter (2008: 97) have both pointed out, his tale is more 'why-' than 'who-dunnit', the focus lying not so much on identifying the culprit and on working out his psychology, but rather on comprehending the unusual nature of the society in which the crime took place. Prentice at one point muses: "I was sure that the solution to the Hollinger murders lay not in Frank's involvement with the retired film producer but in the unique nature of the resort where he had died", and another character explains to him: "I could tell you who started the fire, but you're not ready yet. It's not just a matter of someone's name, but of coming to terms with Estrella de Mar." (*CN* 78 f, 208) In *Cocaine Nights*, therefore, "[t]he detective's work is that of ethnography" (Gasiorek 2005: 171), of what Marc Augé (2008: 7 ff) would refer to as an 'ethnography of the near'.[6] By thus moving the center of interest away from the solving of the mystery, Ballard may be said to crack open the "commodity structure" that Fredric Jameson, following Horkheimer and Adorno, has identified as an essential characteristic of

---

[4] Of course, the specific semantic fields activated by these intertextual allusions vary from intertext to intertext; thus, for instance, the references to Kafka and Hitchcock evoke, among other things, the theme of guilt omnipresent in Ballard's novel, while the mention of Carroll and Escher suggests an inverted, 'nonsensical' realm, in which the laws of reason and common sense are suspended (in this context, cf. Deleuze's [2004a] as well as Lecercle's [1994] illuminating discussions of Carroll's work).
[5] I believe that *Cocaine Nights* can indeed be seen as Ballard's attempt to bring the detective novel somewhat closer to the films of Hitchcock and Lynch – notably *Psycho* and *Blue Velvet* – which he admired (cf. Ballard 1996r, esp. 5).
[6] To a certain extent, already Ballard's early declaration that "[t]he only truly alien planet is Earth" (1996t: 197), made in the context of his call for a radical renewal of science fiction literature, may be understood along the lines of an interest in such an ethnography of the near.

crime fiction, in which, he argues, all elements are 'instrumentalized' for the purpose of consumption-satisfaction, since it is something "you read 'for the end' – the bulk of the pages becoming sheer devalued means to an end – in this case, the 'solution'" (1992: 12). Beyond this, I would argue that Ballard's novel effectively undermines the moral, socio-political and epistemological assumptions that structure the more typical texts of the genre: *Cocaine Nights* completely decenters the unified rational subject generally central to these texts, it turns truth, whose recovery is at the heart of this kind of fiction, into something extremely elusive, and it ends on a note of uncertainty and not, as usual, with the reestablishment and reaffirmation of law and order.[7] In this way, the novel distinctly departs from the traditionally conservative ideology of detective fiction (cf. e.g. Bloch 1988). As Ernest Mandel contends,

> the common ideology of the original and classical detective story [...] remains quintessentially bourgeois. [...] The criminal is always caught. Justice is always done. Crime never pays. Bourgeois legality, bourgeois values, bourgeois society, always triumph in the end. It is soothing, socially integrating literature, despite its concern with crime, violence and murder. (1984: 47f)

Ballard's rewriting of the detective fiction form marks a very clear departure from and, indeed, challenge to this ideology.

As his protagonist begins his investigation of the fire at the Hollinger house and thus his ethnographic study of the Costa del Sol, he quickly realizes that what has materialized on the Spanish coast is a fully developed leisure society, in which work is almost entirely absent. The novel repeatedly emphasizes that as such, the Costa del Sol may well be an embodiment of the future of Europe, a kind of "prototype" for a "leisure-dominated future" (*CN* 187, 35). As the charismatic Bobby Crawford explains to Prentice:

> Our governments are preparing for a future without work [...]. Leisure societies lie ahead of us, like those you see on this coast. People will still work – or, rather, some people will work, but only for a decade of their lives. They will retire in their late thirties, with fifty years of idleness in front of them." (*CN* 180)

Irrespective of the question how plausible such a prognosis may be with regards to reality, in the fictional world of the text, one of mankind's oldest utopian

---

[7] In all of this, Ballard's novel is perhaps closest to the American hardboiled, noir variant of crime fiction. On the differentiation between this branch of detective fiction and what he sees as the 'French' and the 'English' ones, cf. Deleuze 2004b.

dreams, the freedom from work, has evidently been fulfilled.[8] In this context, it is perhaps no coincidence that it is cocaine that is omnipresent in the story and that appears in the novel's title: in light of the text's depiction of the coast as a realm of luxury, pleasure and ease, a place, moreover, which "isn't anywhere" (*CN* 17), the word, through homophony, may possibly evoke the Medieval utopia of the Land of Cockaigne. While there are no rivers flowing with beer or piglets running about with apples in their mouths and carving knives conveniently at the ready in their backs on Ballard's Costa del Sol, it is nevertheless clearly a space to some degree derived from this kind of popular utopianism.

However, the more Prentice sees of the coast, the more he becomes aware that the realization of this utopia in fact assumes an unexpected form and has surprising consequences. One of his earliest observations in this respect is what he identifies as the profound unreality of the spaces of the coast. According to Prentice, "[u]nreality thrive[s] on every side" (*CN* 17) on the Costa del Sol. For one thing, this is due to what Augé has described as "the unprecedented extension of spaces of circulation, consumption and communication corresponding to the phenomenon we identify today as 'globalization'" (2008: ix). The Spanish coast with its "purpose-built villa complexes" and its towns "without either centre or suburbs" that seem to be "little more than [...] dispersal ground[s] for golf courses and swimming pools" (*CN* 15, 16) has plainly fallen victim to this proliferation of non-relational, -historical and -identitarian 'non-places'.[9] When Prentice speaks of "the sense of having a real destination" as "the great undying illusion" of travel and points to the pre-structured sameness of all travel experiences – "[w]e arrive at an airport identical to the one we left, with the same car-rental agencies and hotel rooms with their adult movie channels and deodorized bathrooms" (*CN* 9, 10) – he noticeably echoes Augé's assertion that "the same hotel chains, the same television networks are cinched tightly

---

8 There have, of course, been radically different evaluations of idleness in utopian thought, as, for instance, its vigorous regulation and, indeed, repression in More's classical Utopia on the one hand and its central role in the Medieval visions of the land of plenty or the praise it received from Paul Lafargue (1999) and Bertrand Russell (2004) on the other evince.
9 Unlike the paradigmatic hotel chains, airports, supermarkets, and so forth, not all of the spaces depicted in *Cocaine Nights* are, strictly speaking, ones of transit, the ephemeral, etc. Nevertheless, the world of the novel is unmistakably determined by the spatial logic Augé identifies, and the artificial character, lack of history and identity of the spaces of the coast clearly place them in the category of 'non-place'. In this context, cf. Augé's (2008: 86 f) mention of housing estates as well as his (2008: 64, passim) general comment that places and non-places never exist in pure form but rather mark the opposite poles of a continuum, so that the pairing is best thought of as "an instrument for measuring the degree of sociality and symbolization of a given space" (2008: viii).

round the globe, so that we feel constrained by uniformity, by universal sameness, and to cross international borders brings no more profound variety than is found walking between [...] rides at Disneyland" (2008: xii).[10]

Augé's reference to the theme park is telling. 'Disneyfication' or 'Disneyization' has – with somewhat varying meanings – for some time been a much-used term in urban studies and architectural theory (cf. Zukin 2000; Bryman 2004), and it is one which seems to aptly describe another side of *Cocaine Nights'* Costa del Sol that contributes to Prentice's feeling of unreality. For as a matter of fact, the narrator's descriptions of his surroundings frequently create the impression in the reader that the Spanish coast has well-nigh turned into one gigantic theme park. Again and again, Prentice comes across structures such as an "Aquapark" and "artificial hill[s]" (*CN* 15), villas designed in the style of "a new Arab architecture that owe[s] nothing to the Maghreb across the Strait of Gibraltar" but rather belongs "to the desert kingdoms of the Persian Gulf, reflected through the garish mirrors of Hollywood design studios" (*CN* 16), "King Saud's larger-than-life replica of the White House" and "Aladdin's cave apartments" (*CN* 17), "mock-Andalucian streets" (*CN* 31), and edifices whose "Africanized aspect" appears derived from "a North Africa invented by someone who ha[s] never visited the Maghreb" (*CN* 34 f). Ballard's Costa del Sol is evidently a realm of architectural 'historicism', which is, as Jameson has shown, one manifestation of the cultural practice, even logic, of 'pastiche'. Pastiche in this sense is "blank parody", an imitation of unique styles that is, as it were, entirely "neutral" (Jameson 1991: 17), deprived of any ulterior motive and sense of normality, all idiosyncratic mannerisms and styles having become reified 'codes', to be emulated and combined at will. As such, Jameson argues, pastiche is immediately bound up with what he identifies as the characteristic 'depthlessness' and 'loss of historicity' in postmodernity, that is, "the waning [...] of our lived possibility of experiencing history in some active way" (1991: 21). The novel's coast can thus be read as the product of a postmodern world in which the past "as 'referent'" has been effaced, so that it continues to exist only in the form of "a vast collection of images, [...] a set of dusty spectacles" (Jameson 1991: 18). It is therefore only fitting that Prentice at one point refers to Marbella as a "theme village" and a "stage set" (*CN* 31). Like Disneyland or Las Vegas, the Costa del Sol of the novel is clearly dominated by a "new spatial logic of the simulacrum" (Jameson

---

[10] In this context, it is only appropriate that Prentice, who, ironically, works as a travel writer, intends to write a book on the "history of tourism and its eclipse of the age of travel" (*CN* 289), a project that echoes concerns about the commodified, artificial, standardized and inauthentic nature of the tourist experience as articulated by theorists such as Daniel Boorstin (1975), Dean MacCannell (1999) or Zygmunt Bauman (2003).

1991: 18). When the narrator once more comments on an apartment building adorned with "mock-Roman columns and white porticos apparently imported from Las Vegas after a hotel clearance sale, reversing the export to Florida and California in the 1920s of dismantled Spanish monasteries and Sardinian abbeys" (*CN* 16), it transpires that this is indeed a world of endless simulation, in which authenticity – always a highly precarious quality – is irretrievably lost behind Möbius strip-like chains of simulacra, incessantly assembled by the global flows of capital. Appropriately, the coast appears to Prentice as "a zone as depthless as a property developer's brochure" (*CN* 16). Reality is here wholly consumed by the image, that is, following Guy Debord (2009: 33), accumulated capital. As Jameson points out: "the culture of the simulacrum comes to life in a society where exchange value has been generalized to the point at which the very memory of use value is effaced" (1991: 18).

The spaces of the Costa del Sol can hence be read as materializations of capital, both in their 'spectacular' and their 'cannibalistic' nature. Prentice's identification of architectural languages borrowed from Arabia, Africa and elsewhere may be interpreted as pointing to the "random cannibalization" (Jameson 1991: 18) not only of various styles of the past, but also of other cultural spheres more generally. Commodification and spectacularization apply not only to the old, but also to the other (Augé 2008: 89). It is difference of any kind that is being absorbed here, making Ballard's Costa del Sol an incarnation of the neo-cannibalism that Dean MacCannell has identified as a defining characteristic of late capitalism, which, he avers, "deals with human difference in the most direct way, not merely by doing away with it, but by taking it in completely" (1992: 66).

The coast in *Cocaine Nights* thus emerges as a powerful symbol of global capitalism and its totalizing forces. Frank Prentice's repeated comments on its exemplary role as a prototype for the future – "[e]verywhere will be like this soon" (*CN* 23) – are therefore to be taken quite literally: on the dark horizon of capitalist globalization, the novel implies, looms global sameness. The picture of globalization the text paints is hence a bleak one. Ballard's Spanish coast is at the same time victim and perfect embodiment of what Baudrillard, whose late works develop a similarly gloomy view of global processes, has called "the violence of the global" (2003: 92). More and more, both Baudrillard and Ballard seem to maintain, the homogenizing practices of multinational capitalism sweep away all singularities, swallow all differences, and in this way progressively bring into being "an entirely in-different culture" (Baudrillard 2003: 91).

This culture is among the main contributory factors to another phenomenon undercutting the initial utopian image of the leisure society of the coast: its absolute paralysis. This paralysis is manifest both on the level of the individual and on that of the community, and has a physico-psychological as well as a socio-political dimension. It seems to me that it is with this profound stasis that Ballard's globalization narratives are most centrally concerned. Augé has argued that the worldwide proliferation of non-places means the growing dominance of "spaces in which neither identity, nor relations, nor history really make any sense" (2008: 70), and indeed, these are the main casualties of global homogenization in *Cocaine Nights*. One of Augé's principal arguments is that the space of non-place increasingly produces "a world [...] surrendered to solitary individuality" (2008: 63) by stripping away singular identity and social bonds. In this way, the horizon of human experience under late capitalism becomes determined by isolation and anonymity. Ballard's novel – and, in fact, a large part of his oeuvre generally – explores precisely this horizon and may therefore be considered as part of an "ethnology of solitude" (2008: 98) as envisaged by Augé. Visiting one of the villas of the Residencia Costasol resort, Prentice remarks:

> The outer desert of the Residencia Costasol was reflected in the inner desert of these aseptic chambers. The lighter gravity of this strange planet would numb the brain and maroon the residents in their armchairs, eyes clinging to the horizon lines of their television screens as they tried to stabilize their minds. (*CN* 266)

Again and again, the Costa del Sol is described as a realm of emptiness and silence, characterized by the "absence of any social structure" and an "intense inward migration" (*CN* 35, 216), an extreme form of 'cocooning' (Popcorn 1992: 27–33) facilitated/triggered[11] by the heavy surveillance in the gated communities of the coast, which the text represents as veritable 'scanscapes' (Davis 2000: 363–368). The novel suggests that as these non-places spread, as "the open-plan city" disappears and we move "into the age of security grilles and defensible space" (*CN* 219), our emotional and intellectual capacities increasingly atrophy. Prentice avers: "Total security is a disease of deprivation." (*CN* 293)

Indeed, the residents of the coastal resorts lead a zombie-like existence marked by total apathy and inertia. Their nervous system "fossilized" (*CN* 34), they drift through the days in utter passivity, living a life shorn of serious thought, goals and commitments, passion or, indeed, any other kind of feeling. Similar to the characters of *Crash* and many other Ballardian texts, the residents suffer from the postmodern 'death' or 'waning of affect' (*AE* 116; Jameson 1991: 10–16). As in *The Atrocity Exhibition*, *Crash* and elsewhere, this withering of

---

[11] On the dialectical relation between space and human subjectivity and practice, cf. once again Henri Lefebvre's (2003) thinking on the triad of 'spatial practices', 'representations of space' and 'representational space' as well as Edward Soja's (1989: 76–93) concept of the 'socio-spatial dialectic'.

the emotions is largely due to the colonization of the human psyche by the mass-media systems, above all by television. Thus, the residential enclaves along the coast are described as places where "[t]he sun doesn't shine [...], only satellite TV" and where "[e]verywhere satellite dishes cu[p] the sky like begging bowls" (*CN* 90, 213) – an evocative image suggesting the media's (imperfect) occupation of the vacated position of guarantor of existential meaning after the death of god. Secretly looking into one of the villas of the Residencia Costasol, Prentice gives this chilling description:

> Shielding my eyes from the sunlight, I gazed into one of the darkened lounges. A three-dimensional replica of a painting by Edward Hopper was visible below the awning. The residents, two middle-aged men and a woman in her thirties, sat in the silent room, their faces lit by the trembling glow of a television screen. No expression touched their eyes, as if the dim shadows on the hessian walls around them had long become a satisfactory substitute for thought. (*CN* 215)

Evoking Plato's allegory of the cave as well as Paul Virilio's (2009: 68 f, 2012: 31, passim) notion of the media-generated 'false day', Prentice's account can be read as a powerful image of *alienation*. It seems to me that this, ultimately, is the critical point of convergence of the various impairments exhibited by the residents. They are deeply alienated – from the world, from others, from themselves – a fact that is also expressed through the frequent use of metaphors of sleep ("[w]hen you think of the Costasol complex think of the Sleeping Beauty" [*CN* 213]) and through the portrayal of the residents as, for instance, being afflicted with "an amnesia of self", as existing only as "the ghosts of themselves", or as having "lines of fatigue in [their] faces that have nothing to do with age or tiredness" (*CN* 262, 75, 10).[12] *Cocaine Nights* can be read, in Gasiorek's words, as a veritable "stud[y] in alienation", depicting "an alienated world as capitalism's terminal zone" (2005: 21, 174). It is in light of this alienation consumer capitalism gives rise to that Bobby Crawford's reference to the Residencia Costasol as "a prison" and his observation that "[w]e're building prisons all over the world and calling them luxury condos" (*CN* 220) have to be read. Ballard's leisure society of the Spanish coast thus turns out to be a grim travesty of the Land of Cockaigne, a space in which the capitalist 'overcoding' (Deleuze and Guattari 1987) of utopia with its flattening and immobilizing forces produces a paralyzed and apathetic people similar to Nietzsche's (2006: 9 f) 'last men'

---

[12] It should be added that, as in some of Ballard's other works, the characters of *Cocaine Nights* to some extent actually *welcome* their anonymity and isolation, so that once again, two incompatible discourses clash here. Yet, this very attitude can of course itself be contemplated as a form or effect of alienation.

(sic). This similarity extends beyond lethargy and ennui. Indeed, the inertia of the novel's characters can be understood as both symptom and symbol of a much deeper, socio-political malaise, connected in theoretical discourse with the figure of the last man (sic).

One thing the text repeatedly emphasizes is that the Costa del Sol has effectively become "an eventless world", in which "nothing [will] ever happen again" (*CN* 33, 75). In fact, time itself seems to have come to a standstill: Prentice muses that "time ha[s] died in the Residencia Costasol" and speaks of "the timelessness of a world beyond boredom, with no past, no future and a diminishing present. [...] Nothing could ever happen in this affectless realm, where entropic drift calmed the surfaces of a thousand swimming pools."[13] (*CN* 224, 35) I would argue that the insistence with which the novel returns to these notions of time- and eventlessness – underscored throughout the text by an imagery of completely smooth and undisturbed pool surfaces as well as by the recurring emphasis on the absolute silence governing the coast – strongly suggests a larger significance and context, which, in my opinion, can only be the 'end of history'.[14] This theorem was the subject of fierce debate in the early and mid-1990s and *Cocaine Nights*, published as it was in 1996, seems to me to be part of this debate.

Its origins, of course, lie elsewhere: in the works of Hegel and Marx and the interpretation of them in the 1930s by the Russian-born French philosopher Alexandre Kojève. Some of the latter's ideas echo powerfully in Ballard's novel. In a long footnote to his lectures on Hegel's *Phenomenology of Spirit*, held in Paris between 1933 and 1939 in front of an audience that included Georges Bataille, Jacques Lacan, Jean-Paul Sartre, Maurice Merleau-Ponty, André Breton, and Pierre Klossowski, Kojève for one thing shifts the locale of the end of history from the Prussian state, where Hegel localized it, to America, and for another to some extent reinterprets this 'event'.[15] Whereas for Hegel (1978), who saw world history as a continuous progress towards 'the Absolute' driven by reason (specifically, by its 'cunning'), the end of history marked the final self-realization of 'the Spirit' and the resolution of all conflicts in an ideal social order, Kojève was rather less sanguine. Since the essence of man (sic), according to the French philoso-

---

[13] The mention made of entropy in this passage of course also hints at a 'winding down' of time and history.

[14] For an informative investigation of this notion, cf. Niethammer 1994.

[15] The fact that, in the course of their careers, both Hegel and Kojève revised their identification of the 'destination' of the historical process – the former first recognized it in Napoleonic France before shifting it to Prussia, while the latter (1980: 158n6 – 162n6) changed it first from France to Stalinist Russia, then back to the First French Empire, then to the USA, and finally to Japan – reveals how much such diagnoses are products of historical circumstance.

pher, is "Action negating the given", the termination of history, understood as the end of this dialectical work of negation and the 'struggle for recognition' between masters and slaves, can only mean "the definitive annihilation of Man [sic] properly so-called" (1980: 158n6, 159n6) and hence a (re-)animalization of man (sic). Considering "the 'American way of life' [...] the type of life specific to the post-historical period, the actual presence of the United States in the World prefiguring the 'eternal present' future of all of humanity" (1980: 161n6), Kojève predicted a future of trivial frivolity and ennui, in which art, love and play would lose all significance and become 'natural' again, and in which philosophy and discourse would disappear all together.[16]

It would seem that it is this future that Ballard's *Cocaine Nights* delineates. The novel's characters are living in the eternal present the French thinker foresaw and have effectively become the "post-historical animals of the species *Homo sapiens*" Kojève announced, living "amidst abundance and complete security", being no longer truly happy but merely "*content*" (Kojève 1980: 159n6). The overall image of total stasis, the residents' lack of emotion and relationship, their life on "the far side of boredom", deprived of any conflict and significance, the complete absence of art, culture, thought and philosophy – "[t]he only real philosophers left are the police" (*CN* 177, 117), one character tellingly declares – even the omnipresent silence, almost heralding the loss of human language Kojève expects, all point to a Kojèvian state of *posthistoire*. Like the suburbs in *Millennium People*, then, *Cocaine Nights*' Costa del Sol clearly emerges as "one of the end-states of history" (*MP* 91).

In response to the fall of the Berlin Wall in 1989 and the ensuing dissolution of the Soviet Union, the discourse of the end of history rose to prominence again in the 1990s,[17] and it is this that marks the historico-cultural horizon of Ballard's text. In fact, the end of history as it manifests itself in philosophical-cultural discourse in this decade is not only derived from Kojève's thought, but also from an earlier historico-cultural moment. Already in the 1950s, following the death of Stalin, Khrushchev's 'secret speech', and anti-regime protests and revolts in several Eastern European countries, and against the background of the optimism of the Eisenhower era, numerous scholars and commentators, most notably Daniel

---

[16] In the 1960s, the conservative German philosopher Arnold Gehlen expressed a somewhat related view of the end of history (cf. Niethammer 1994: 10 ff).

[17] A more general crisis of temporality and historicity which has come to be seen as a defining characteristic of postmodernity was, however, already diagnosed in the late 1970s and early 80s (cf. Lyotard 1984; Jameson 1991: 1–54). In this context, cf. also Ballard's fascinating remarks on time and history in the introduction to *Crash*, including his sense that "[i]ncreasingly, our concepts of past, present and future are being forced to revise themselves" (*C* n.pag.).

Bell, had proclaimed the 'end of ideology' and/or the 'end of utopia'. Bell argued that in view of the failures and horrors of Soviet communism and the prosperity of the Western liberal capitalist democracies, "the old passions [were] spent", "the old politico-economic radicalism [...] ha[d] lost its meaning", and that therefore "the ideological age ha[d] ended" (2001: 404, 403). Even though there was, among younger intellectuals, "a restless search for a new intellectual radicalism" (Bell 2001: 404), nothing could be found. All of this, of course, changed in the following decade, when history, ideology and utopia 'returned' with a vengeance. For some time, political struggle and idealism seemed here to stay. Yet, 'after the orgy', as Baudrillard (1993c: 3) has it, that is, in the 'liberated'/'liberalized' postmodern world, and after the collapse of communism, history to many thinkers in the 1990s seemed once more, and this time irrevocably, over. Thus, the neo-conservative political scientist Francis Fukuyama, one of the most prominent proponents of the end-of-history thesis, boldly declared the "unabashed victory of economic and political liberalism" (1989: 3). "[T]he triumph of the West, of the Western *idea*", Fukuyama argued, was "evident [...] in the total exhaustion of viable systematic alternatives to Western liberalism" and the plain fact that "the *ideal* of liberal democracy could not be improved upon" (1989: 3, 1992: xi).[18] Since fascism and communism were defeated and religion and nationalism represented no serious alternative ideologies but only "irrational forms" (1992: 207) of the desire for recognition, capitalist liberal democracy had to be considered as the winner of the world-historical ideological struggle and therefore signaled the end of history. Drawing on Hegel and Kojève – Fukuyama speaks of "a new, synthetic philosopher named Hegel-Kojève" (1992: 144) – as well as Plato's theory of the soul, Fukuyama proposed a teleological view of history according to which what he (1992: 204) sees as the two motors of history, modern natural science on the one hand and the struggle for recognition on the other, had finally brought about the satisfaction of all material needs through capitalism in the realm of economics and the satisfaction of the desire for recognition through universal and equal recognition guaranteed by liberal democracy in the realm of politics. Fukuyama concluded that the "Universal History of mankind" would culminate in a "universal and homogeneous state" (1992: 48, 204) – a term adopted from Kojève – so that all that remained, according to a distinctly neo-

---

[18] As Russell Jacoby (1999: 8f) points out, despite Fukuyama's declared intention to somewhat distance himself from Bell, he nevertheless defends a very similar proposition, even – for example in his talk of an 'exhaustion' of ideologies – echoing Bell's words.

imperial logic, was for 'the rest' to catch up with 'the West' (Hall 1996) in their inevitable evolution towards economic and political liberalism.[19]

Very similar to Bell, Raymond Aron, Seymour Martin Lipset and other conservatives in the 1950s, Fukuyama thus hailed the end of history and ideology as a victory for capitalism and the universal values of liberal humanism. Yet, by far not all intellectuals shared his optimism. In fact, in an early essay, which predates the revolutions in the East and in which he formulated his thesis of the end of history for the first time, Fukuyama himself – somewhat like Bell – had adopted a more ambivalent attitude. Tellingly, the title of this article contained a question mark – "The End of History?" – that would disappear from that of his book-length study published three years later. In a passage of the essay that recalls Kojève's account of *posthistoire* and that resonates powerfully with Ballard's portrayal of the Spanish coast, Fukuyama predicts "centuries of boredom" and asserts:

> The end of history will be a very sad time. The struggle for recognition, the willingness to risk one's life for a purely abstract goal, the worldwide ideological struggle that called forth daring, courage, imagination, and idealism, will be replaced by economic calculation, the endless solving of technical problems, environmental concerns, and the satisfaction of sophisticated consumer demands. In the post-historical period there will be neither art nor philosophy, just the perpetual caretaking of the museum of human history. (1989: 18)

Many thinkers on the left shared the sense that with the events of 1989/90, history had been irreversibly ruptured or ended, and, predictably, were far from cheerful. Thus, Perry Anderson writes:

> Ideologically, the novelty of the present situation stands out in historical view. [...] For the first time since the Reformation, there are no longer any significant oppositions – that is, systematic rival outlooks – within the thought-world of the West; and scarcely any on a world scale either, if we discount religious doctrines as largely inoperative archaisms [...]. Whatever limitations persist to its practice, neo-liberalism as a set of principles rules undivided across the globe: the most successful ideology in world history. (2000: 13)

In the face of this situation, Anderson concludes, "[t]he only starting-point for a realistic Left today is a lucid registration of historical defeat", "a lucid recognition of the nature and triumph of the system, without either adaptation or self-

---

19 The significance of Fukuyama's study as a philosophical diagnosis of the times, specifically of the 'postcommunist situation', has been emphasized, among others, by Peter Sloterdijk (2010: 36ff). For an elaborate critique of Fukuyama's argument, cf. e.g. Derrida 2006: 61–95. Dean MacCannell (1992: 61ff) interprets the discourse of the end of history as another instance of the capitalist neo-cannibalism discussed above.

deception, but also without any belief in the chance of an alternative to it" (2000: 12, 9n5).

While, as I argue, Ballard's entire oeuvre can be read as an acute reaction to the unprecedented expansion of capital in the late 20th and early 21st century and the concomitant annulment of received forms of critique and resistance, these developments and the awareness of them intensified to a considerable degree after the events of 1989/90, and this intensification forms the more specific historico-cultural horizon of the novels *Cocaine Nights* and *Super-Cannes*. The overwhelming impression, particularly on the left, of a "universal triumph of capital" and a total "cancellation of political alternatives" (Anderson 1998: 91, 92) as expressed in the discourse of the end of history echoes throughout the two texts. Thus, in the former, a conversation between Prentice and the psychiatrist Irwin Sanger characterizes the present historical moment in terms of "a final goodbye to wars and ideologies" and as one in which hardly anyone can muster the "vast effort of imaginative and emotional commitment" demanded by religion anymore and in which politics has become "a pastime for a professional caste", "fail[ing] to excite the rest of us" (*CN* 180). Similarly, Bobby Crawford maintains that religions and their symbols are "as dead as a line of totem poles" and that "[p]olitics is over, [...] it doesn't touch the public imagination any longer" (*CN* 245).[20]

Beyond the general thematic of the end of history, the novel's radicalized vision of 'post-political' or 'post-democratic' (Crouch 2005) apathy, paralysis and exhaustion can arguably be contextualized even more specifically. After all, the 1990s was also the decade that saw the development of 'New Labour' and the 'Third Way'. The term 'New Labour' was first introduced by Tony Blair in 1994, the same year he was elected leader of his party, and subsequently became the slogan for the ensuing restyling of the party's political philosophy, enshrined, for example, in the 1996 manifesto *New Labour, New Life for Britain* (Labour Party 1996). The party's new 'center-left' approach to politics was heavily influenced by sociologist Anthony Giddens' (1994, 1998) argument that the lack of a viable systemic alternative to liberal capitalism and the concomitant obsolescence of the old political fronts of left and right called for a Third Way 'beyond left and right' in politics. To many critics, this doctrine of the Third Way was not much more than a neo-liberalism with a human face (or even mask), and its espousal by the Labour Party effectively signaled the disappearance of a socialist

---

[20] The fact that the otherwise antagonistic characters of Sanger and Crawford agree on this characterization makes it even more compelling.

alternative in Britain's political landscape and thus the final victory for the neo-liberal consensus. As Perry Anderson writes:

> Ideologically, the neo-liberal consensus has found a new point of stabilization in the 'Third Way' of the Clinton-Blair regimes. [...] The hard core of government policies remains further pursuit of the Reagan-Thatcher legacy, on occasion with measures their predecessors did not dare enact [...]. But it is now carefully surrounded with subsidiary concessions and softer rhetoric. The effect of this combination, currently being diffused throughout Europe, is to suppress the conflictual potential of the pioneering regimes of the radical right, and kill off opposition to neo-liberal hegemony more completely. [...] For the quietus to European social-democracy or the memory of the New Deal to be consummated, governments of the Centre-Left were indispensable. In this sense, adapting Lenin's maxim that 'the democratic republic is the ideal political shell of capitalism', we could say that the Third Way is the best ideological shell of neo-liberalism today. (2000: 7; cf. also Hall 2003)

By 2000, the year *Super-Cannes* was published, this development was clearly attested by the increasing implementation of essentially neo-liberal policy by the newly elected social democratic governments in several West European states. It seems to me that this hollowing-out of socialism, especially in Britain, constitutes the historical background for the hyperbolic portraits of the end of history and politics in *Cocaine Nights* and *Super-Cannes*. In an interview conducted in 1998, Ballard himself explicitly refers to these issues and does so in a way that chimes with the thematic of the end of history in a remarkably distinct manner. In the interview, Ballard acknowledges having felt "a distinct pain" at the collapse of the Berlin Wall and the end of the "heroic experimen[t]" of communism and elaborates:

> Bourgeois life has triumphed, and the suburbanisation of the planet [a favorite phrase of Ballard's] and the universal acceptance of the shopping mall have now virtually put an end to politics. What we have is the commodification of everything, including ideologies, and government by advertising agency – as in Blair's New Britain. (in Zinik 2012: 356f)

On a metaphorical level, the end of history is also expressed in the ubiquitous whiteness of the novels' worlds. Of course, white is in fact the dominating color of most leisure retreats on the Costa del Sol and of the business park of Sophia-Antipolis, on which *Super-Cannes*' Eden-Olympia is modeled. Yet, by means of their representation in the texts, these actual 'whitescapes' are endowed with (additional) signifying function: when Prentice is reminded by the white-walled structures of the coast of the "architecture dedicated to the abolition of time" of Paolo Soleri's experimental town in Arcosanti, Arizona, when he compares them to "blocks of time that ha[ve] crystallized beside the road"[21] and describes them as "immobile as chalk tombs in their whiteness" (*CN* 34, 75, 276), or when Crawford reminds him that "white is the colour of silence" (*CN* 209), it becomes clear that the buildings' white exteriors are also figurations of the newly 'blank slate' of history, on which nothing will ever again be written. In addition to that, the omnipresent and immaculate white surfaces may also be taken to symbolize the friction- and tensionless ennui of life after the end of history, what Baudrillard has referred to as the "boredom of paradise" (2005: 145). Interestingly, Baudrillard, too, uses an imagery of whiteness to characterize the sterile world after the termination of history: "we are doomed [...] to a complete aseptic whiteness." (1993c: 50) It is certainly no coincidence that at one point in *Super-Cannes*, the renegade psychiatrist Wilder Penrose gazes at the white walls surrounding him "searching for a blemish" (*SC* 257). The spotless whiteness of the novels' spaces thus points us to "the crisis of an achieved utopia" deprived of all negativity, to the fact that its realization is only ever paradoxical or "parodic" (Baudrillard 1999: 77, 1994f: 52): "We mustn't believe we are living the realization of some evil utopia – we are living the realization of utopia, period." (Baudrillard 2008: 86) According to the somewhat neo-Hegelian logic underlying the discourse of the end of history as it manifests itself in the works of both Ballard and Baudrillard, with the disappearance of an outside or other to the system which the realization/end of history and utopia entails and the consequent end of all major conflicts, life is reduced in all of its dimensions – politically, culturally, mentally – to a monotonous and static tedium.[22]

What *Cocaine Nights* ultimately stages, then, is the failure of what Jürgen Habermas (1990, 1997) has termed 'the project of modernity'. If modernity is marked by a "maelstrom of perpetual disintegration and renewal" (Berman 1983: 15), if it is "the epoch that lives for the future, that opens itself up to the novelty of the future" (Habermas 1990: 5), and if its 'project' is therefore centered on the idea of individual and collective autonomy, Ballard's novel unmistakably rings its death knell – for any notions of emancipated subjectivity, rational progress and political responsibility have no place in its world, a world in which, according to Crawford, "the late twentieth century ran into the buffers" (*CN* 235).[23] What looms at the end of history here are not the enlightened citizen and the

---

[21] This phrase distinctly recalls Ballard's earlier novel *The Crystal World*, in which, however, the 'crystallization' is presented in much more positive terms.
[22] The theme of the complete erasure of negativity is even more prevalent in *Super-Cannes* and will therefore be discussed in more detail in the next section.
[23] Gasiorek makes a similar point when he argues that the novel is "preoccupied with modernity's failure to deliver its emancipatory promises" (2005: 21).

integrated, democratic community based on communicative rationality (Habermas 2004a, 2004b), but rather the alienated, apathetic vacationer and social fragmentation and anomie. On Ballard's Costa del Sol, the project of modernity will never be completed, or rather, has paradoxically obliterated itself through its very realization. The end of history and utopia depicted in the novel thus points to a "paradoxical state of affairs, which is simultaneously the complete actualization of an idea, the perfect realization of the whole tendency of modernity, and the negation of that idea and that tendency, their annihilation by virtue of their very success" (Baudrillard 1993c: 10).

The novel's coast can thus be read, not so much – or at least not only or even primarily – as the result of extrapolation, but as a hyperbolic reference to the 1990s' (Western) world after the end of history, utopia, ideology and politics, marked by a complete "saturation of social existence by capitalist logics" and lingering on in "an eternal present, [in which] no imaginable alternative exists, and the dream of revolutionising socio-political life melts into the air" (Gasiorek 2005: 174, 21). Yet, there is one exception in the novel, one community which actually deserves the name: Estrella de Mar. As Prentice immediately notices, this enclave is teeming with life: unlike the somnambulant residents of the other resorts, the people of Estrella de Mar have "returned to life, to a realm of aroused emotions and woken dreams", are "alert and confident", and infused with "optimism and creativity" (*CN* 276, 36, 289). A "civic renewal" (*CN* 254) has taken place here, manifest in countless activities from town council assemblies and church gatherings to sports and film clubs, parties and barbecues. In particular, "a thriving arts community" (*CN* 36) has sprung into being, including theater groups, art studios and exhibitions, craft centers, choral societies, and so forth. Indeed, one character compares the resort to "Chelsea or Greenwich Village in the 1960s" (*CN* 43), thus also indicating a somewhat counter-cultural dimension. Crawford points out that "a real civic pride [is] being born for the first time" (*CN* 279) on the coast. All of this, the novel repeatedly insists, makes Estrella de Mar "a true community", successfully resisting the colossal alienating and "inertial forces" (*CN* 66, 239) of global capitalism.

As Prentice soon discovers, this socio-cultural, political and psychological regeneration is the result of another catastrophic strategy: a wide network of criminal and transgressive activities instigated and coordinated by Bobby Crawford. The central topic of transgression is already implied at the very beginning of the novel. Not only does it open with Prentice's declaration "[c]rossing frontiers is my profession" – a comment whose meaning, in hindsight, is not exhausted within the immediate context of his work as a travel writer – and with his assertion that the "strips of no-man's land between the checkpoints always seem such zones of promise, rich with the possibilities of new lives" (*CN* 9), the territory of Gibraltar, in which his plane lands, is also described as a liminal zone (in-between Britain and Spain), a "frontier town", whose main "business clearly ha[s] nothing to do with peace, order and the regulation of Her Majesty's waves" (*CN* 10). Already at this point, transgression and the associated state of liminality are depicted as enabling and invigorating. Victor Turner, following Arnold van Gennep, famously characterized liminality and liminal persons as "necessarily ambiguous, since this condition and these persons elude or slip through the network of classifications that normally locate states and positions in cultural space", maintaining that "[l]iminal entities are neither here nor there; they are betwixt and between the positions assigned and arrayed by law, custom, convention, and ceremonial" (1995: 95). This characterization rings true with regards to Ballard's novel, in which Gibraltar's liminality anticipates Prentice's imminent passage into the equally liminal space of Estrella de Mar, where the conventional structures of law and order are revealed to be suspended.[24] It is interesting that Turner (1995: 94–130) emphasizes the experience of solidarity and 'communitas' connected with transgression and liminality, for the catastrophic strategy at the heart of *Cocaine Nights* is based on a somewhat similar assumption. The novel's controversial thesis is that in the post-historical period, it is solely through transgressive behavior, through "anything that breaks the rules, sidesteps the social taboos" (*CN* 245), that the paralyzing forces of global capitalism can be overcome and that a sense of community can be created. In Estrella de Mar, Crawford explains, "transgressive behaviour is for the public good"; here, illicit and deviant acts function as "means to an end": a "living community" (*CN* 181, 279). After the end of politics, the novel maintains, such acts are the only way left to "energize people, give them some sense of community" (*CN* 180).[25] Prentice asserts:

> [Crawford] stumbled on the first and last truth about the leisure society, and perhaps all societies. Crime and creativity go together, and always have done. The greater the sense of crime, the greater the civic awareness and richer the civilization. Nothing else binds a community together. It's a strange paradox. (*CN* 281)

---

[24] Of course, the novel's concern with post-historical time points to another kind of limbo, and the holiday many of the coast's residents are on – itself a liminal state – may be read as a metaphor for it.

[25] Such references to the 'energizing' and 'rousing' of people, to "provok[ing] [them] and tap[ping] [their] need for strong emotion, quicken[ing] the nervous system and jump[ing] the synapses deadened by leisure and inaction" and in this way "returning [people] to their true selves" (*CN* 180, 240), once again present a discourse we already encountered in our discussion of *Crash*.

Thus, Crawford's subversive re-reading of history through the lens of delinquency – "[n]ame me a time", he challenges Prentice, "when civic pride and the arts both flourished and there wasn't extensive crime" (*CN* 261) – yields a strategy for countering the social and psychological inertia brought about by the unrivalled reign of capitalism. In light of the focus of this reading on the novel's staging of the end of history, it is therefore only appropriate that Prentice links Crawford's unlawful actions with the feeling that "the clocks [...] begin to race again" (*CN* 266).

Hence, *Cocaine Nights* is clearly informed by and part of what Chris Jenks (2003: 92), especially with reference to Bataille and Foucault, has termed the 'transgressive turn' in contemporary thought. In the novel, the characters' indulgence in transgression is consistently coded in terms of a 'willed psychopathy', a notion that would remain a principal concern for Ballard in all his subsequent novels. In fact, with their explicit and extended preoccupation with madness, *Cocaine Nights* and the succeeding works *Super-Cannes*, *Millennium People* and *Kingdom Come* together may be considered as marking the point of culmination of an ongoing interest in the subject that can be traced throughout Ballard's entire oeuvre, right back to such early stories as "The Overloaded Man" or "The Insane Ones". There are two sides to this interest: on the one hand, an attention to the constructedness of 'madness', and on the other, an exploration of its emancipatory potential. In this, Ballard is, of course, in good company. In particular since the 1960s – the time, in which his literary career took off – numerous thinkers and groups, most notably the anti-psychiatry movement, contested the established conceptualization of madness as a 'mental illness' and challenged the practices of psychiatry and psychoanalysis. As early as 1954, Michel Foucault (1976) confronted dominant medical paradigms by arguing for a phenomenological analysis of mental illness, aiming at a non-objectifying, intersubjective *understanding* of it on its own terms, which, he maintained, had to be combined with a materialist reconstruction of what he argued must be its necessarily socio-historical causes. In his subsequent *History of Madness*, published in 1961, Foucault then radicalized his own perspective, no longer merely attributing existing pathologies and deviations to social conditions but questioning the very classification of certain phenomena *as* pathological and deviant. Such classifications, Foucault maintains, themselves have to be recognized as social products. In a magisterial reconstruction of the various discursive constructions of madness throughout history, Foucault shows that it is only in the 17th and 18th century, during the age of the Enlightenment, that "[t]he caesura that establishes the distance between reason and non-reason" (2006: xxviii), which already loomed on the horizon of Renaissance humanism, is fully instituted. Only on the basis of this division, according to Foucault, could the sovereign rational subject erect its unbounded reign. Its very constitution is based on the exclusion of the other of madness, now conceived essentially as unreason – an exclusion that can be discerned on numerous levels: philosophical (Descartes), political (the 'great confinement'), medical, etc. For Foucault, the increasing 'scientification' of psychiatry and the concomitant 'humanization' of its practices through medicalization at the end of the 18th century, when madness comes to be objectified as an illness, are not much more than a subtle continuation and intensification of the practices of domination inaugurated by the Enlightenment. In Foucault's work, madness thus emerges as a historically variable construct, as the result of "a division and a rejection" (1972b: 216).[26]

This idea, shared by thinkers such as Thomas Szasz, R.D. Laing, David Cooper, Gilles Deleuze and Félix Guattari, also informs many of Ballard's texts, which again and again confuse the boundary between sanity and insanity and deconstruct notions of 'normality', frequently featuring highly ambiguous, if not plainly mad psychiatrists, societies which have themselves become insane, so that abnormal behavior comes to seem as a reasonable option – a characteristic notion of antipsychiatry[27] – as well as, on a more formal level, a narrative perspective that initially portrays central characters as though they were deluded while conventional reality appears as unobjectionable and eventually reverses this perception (Gasiorek 2005: 7). A notable example is certainly *The Atrocity Exhibition*, whose protagonist is both psychiatrist and patient, and who welcomes his psychosis as a way to make sense of the violent chaos of the 1960s as well as of his individual traumata – a strategy that, in a sense, the novel as a whole draws on, too.[28]

Cocaine Nights similarly subverts the binary opposition of the normal and the insane, represented by the antagonists Dr. Sanger and Crawford. Here, too, the psychiatrist, who is morally compromised because he exploits his position in order to have sexual relationships with his female patients, does not present a stable sense of normalcy. Indeed, one character at one point refers to him as "the one mad person in the whole of Estrella de Mar" (*CN* 64), an impression apparently confirmed by a later scene, in which the absconding of one of his patients fully overturns his mental balance, leaving him, in what is evidently a clas-

---

[26] For another historical overview – and one that does not always concord with Foucault's, especially with regards to his thesis of a 'great confinement' – cf. Porter 1987 and 2003.

[27] Laing, for instance, declares: "The texture of the fabric of [our] socially shared hallucinations is what we call reality, and our collusive madness is what we call sanity." (1967: 73) Ballard echoes such anti-psychiatric notions almost verbatim when, in an interview, he asserts that we are now living in "a paradoxical realm where the psychopath is the only person who can imagine – who is capable of imagining – sanity, of conceiving what sanity is" (in Revell 1984b: 44).

[28] As was already observed, this, of course, is part of Ballard's Surrealist heritage (cf. *AE* 139), recalling, for example, Salvador Dalí's 'paranoiac-critical method' (Luckhurst 1997: 92f).

sical image of derangement, "[m]urmuring to himself, [...] slowly clapping his hands at the silent trees" (*CN* 283). In *Cocaine Nights*, and even more so in Ballard's other late novels, this decentering of 'sanity' is underscored by a textual strategy consisting in a striking proliferation of words derived from the semantic field of 'madness', an excess that connects the concept to so many persons and contexts that it finally loses any definite meaning, turning it into a floating signifier, nothing but an empty shell. Thus, all these works profoundly destabilize the category of madness; it is revealed as the result of an ultimately arbitrary division and exposed as intimately caught up in 'power-knowledge' relations (cf. Foucault 1979: 27). In these texts, madness emerges as not much more than a discursive artifact fashioned by power to legitimize its own hegemonic constructions of social reality, allowing it to denounce any deviance from and challenge to the established norms of bourgeois rationality. It is in this sense that, in *Millennium People*, one must read the narrator's prediction that after the end of the middle-class uprising, "[t]he kingdom of the double yellow line [will] be restored, and *the realm of sanity* and exorbitant school fees [will] return" (*MP* 229, emphasis added). As Szasz puts it: "what people now call mental illnesses are, for the most part, *communications* expressing unacceptable ideas, often framed in an unusual idiom" (1991: 19). It is no wonder, then, that Ballard's Sanger "find[s] it difficult to talk to Crawford" (*CN* 283).

Cocaine Nights continually casts the opposition between the two men in terms of different 'drugs', with cannabis and cocaine on the one hand and Largactil and Prozac on the other. In an anti-psychiatric vein, the novel frequently equates both kinds of drugs, suggesting that the latter are simply "the drugs that society approves" (*CN* 141), and frames the opposition in terms of contrasting ideologies and questions of power. Repeatedly, different characters suggest that Sanger's, not Crawford's, are "the really dangerous drugs" (*CN* 131) and that the actual difference between the two is the one between being put "under house arrest inside [one's] own hea[d]" by the "men in white coats who know best", effectively becoming "a prisoner of the medical profession's good intentions" (*CN* 199f, 208, 268), and "freedom, the right to be a crashed-out bar-kook" in "a free and unrooted world" "where moral judgements [are] never made" (*CN* 200, 268). While the novel never fully endorses such a position,[29] the view that psychiatric practice constitutes an exercise of power and

---

[29] I would argue that in some instances, Ballard even consciously exaggerates this discourse in order to expose and criticize its underlying Romantic naivety, as in the following excerpt: "Bibi was a free spirit – her best friends were acid and cocaine. When she took acid she made us part of her dreams. Sanger and the Hollingers reached inside her head and took out the small white bird. They broke its wings, closed the cage again and said to everyone: 'Bibi is happy.'" (*CN* 141)

a form of violence, a condensation and intensification of the 'normative violence' that is part of everyday life and 'normal' or 'intelligible' subjecthood (cf. Butler 1999), remains a persistent and accented one.

In *Cocaine Nights*, madness, that is to say, forms of action and speech rejected or abjected by the dominant bourgeois culture, is clearly ascribed with liberatory power: it is what makes possible the overcoming of post-historical paralysis and anomie. Therefore, today, according to Crawford, "the psychopath plays a vital role. He meets the needs of the hour, touches our graceless lives with the only magic we know" (*CN* 271), namely that of transgression. For this reason, Prentice comes to consider Crawford as "the saint as psychopath, or the psychopath as saint" (*CN* 280). Here, too, of course, the novel inscribes itself in a long tradition in the history of thought. Not only was madness quite commonly associated with divine (or demonic) possession in a number of cultures and epochs up until the Renaissance (incl. Christian beliefs in the ecstatic revelations of mystics and saints) (Porter 1987, 2003; Foucault 2006) as well as with the figure of the 'inspired' artist – an idea powerfully revived, after it had been discredited during the Age of Reason, in the Romantic notion of the genius – there is also a long tradition of writers, thinkers and artists who have actively championed madness and transgressive behavior as a potent means to subvert bourgeois-capitalist morality and rationality. This line of thought includes William Blake and the 'Dark Romantics', Edgar Allan Poe, Charles Baudelaire and the Symbolists, Friedrich Nietzsche, Dadaism and Surrealism, Georges Bataille, the writers of the Beat Generation, as well as Foucault and Deleuze. Thus, Foucault speaks of the "fundamental liberty of the madman" (2006: 513),[30] while Deleuze sees

---

In this context, cf. Ballard's (1996q) comments on the subject in his review of Roy Porter's *The Faber Book of Madness* as well as his (in Self 2006: 383f) remarks on Laing in an interview with Will Self. This, however, does not invalidate the novel's critique of psychiatry. One could argue that the fact that the novel continually juxtaposes Sanger and Crawford and their respective discourses and ideologies without ever conclusively settling this debate is meant to provoke attention to another subject position, namely that inhabited by Bibi Jansen and Laurie Fox, the two patients Sanger and Crawford mainly fight about. They, and particularly their bodies, are constantly rewritten by the two men's discourses, while *their* voices, tellingly, are not heard even once in the entire novel. This, it seems to me, must be read as a textual strategy to show up their 'subaltern' status; in this context, it is certainly no coincidence that the division separating the subject positions occupied by the four characters is plainly gendered (cf. Spivak 1988).

30 It should be noted that, while in his *History of Madness*, Foucault still proceeded from the quasi-Nietzschean assumption of a 'truth' of madness unveiling the 'tragic' nature of being, a truth that he saw as having gotten increasingly lost since the Renaissance and particularly since the 'classical age', he later distanced himself from such anthropological assumptions and instead favored a more radical historicism. Cf. his (1972a) explicit self-criticism in *The Archaeology of Knowledge*.

madness as today "testifying all alone for deterritorialization as a universal process" (Deleuze and Guattari 1983: 321). In particular, Ballard's notion of the saintliness of the insane chimes with similar views held by previous thinkers such as Laing's understanding of the schizophrenic as shaman or Bataille's conceptualization of the sacred, as well as with the latter's declaration "I am not a philosopher, but a *saint*, perhaps a madman" (qtd. in Richardson 1998: 1). Of course, Ballard himself has in interviews and elsewhere repeatedly emphasized the significance and potential of madness, claiming, for instance, that "the psychopathic should be preserved as a nature reserve, a last refuge for a certain kind of human freedom" (in Self 2006: 380).

This freedom, regained through transgression and madness, effectively turns Estrella de Mar into a 'carnivalesque' (Bakhtin 1984) and 'heterotopic' (Foucault 1986a) site, a reclaimed 'counter-space' to the surrounding spaces of global capitalism.[31] If Ballard's depiction of the Spanish coast, its spaces, people and lives, is meant as a hyperbolic representation of a world fully conquered by capital, in which history has effectively ended and all utopian aspirations have expired, leaving only paralysis and anomie, then Estrella de Mar clearly signals the possibility of resistance. Yet, this resistance can once again only consist in a catastrophic strategy, involving a spiral of violence.

The novel's portrayal of this strategy, as well as of its main proponent, Bobby Crawford, is an ambivalent one. While many characters, the narrator and, I would argue, by and large the implied author of the text, are essentially sympathetic to Crawford and his actions, he is nevertheless repeatedly viewed in a more critical light. It is mainly through the characters of Dr. Sanger and Paula Hamilton that an alternative moral framework emerges, but Prentice, too, on more than one occasion questions Crawford's ideas on social regeneration, debunking them as mere "rhetoric", "an amalgam of alarmist best-sellers, *Economist* think-pieces and his own obsessive intuitions", which is used to justify what in truth is nothing but a "criminal conspiracy" (*CN* 240, 219, 298) and a playing out of Crawford's personal fantasies and desires – in fact, the novel implies that his philosophy of transgression may largely be traced back to (traumatic) childhood experiences (*CN* 246). In addition, a rich imagery drawn from the field of imperialism, especially militarism and evangelism, that appears in connection with Crawford – he is, for example, frequently compared to "a young district commissioner in the days of Empire", who is filled with "a strange missionary fervour" (*CN* 218, 219) – suggests, as Baxter argues, that "Crawford advances

---

[31] It seems to me that the most paradigmatic carnivalesque and heterotopic space in Ballard's fiction is the eponymous building in his novel *High-Rise*.

a project of cultural and psychological decolonisation which is, in actuality, a reverse process of colonisation" (2009: 196), an argument for which Crawford's military past provides further support.

And yet, Crawford's project cannot be reduced to a mere "psychopathology of imperialism", just as the notion of 'community' in the text should not be discarded as nothing but "a euphemism for a network of corruption and exploitation" (Baxter 2009: 196, 2008: 100). On the whole, I see the novel as being much more ambivalent than critics such as Baxter acknowledge. Among other things, this ambivalence results from the actual sense of community felt by the residents of Estrella de Mar, the fact that 'crime' and 'victimhood' are not perceived as such by the people involved (*CN* 304), the text's repeated emphasis on Crawford's "idealism", his "selfless commitment" (*CN* 248, 254) to his fellow residents and his genuine desire to help everyone (*CN* 280), the fact that his detractors are themselves highly ambiguous, morally questionable characters, and the fact that even *these* concede that despite all, Crawford is (in the case of Sanger) or may be (in the case of Hamilton) a force for good (*CN* 176, 179 ff, 293). As in many of Ballard's other works, the behavior of the novel's protagonists is largely overdetermined, diverse discourses are overlaid, and different positions, arguments and evaluations constantly cancel each other out, creating a finally irreducible ambivalence or, indeed, polyvalence.

Even the meaning of the frequent religious similes and metaphors is ultimately ambiguous, for in light of Crawford's belief in the vital role of deviant and transgressive behavior, they may not (only) point us towards his own colonizing ambitions, but to the fact that a different conception of 'religion' might be at stake here, one that is rather close to that developed by Georges Bataille. For Bataille, "[r]eligion is the satisfaction that a society gives to the use of excess resources, or rather to their destruction" (2007: 120), and consequently, all forms of 'expenditure', such as transgression, eroticism, violence, madness, and festivals, are considered as constituting the essence of the 'sacred'.[32] Tellingly, Bataille sees such forms as indispensable for any true community, which, in his eyes, always occurs when social rules and laws are broken and 'profane', capitalist society is undone. The paradigm for this, according to Bataille, is the sacrifice, and interestingly, the death of the Hollingers in Ballard's novel fulfills a very similar function and is at one point actually referred to as a "sacrifice" (*CN* 324). In view of Bataille's (e.g. 2007: 45–61) repeated discussion of the Aztecs as a civilization that, unlike our own, had a genuine place for the sacred in the form of sacrifice, it is furthermore telling that the charred ruin of the Hollinger mansion is once

---

[32] Cf. the more detailed discussion of Bataille's thought in chapter 2.

likened to "the remains of a funeral pyre on a Central American mesa" (*CN* 35). To some extent, the community of Estrella de Mar, based as it is on an elaborate economy of transgression, seems to be a recreation of the kind of society that Bataille approves of.[33] Of course, the element of collective loss and the restoration of 'intimacy' or 'continuity' that is crucial to Bataille's conception of community is largely absent from Ballard's novel, but the correspondences are nevertheless striking. The fact that most of the religious imagery in the text is derived from a Christian context, too, does not properly fit into the Bataillean framework – after all, Bataille, following Max Weber, considers Christianity as a major force in the exclusion of the 'sacred' and the 'profanation' of the world[34] – yet, Crawford is also compared to a shaman and to Zoroaster (*CN* 310, 289), comparisons that call to mind Bataille[35] and Nietzsche (2006) and thus evoke alternative horizons of meaning to the one of aggressive evangelism and imperialism highlighted by Baxter.

In this regard, too, then, *Cocaine Nights* remains deeply ambivalent. Like the other works discussed in this study, the novel unfolds a universe of Nietzschean 'dangerous' thought, in which, in the protagonist's words, "[t]here's a different set of social conventions" (*CN* 304) and all received moral coordinates are critically unhinged. This revaluation of values presents a radical challenge to readers, a challenge to which some critics respond by a moralistic reading that stabilizes the faltering coordinates. Thus, in Baxter's interpretation, Prentice's experiences in Estrella de Mar are ultimately made into an unambiguous story of "moral corruption" and the novel as a whole turns out to be an almost cautionary tale about an "erosion of moral values which Ballard encourages the reader to challenge" (2009: 196, 193). While Baxter is generally very perceptive of the many complexities of Ballard's works, her readings in the end occasionally erase the genuine subversive dimension of the texts. I have, therefore, proposed the concept of the 'catastrophic strategy' as a tool for readings that attempt to do

---

[33] Beyond that, there are also unmistakable parallels with other theories considering violence as constitutive of human community such as Girard's (1989, 2005) concept of the 'scapegoat mechanism', in which murder ends the violent spiral of 'mimetic desire', as well as Freud's (1999) notion of the original murder of the tyrannical 'primal father' by the 'primal horde'. With regards to the latter, cf. especially the fundamental role of collective guilt in the novel, whose significance Freud emphasizes, too, and the fact that the people of Estrella de Mar are at one point referred to as a "clan" and a "tribe" and that the Hollinger house is once compared to a "tribal totem" (*CN* 60, 324, 207). For other discussions of sacrifice in the novel, which come to different conclusions, cf. Baxter 2008: 101f; Tew 2008: 108f.

[34] It should, however, be noted that Bataille, too, nonetheless frequently describes the experience of continuity in a terminology clearly derived from Christian mysticism.

[35] On Bataille and shamanism, cf. Richardson 1994: 112ff.

justice to this politically significant dimension by not eliminating the fundamental ambivalence of Ballard's works.

This tool leads me to a conclusion that is rather close to the one arrived at by Paddy in his discussion of *Super-Cannes*, namely that "the real danger" in *Cocaine Nights* "is not the exercise of violence itself, but the way it has been systemized and controlled" (2012: 192). For the novel repeatedly indicates that Crawford's subversive strategy is, to use again Deleuze and Guattari's (1987) terminology, ultimately 'overcoded' and contained by the powers of capital. These are represented in the novel by the character of Elizabeth Shand and her associates, who effectively harness Crawford's actions to a capitalist logic, utilizing the psychological and social revitalization he initiates as an opportunity to establish ever new circuits of profit. To them, the overcoming of paralysis means above all "a boost to business" and "a fortune to be made" (*CN* 229, 211) through both legal and illegal commercial operations. When Prentice, referring to a comment by Shand on his deviance and to the fact that he is being watched by her suspicious chauffeur, notes that "[d]eviance in Estrella de Mar [is] a commodity under jealous guard" (*CN* 135), this should therefore also be taken quite literally: Estrella de Mar's transgressive activities are finally all "tied up within an insidious capitalist process" (Baxter 2009: 195). Thus, Crawford might have defeated the immobilizing forces of consumer capitalism, but he stands no chance of undermining the system as such, into whose infinitely flexible and adaptive networks he is smoothly integrated. Shand's repeatedly mentioned "steely gaze" (*CN* 252) under which life in Estrella de Mar takes place signifies the panoptic vision and unshakeable grip of power. In one scene, the narrator provides a particularly striking description of Shand: "As she gazed at the scene around her, like a silken cobra sated after digesting a succulent goat, I could almost see the accumulating cash totals flicker past her eyes." (*CN* 290) This, surely, is a remarkable expression of "the nature of the beast" (Lotringer 2007: 11), a powerful image for the predatory, cannibalistic monster of capital.

Another reason why Crawford's project is so easily absorbed into the capitalist system he set out to challenge perhaps lies with the fact that the type of community he recreates through his economy of transgression and the virtues and values he rekindles are essentially those historically coinciding with and to some extent conducive to the rise of capitalism. As Prentice at one point observes, Estrella de Mar, with its local council assemblies, good schools, church gatherings, numerous arts groups and so forth, is at heart deeply "[b]ourgeois" – and Shand agrees that "[i]t's all so earnest and middle-class" (*CN* 130). Prentice notes: "Here, there were no gangs of bored teenagers, no deracinated suburbs where neighbours scarcely knew each other and their only civic loyalties were to the nearest hypermarket and DIY store." (*CN* 66) This, of course, sounds very much like the bourgeois ideal of the 'healthy community' – and there has always been something quasi-fascistic, very stifling and staid about it. What, above all, underlies the countless communitarian activities that develop due to Crawford's regime of transgression is, in effect, a bourgeois work-ethic and ideology of self-realization. As one character remarks with regards to the resort's excessive activity and productivity: "Sometimes I dream of pure idleness, but not a hope. Stand still for a moment and you find yourself roped into a revival of *Waiting for Godot*." (*CN* 43)

It seems to me that, in the end, Ballard's novel is somewhat pulled in two opposite directions: on the one hand, it subscribes to a genuinely postmodern[36] catastrophic strategy of transgression and willed psychopathy, subverting the modern binaries, laws and hierarchies, while on the other, it appears, in the final analysis, to harbor something of a nostalgia for the 'project of modernity' it initially declared dead, since it remains rather devoted to the autonomous subject and since the community that is reestablished by means of this catastrophic strategy assumes a decidedly modernist shape: an "intact and self-sufficient community", in which "[t]ogether [all] begin to thrive" and "find [their] full potential as individuals and as a community" (*CN* 288, 245). At the heart of *Cocaine Nights*, we thus find a profoundly paradoxical dialectic, whereby Crawford's postmodern, trans-political subversive acts are finally driven by a contradictory desire to re-enter bourgeois modernity and re-animate its politics, history, subjectivity, and rational and communicational society (incl. civic responsibility, a functioning public sphere, etc.). It is, then, not least Crawford's inability to initiate a new kind of collectivity[37] that allows for the eventual capitalist overcoding and containment of his resistance. This problem is even more pronounced in *Super-Cannes*, to which I now want to turn.

5.2 The Spectral Reign of Global Capital

With Paul Sinclair, the narrator-protagonist of *Super-Cannes*, we encounter another sleuth-cum-ethnographer. The novel opens with his and his wife Jane's ar-

---

36 Of course, transgression as such is a phenomenon existent in all societies and at all times, even though it can be argued to be a distinctive feature of modernity and "a primary postmodern topic" (Jenks 2003: 8). In Ballard's novel, it is the fact that it arises out of the context of late capitalism and reacts against it that makes it 'postmodern'.
37 For interesting philosophical attempts to re-conceive the notion of 'community' (in the wake of Bataille), cf. e.g. Blanchot 1988 and Nancy 2008.

rival at Eden-Olympia, a fictional business park in the south of France, where Jane is about to take up a position as a pediatrician. While his wife quickly integrates into the busy world of the enclave, Sinclair, recovering from a flying accident and thus having a lot of free time on his hands, soon begins to investigate the "unsolved mystery" (*SC* 4) surrounding the death of Jane's idealistic predecessor David Greenwood, who, inexplicably, set out on a killing spree one morning in late May. In the course of his investigations, Sinclair, like Prentice in *Cocaine Nights*, discovers the truth about the society of Eden-Olympia, a society that, contrary to the one in Ballard's previous novel, is dominated not by leisure but by work. Hosting not only big but "[t]he biggest" international companies (Mitsui, Siemens, Unilever, Sumitomo and many others) and employing over 10,000 people, essentially "a new elite of administrators, *énarques* and scientific entrepreneurs", "the most highly paid professional caste in Europe" (*SC* 15, 5), the business park is a veritable "temple of efficiency", a realm of "ceaseless work" (*SC* 65, 155). According to its neo-liberal ideology, "[f]reedom [is] the right to paid work, while leisure [is] the mark of the shiftless and untalented" (*SC* 46). In fact, as Sinclair observes, with "[w]ork dominat[ing] life in Eden-Olympia [...] and driv[ing] out everything else", the very "concept of leisure [is] dying in the business park, replaced by a grudging puritanism" (*SC* 254, 46). It seems to me that the repeated reference that is made in the text to the emergence of this "rule of the new corporate puritanism" (*SC* 169) points to more than the universalization of the work-ethic. I would argue that beyond this, it suggests, just like the comparison of the business park's professionals to "an order of computer-literate nuns, committed to the sanctity of the workstation and the pieties of the spreadsheet" (*SC* 8), that capitalism is not just, following Max Weber (1958), a secularization of the Protestant faith, but, as Walter Benjamin argues in a posthumously published fragment, by its nature constitutes itself a religious phenomenon, "a pure religious cult", as he writes, "perhaps the most extreme there ever was" (2005: 259).[38]

I want to argue that in its utter dedication to the sacred objects, truths and rituals of the capitalist religion and its manifest multinational, big business character, Eden-Olympia can be read as an embodiment of what the political theorists Michael Hardt and Antonio Negri have called 'Empire'. This is the name they give to the contemporary, genuinely postmodern and global structure of domination, composed of a series of nation-states, transnational corporations and supranational organisms and built on a symbiosis of economic and political power. The two thinkers write:

---

[38] This notion of Benjamin's has recently been picked up by Giorgio Agamben (2007: 80ff).

Along with the global market and global circuits of production has emerged a global order, a new logic and structure of rule – in short, a new form of sovereignty. Empire is the political subject that effectively regulates these global exchanges, the sovereign power that governs the world. (2001: xi)

Unlike the old imperialisms, Empire does not designate an extension of the nation-state, but is decentered and deterritorializing, a network power, whose open frontiers are ever expanding as it "progressively incorporates the entire global realm" (Hardt and Negri 2001: xii). Empire thus signals the 'real subsumption' of global society under capital (cf. Marx 1977: 948–1084), achieved through an unprecedented 'extensive', geographical and 'intensive', domestic expansion of capital (Massumi 1992: 132). As we will see, both dimensions are clearly present in *Super-Cannes*.

Ballard's Eden-Olympia epitomizes Empire. Its tenants evidently inhabit what Manuel Castells (1996: 446f) has referred to as the 'third layer' of the 'space of flows' (Shaviro 2003: 134ff), that is, the segregated, homogeneous space of the global elites. When Wilder Penrose, Eden-Olympia's deviant psychiatrist, declares that "[t]he middle classes have run the world since the French Revolution, but they're now the new proletariat" and asserts that "[i]t's time for another elite to set the agenda", and when another member of this elite refers to herself and her peers as "the vanguard of a new world-aristocracy" (*SC* 97, 115), all of this distinctly chimes with Hardt and Negri's talk of the new "global aristocracies" (2005: 61) and their contention that since "[t]oday nearly all of humanity is to some degree absorbed within or subordinated to the networks of capitalist exploitation" (2001: 43), the concept of the 'proletariat' needs to be redefined (e.g. 2001: 52f).[39] Likewise, the intellectual – rather than physical – nature of the various kinds of work carried out in the business park, exemplified by Penrose's statement that the "raw material processed at Eden-Olympia is high-grade information" (*SC* 29), reflects the transformation at the heart of the dominant productive processes that goes along with the development from monopoly capitalism and imperialism to multinational, 'cognitive capitalism' (Moulier Boutang 2011) and Empire, the shift, that is, from industrial factory labor to what Hardt and Negri (e.g. 2001: 290–294) term 'immaterial labor'. Needless to say, Penrose's contention that this shift automatically entails a clean slate of the business park's corporations since, as he claims, "[c]ompanies here aren't involved with the Third World" (*SC* 28) is nothing but ideology. It is through the poor, industrial town of La Bocca that the novel points to the continuing injustice and inequality

---

[39] The notion of the proletarianization of the middle class already anticipates Ballard's next novel *Millennium People* and will be taken up again in the following chapter.

in the international division of labor, to which, *of course*, Eden-Olympia's multinationals in one way or another contribute (cf. *SC* 11). The dilapidated and impoverished migrant enclave functions as the dark underbelly of the business park, and the radical opposition of these two spaces signals the "ever more extreme separation of a small minority that controls enormous wealth from multitudes that live in poverty at the limit of powerlessness" and thus unmistakably makes clear that the "geographical and racial lines of oppression and exploitation that were established during the era of colonialism and imperialism have in many respects not declined but instead increased exponentially" (Hardt and Negri 2001: 43). As Sinclair observes: "La Bocca was a long way from Cannes, but separated by a universe from Eden-Olympia." (*SC* 152) At the same time, the geographical closeness of the two places seems to confirm Hardt and Negri's argument that "the international divisions and flows of labor and capital have fractured and multiplied", so that the First and Third World, center and periphery, etc. "no longer define an international order but rather have moved closer to one another" (2001: 335, 336). Eden-Olympia and La Bocca hence demonstrate that "Empire is characterized by the close proximity of extremely unequal populations" (Hardt and Negri 2001: 336f), and the fact that it is mainly immigrants who live and work in La Bocca underscores that there are very different kinds of flows beyond those creating the 'ethno-', 'finance-', 'technoscapes', and other landscapes (Appadurai 1996: 27–47) that make up Eden-Olympia, namely the migratory movements of the marginalized, exploited and disenfranchised, which take place under fundamentally different circumstances and conditions from those of capital, goods, information or the global elites and are, indeed, often considered by the latter as an obstacle to the desired flows, therefore requiring intensified regulation.

Hence, the radical difference of the business park on the one hand and Cannes' industrial suburb on the other does not hide the fact that the two are in fact reverse sides of the same coin: global capitalism. Here, then, Ballard's acute political vision once again manifests itself. That Eden-Olympia regularly donates "generous funds" (*SC* 150) for the improvement of the living conditions of the people in La Bocca (especially for the refuge for orphaned and abandoned daughters of migrant workers) only adds to the paradigmatic nature of Ballard's arrangement. These are only 'the two faces of Bill Gates' (Žižek 2009: 19) – or, in fact, of multinational capitalism itself. As Slavoj Žižek points out, such charity, considered from a sober point of view, is really an almost cynical act, "the humanitarian mask hiding the face of economic exploitation" (2009: 19). Eden-Olympia's 'generous' donations may therefore be read as symbolic of the 'help' for the destitute parts and peoples of the world provided by the leaders of Empire, which, in the end, always deflects attention away from the latter's actual responsibility for the miserable situation of the former.[40]

In the novel, La Bocca thus functions as capitalism's abject other, its people, though vital for the functioning of the system, reduced by that system to the status of "waste products destined for expulsion" (Baxter 2008: 104). Already its name, the Italian word for 'mouth', points towards these Bataillean thematics of 'appropriation' and 'excretion', of 'homo-' and 'heterogeneity' (Bataille 1985d, 1985e). In fact, La Bocca appears as the domain of all the heterogeneous elements which had to be excluded from homogeneous capitalist society. This homogeneity manifests itself on various levels in the text. For one thing, it is evident in the conformity of subjectivities. This is most drastically – though, perhaps, a little too simplistically – illustrated by the transformation Sinclair's wife undergoes at Eden-Olympia from an unconventional, adventurous, scruffy and unruly "hippie doctor" and "rebel" (*SC* 39, 43) to her "newfound role as international career physician" and "busy consultant with an eye on her watch" (*SC* 279, 66). The business park, Sinclair observes, has quickly "adopted" Jane, "setting up a branch office inside [her] head" and "stifl[ing] [...] her hunger for freedom" (*SC* 79, 212, 45), and on several occasions, Ballard's protagonist mourns the growing alienation between himself and his wife, who, he observes, is "barely recognizable in trim business suit and court shoes" and soon seems to "merg[e] into the corporate space" (*SC* 39, 54) of Eden-Olympia seamlessly. As Hardt and Negri point out, contemporary capitalist organizations have largely adopted the precepts of postmodernist thought, so that, on one level, their structures and 'culture' no longer rely on binary divisions and practices of exclusion and homogenization. Instead, these corporations appear as "leaders in a very real politics of difference", trusting in "the efficiency and profitability of diversity and multiculturalism" (Hardt and Negri 2001: 153). At the same time, however, all the differences such organizations include within their realm are of course organized in the interests of profit and thus, the multiplicity of identities must on another level always be overcoded and subsumed into the ultimate homogeneity of capitalist subjectivity. This is plainly expressed in Penrose's metaphor of the 'melting pot'. He explains: "There's nothing racist [...]. We're truly multinational – Americans, French, Japanese. Even Russians and east Europeans. [...] We're a melting pot [...]. The solvent now is talent, not wealth or glamour." (*SC* 19) Implicit here is the same problematic dimension that has also led theo-

---

40 Žižek (2009: 19f) also refers to Peter Sloterdijk (2010: 31f) and his use of Bataille's notion of the 'general economy' and posits that such an 'expenditure' of accumulated wealth is furthermore necessary for the postponement of crisis and the reestablishment of balance within the capitalist system.

rists of ethnicity to replace the melting pot as an image for the United States with other metaphors such as the 'mosaic', the 'quilt' or the 'salad bowl' (which, however, never fully get rid of the problem and bring with them other ones instead), namely the eventual 'solving' of all varieties into a larger unity.

Beyond this production of adequate subjectivities, the homogeneity of the capitalist system also finds expression in Eden-Olympia's dream of complete order and total control, an ideal symbolized, among other things, in the recurrent imagery of absolutely calm and undisturbed surfaces of swimming pools and lakes – as Sinclair at one point remarks, "disturbing the surface would probably trigger a full-scale alert" (*SC* 88). To this "excessively ordered world", in which "even nature knows her place" (*SC* 77, 83), contingency is intolerable: one character points out that "[t]here are things Eden-Olympia can't cope with – they key that breaks in the lock, the toilet that backs up, the druggy woman you fall in love with. [...] Eden-Olympia can fight off a billion-dollar takeover bid, but a little dog shit on the shoe leaves it helpless." (*SC* 378) It is, of course, no coincidence that these words are uttered by the security guard Frank Halder and that the business park constitutes a high-security gated community, continuously obsessed "with the invisible intruder in the fortress" (*SC* 257).[41] What all of this brings into sharp focus is what Bataille (1985d) has identified as the essential homogeneity of capitalism as well as fascism[42] and the rather close relation between the two.[43]

The business park thus has more than one trait in common with its namesake in ancient Greek mythology: not only does it represent, just like the mythical mountain, the home of the gods – only that now, it is no longer Zeus and his fellow deities but the very earthly leaders of Empire that decide mankind's destiny. Both also share their dissociation from "the contingent world" (*SC* 370): just as Eden-Olympia's purity and order are never disturbed by even a single drifting leaf (*SC* 9), so Mount Olympus, according to the description given in the *Odyssey*, "stands unmoved": "never rocked by galewinds, never drenched by rains, / nor do the drifting snows assail it, no, the clear air / stretches away without a cloud, and a great radiance / plays across that world" (Homer 2006: 169). Unlike that of Homer, however, Ballard's image is clearly a dystopian one. In fact, his Eden-

---

41 The paragraph quoted here distinctly echoes Ballard's short story "Motel Architecture". Beyond this, the novel's focus on a self-enclosed community characterized by absolute order and functionality also recalls the earlier works *High-Rise* and *Running Wild*.
42 Bataille emphasizes, however, that what he terms 'imperative heterogeneity' plays a much more important role in fascism than in, for example, liberal or monarchical societies (see below).
43 Ballard further explored this topic in his last novel, *Kingdom Come*.

Olympia, "in which virtually every aspect of the individual's life is subject to a routine, all human needs have been anticipated, and the entire social mechanism has been calibrated to minimise friction and disturbance" (Gasiorek 2005: 21), suggests that late capitalism effectively marks the endpoint of the development towards the fully "administered world" (Horkheimer and Adorno 2002: xi) that the thinkers of the Frankfurt School so vehemently warned about.

Finally, similar to *Cocaine Nights*, capitalist homogeneity also manifests itself in the text's representation of space. Like Ballard's previous novel, *Super-Cannes*, too, presents multinational capitalism as a force that increasingly erases all local differences and in this way homogenizes the globe. In this context, the book's third and final part opens with a revealing event: the celebration ceremony held on the occasion of the foundation of "Eden-Olympia Ouest, better known in the international business community as Eden II" (*SC* 355). Sinclair explains: "The future was a second Eden-Olympia, almost twice the size of the original", a big step towards "the planned expansion of Eden-Olympia into a vast urbanization larger than Cannes itself" (*SC* 356, 295). Here, corporate space clones, enlarges and extends itself, and it is certainly no coincidence that the direction of its expansion is westwards (*ouest*); after all, through such related concepts as *translatio studii*, *translatio imperii* and 'Manifest Destiny', the movement of 'civilization' – often an imperial movement – has for many centuries been conceived as a westward one. Thus, it is only fitting that Penrose feels "[p]rogress" to be "palpable" (*SC* 356) at the ceremony and, alluding to John Winthrop's (2003) religious version of the historiographic topos, sees the future as "[a] hundred cities on a hundred hills" (*SC* 357).

In this way, the scene paints the gloomy picture of a triumphant neo-imperialism and thus seems to confirm one character's fear that "[t]he whole world will soon be a business-park colony" (*SC* 344f). This, of course, is precisely the goal Empire aspires to: "Eden-Olympia is the face of the future" (*SC* 254), Penrose proclaims. Shortly after the end of the groundbreaking ceremony, the psychiatrist elatedly declares that "[t]here are times when you feel the wind of history under you wings" (*SC* 362). Penrose here appears as Walter Benjamin's (1969b: 257f) 'angel of history'. Yet, it is an inverted angel, less angel than demon. For whereas Benjamin's figure is looking back into the past, desperately aware of the catastrophic course of history and yearning for redemption, Penrose's face is turned straightforward towards the future, about which he likes to talk so much. Unlike Benjamin's angel, Penrose has no desire to close his wings for contemplation, but instead wants to fly on the winds of history as fast as possible. As he himself explains: "Nothing can overtake us, so why look back into the past?" (*SC* 356) Wielding his rhetoric of 'progress', Penrose is fully ignorant of the fact that this progress is actually a violent "storm", which keeps piling debris that "grows skyward" (Benjamin 1969b: 258).[44]

The wreckage global capitalism keeps piling up is everywhere evident in Ballard's novel. The laying of the groundwork for Eden II, for example, is described in the following terms: "The site-contractors were already at work, clearing the holm oaks and umbrella pines that had endured since Roman times, surviving forest fires and military invasions. Nature, as the new millennium dictated, was giving way for the last time to the tax shelter and the corporate car park." (*SC* 356) What we are being alerted to here is clearly the postmodern 'end of nature'. As Fredric Jameson argues, "[p]ostmodernism is what you have when the modernization process is complete and nature is gone for good." (1991: ix) When, in the process of laying the groundwork, the grass cover is pared away and the granitic marl thus exposed "to a few moments of sunlight before it [is] sealed away for ever under a million tons of cement", or when, in another scene, all the plants in the business park appear "pallid and defeated, the ground beneath them so crammed with electronic ducting that no roots [can] prosper" (*SC* 356, 133), Jameson's claim that "the prodigious new expansion of multinational capital ends up penetrating and colonizing [all] [...] precapitalist enclaves" (1991: 49) is dramatically verified. With the advent of Empire, any outside to the system disappears and the modern dialectic between inside and outside is replaced by "a play of degrees and intensities, of hybridity and artificiality" (Hardt and Negri 2001: 188).

Beyond this death of nature, the totalization of capitalist space and the concomitant homogenization of the globe are still more urgently conveyed through the novel's suggestion of an accelerating disappearance of all singularities in the emerging world system. Like *Cocaine Nights*, *Super-Cannes* unmistakably subscribes to Baudrillard's grim view that the globalization of capital entails a violent erasure of any form of alterity, negativity or singularity. Eden-Olympia clearly represents what the French philosopher describes as "the all-powerful global technostructure", whose defining characteristics are "the supremacy of positivity alone and of technical efficiency, total organization, integral circulation, the equivalence of all exchanges" (2003: 91, 92). The text continuously stages the materialization of this all-encompassing global order through what it depicts as the increasing elimination of "the Riviera of old" (*SC* n.pag.). As one character suggests, "a war [is] on": "Eden-Olympia versus the rest of the Côte" (*SC* 128). The certain winner of this battle is not hard to identify: unstoppable, the homogeniz-

---

[44] The reference to Benjamin is also fitting because, as at the time that his essay was written, 'progress' in the novel appears in the shape of fascism.

ing forces of global capitalism progressively erase the idiosyncratic spatial, architectural and cultural textures of the French coast, thus effectively "reshaping the [entire] geography and character of the Côte d'Azur" (*SC* 133). Hence, more and more, the landscape of the Riviera is being remodeled according to the "drawing board" of corporate planning and the coast in this way turned into "Europe's California" or "silicon valley" (*SC* 224, 128, 5). In a kind of 'synecdochal spiral', this transformation of the old into "the new Riviera" comes to stand in for larger processes signaling the emergence of a "new France" and a "new Europe" (*SC* 126, 5, 93).[45] This change is most evident in the way in which business enclaves and science parks, vast apartment complexes and freeways now dominate the landscape. As opposed to the former spaces of the coast, the novel portrays this new environment as a cold, sterile and artificial one, consisting of all kinds of simulacra, such as "artificial lakes", "simulated nature trails that en[d] abruptly when they [are] no longer visible from the road" and "[o]rnamental pathways" (*SC* 37) that only lead to electricity substations. Appropriately, this "faked-up landscape" is repeatedly compared to "a film set", the crucial point being, of course, that this set "just happens to be real" (*SC* 94, 216). What better image for the age of Baudrillardian hyperreality?

Beyond this, the new buildings of the Riviera bare a conspicuous similarity to the architecture that thinkers like Jameson and Baudrillard have identified as a product and expression of late capitalism. Their "glass" or "mirror curtain-walling" (*SC* 8, 91), for instance, distinctly recalls Jameson's famous analysis of John Portman's Westin Bonaventure Hotel in Los Angeles with its "great reflective glass skin" (1991: 42) repelling the world outside, a structure that, Jameson argues, is a paradigmatic manifestation of postmodern 'hyperspace'. Certainly, Ballard's Eden-Olympia signals such a space as well, aspiring as it does to be "a total space, a complete world" (Jameson 1991: 40). It is only fitting that else-

---

45 In light of the novel's mostly European cast of characters, David Pringle – in a response to a short essay on Ballard on Steven Shaviro's blog – has suggested that *Super-Cannes* can be regarded as Ballard's "Euro-novel" and perhaps even as an "anti-European Union" (in Shaviro 2009: n.pag.) one. This is an interesting idea, especially when considered against the background of the political debates concerning the Maastricht Treaty, the introduction of the Euro, and Europe generally during the Major years and the continued (from the Thatcher era) Euro-skepticism or even Europhobia among large parts of Britain's population, reinforced by such events as the EU's embargo on British beef exports, imposed in reaction to the BSE crisis and effective from 1996 until 2006. In this context, it is certainly telling that England is at one point in the novel referred to as "the village idiot of the new Europe", "[t]he misfit, the holy fool" (*SC* 105). On the whole, however, I would agree with Shaviro that national distinctions become less important in the world of Empire and read the novel as an engagement with global capitalism rather than with (just) Europe.

where in the text, the business park is compared to "a vision of glass and titanium straight from the drawing boards of Richard Neutra and Frank Gehry" and that its buildings are said to "[wear] their ventilation shafts and cable conduits on their external walls" (*SC* 5, 8),[46] an obvious allusion to the Centre Georges Pompidou in Paris: both the Beaubourg, as the French cultural center is also known, and the Gehry house in Santa Monica are discussed by Jameson (1991: 40, 115–118) as further examples of hyperspace.[47] According to the American theorist, all these buildings in their different ways are characterized by the postmodern abolition of the distinction between the inside and the outside and can therefore be considered as perfect spatial analogies of the capitalist world system. The novel's reference to the Beaubourg is furthermore significant if one takes into account Baudrillard's brilliant analysis of it, in which he reads the center as a "[m]onument to the games of mass simulation", whose external architecture signals the age of networks, flows, circuits and acceleration, and which, moreover, presents

> the model of all future forms of controlled socialization: retotalization in a homogeneous space-time of all the dispersed functions of the body and of social life [...], retranscription of all the contradictory currents in terms of integrated circuits. Space-time of a whole operational simulation of social life. (1994e: 61, 67)

In Ballard's Eden-Olympia, this space-time has clearly fully materialized.

When Sinclair at one point describes the expression on his wife's face as "as depthless as the artificial lakes in Eden-Olympia" (*SC* 321), it becomes evident that space and subjectivity are reshaped by global capital according to a similar logic of simulation,[48] performance, functionality and effacement of the distinction between inside and outside (demolishing the 'enclosure' of the centered ego just like the solid walls of bourgeois privacy; cf. Jameson 1991: 115). Again and again, the novel posits a link between the transformation and homogenization of space and that of human identity – here, we once again encounter Soja's (1989: 76–93) 'socio-spatial dialectic' – and generally indicates global capital-

---

[46] In fact, like a good semiotician, the narrator himself reads this architecture as symbolic of late capitalism, interpreting the external tubes and channels as "an open reminder of Eden-Olympia's dedication to company profits and the approval of its shareholders" (*SC* 8).
[47] It should be noted, however, that the three buildings are by no means interchangeable for Jameson. He particularly distinguishes the Gehry house, which he considers to be far more complex and which he ultimately reads, unlike the others, as an attempt at "a new Utopian spatial language" (1991: 128).
[48] In another scene, the narrator refers to the thick layer of cosmetic cream covering his wife's face as "a mask that hid[es] nothing" (*SC* 321).

ism's production of a new type of subjectivity. Pondering the transformation of his wife, Sinclair muses:

> After another six months she would be as institutionalized as any long-term convict, locked inside a virtual cell she called her office. Eden-Olympia demanded a special type of temperament, committed to work rather than to pleasure, to the balance sheet and the drawing board rather than to the brothels and gaming tables of the Old Riviera. (*SC* 81f)

Extinct are thus not just the distinctive buildings and landscapes of the coast, but also its characteristic personalities. From the start, the novel contrasts "[t]he new Côte d'Azur [that] doesn't have time for fun" and that is peopled with conformized, isolated, 'mediatized' and 'securitized' (Hardt and Negri 2012: 14–24) subjectivities bent on nothing but work to "an older Côte d'Azur where the hallowed traditions of crime and social pathology still flourished" (*SC* 103, 83f). In this past, the novel suggests, human subjectivity was still produced along different lines[49] and thus not as completely or effectively adjusted to the demands of capital as in the contemporary era of global capitalism, so that, in place of today's omnipresence of "agentic subjectivities" (Hardt and Negri 2001: 32), there was still room for a host of deviant and unruly identities. The text repeatedly evokes this past through references to renowned writers and artists such as Graham Greene, F. Scott Fitzgerald, Pierre Bonnard, Pablo Picasso, or Henri Matisse, who, at some point during their lives, resided on the Riviera. Sinclair remarks that theirs was "another Riviera, as remote from this futuristic apartment complex [Marina Baie des Anges] as the casino at Monte Carlo was from the temple of Karnak" (*SC* 224). Wistfully, he observes: "Picasso and Matisse have gone, and the business parks have taken their place." (*SC* 103) As the comparison to Monte Carlo and Karnak once again makes clear, the disappearance of the coast of the old writers and painters signals not only the end of the transgression and excess their lifestyle and modernist, avant-garde art stood for, but is also coded in terms of a transition from 'history' and 'civilization' to the age of simulacra and simulation.

Even more than in the case of *Cocaine Nights*, *Super-Cannes*' critique of late capitalism is thus predicated on a series of binary oppositions, whose unambiguous division and valuation occasionally make the novel lapse into nostalgia for a largely mythological past (Baxter 2009: 202): the text consistently works with the dichotomy of a homeostatic, artificial and technocratic late-capitalist present deeply marked by 'homogeneity' and a somewhat idealized more liberal past in

---

[49] We could say that these were the lines of the 'disciplinary society' and not yet the ones of the 'society of control' (cf. Hardt and Negri 2001: 195–198; see below).

which 'heterogeneous' elements, including madness, addiction, violence, and the (radical) imagination, still had a place.[50] We might say that through Sinclair's 'walks' across the Riviera, in the course of which certain places frequently trigger references to the older coast, the Riviera gets mentally remapped, and in this way something like an alternative 'psychogeography' is achieved, one that is opposed to its current shape and official representation.[51] Being traced by no one but Sinclair, however, this alternative does not get translated into political praxis. The past remains in the past.[52]

The portrait of the world of Empire painted by the novel is hence clearly that of a 'hyperintegrated system' or 'integral reality' (Baudrillard 1993c: 69, 2005: passim), resulting from the world being subjected to "an unlimited operational project", whose goal, practically realized on the novel's French coast, is "a systematic de-programming not only of all crime, but of anything that might disturb the order of things, the policed order of the planet" (Baudrillard 2005: 17, 118).[53]

---

[50] This dichotomy, which is already evident in an 1989 essay in which Ballard (1996g) comments on the changing Côte d'Azur, finds further expression in the opposition between different types of machines, with the cool functionality of the Mercedes and of advertising planes – ubiquitous in the novel – on the one hand and the charm of the Jaguar and of older aircraft such as the Harvard on the other (cf. the latter's emphatic association with a time past in the episode in which Sinclair visits the offices of Nostalgic Aviation [SC 149]). Cf. the following passages, in which the latter's connection with heterogeneity, contingency, and freedom is unmistakable: "The Jaguar waited for me in the sun, its twin carburettors ready to do their best or worst. Starting this high-strung thoroughbred was a race between hope and despair. By contrast, thirty feet from me, was the Delages' Mercedes, as black and impassive as the Stuttgart night, every silicon chip and hydraulic relay eager to serve the driver's smallest whim"; "I watched until it [the publicity plane] disappeared, wishing that I sat in the cockpit of my old Harvard, deafened by the roar of the engine and gagging on the stench of lubricating oil, [...] three bottles of iced beer in a cool-bag hanging from the throttle mount, cigar smouldering in the ashtray sellotaped to the instrument panel. I needed the rush of icy air over the canopy, and the flood of light that irrigated every cell in the retina, every waiting space in the soul." (SC 51f, 107) Against this background, it is certainly no coincidence that, at the end of the novel, Sinclair prepares for his attack against Eden-Olympia at the small Cannes-Mandelieu airport near La Bocca, right next to the showroom of Nostalgic Aviation (SC 387ff).

[51] On psychogeography and its interesting genealogy, one that extends back far beyond the Situationist International, cf. Coverley 2006. In the present context, cf. Coverley's observation that psychogeography as an artistic and political project usually involves "an antiquarianism that views the present through the prism of the past" (2006: 14).

[52] If it continues to be of relevance in the present, it is mostly in recycled, simulacral, fetishized and commodified form, as the example of Nostalgic Aviation (SC 149) (or museums such as the one at the Château Grimaldi, Picasso's home in 1946) illustrates.

[53] For a related, stimulating reading of the novel, which also draws on the thought of Baudrillard, cf. Noys 2007.

Eden-Olympia is thus an embodiment of what Baudrillard (2002) has referred to as the 'perfect crime', that is, the crime of perfection, of the virtual completion and total realization of the world, of the achievement of the system's fantastic aim "to quell any refractory zone, to colonize and tame all the wild spaces, whether in geographical space or in the realm of the mind" (Baudrillard 2003: 98). As we have seen, it is precisely with regards to these two realms that the novel principally depicts the process of homogenization.

With this transition to the homogeneous 'smooth space' (Deleuze and Guattari 1987: 474–500) of imperial sovereignty that knows no more negativity or outside, we find ourselves once again confronted with the 'end of history' – "[t]ime stands still at Antibes-les-Pins" (*SC* 326), one character remarks. When Penrose confidently declares "I'm not worried by any rival ideology – there isn't one" (*SC* 361), he clearly bears out Hardt and Negri's thesis that with the emergence of Empire, "the era of major conflicts has come to an end: sovereign power will no longer confront its Other and no longer face its outside, but rather will progressively expand its boundaries to envelop the entire globe as its proper domain." (2001: 189) As in *Cocaine Nights*, this 'end of ideology' entails the utter failure of the 'project of modernity':

> The twentieth century ended with its dreams in ruins. The notion of the community as a voluntary association of enlightened citizens has died forever. [...] Sanity and reason are [...] a vast illusion, built from mirrors that lie. Today we scarcely know our neighbours, shun most forms of civic involvement and happily leave the running of society to a caste of political technicians. (*SC* 263)

It is hard to imagine a more drastic swan song for Habermasian liberal politics. In *Super-Cannes*, the (Western) world has moved fully into the age of 'post-democracy', in which, with the victory of neo-liberalism, history as the movement of a dialectic of ideological contradictions has come to an end, political apathy reigns supreme, and politics is – to use a favorite phrase of Ballard's – "conducted as a branch of advertising" (*C* n.pag.), reduced to policy, management and administration, and in large parts determined by the economic elites (cf. Rancière 1999; Crouch 2005). "No democratic accountability. No one votes. So who runs things?" Sinclair asks, and Penrose, with unabashed honesty, replies: "We do. We run things." (*SC* 94) Again and again, the enormous power of capital is conveyed in hyperbolic images: not only, as different characters emphasize, do "[t]he people who run Eden-Olympia have a lot of power", they have, it seems, even "gone beyond God", being able to "get away with anything" (*SC* 130, 202, 344) and having effectively freed themselves from all moral constraints: "A giant multinational like Fuji or General Motors sets its own morality" (*SC* 95), Penrose declares.

Unlike *Cocaine Nights*, *Super-Cannes* suggests yet another dimension of or contributory factor to the end of history: acceleration. Clearly, life in the corporate world of Eden-Olympia is of the fast kind, and its people – as the case of Sinclair's wife vividly illustrates – are always under stress and pressure. Sinclair observes, once again reiterating the profound difference between past and present: "Jane belonged to an epoch that accelerated and braked, but never cruised." (*SC* 321) With its emphasis on the new rhythm and pace of life under late capitalism, Ballard's novel chimes in with thinkers such as Baudrillard, Paul Virilio, Marc Augé and Hartmut Rosa, who, in different contexts, have all called attention to acceleration as a central characteristic of the contemporary.[54] Thus, Baudrillard, for one, diagnoses "an inflation, a galloping acceleration, a dizzying whirl of mobility, an eccentricity of events and an excess of meaning and information" which combine "with an exponential tendency towards total entropy" (1994f: 112). According to the French philosopher, as well as to the other above-mentioned theorists, the acceleration at the heart of modernity has now reached a point at which things happen too quickly to make sense: "the acceleration of modernity, of technology, events and media, of all exchanges [...] has propelled us to 'escape velocity', with the result that we have flown free of the referential sphere of the real and of history" (1994f: 1). The end of history is therefore (also) due to the fact that the "degree of slowness", the "degree of distance" and the "degree of liberation" which "are needed to bring about the kind of condensation or significant crystallization of events we call history" (Baudrillard 1994f: 1) have been lost in the era of postmodernity. Typically, Baudrillard sees the major reason for this in the way the electronic media filter, process and package 'reality' for us and reduce all events to an uninterrupted stream of signifiers without definite referents or signifieds, a stream that tends to level the differences not just between the events, but also between them and other elements such as advertisements and entertainment, to deprive them of their 'eventness' and turn them into spectacles, and thus to divest them of any real significance. He explains:

> Events now have no more significance than their anticipated meaning, their programming and their broadcasting. Only *this event strike* constitutes a true historical phenomenon – this refusal to signify anything whatever, or this capacity to signify anything at all. This is the true end of history, the end of historical Reason. (1994f: 21f)

---

[54] In fact, with the notion of 'accelerationism', acceleration has, of late, become a major topic in (leftist) critical theory (cf., e.g., Avanessian 2013; Avanessian/Mackay 2014; Mackay/Avanessian 2014; Noys 2014).

In Ballard's novel, something of this sort transpires in a scene in which Sinclair listens to the radio:

> I listened to the stream of pop music and plugs for video-rental shops and pool cleaners. Snatches of international news broke the flow, references to civil war in the Cameroons and an assassination attempt on the Israeli prime minister, but they seemed inconsequential compared with the graphic accounts of a yacht fire in the Golfe-Juan marina, or a landslip at Théoule that had cracked a swimming pool. On the new Riviera, only the trivial had any importance. (SC 126)

Not only are grave events of international political import here reduced to the same status as local yacht fires and advertisements for pool cleaners, they are even deemed significantly *less* significant than the latter and are actually perceived as something akin to white noise, 'breaking the smooth flow' of transmission.

In a similar vein as Baudrillard, Augé, too, has spoken of an "acceleration of history" and an "overabundance of events" (2008: 22, 23) which he considers as characteristic of what he terms 'supermodernity', yet the most comprehensive analysis of the phenomenon of acceleration has been conducted by the German sociologist Hartmut Rosa (2005). In his illuminating study on the historical transformation of the temporal structures of society, Rosa shows that with the advent of globalization, the social acceleration which is a constitutive part of modernity exceeds a critical point beyond which the (modernist) objectives of individual coherence and social synchronization and integration can no longer be upheld. Similar to *Super-Cannes*, Rosa maintains that this end of the claim to individual as well as collective autonomy which the passage to post- or 'late modernity' entails signals the collapse of the project of modernity, which originally fueled the process of acceleration but is now undermined by it. Significantly, in light of my discussion of the novel, Rosa (esp. 2005: 352–427) identifies two major consequences of the new surge of acceleration we have witnessed since the late 20th century, both tied to a novel experience of time he refers to as the 'temporalization of time' itself (*Verzeitlichung der Zeit*): on the socio-political level, the level of 'historical time', we witness an increasing desynchronization of systemic developments on the one hand and political action on the other, which results in a growing impotence of politics in the face of ever more rapid social and especially economic change. Consequently, Rosa argues, society loses its character as a political 'project', and this change and the concomitant exhaustion of all utopian energies in turn make political events appear to us as mere situational episodes, so that history ceases to be understood as a directional and controllable movement. The outcome is a dialectical reversal whereby hyperacceleration paradoxically leads to a 'detemporalization of history' (*Entzeitlichung der Geschichte*), that is, to the impression that it has effectively ended.[55] As we have seen, this notion of the end of history and politics is at the heart of the thematic of globalization presented in *Super-Cannes*. As I want to show, the second consequence of this acceleration identified by Rosa is highly pertinent to the novel as well.

Rosa argues that while, at a collective level, the paradoxical experience of what Virilio (1999) has called 'polar inertia', that is, of stasis despite, or rather because of acceleration, leads to *posthistoire*, at the level of the individual and its 'daily-life time', it gives rise to feelings of loss of control, anxiety and strain in the face of the quickened rhythms of life, the increasing speed of change and the contemporary excess of options and obligations. Here, the temporalization of time implies a 'detemporalization of life' (*Entzeitlichung des Lebens*), so that life tends to be experienced as an erratic and aimless 'drift' (Sennett 1998: 15–31). More and more, Rosa points out, this experience today comes to assume pathological form in feelings of permanent exhaustion or in depression. At the end of his study, Rosa convincingly concludes that all these related phenomena testify to the fact that the temporal structures of our 'society of acceleration' effectively produce *alienation*. They are, he (2005: 480–486) argues, a potent locus for the exercise of power, translating systemic imperatives into the very 'habitus' of the subject.

Certainly, the ennui, death of affect and anomie experienced by the characters of *Super-Cannes* are testament to this alienation caused by acceleration. Moreover, here, too, 'turbo-capitalism', to borrow a term of Edward Luttwak's (2000), generates pathological exhaustion. As Wilder Penrose observes, "[w]ork dominates life in Eden-Olympia, and drives out everything else", and consequently, all the professionals at the business park suffer from "[t]oo much work" and having "no energies to spare" – they are, in Penrose's words, utterly "creatures of the treadmill" (*SC* 254, 255, 264). The results are not only insomnia, migraines and infections, but "depression", a general "inability to rest the mind, to find time for reflection and recreation", an overall "loss of mental energy" (*SC* 258, 251, 253) and anxieties that cannot be properly identified (*SC* 253). In a word: "Chronic fatigue syndrome haunt[s] the place." (*SC* 253) Once again, this is most dramatically illustrated by Sinclair's wife Jane, who at one point remarks: "Outside the clinic [where she works] I hardly exist. I'm tired all the time" (*SC* 270).

With this emphasis on the characters' fundamental tiredness and lack of energy, the novel distinctly echoes the view proposed by Alain Ehrenberg (2010),

---

[55] Baudrillard (1994f: 3–5) similarly posits a second mode of history's vanishing, one of slowing down, besides the already mentioned one of speeding up.

Byung-Chul Han (2010, 2011) and others that exhaustion and depression constitute *the* characteristic pathology of postmodernity and as such are symptomatic of the changed condition and mental state of the subject under late capitalism. According to the work of these thinkers, the contemporary spread of exhaustion is connected with three interrelated factors, all of which are pertinent to *Super-Cannes:* for one thing, as especially Han points out, today's 'psychic infarcts' are due to an excess of positivity and sameness. The German philosopher follows Baudrillard's thesis of the postmodern erasure of negativity and radical otherness, which, as we have seen, Ballard's novel subscribes to as well, and argues that burnout, depression, etc. must be considered as mental abreactions against this 'violence of positivity'. Lack of an other or outside thus causes political-collective (end of history) as well as psychological-individual (depression) 'exhaustion'.[56] It is therefore once again only fitting that *Super-Cannes* brings these two aspects together.

Beyond this, as both contemporary critical theory and the novel aver, mental collapse also results from the fact that we now live in a *Leistungsgesellschaft* (Han 2010: 17 ff, passim), an exclusively achievement-oriented society which exerts a continuously growing pressure on individuals to always 'function' in a faultless way and to optimize their performance. The fact that Jane finds it increasingly hard to relax and to function in her job without the use of drugs, eventually becoming a virtual "heroin addict" (*SC* 345), illustrates this well and seems to confirm Han's (2010: 54) argument that the *Leistungsgesellschaft* is gradually turning into a *Dopinggesellschaft*. As Han (2010: 43) puts it, the modern imperative to achieve turns the individual as well as society as a whole into an 'autistic performance machine' – a phrase that brilliantly captures Eden-Olympia and its resident professionals – and eventually leads to fatigue and nervous breakdown.

Finally – this being the central argument of Ehrenberg's study on the 'weariness of the self', one closely connected with the previous aspect – psychic exhaustion is furthermore the (paradoxical) result of the dominant form of subjectivation in the era of late capitalism. As Ehrenberg shows,

> [d]epression began its ascent when the disciplinary model for behaviours, the rules of authority and observance of taboos that gave social classes as well as both sexes a specific destiny, broke against norms that invited us to undertake personal initiative by enjoining us to be ourselves. [...] Depression presents itself as an *illness of responsibility* in which the dominant feeling is that of failure. The depressed individual is unable to measure up; he [sic] is tired of having to become himself [sic]. (2010: 4)

---

56 In this context, cf. Dominic Pettman's (2002) attempt – also conducted in the wake of Baudrillard – to think a 'politics of exhaustion'.

According to Ehrenberg, with the end of the disciplinary society brought about by the social movements of the 1960s, discipline and the moral law with all its precepts and prohibitions lost much of their social relevance. In the 'permissive society', the social rules no longer primarily demand obedience and conformity but personal responsibility and initiative: "Notions like 'projects,' 'motivation,' and 'communication' are now the norm." (Ehrenberg 2010: 8) Ehrenberg argues that this transformation entailed a corresponding change in the nature of the dominant psychopathologies, so that the neurosis of the 19th and first half of the 20th century, essentially an affliction centered on bourgeois guilt, has been increasingly replaced by depression, which occurs when the individual is no longer able to live up to the "gospel of personal fulfilment" and the "commandments of individual initiative" (2010: 164).

While the characters in *Super-Cannes* do not, strictly speaking, suffer from the identity insecurity and the incapacity to act that Ehrenberg identifies as the two principal characteristics of depression, their exhaustion can nevertheless only be properly understood if considered in the light of the general genealogy he traces – for clearly, the subjectivity of all the professionals at Eden-Olympia is precisely the one that Ehrenberg talks about, a subjectivity that Baudrillard, himself referring to Ehrenberg, terms 'athletic' or 'neo-individualism', because it is "bent on performance and entrepreneurial heroism" (1994f: 105). In view of our discussion of the novel so far, it is certainly telling that Ehrenberg (2010: 183f) links this transformation of the image of the entrepreneur into "everyone's role model", "a style of action that each individual [is] exhorted to use" (2010: 183), to what we have referred to as the 'end of ideology' and 'of utopia' and the total victory of neo-liberalism in the Western world. Ballard's characters have fully imbibed this model. Evidently, the subjectivities manufactured at Eden-Olympia are no longer produced along Taylorist and Fordist lines, but according to a model that promotes autonomy, creativity, initiative, responsibility, motivation, and flexibility – the 'entrepreneurial self'.[57] This model is most succinctly expressed in the business park's oft-repeated mantra that "work is the ultimate play, and play the ultimate work" (*SC* 94). As Penrose explains: "Work is the new leisure. Talented and ambitious people work harder than they have ever done, and for longer hours. They find their only fulfilment through work. [...] Creative work is its own recreation." (*SC* 254) Eden-Olympia's professionals are thus no longer *Gehorsamssubjekte*, the repressed subjects of the old disciplinary society, they are *Leistungssubjekte* (Han 2010: 17):

---

[57] This neo-liberal mode of subjectivation has been investigated in detail in the field of governmentality studies (cf. esp. Bröckling 2013).

> organization man died out in the 1960s [...], our worried friend in the grey-flannel suit. [...] He was locked into a low-tech bureaucratic cave, little more than a human punch card. Today's professional men and women are self-motivated. The corporate pyramid is a virtual hierarchy that endlessly reassembles itself around them. They enjoy enormous mobility. (*SC* 95f)

As numerous theorists have pointed out, this disappearance of the conformed subjectivity theorized by William H. Whyte, to whom the novel here alludes, David Riesman and others should, however, not be understood as a sign of emancipation. On the contrary, exploitation becomes even more severe since its source is no longer an oppressive power external to the subject but *the subject itself*. Thus, coercion does by no means cease to exist but is merely internalized – as Sinclair quickly realizes, people at Eden-Olympia are "self-disciplined" (*SC* 54). Even more than in the era of the Foucauldian disciplines, then, the individual today is both victim *and* perpetrator of its own subjection. Echoing Benjamin's notion of capitalism as a religious formation which we identified in the novel as well, Baudrillard therefore speaks of a "terroristic fundamentalism" of the new "sacrificial religion of performance, efficiency, stress and time-pressure" to which the individual is "a convert", a fundamentalism whose aim is the subject's "total mortification and unremitting sacrifice to the divinities of data, total exploitation of oneself by oneself, the ultimate in alienation" (1994f: 106). Despite the fact that the system is more individualizing than ever, the contemporary individual, Baudrillard asserts, is consequently "not an individual at all" but "a *pentito* of subjectivity and alienation, of the heroic appropriation of himself [sic]" (1994f: 106).[58] Baudrillard explains:

> 'post-modern' individualism arises not out of a problematic of *liberty* and *liberation*, but out of a *liberalization* of slave networks and circuits, that is, an individual diffraction of the programmed ensembles, a metamorphosis of the macro-structures into innumerable particles which bear within them all the stigmata of the networks and circuits – each one forming its own micro-network and micro-circuit, each one reviving for itself, in its micro-universe, the now useless totalitarianism of the whole. (1994f: 107)

As Han (2010: 18f) points out, there is hence an underlying continuity between the disciplinary society and the contemporary one: the goal to maximize productivity. Late capitalism's great discovery: the subject that exploits itself is far more productive than the one exploited by others because its exploitation is coextensive with the impression of freedom (Han 2010: 22).

---

[58] Similarly, Gilles Deleuze (2011: 140) speaks of the replacement of the individual by the 'dividual'.

As a realm in which the prohibitive law, submission, discipline and anonymous conformity have been largely replaced by possibility, motivation, initiative and individuality, Ballard's Eden-Olympia must be read as an embodiment of what Gilles Deleuze (2011) has termed the 'society of control'.[59] This society appears far more liberal and democratic than its disciplinary predecessor, yet in truth, the structures of domination do not disappear but are only transformed into ever modulating and free-floating forms of control, which produce subjectivities – less standardized, more 'autonomous', flexible and hybrid – better geared to the demands of global capital. With this transformation, the grip of power is far from being loosened; in fact, it encloses the individuals ever more tightly, fully permeating their bodies and minds as well as the entirety of social relations. More than ever before, the subjects today willingly participate in their own subordination. Hence, as Hardt and Negri point out, the passage to the society of control does not signal the end of discipline, that is, of the self-disciplining of the subject, but, on the contrary, entails "an intensification and generalization of the normalizing apparatuses of disciplinarity", in such a way that "the elements of transcendence of disciplinary society decline while the immanent aspects are accentuated" (2001: 23, 331). Sinclair's sarcastic response to Penrose's paean on the merits of Eden-Olympia's "regime of fulfilment through work" captures the nature of this society well: "It sounds like a ticket to 1984, this time by the scenic route."[60] (*SC* 39, 95)

According to Hardt and Negri, the transition from disciplinary society to the society of control is a central element in the materialization of Empire, since it is in this transition that the 'real subsumption' of society under capital, that is, "the increasingly intense relationship of mutual implication of all social forces that capitalism has pursued throughout its development[,] has now been fully realized" (2001: 24f). At this point, another crucial element emerges, one that is also relevant with regards to *Super-Cannes*: 'biopower'. Hardt and Negri contend that

> only the society of control is able to adopt the biopolitical context as its *exclusive* terrain of reference. In the passage from disciplinary society to the society of control, a new paradigm of power is realized which is defined by the technologies that recognize society as the realm of biopower. (2001: 24)

---

[59] Gasiorek (2005: 194), too, briefly notes that the new type of society outlined by Deleuze is a key reference point for Ballard's late work, but does not flesh out this observation.

[60] Besides its explicit reference to Orwell's dystopia, this statement also distinctly echoes the latter's characterization of the 1930s as "a scenic railway ending in a torture-chamber" (1968: 534). Penrose's statement, in turn, recalls the Nazi slogan "Arbeit macht frei", which was placed over the entrances to various concentration camps. Cf. also the repeated comparisons of Eden-Olympia to a prison (e.g. "corporate cage" [*SC* 258]).

The two thinkers here draw on the work of Michel Foucault, who described this new kind of power which slowly emerged in the 17th century and came into its own in the 19th century as one that was no longer based on the "ancient right to *take* life or *let* live", as sovereign power had been, but on the ability "to *foster* life or *disallow* it to the point of death" (1978: 138). Organized around the two poles of the disciplines on the one hand, focused on the individual human body, and 'biopolitics' on the other, centered on the species body, that is, the regulation of the population, this is a power that is "bent on generating forces, making them grow, and ordering them, rather than one dedicated to impeding them, making them submit, or destroying them" (Foucault 1978: 136). 'Deduction' is no longer its primary form; instead, its principal task is the administration of life. With the emergence of this power, then, we witness "the entry of life into history, that is, the entry of phenomena peculiar to the life of the human species into the order of knowledge and power, into the sphere of political techniques" (Foucault 1978: 141f). Building on Foucault's thesis that biopower was an indispensable element in the development of capitalism since it made possible "the controlled insertion of bodies into the machinery of production and the adjustment of the phenomena of population to economic processes" (1978: 141), Hardt and Negri argue that this investment of life by power, which was still only partial in the age of disciplinary society and industrial capital, has become total with the transition towards the society of control and late capitalism. It is Empire that both "structure[s] global territories biopolitically" (Hardt and Negri 2001: 31) and at last puts all individual and collective forces of life in the service of the production of surplus value. Hardt and Negri assert that "[t]he absoluteness of imperial power is the complementary term to its complete immanence to the ontological machine of production and reproduction, and thus to the biopolitical context." (2001: 41)

It is a mark of the brilliant astuteness of Ballard's vision of Empire that *Super-Cannes* comprises this complementarity as well. The novel not only demonstrates how power seizes all productive capacities of life and organizes the totality of its subjects' activities in the domain of value and utility, something well illustrated by Eden-Olympia's view of their staff as their "biggest investment" (*SC* 16), a phrase that distinctly echoes biopolitical concepts such as 'human resources' or 'human capital'. The text also shows that in line with this, power multiplies and refines the political technologies that "inves[t] the body, health, modes of subsistence and habitation, living conditions, the whole space of existence" (Foucault 1978: 143f). The novel depicts Eden-Olympia as a 'caring' regime making numerous and vast interventions in the lives of its people, reaching ever further into all kinds of areas of their existence and subjecting these to legislation and a management geared at the 'well-being' of the individual (cf. esp. *SC* 95).⁶¹ As Sinclair is repeatedly reminded, "Eden-Olympia looks after everything"; "[o]nce you are there, they look after you forever" (*SC* 147, 138). Particularly the long conversation between the narrator and Penrose in chapter 29 reveals the business park's immense concern for the health of its employees, which, according to Penrose, "is under constant threat" (*SC* 251). As the latter's obsessive worries about "resistance levels", "energy levels", "immune levels" (*SC* 253, 257, 258), and so forth, and his observation that "compared with the health of executives in Manhattan, Zurich and Tokyo, the physical and mental well-being of the five hundred most senior people at Eden-Olympia is extremely high" (*SC* 252) make clear, the exact and continuous measurement, recording and improvement of the state of health of its subjects has become a critical task of power. To that end, the business enclave conducts all kinds of "careful tests", subjects the professionals to "endless check-ups" (*SC* 253, 111), and immediately responds to afflictions thus identified by developing appropriate therapy programs. The extreme nature of this preoccupation with the well-being of its people transpires – in an almost caricatural way – when Sinclair's wife uses a new computer model to trace the spread of nasal viruses across Eden-Olympia and comes to surmise that "if people moved their chairs a further eighteen inches apart they'd stop the infectious vectors in their tracks" (*SC* 98). It is furthermore evident in the business park's plan to install newly devised "self-diagnostic kits" in all households by using the already existing network of modem links that connect virtually all houses and apartments in this "'intelligent' city" to its clinic and other institutions (incl. the nearest Tiffany's [*SC* 16] – after all, people are not only required to be fully operative producers but also zealous consumers):

> Every morning when they get up people will dial the clinic and log in their health data: pulse, blood-pressure, weight and so on. One prick of the finger on a small scanner and the computers here [at the clinic] will analyse everything: liver enzymes, cholesterol, prostrate markers, the lot. (*SC* 122, 16, 67)

---

61 Ballard's understanding of and interest in contemporary biopower also transpires in an interview with John Gray conducted in 2000, the year of the publication of *Super-Cannes*. In this interview, Ballard states: "We all subscribe to the humane and liberal values of our welfare-state democracies, we all accept enormous interventions in our lives by the state: the right way to bring up our children, the right way to treat our wives and husbands, the right way to behave in the office. Our lives are circumscribed by enlightened legislation almost every minute of the day. The purity of the food we eat, the water we drink, the sorts of plants we can grow in our gardens virtually: [sic] all are legislated out of this benign and sensible and caring administration that governs the Western world." (in Gray 2012: 377f)

The novel is unambiguous with regards to the ultimate motivation behind all these biopolitical measures. Similar to Foucault, *Super-Cannes* suggests that the increasing concern for and administration of life is not primarily a matter of a more civilized, humane and benevolent paradigm of power, but is in fact largely driven by the capitalist goal of process optimization and efficiency enhancement. To improve and prolong life means to be able to exploit it ever more fully.[62] As Sinclair at one point notes: "as long as there's a pulse, the money flows" (*SC* 307). When Penrose remarks that Eden-Olympia has "[made] the office feel like a home – if anything, the real home" – a characteristic element of today's society of control[63] – and has turned people's apartments and houses into "[s]ervice stations, where people sleep and ablute" (*SC* 17), it becomes clear that the human body has been effectively reduced to a docile, disciplined machine which has to function smoothly at all times and whose usefulness has to be maximized. In the novel's imperial regime, the human body is nothing but "an obedient coolie, to be fed and hosed down, and given just enough sexual freedom to sedate itself" (*SC* 17). What these rather drastic images express is not an aberrance or perversion of the biopolitics of liberal democratic capitalism but, in fact, its basic logic, one that becomes ever more evident in the contemporary age of Empire, in which "the whole social body is comprised by power's machine" (Hardt and Negri 2001: 24).

With its emphasis on the biopolitical nature of contemporary power and the concomitant reduction of the body to a coolie, a tool or a machine, Ballard's novel indicates that life under global capitalism is, to use Giorgio Agamben's term, increasingly becoming 'naked'. Drawing on Aristotle's distinction between *zoē* and *bios*, Agamben distinguishes between 'naked' or 'bare life' on the one hand and a politically qualified form of life on the other, and argues that it is on the basis of this division and, specifically, on the exclusion of *zoē* from the political sphere of the *polis*, that the political tradition of the Occident established itself. Yet, according to the Agambean logic of 'exception', this exclusion takes the form of an "inclusive exclusion" (Agamben 1998: 7) whereby a connection with what is rejected is always upheld. What Agamben calls the 'logic of sover-

---

62 The nature of life in the contemporary society of control and subject to biopolitical measures and imperatives is brilliantly captured in the track "Fitter Happier" by the English band Radiohead. Its beginning and end – "fitter [sic] happier [sic] more productive" and "fitter, healthier and more productive" (Radiohead 1997) respectively – which distinctly parody the lifestyle slogans of the 1990s, are somewhat echoed in Ballard's novel when Penrose encapsulates the nature of "Eden-Olympia and the future" with the words "[r]icher, saner, more fulfilled" (*SC* 297).
63 Of course, this fusion of the two spaces is today often also realized through the inverse development, the home turning into one's office.

eignty' consists in this paradox according to which mere life and law are on the one hand separated, yet on the other always remain deeply linked at the heart of sovereignty and blend into each other. 'Threshold' is the term the Italian philosopher uses to designate this point at which exclusion and inclusion, bare life and political existence, exception and norm, violence and law are indistinguishable, and the *homo sacer* – just like the sovereign, at the opposite end of the power spectrum – is the emblem of this threshold, a figure of archaic Roman law that designated a man who could be killed with impunity but not be sacrificed and who was thus excluded from – and at the same time included in – the secular as well as the religious legal order and reduced to the status of his physical existence (Agamben 1998: 71–115). Unlike Foucault, then, Agamben claims that biopolitics is as old as and, indeed, at the root of Western politics, since "the inclusion of bare life in the political realm constitutes the original – if concealed – nucleus of sovereign power. *It can even be said that the production of a biopolitical body is the original activity of sovereign power.*" (1998: 6) Whereas for Foucault, sovereign power and biopower are distinct forms and the politicization of life that distinguishes the latter is a genuinely modern phenomenon, Agamben argues that, by "[p]lacing biological life at the center of its calculations, the modern State [...] does nothing other than bring to light the secret tie uniting power and bare life" (1998: 6). Agamben therefore asserts:

> The Foucauldian thesis will [...] have to be corrected or, at least, completed, in the sense that what characterizes modern politics is not so much the inclusion of *zoē* in the *polis* – which is, in itself, absolutely ancient – nor simply the fact that life as such becomes a principal object of the projections and calculations of State power. Instead the decisive fact is that, together with the process by which the exception everywhere becomes the rule, the realm of bare life – which is originally situated at the margins of the political order – gradually begins to coincide with the political realm, and exclusion and inclusion, outside and inside, *bios* and *zoē*, right and fact, enter into a zone of irreducible indistinction. (1998: 9)

Thus, according to Agamben, bare life, whose connection with power was initially only given in the form of the inclusive exclusion, becomes its privileged object with the advent of modern biopower, which thus merely generalizes and radicalizes what has always been a (latent) part of Western politics. Agamben goes on to argue that since then, the biopolitical problematic has been continually aggravated and the state of exception has progressively become the rule. For this reason, the Italian thinker claims that the camp, whose essence "consists in the materialization of the state of exception and in the subsequent creation of a space in which bare life and the juridical rule enter into a threshold of indistinction", must be considered as "the hidden matrix and *nomos* of the political space in which we are still living" (1998: 174, 166). The camp, Agamben declares, "is the very paradigm of political space at the point at which politics becomes biopolitics and *homo sacer* is virtually confused with the citizen" (1998: 171). This, according to Agamben, is today more and more the case. While the totalitarian concentration camps proper have disappeared, life has nevertheless continued to be invested by power to an ever greater extent, and consequently, the systematic production of bare life now escalates, so that "in our age all citizens can be said, in a specific but extremely real sense, to appear virtually as *homines sacri*" (Agamben 1998: 111).

It seems to me that Agamben's apprehension that the camp "is the new biopolitical *nomos* of the planet" and that "[b]are life is no longer confined to a particular place or a definite category" but "now dwells in the biological body of every living being" (1998: 176, 140) to some extent also animates *Super-Cannes*. As different commentators have pointed out, Agamben's remarks on the universalization of bare life largely remain vague and suggestive. Yet, critics such as Byung-Chul Han, Slavoj Žižek or Thomas Lemke have attempted to specify, develop and rethink his theory, particularly by going beyond the exclusive focus on the divestment of rights and on death and by taking into account how the politicization of life is always intertwined with its economization (Lemke 2011: 116). It is in light of this argument, according to which it is essentially the late-capitalist "'bioeconomic' imperative" (Lemke 2011: 60) of maximizing value and optimizing one's performance that reduces people to a state of bare life (Han 2010: 34–36, 2011: 106f, 164–170; Žižek 2011: 124f), that the professionals of Eden-Olympia can be considered *homines sacri* – their "most elementary, 'zero' position is that of being an object of biopolitics" (Žižek 2011: 125). Given this intensified politicization of life, as well as the total homogeneity of the business park's social space discussed earlier, it is perhaps not all that surprising that Eden-Olympia eventually turns to fascism.[64] After all, Agamben's analysis, by unveiling their shared biopolitical foundation, has posited "an inner solidarity between democracy and totalitarianism" (1998: 10) and exposed the indissoluble nexus between the granting and the withdrawal of rights, between human rights and the concentration camps, between the sanctity and the total destructibility of life. Consequently, Agamben declares:

> Today politics knows no value (and, consequently, no nonvalue) other than life, and until the contradictions that this fact implies are dissolved, Nazism and fascism – which transformed the decision on bare life into the supreme political principle – will remain stubbornly with us. (1998: 10)

---

[64] Cf. also the fact that references to totalitarianism are repeatedly made in connection with Eden-Olympia's biopolitical regime (e.g. *SC* 67, 122).

In *Super-Cannes*, the fascist tendencies taking hold of Eden-Olympia are paradoxically closely connected to the catastrophic strategy of a willed madness. Similar to *Cocaine Nights*, the novel suggests that the alienation, exhaustion and anomie caused by global capitalism can only be countered by means of "a voluntary and elective psychopathy" (*SC* 264). No 'fundamental tiredness', then, that would bring with it calm, a slowing down of life, serenity, contemplation and inspiration, and a new kind of community (a *Müdigkeitsgesellschaft*) and that Han (2010: 54–61) proposes as an alternative to the isolating 'tiredness of fatigue' caused by contemporary acceleration and the economic imperatives of the system. No rebellion by the exploited masses either, as Hardt and Negri (2001, 2005) hope and predict, no constitution of a new revolutionary subject such as the 'multitude' that would eventually destroy the current global order, reorganize global flows and exchanges, invent new democratic forms, and thus construct a just and egalitarian 'counter-Empire'. With regards to the hyper-integrated, perfectly operational world of the text, all such alternatives appear as nothing but utopian fantasies. Instead, as Penrose explains, encapsulating what we have identified as the driving hypothesis behind Ballard's oeuvre, once again, "[e]xtreme problems call for extreme solutions" (*SC* 365). As in *Cocaine Nights*, the solution here is "a new kind of psychopathology" (*SC* 96), and *Super-Cannes* rehashes the preceding novel's insistence on the constructedness and relativity of 'madness' as well as on its liberating energies. Thus, Penrose speaks of "a struggle between competing psychopathies", the other one being consumer capitalism (cf. also *SC* 363), declares that "[g]oing mad is [the] only way of staying sane", and contends that "psychopathy is freedom" (*SC* 365, 202, 263). Echoing a fundamental conviction of Ballard's, restated numerous times (e.g. in Revell 1984b: 44, in Self 2006: 380, as well as *RW* 83), Penrose emphasizes the emancipatory character of insanity: "In a totally sane society, madness is the only freedom. Our latent psychopathy is the last nature reserve, a place of refuge for the endangered mind." (*SC* 264) Such a view of madness as a form of resistance against an administered world was in some ways already anticipated by Friedrich Nietzsche, who proclaimed the "*dignity of foolishness*" and speculated that a "tyranny of prudence" could eventually produce "a new kind of nobility" and that "[t]o be noble might then come to mean: to entertain follies" (2001: 43). Similarly, Baudrillard has spoken of "the brutalizing effects of rationality, normative socialization and universal conditioning" and declared that "[w]hen intelligence becomes hegemonic, becoming a mode of technical, collective, automatic adaptation, then any other hypothesis than intelligence becomes preferable"; "at this point", he maintains, referring to Nietzsche, madness may "recover a degree of nobility in abreaction to Integral Reality" (1993c: 75, 2005: 178 f, 178). Clearly, the commitment of Ballard's characters to violence, crime, drugs, and sadomasochistic, excretory and other kinds of 'perverse' sexual acts must be read as a powerful reassertion of Bataillean heterogeneity in the face of the universal homogeneity of global capitalism, which, as we have seen, excludes every useless element and reduces man (sic) to "a function, arranged within measurable limits, of collective production" (Bataille 1985d: 138).[65]

Yet, as the novel makes unmistakably clear, in the end, there is nothing subversive about Penrose's strategy of a willed psychopathy. Whereas *Cocaine Nights* portrayed the eventual *failure* of Crawford's project due to its inscription into an essentially modernist imaginary of community and to its containment by the powers that be, but nevertheless seemed to affirm the project as such and to uphold at least the *possibility* of resistance implied by it, *Super-Cannes* allows for absolutely no ray of light to pierce through the unshakable walls of the closed and claustrophobic world of Eden-Olympia. For whereas Crawford's madness was merely *incorporated* by the forces of capital, Penrose's is *from the outset* destined for nothing but the consolidation of the system. In the business park, expenditure is not 'nonproductive', as Bataille maintains it should be, but, on the contrary, part of a psychiatric treatment – "madness as a form of therapy" (*SC* 251) – fully enlisted in the capitalist project of maximizing efficiency. Thus, the ultimate goal of the transgressive actions the characters engage in – which are always "carefully monitored", theirs finally being "a controlled and supervised madness" – is to cure the professionals of their afflictions in order to optimize their economic performance and thereby make "[c]orporate profits and equity values [...] climb again" (*SC* 261, 251, 260). In *Super-Cannes*, madness and transgression are therefore not attempts to elude and resist the late-capitalist biopolitical paradigm, but are entirely subjected to its logics. And, as Sinclair observes:

> the radical therapy clearly worked. The members of the bowling teams [who carry out the diverse criminal acts] glowed with health, and Eden-Olympia had never been so successful. The flow of adrenalin, the hair-triggers of fear and flight, had returned the corporate nervous system and pushed profits to unprecedented heights. (*SC* 280)

What was still a means of resistance in *Cocaine Nights* here turns out to be a sign of the total perversion of the system, which itself is revealed to be the greatest transgressor – in the words of Wilder Penrose: "Eden-Olympia is the biggest rebellion of all" (*SC* 361). Hardt and Negri (2001: 325 ff), following Deleuze and

---

[65] As in *Crash* and so many other Ballardian texts, the characters' reconnection with heterogeneity is here, too, repeatedly described as an "energizing" (*SC* 172) experience that entails the (re-)discovery of a more authentic being (e.g. *SC* 173, 258, 265).

Guattari, have pointed out that capital is by nature a force of decoding and deterritorialization, and ever more so at a time in which it has become global. In Ballard's novel, this tendency has become radicalized and now affects all areas of life. *Super-Cannes* portrays late capitalism as a practically omnipotent power system transcending every conceivable boundary and violating virtually all taboos for the sake of the generation of profit, and suggests that it can – as Baudrillard has long argued – therefore no longer be effectively attacked according to a logic of transgression, which it has fully assimilated to itself. Indeed, the novel maintains that consumer capitalism increasingly transforms transgression itself into a commodity: "The consumer society hungers for the deviant and unexpected. What else can drive the bizarre shifts in the entertainment landscape that will keep us 'buying'?"[66] (*SC* 265)

At Eden-Olympia, all heterogeneous elements are hence from the start overcoded by capitalist homogeneity. In the world of the business park, "a society which seeks – by prophylactic measures, by annihilating its own natural referents, by whitewashing violence, by exterminating all germs and all of the accursed share, by performing cosmetic surgery on the negative – to concern itself solely with quantified management and with the discourse of the Good", these elements function like a homeopathic remedy[67] that wards off the threat of "immunodeficiency" towards which all hyperintegrated systems in their "hyperbolic positivity" (Baudrillard 1993c: 92, 69, 121) tend and in this way maintains the system's stability. The heterogeneous elements thus correspond to what Bataille has termed the 'imperative' form of heterogeneity (Baxter 2008: 104f), one that operates in the service of the homogenous forces. Bataille explains: "the protection of *homogeneity* lies in its recourse to imperative elements that are capable of obliterating the various unruly forces or bringing them under the control of order" (1985d: 139). Given that Bataille saw in fascism "the accomplished uniting of the [imperative] *heterogeneous* elements with the *homogeneous* elements" (1985d: 155), it seems only logical that the society of Ballard's business park increasingly transforms into a fascist one.[68]

---

[66] This idea has been taken up by John Gray, who argues that after its economic exhaustion, the commodification of deviance, violence, etc. will be followed by a marketing of 'morality' "as a new brand of transgression" (2003: 166), something we are arguably already witnessing today.
[67] Notably, Ballard's novel (*SC* 251) and Baudrillard (1993c: 77, 121) both employ the term 'homeopathic' to describe the function forms of heterogeneity or negativity have in such an aseptic, transparent and operational environment, a term that once again signals the contemporary omnipresence of biopolitics. In this context, cf. also Noys 2007.
[68] These dynamics in the novel could also fruitfully be analyzed in terms of the Deleuzoguattarian model and its explication of the complex relations between the schizoid-revolutionary

We have already seen that the destitute and mostly migrant enclave at La Bocca functions in the text as global capital's abject other, and it is on the continuous violent expulsion of this 'impoverished', 'impure' heterogeneity that Eden-Olympia's homogeneity is founded and by means of which it is maintained. As Bataille professes in his analysis of fascism, "the destructive passion (sadism) of the imperative agency is as a rule exclusively directed either toward foreign societies or toward the impoverished classes, toward all those external or internal elements hostile to *homogeneity*" (1985d: 147). It thus quickly transpires that Eden-Olympia's social order is based on strict 'racial' and social divisions and hierarchies and that these are not contested but reaffirmed and reinforced by Penrose's 'therapy program'.[69] In fact, the psychopathy he prescribes to his 'patients' takes the form of brutal acts of violence perpetrated by a (mostly) white economic elite against workers and, above all, immigrants[70] – in short, against what fascist identitarian logic, in its need to create an other in contrast to whom the self can be defined, constructs as "[p]eople of the 'other' side" (*SC* 193).[71] Like "lords of the chateau, free to ride out and trample down the peasantry for their own amusement", Penrose's "playgroup Nazis" cruelly mistreat anyone whose skin color is not, in the words of the black security guard Frank Hald-

---

and the paranoiac-fascisizing poles of social libidinal investment, between de- and reterritorialization, decoding and overcoding, etc. Jake Huntley's (2012: 225–227) discussion of Ballard's late fiction goes some way in this direction. In this context, cf. also my analysis of *Concrete Island* in chapter 3. One might add that the fascist dimension is already implied in the business park's name, which could be read as an allusion to Leni Riefenstahl's film *Olympia*, which documents the 1936 Summer Olympics held in Berlin.

69 Thus, whereas Hardt and Negri (2001: 190–195), drawing on the work of Etienne Balibar (1991), argue that in the age of Empire, the modern form of racism is increasingly replaced by its postmodern form, in which culture fills the role previously played by biology, in the global order of Ballard's novel, the older racism not only persists but forcefully reasserts itself and continues to exist alongside the novel form.

70 In the world of the novel, these two groups largely coincide – at least, the more 'unqualified' jobs are almost exclusively performed by migrant workers – a fact that points up that the late-capitalist division of labor (still) clearly follows 'racial' lines. One character's observation that the "top managements at Eden-Olympia are deeply racist, but in a new way", the "corporate pecking order [being] all that counts" (*SC* 343f), must be read along these lines as well. Tellingly, the attacks against the immigrants are collectively known as *ratissages* in the text (*SC* 210), a term closely connected to the bloody history of the Algerian War.

71 In contrast, the victims in *Cocaine Nights* are all "willing" (*CN* 188), a fact that obviously raises the question whether 'victimhood' is an appropriate concept in this context at all. Cf. also Prentice's observation that nobody ever reports a crime because "no one thinks of it as crime. Neither the victims nor the people who take part. There's a different set of social conventions [...]. Theft and prostitution exist here, but everyone sees them as 'good works' of a new kind." (*CN* 304)

er, "pinko-grey" (*SC* 203, 352, 193). Halder notes that the political climate of Eden-Olympia is "so right-wing it's off the scale", and Sinclair likewise remarks: "We're back in Weimar Germany, with a weekend Freikorps fighting the Reds." (*SC* 193, 344) Consequently, Ballard's protagonist predicts: "The Adolf Hitlers and Pol Pots of the future won't walk out of the desert. They'll emerge from shopping malls and corporate business parks." (*SC* 256) The novel pushes neo-liberal rhetoric and ideology over the edge when Penrose, himself already a semi-messianic figure, for his part maintains: "on the whole the immigrant community benefits. Eden-Olympia is a scrupulous equal-opportunities employer, with no racial bias. We hire a disproportionate number of north Africans as gardeners and road sweepers. The immigrant population gains from the clearer heads of the people who do the hiring." (*SC* 260) This shocking reasoning is pushed to the extreme when Penrose, with regards to a video of the professionals' racist violence, advises Sinclair to simply think of the victims "as film extras, paid for a few minutes' discomfort", and comes to the outrageous conclusion that really, the victims "expect to be abused", so that all those violent managers are actually "doing them a good turn by satisfying their unconscious expectations" (*SC* 298, 297). These exploited and abused immigrants and workers are the real *homines sacri* of the text, living in the ghetto- or camp-like town of La Bocca, where, by the power of the 'sovereign' global elite, the law appears permanently suspended, stripped of their rights and thus reduced to a state of naked life. If, as I argued earlier, the neighboring spaces of Eden-Olympia and La Bocca can be read as a microcosmic representation of the international division of labor, then certainly Ballard's novel bears out Agamben's claim that the current global order "transforms the entire population of the Third World into bare life" (1998: 180).[72]

In *Super-Cannes*, willed madness can thus be considered a 'catastrophic strategy' only in one sense of the term: it does not attempt to 'overturn' power but merely yields disastrous consequences. No longer a means of resistance, it is on the contrary fully incorporated into the system's drive towards rationality, productivity and order. Similar to Aldous Huxley's *Brave New World* and George Orwell's *1984*, both of which *Super-Cannes* alludes to (*SC* 59, 95), the novel's vision is a deeply dystopian one, in which any challenge to the existing order is doomed from the outset (Baxter 2009: 206–208). Even though the disciplinary society of Airstrip One has been replaced by Eden-Olympia's society of control, this vision is no less nightmarish. As the narrator at one point observes: "Taking

---

[72] Of course, this notion of the reduction of subaltern peoples to bare life is, however, not unproblematic, reinforcing as it does the figure of 'the other-as-victim' (cf. e.g. Margaroni 2007: 113ff).

their cue from Eden-Olympia and Antibes-les-Pins, the totalitarian systems of the future would be subservient and ingratiating, but the locks would be just as strong."[73] (*SC* 133)

As if to drive home its fatalistic outlook, Ballard's text ends with an image of hopeless rebellion. Having realized the full extent of Penrose's neo-fascist regime, in which he, too, has become implicated, Sinclair finally resolves "to finish the task that David Greenwood [...] begun" (*SC* 392).[74] The novel's conclusion has the protagonist, shotgun in hand, preparing for another killing spree, in which he plans to murder Penrose and the other key players of the 'therapy program' and with which he intends to expose Eden-Olympia's secret history to the world.[75] Yet, for the reader, there is a strong sense of history repeating itself here, of an originally tragic event occurring for a second time, but this time as farce (cf. Marx 1979: 103). For not only does Sinclair's plot, as Gasiorek observes, read like "a parody of male heroism" (2005: 174), driven as he is by an absurd "delusion of celebrity" (Baxter 2009: 208), attempting to fashion a public image of martyrdom, imagining himself "on the international news, the bodies of the guilty laid out behind [him] like hunting trophies" and fantasizing about a "Presidential pardon" (*SC* 390, 391). More than that, the reader is also fully aware that, just like Greenwood's, Sinclair's rampage will not change anything. While individual agents such as Penrose may be removed, the system as such will go on as before, and the protagonist's 'subjective' violence will not be able to abolish 'systemic' violence (Žižek 2009: 1f) at all. Like those committed by Greenwood, Sinclair's murders will be 'rewritten' so that they can be securely assigned to one of the existing 'maps of problematic social reality' (Hall 1993: 98), and in the end, he will meet the same fate as his predecessor: "nearly six months after the event, a relieved Eden-Olympia had erased David Greenwood from its collective memory, filing the tragedy in some administrative limbo assigned to earthquakes and regicides" (*SC* 88). The fact that Sinclair's supporter and fellow conspirator Halder, who, through graffiti, arson, vandalism

---

73 This is a point Ballard has repeatedly made (e.g. 1996h, in Baxter 2004: 31f).
74 This resolution marks the culmination of a doubling of Sinclair and Greenwood that runs through the entire narrative. Cf. e.g. one scene in which, wearing the latter's tuxedo, Sinclair remarks: "Gazing at myself in the wardrobe mirror, I sensed that I had become Greenwood and assumed his role." (*SC* 288)
75 Interestingly, the murders perpetrated by Greenwood were carefully 'staged' by him so as to endow them with a distinctly retributive, moralistic and almost allegorical character – according to Sinclair, "[e]ach murder scene is a kind of tableau. Bachelet with his crack pipe and stolen jewellery. Berthoud with his suitcase of heroin. Vadim and the kiddie porn. Each photograph isn't Greenwood's crime scene – it's theirs." (*SC* 203) I feel that in this, the novel somewhat echoes director David Fincher's postmodern morality play *Seven*.

and sabotage, for his part attempts to destabilize the system by reintroducing heterogeneous elements into it, does not intend to subvert it but merely to displace his superiors and take their place, and that he manipulates and uses the protagonist in order to achieve this end (e.g. *SC* 378, 338), further strengthens the reader's impression of the ultimate futility of Sinclair's impending revolt. Empire will prevail.

Super-Cannes is therefore perhaps the most pessimistic and unambiguously dystopian novel in the Ballardian oeuvre. Here, in the words of Gasiorek, "the subject is figured as a puny entity whose interventions have no capacity to disturb the flows and exchanges of globalised multinational networks of power" (2005: 174). The ending of the narrative thus emerges as a highly ironic one: Ballard's only novel to close with a character's explicit act of critique and deliberate plan for a political (albeit destructive) act of resistance is at the same time his bleakest, making it clear that no such struggle will ever be of any avail. In this late text, not even the 'extreme possibility' of a catastrophic strategy seems to be able to challenge, let alone destroy, the truly "spectral reign of globalized capitalism" (Hardt and Negri 2001: 48).

6 In Pursuit of the 21ˢᵗ Century: The Revolutionary Imagination and the Spectacle of Terrorism in *Millennium People*

Rioters in business suits, Molotov cocktails fashioned out of Perrier bottles and regimental ties, sit-ins accompanied by Verdi operas, doctors and lawyers torching their own houses. In Ballard's *Millennium People*, it is not the proletariat but the middle class, traditionally conceived as "society's keel and anchor" (*MP* 5), who revolt. Not workers but architects and academics, surgeons and managers give up their jobs, responsibilities and lifestyles, take to the street and start a revolution. Considering themselves "the new proletariat" (*MP* 9), they set about dismantling the entire bourgeois way of life. Perhaps, the very idea of a middle-class rebellion may incite laughter, and there is a rich texture of humor in Ballard's novel indeed (cf. Baxter 2009: 209 f). It is particularly the juxtaposition between the dissenters' radical rhetoric and their affluent and protected existence – "Kropotkin with pink gins and wall-to-wall Axminster" (*MP* 67), as the autodiegetic narrator David Markham at one point puts it – as well as numerous rather inappropriate similes that are occasions for laughter. The protesters frequently compare their own situation to historical moments of social upheaval and revolution, which, again because of the repeatedly blatant disparity between those moments and the conditions of their own insurrection, is often quite amusing. They make reference, for example, to the October and the French Revolution as well as to the British miners' strike (*MP* 77, 156, 80), consider Twickenham "the Maginot Line of the English class system" (*MP* 85), link their plan of storming the V&A and pulling the copy of Michelangelo's *David* from its pedestal to the toppling of the statues of Stalin and Lenin after the fall of the Berlin Wall (*MP* 154), and see themselves as "little more than an indentured coolie force" (*MP* 104). It is mainly because of these humorous elements of the text that critics have tended to dismiss the rebellion as "superficial" and mere "farcical pseudo-politics" (Gasiorek 2005: 195), as a "protest driven more by convenience than the desire for change" and as fundamentally lacking "ideological integrity" and "political and historical authenticity" (Baxter 2009: 209 f, 210). Yet, it seems to me that these judgments may have been made rather too quickly. I would argue that the novel's portrayal of the middle-class revolution is much more ambivalent than critics have let on and that its humor should not eclipse the basic seriousness of the revolt. Ballard himself has implied as much in an interview: "Readers say that *Millennium People* made them laugh aloud, which is wonderful news, but then there is something inherently funny about the idea of a middle-class revolution. But perhaps that in itself is a sign of how brain-washed the middle-classes are. The very idea that we could rebel seems preposterous." (in Baxter 2004: 34) Therefore, I propose to take the rebellion seriously and to analyze its ideological thrust, its methods and goals, which have so far been widely ignored due to overhasty dismissals. Further, I will argue that the frequent inapt comparisons are not so much signs of a lack of authenticity, but rather indicators of the state of revolutionary discourse under late capitalism – a state, as we will see, in which the very appeal to authenticity appears increasingly futile.

Similarly, the following reading of the novel will also break with previous analyses of the violent terrorist attacks carried out by the charismatic Richard Gould and his followers. Critics have read his revolt as "primarily a metaphysical one" (Gasiorek 2005: 195), resulting from an overpowering nihilistic despair. While such a reading certainly suggests itself, it does not exhaust the polyvalence of the text. As in Ballard's other works, several discourses are overlaid in *Millennium People*, which allows us to place Gould's actions in a different, namely postmodern, context. By doing so, I will also depart from evaluations of his acts which consider them as an "empty gesture, [...] a blank protest", in which violence turns into a "voyeuristic spectacle" and is thus "[n]o longer experienced as shocking, no longer understood as *real*, [...] as suffering, as horror" (Gasiorek 2005: 198 f, 199); which, furthermore, reject his doings as nothing but a "highly articulate experiment in psychopathic imperialism" (Baxter 2009: 215) devoid of "any political programme" as well as "any notion of ethical truth or programmatic social change", thus amounting to a "revolt against sociality itself" (Gasiorek 2005: 212); and which, finally, see his rebellion as fueled by Romantic-expressive philosophies asserting the absolute primacy of the self and of its desire (Gasiorek 2005: 196 f). Against these readings, Gould's revolt will here be construed as a deeply (trans-)political one, based on another catastrophic strategy in which the subject is not prioritized but erased and whose spectacular nature, lack of political agenda and attack against sociality itself are not things to be lamented but, in fact, its very point. As I will argue, Ballard's late novel once again brings into sharp focus the topics that form the subject matter of this study – indeed, it arguably does so even more pointedly than all his other texts. *Millennium People* can be read as a profound investigation into the possibilities for critical thought and dissident action in the 21st century. As such, it points toward a continued, perhaps even renewed, need for political practice and critique in the new century, yet at the same time underscores once more that their received forms are no longer viable or effective and that the only way out is thus a veritable pataphysics of resistance.

6.1 Escaping the Soft-Regime Prison

As the title of Ballard's novel has it, its protagonists are 'millennium people', all "[i]n pursuit of a new millennium" (*MP* 65). The 20th century from which they are trying to escape is said to "shap[e] everything we do, the way we think"; by doing so, according to Richard Gould, it "lock[ed] the doors on us. We're living in a soft-regime prison built by earlier generations of inmates. Somehow we have to break free." (*MP* 63, 139) The characters' desire to usher in a new millennium is thus an attempt to liberate themselves from the kinds of subjection that determine their lives under consumer capitalism and its diffuse networks of power. The metaphor of the inmate-built soft-regime prison is central here. It expresses in nuce all the crucial elements of the revolutionaries' social and political critique. For much more important than the 'material' dimension of the protest is its 'ideological' dimension. On the one hand, the rebels demonstrate against their increasingly precarious social existence due to ever higher rents, stagnating salaries, rising interest rates, etc. There is considerable humor here, for, as Markham points out, "[t]hese people want to change the world, use violence if they need to, but they've never had the central heating turned off in their lives" (*MP* 67). Yet even here, the narrator's wit should not lead us to overlook the serious side to the dissenters' claim to be a new kind of proletariat and to write them off as hypocritical imposters. Rather, it is the category of the 'proletariat' itself that needs to be redefined in view of the changes in the schemata of capitalist production and exploitation effected by global capitalism. According to Michael Hardt and Antonio Negri,

> [w]e need to recognize that the very subject of labor and revolt has changed profoundly. The composition of the proletariat has transformed and thus our understanding of it must too. In conceptual terms we understand *proletariat* as a broad category that includes all those whose labor is directly or indirectly exploited by and subjected to capitalist norms of production and reproduction.[1] (2001: 52)

Much more central to the novel, however, is the (in a stricter sense) ideological aspect of the rebellion: the insurgents' deconstruction and rejection of the dominant, bourgeois ideology. This principal element of the revolt is already intimated in the very first chapter. Walking through the deserted and ruined estate of Chelsea Marina in the novel's present – most of the plot is presented in analepsis – Markham spots "an almost new worsted suit, the daytime uniform of a mid-

---

[1] As early as 1967, Guy Debord similarly remarked that the new economic system "*proletarianize[d]* the whole world" (2009: 31). In this context, cf. also Gray 2003: 161.

dle-ranking executive, lying among the debris like the discarded fatigues of a soldier who had thrown down his rifle and taken to the hills. The suit seemed strangely vulnerable, the abandoned flag of an entire civilization" (*MP* 8). Like the briefcase, hat and raincoat in *Concrete Island*, the suit is, of course, a metaphor for the bourgeoisie. The fact that it has been discarded despite its impeccable condition is, then, clearly equally metaphoric, something that is underlined by the simile of the deserted soldier. According to Hardt and Negri, forms of 'being-against' such as desertion and "[t]he refusal of work and authority" are "the beginning of liberatory politics" (2001: 204, cf. also 210–214). What we are presented with as early as in the opening pages of the book is thus an image of desertion from the dominant ideology and the established social order, an act which potentially renders that order 'vulnerable'.

But how, precisely, is the ideological battle against this order fought? What kind of social critique is the middle-class revolution based on? The aversion towards theory of the Film Studies lecturer Kay Churchill, the leader of the rebellion, notwithstanding – she feels there is "too much jargon around" and condemns "Marxist theory-speak swallowing its own tail" (*MP* 53) – the thought underlying the revolt is clearly derived from the (Neo-)Marxist tradition.[2] This legacy occasionally manifests itself in the revolutionaries' rhetoric as well, as can be seen in the following passage: "As in the past, we all agreed, the police were doing the dirty work for a ruthless venture capitalism that perpetuated the class system in order to divide the opposition and preserve its own privileges." (*MP* 216) In their criticism of the capitalist system, Kay and her followers address several different ways by which power is exercised and maintained. Among their main targets are cultural institutions such as the National Film Theatre, the BBC and video stores, which, just like tourism and consumerism, they attack for "making [the middle class] docile" (*MP* 61). Recalling Marx's (1982: 131) famous condemnation of religion, they see these institutions as performing a crucial socio-political role, functioning as an "opiate", whose "corrupting fantasies" (*MP* 92, 120) serve to reconcile people to their existence. The rebels' critique, especially of the mass media, clearly recalls Theodor Adorno and Max Horkheimer's prescient analysis of the 'culture industry' of the 1940s. This industry, the two philosophers argue, expresses the "regression of enlightenment to ideology", whose content "is exhausted in the idolization of the existing order and of the power by which the technology is controlled" (2002: xviii, xix). According-

---

[2] In fact, one might perhaps argue that Kay's commitment to practice is itself a typical element of the Marxist legacy. Cf. e. g. Marx's famous pronouncement that "[t]he philosophers have only *interpreted* the world in various ways; the point is, to *change* it" (1994: 101).

ly, the products of the culture industry are propelled by the system's imperative of "not for a moment allowing [the recipients] to suspect that resistance is possible" and, quite the reverse, of getting them to "insist unwaveringly on the ideology by which they are enslaved" (Horkheimer and Adorno 2002: 113, 106). These ideas are reflected in a number of passages in Ballard's novel, as for instance in the following:

> the BBC had played a leading role in brainwashing the middle classes. Its regime of moderation and good sense, its commitment to the Reithian aims of education and enlightenment, had been an elaborate cover behind which it imposed an ideology of passivity and self-restraint. The BBC had defined the national culture, a swindle in which the middle classes had colluded, assuming that moderation and civic responsibility were in their own interest. (*MP* 149f)

While the Chelsea Marina revolutionaries occasionally still seem to hold to a rather orthodox understanding of ideology as 'false consciousness', that is, as a static set of deceiving ideas simply imposed 'from above', most of their remarks and activities clearly evince a more complex conception of control, with attention being given to the essentially processual dimension and the material existence of ideology as well as to the largely productive nature of power. As the dissenters have realized, subjugation in late capitalism has to be rethought beyond manipulation and repression. This realization stands behind the numerous comments proposing the idea that today, "[t]here are no Mr Bigs" because "[t]he system is self-regulating" in that the middle classes "police themselves" (*MP* 104, 89). As Antonio Gramsci has pointed out, domination can only be permanent if it is based on both what he terms 'political society' as well as 'civil society'. To coercive power which *enforces* discipline must thus always be added 'hegemony', "[t]he 'spontaneous' consent given by the great masses of the population to the general direction imposed on social life by the dominant fundamental group" (Gramsci 1971: 12, emphasis added). The state, Gramsci writes, equals "political society + civil society, in other words hegemony protected by the armour of coercion" (1971: 263).[3] The notion of 'hegemony' is crucial to Kay's critique in the novel: according to her, it is precisely "the whole middle-class dream" (*MP* 86) that people aspire to – a dream that includes such elements as a higher education, employment, wealth and security, a sense of civic responsibility and moderation, respect for the law, and liberal values – that is a key instrument in their subordination. Thus, when Gasiorek dismisses the protesters' actions because they "really mark the final dissolution of civic responsibility"

---

[3] As will become clear below, both aspects are emphasized in Ballard's novel.

(2005: 195), he fails to see that this is precisely the point, that this dissolution represents a conscious act of subversion, since the notion of responsibility in question was itself fashioned by power for the purpose of stabilizing the status quo. Through their very ambitions and ideals, their values and norms, even their most intimate desires and beliefs, people actively reaffirm the system that ensures their subjection. Even the bourgeoisie's dearly-held 'common sense', all that can supposedly safely be 'taken for granted', must be recognized as a product of power that binds them to it.

Gramsci's view of ideology as a process constantly at work, his interest in its material nature, as well as his notion of the two fundamental levels of force and of consent reappeared later in modified form in the work of Louis Althusser. The French Marxist philosopher argues that ideology is continuously reproduced in people's everyday practice, in their speaking, thinking and acting. In particular, he emphasizes the central role of 'ideological state apparatuses' (ISAs) such as the family, school, university, church, and the media in constituting us as subjects in, and to, ideology. These institutions, according to Althusser, hail or 'interpellate' the individuals into determinate subject-positions constructed for them by the system; through their responding and inhabiting of the designated subjectivities, the existing social relations are reproduced. Analogous to Kay's notion that "[t]he prisoners polish their chains" (*MP* 90), Althusser explains that in this way, power guarantees that "the vast majority of (good) subjects work all right 'all by themselves'", that "the individual *is interpellated as a (free) subject in order that he shall submit freely to the commandments of the Subject, i.e. in order that he shall (freely) accept his subjection*, i.e. in order that he shall make the gestures and actions of his subjection 'all by himself'" (1971: 181, 182). Althusser maintains that of all ISAs, the school is of particular importance today: "I believe that the ideological State apparatus which has been installed in the *dominant* position in mature capitalist social formations [...] is the *educational ideological apparatus*." (1971: 152) A very similar conviction appears to motivate the residents of Chelsea Marina when they decide to withdraw their children from their schools, "rejecting the entire ethos of private education" as "a vast obedience-training conspiracy" (*MP* 152, 152f). Education now presents itself to them as not much more than a vital tool in the reproduction of the relations of production, with "[e]ach mass ejected *en route*", in the words of Althusser, "practically provided with the ideology which suits the role it has to fulfil in class society" (1971: 155). Inspired by Kay and Gould, according to the reverend Stephen Dexter, the rebels "see that private schools are brainwashing their children into a kind of social docility, turning them into a professional class who will run the show for consumer capitalism" (*MP* 104).

In their critique of the ways power is internalized by those it subordinates, the middle-class revolutionaries are sometimes closest to the thought of Althusser's student Michel Foucault. Similar to his teacher, Foucault has shown that power no longer has to be enforced externally because it now produces subjects which are completely amenable to it. At one point in the novel, Kay sardonically states that "[o]ur ancient democracy has its eyes and ears everywhere – cameras in teapots, microphones behind the chintz. Every time you take a pee some security man at MI5 is making a note of your manhood. We all do it." (*MP* 49) The rebel leader here does not only point to the erosion of such democratic pillars as civil rights through the steady increase of public surveillance (CCTV) – and that in a country that has always prized itself on its libertarian tradition (it is no coincidence that the cameras are placed in *teapots*; as a symbol of national culture, Kay's image suggests that this British tradition is now hollowed out). Beyond that, Kay also implies that contemporary power is of what Foucault terms the 'disciplinary' type, which has already been mentioned in earlier chapters. In 'panoptic' societies as ours, she seems to suggest, in which disciplinary mechanisms are no longer confined to certain specific institutions but instead pervade the entire social body, control functions entirely automatically. As Foucault puts it, "[h]e who is subjected to a field of visibility, and who knows it, assumes responsibility for the constraints of power; he makes them play spontaneously upon himself; he inscribes in himself the power relation in which he simultaneously plays both roles" (1979: 202f). As Kay's example of 'peeing' makes clear, 'discipline' is a modality of power primarily exercised on the body, which it "invests [...] in depth" (Foucault 1979: 217): it adjusts individuals to a norm by structuring and regulating their gestures, postures and movements. The singular importance of the norm in modern societies has repeatedly been stressed by Foucault. He explains that "[t]he discourse of discipline has nothing in common with that of law, rule, or sovereign will. The disciplines may well be the carriers of a discourse that speaks of a rule, but a natural rule, a norm. The code they come to define is not that of law but that of normalisation." (1980: 106) According to Foucault, in connection with the interdependent rise of capitalism and life-centered 'biopower', the law gradually changes its form: it no longer "refers to the sword", but instead "operates more and more as a norm, and [...] the judicial institution is increasingly incorporated into a continuum of apparatuses (medical, administrative, and so on) whose functions are for the most part regulatory. A normalizing society is the historical outcome of a technology of power centered on life." (1978: 144)

This normalizing power is another main target of the revolutionaries' social critique. Kay expounds that "the middle class have to be kept under control. They understand that, and police themselves. Not with guns and gulags, but with social codes. The right way to have sex, treat your wife, flirt at tennis parties or start an affair. There are unspoken rules we all have to learn." (*MP* 89) Like Foucault, Ballard's heroine thus underscores that the system does not need to make use of repression anymore, but instead can rely on the self-surveillance and -regulation of its subjects. Her statement that 'we all' internalize these norms and that 'we all' keep watch over their observance (see above) echoes Foucault's declaration that "[t]he judges of normality are present everywhere" (1979: 304). These omnipresent judges continually reinforce "the barriers set out by the system": "Try living with a teenage girl or having sex with your stepson. Try saying you believe in God and the Holy Trinity, or giving a free room to a refugee family from black Africa. Try taking a holiday in Benidorm, or driving a brand-new Cadillac with zebra upholstery. Try bad taste." (*MP* 86) Particularly in her last examples, Kay displays an understanding of aesthetic sense not only as something constructed and relative, not natural and universal, but also as a powerful bearer of class differences. In this, she seems to follow the French Neo-Marxist sociologist Pierre Bourdieu, who has argued that all our dispositions of the mind and body – the so-called 'habitus' – are a product of our place in the social world. Bourdieu reveals cognitive structures to be "'embodied' social structures" and bodily behavior as "social necessity made second nature, turned into muscular patterns and bodily automatisms" (1989: 468, 474). Thus, people's likes and dislikes, that is, their perceptions and classifications, even their very schemes of perception and classification, as well as their most automatic and apparently insignificant bodily techniques – their ways of walking, talking or eating – are ultimately all based on class.[4] According to Bourdieu, practices of 'distinction' enacted in the medium of taste (cultural products, food, lifestyle, clothes, etc.) as well as in all the little details of bodily hexis continually mark and re-mark class divisions, while at the same time, the habitus of the dominant social groups is universalized out of its class origin into a hegemonic position for all members of society. The function of the habitus is therefore ultimately a conservative one:

> One of the most important effects of the correspondence between real divisions and practical principles of division, between social structures and mental structures, is undoubtedly the fact that primary experience of the social world is that of doxa, an adherence to relations of order which, because they structure inseparably both the real world and the thought world, are accepted as self-evident. [...] Thus the conservation of the social order is decisively reinforced by [...] the orchestration of categories of perception of the so-

---

[4] In an interview, Ballard himself evinces a similar sense for the social conditioning of perception, taste, etc.: "I like Indian food, but that's not an artificial need, it's a genuine thing, a taste, though it was artificially imposed on me." (in Burns/Sugnet 1981: 21)

cial world, which, being adjusted to the divisions of the established order (and thereby to the interests of those who dominate it) and common to all minds structured in accordance with those structures, present every appearance of objective necessity. (Bourdieu 1989: 471)

Hence, when Ballard's Kay organizes attacks not only against the institutions of the culture industry but also against the places of 'high culture' such as Tate Modern, claiming that the fine arts "delud[e] the middle classes that a developed 'cultural' sensibility endow[s] them with a moral superiority denied to football fans or garden gnome enthusiasts" (*MP* 154), this can be read as a critique of the ideology of taste and distinction and of the whole economy of 'cultural capital' in which it has its place (Bourdieu 1986).

The deconstruction of the dominant ideology and the exposure of the various mechanisms of control securing the perpetuation of the status quo, largely neglected by academic criticism on Ballard's novel to date, are thus central elements of the uprising in Chelsea Marina. As the analysis of the ideological thrust of the protesters' critique and the disclosure of its many parallels with the theories developed by the philosophers of the Frankfurt School, by Gramsci, Althusser, Foucault, and Bourdieu has shown, the rebellion is clearly an heir to the critical thought of the (Neo-)Marxist tradition. In particular, it shares with this tradition a concern for the diverse ways in which power is internalized today, so that domination under late capitalism is more complete than ever before. This is the meaning of the metaphor of the soft-regime prison built by its inmates. It is a perfect image for the self-regulating postmodern 'society of control' (Deleuze 2011), in which subjects are produced in and through relations of power, in which the mechanisms of rule become ever 'softer' and more 'democratic', and whose members ever more avidly desire precisely that which subjects them. Thus, when the rebels, in the words of Gould, which once again evoke the image of the soft-regime prison, begin to "pee[l] the velvet off the bars and tast[e] the steel" (*MP* 170) and attack contemporary forms of subjugation, they are clearly engaged in an attempt at 'desubjectivation' or 'disidentification' (Pêcheux 1982), that is, at dismantling subjectivities manufactured by power. The narrator's repeated declaration that the revolutionaries are "protesting against themselves" because "[t]hey know *they* are the enemy" (*MP* 109) must be read in this light: they question their deepest beliefs and convictions, distrust their most unconscious and spontaneous perceptions and evaluations, and try to disrupt their sense of who they are. In this context, Kay's assertion that she is "unlearning" (*MP* 89) the norms which she, like everyone else, has internalized resonates with Raymond Williams' claim that "we have to unlearn [...] the inherent dominative mode" (1958: 336).

Perhaps, the fact that the dissenters are repeatedly referred to as "a new tribe of [...] gypsies" (*MP* 7) can be taken as an indication of their attempt to fashion a new, resistant kind of subjectivity and lifestyle, and at the same time of the anxieties their transgressions provoke in other people. The 'gypsy' – understood not as a specific ethnic group, but as a discursively constructed category that has historically been applied to a number of different people(s) – of course, has a long history of such provocation, whose most recent major expression in England was possibly the 1985 Battle of the Beanfield, which saw the mass arrest and violent abuse of several hundred New Age travelers at the hands of the Wiltshire police force, ideologically backed by the conservative Thatcher government and various mainstream media.[5] The new nomadism of Ballard's rebels – according to Hardt and Negri (2001: 210–214, 361–364), an important element of contemporary political resistance – may be *socially* peripheral, but like that of the New Age travelers and numerous 'gypsies' before them, it is *symbolically* central (Stallybrass and White 1986: 5). As with so many symbolic inversions, the protesters' transgression of cultural values and norms is somewhat transcoded into a discourse of the (grotesque) body pointing to the fundamental exclusions and denials that accompany and make possible the constitution of the dominant, 'proper' ('actual'/'clean') culture. Thus, when a woman watching the departure of the protesters, who at one point desert Chelsea Marina, disapprovingly comments that "[t]here's more than a touch of the gypsy in them" and shakes her head "in disgust" (*MP* 265), it is precisely this expulsion of all that the bourgeois subject, in its self-definition, marked out as 'low' and "internalized under the sign of negation and disgust" (Stallybrass and White 1986: 191) that is at stake.

As we have seen, the middle-class rebellion in *Millennium People* is characterized by a genuine political impetus and by dedicated emancipatory practice and should thus not be dismissed as superficial and dishonest pseudo-politics. It is because of the insurrection's seriousness, of its pointed ideological critique and its sincere goal of achieving liberation from late-capitalist subjection that the narrator, at the very end of the novel, looks back on the events that took place in West London as "a brief period when Chelsea Marina was a place of real promise" (*MP* 293 f).

---

[5] Notably, in Ballard's novel, it is the traditionally conservative *Daily Mail* that dubs the Chelsea Marina revolutionaries "'the first middle-class gypsies'" (*MP* 153).

6.2 Subversion, No End of Subversion – Only Not for Us

In the end, however, the revolution at Chelsea Marina fails. Baxter rightly observes that the novel "opens on a note of post-apocalyptic fatigue" (2009: 208), and protagonist David Markham notes that what has changed after the uprising is hard to elicit – if anything has changed at all (*MP* 231, 234, 289). Baxter identifies the main cause of this failure in what she sees as the rebellion's lack of integrity and authenticity, which ultimately makes it nothing more than "a postmodern performance of political pastiche" (2009: 210). I want to argue, however, that much of what Baxter considers to be signs of hypocrisy and deceit inherent to the protest are really markers of the fundamental ineffectualness of received forms of political critique and resistance in late-capitalist postmodernity. As this section will show, Ballard's novel indicates that the reason for this ineffectualness is threefold: the revolution does not succeed because its subversive energies are ultimately contained and reterritorialized by the all-encompassing market and the ever more flexible mechanisms of social control; because cultural conditioning in the end proves to be too powerful, so that all attempts at desubjectivation eventually fail; and, most importantly, because it does not take into account the simulative nature of the system, attacking it according to a logic power itself has prescribed.

After 'the bonfire of the Volvos' (the title of chapter 27), a culminatory violent conflict between the middle-class insurgents and the police, it seems that Kay and her followers have carried the day. The police withdraw, acquiesce not to bring any charges, quietly forget the attacks against public institutions such as Tate Modern or the National Film Theatre, and agree to examine the residents' complaints and to negotiate. Subsequently, Kay's face is "flushed with victory" (*MP* 231) – yet, as the attentive reader already surmises, and as will become ever clearer in the rest of the novel, this truce is far from a victory; indeed, what follows is not a history of triumph but a veritable case study of containment. In this process, the revolution falls prey to the two forms of incorporation identified and described by Dick Hebdige (1979: 92–99), the 'ideological' form and the 'commercial' one.

At the end of the text, it appears like the authorities have given in:

> Kensington and Chelsea Council [...] ordered an army of workers into the estate. They dragged away the burnt-out cars, asphalted the streets and repaired the damaged houses. [...] Amicable negotiations with the management company ended with the promise of a financial sweetener from the council. In return, the company postponed the rise in maintenance charges that had set off the revolt. [...] Like nurses, bus drivers and traffic wardens, the middle-class professionals of Chelsea Marina were now seen as poorly paid but vital contributors to the life of the city. This sentiment, repeated by a relieved Home Secretary in many television interviews, confirmed the residents' original belief that they were the new proletariat. (*MP* 289)

The residents' protest and its legitimacy are finally officially recognized and the problems addressed – and yet, it is precisely this that spells defeat, not success. It is not in spite but *because* of this recognition that the revolution fails to have any significant political effect. Raymond Williams points out that "much incorporation looks like recognition, acknowledgement, and thus a form of *acceptance*" (1977: 125). By confirming the rebels' self-perception and acknowledging/ascribing to them their role as 'poorly paid but vital contributors' to society, the system is eventually able to firmly place them within its 'maps of meaning' (Hall 1993: 98) and absorb them into the orderliness and regularity of its received procedures. The protest is redefined in the terms of the political establishment and its subversive otherness thus minimized, indeed, reduced to sameness. In this way, the status quo remains utterly untouched. It is no wonder the Home Secretary feels 'relieved'. This kind of 'hermeneutic appropriation', of containment through recognition, is, of course, a core element of Western liberalism. As Markham so aptly puts it: "We had won, but what exactly? Gazing at the quiet streets, I was conscious of an emotional vacuum. Our victory had been a little too easy [...]. I had overturned cars and helped to fill Perrier bottles with lighter fuel, but a tolerant and liberal society had smiled at me and walked away" (*MP* 234). Notably, in the process of recognition, the revolution is entirely reduced to its material dimension. By presenting themselves as responsive to some of the concrete grievances that initially started the revolt, the authorities cleverly transform these into the sole matter of contention and utterly cast aside its much more important ideological dimension. Integrated into the system's finely attuned structures of political and social decision-making – what Jacques Rancière (1999) has referred to as the order of the 'police', the opposite of true 'politics' – the protesters are forced to submit to its discursive rules and boundaries, which allow only certain demands to be heard or, in fact, to be voiced.[6] It is striking, and truly disheartening, to witness how the idealistic Kay, upon entering this order, compromises all her far-reaching claims and ideas and quickly becomes "a voice of moderation" (*MP* 162). No longer an agent of radical dissent, she now leads residents' delegations, conducts 'amicable negotiations' (see above) and thus turns into yet another "political figure, arguing her case on discussion programmes, profiled in the Sunday broadsheets and backed by ambitious young lawyers with time on their hands" (*MP* 166). Kay is immediately assimilated into "the corporate world of corridor politics" (*MP* 140) ruled by the dictum of consensus, by political rationality and common

---

[6] Rancière's brilliant thought on these issues is captured in his crucial, but untranslatable, term *la mésentente*.

sense, which makes any kind of rigorous disruption of the social order impossible through the very conditions of political articulation it prescribes.

The fact that, regardless of the high number and the extreme nature of the insurrectionists' attacks, astoundingly, no charges are brought against them indicates the system's profound anxiety and desperate concern to preserve or re-create the existing social order. This, needless to say, includes – is, quite probably, even mainly driven by – the smooth functioning of the capitalist economy, as the novel's almost obsessive focus on property values makes clear. Again and again, the authorities are depicted as extremely "nervous of the effects that a social revolution would have on [...] property values", and it is no coincidence that, at the very end of the text, Markham comes across a "retouched aerial photograph" of Chelsea Marina that represents it as "a place of almost millennial charm, with crime-free streets and ever-rising property values" (*MP* 289, 293). In a way, this picture is the absolute symbol of defeat: no trace of the revolution is left, it has become entirely reabsorbed into the capitalist spectacle of space as commodity, and the '*millennial* charm' of this spectacle is the very negation of all the dissenters' ambitions, a cynical cancellation of their pursuit of a new, liberated millennium.

The restoration of the status quo is further supported by the mass media, which devise convenient narratives that reshape reality in accordance with the dominant discourses and paper over anything that might prove harmful to hegemonic definitions of the world. Thus, for example, Markham picks up an evening paper whose headline reads "'Luxury Rent Rebels Surrender'" (*MP* 269), which actually was not the case, and is at the end identified as the man who killed Gould and thus saved the Home Secretary, even though it was Stephen Dexter who shot Gould and Markham seriously doubts that even the Home Office believes its own story (*MP* 290). Yet, a neat narrative is needed, so Markham is not questioned too closely or put through a powder test of his hands, and he soon turns into Gould's killer. As he himself observes: "media speculation is today's crucible of accepted truth" (*MP* 290). More than that, the media also play a crucial role in the commodification of the revolution. After the end of the uprising, Kay, for instance, "secure[s] a large advance for her book-of-the revolution" and goes on to become "a successful columnist and TV pundit" (*MP* 290), proclaiming the revolution on an afternoon cable channel (*MP* 7), making "a television documentary about middle-class radicalism in the London suburbs" (*MP* 234), etc. Though somewhat still committed to the struggle for change, the former leader of the rebellion has become wholly sucked into the capitalist media-machine, which exploits her experiences and personality and, of course, always prescribes the forms her reports may take (and, possibly, the content as well). If this is still rebelliousness, it is, in the words of Debord, "spectacular rebelliousness": here, "dissatisfaction itself becomes a commodity" (2009: 48). This recuperation into the media-capitalist spectacle comprises the narrator as well: he, too, plans to write a book about the background and aims of the revolution (*MP* 293). It thus seems only a matter of time until Markham, like Kay, the newly crowned 'pundit', will become part of the army of countless self-designated 'experts' who swamp today's media landscape and who are such a useful tool in the continuous struggle of the dominant social groups to shape public opinion and the 'common sense' and thus secure their hegemony. Gould is therefore right when, at one point in the novel, he predicts the fate of the revolt: "Nothing will happen. [...] The storm will die down, and everything will peter out in a drizzle of television shows and op-ed pieces." (*MP* 170)

In the end, we see the Chelsea Marina protest as deprived of all its political potential, fully incorporated and commodified, and about to take its illustrious place among "the country's civic traditions, along with the Lord Mayor's parade, Ascot week and Henley Regatta" (*MP* 38). What was initially a highly subversive movement now faces a bitter end: "Our modest revolution would become part of the folkloric calendar, to be celebrated along with the last night of the Proms and the Wimbledon tennis fortnight." (*MP* 10) What Hebdige says about subcultures hence turns out to apply to the rebellion as well: "It is through [a] continual process of recuperation that the fractured order is repaired and the [revolt] incorporated as a diverting spectacle within the dominant mythology" (1979: 94). In fact, as with punk and mod culture, which, as Hebdige shows, "begin by issuing symbolic challenges, but [...] must inevitably end by establishing new sets of conventions; by creating new commodities, new industries or rejuvenating old ones" (1979: 96), the middle-class revolution, too, soon inspires a "new guerrilla chic", quickly "featured in an *Evening Standard* fashion spread" (*MP* 234). In nearly all respects, the rebellion is thus eventually absorbed into the capitalist spectacle and entirely taken up in the commodity form, on which the ideological and commercial types of incorporation converge (Hebdige 1979: 96). The system's effectively limitless power of containment is aptly expressed by the narrator: "The infantilizing consumer society filled any gaps in the status quo as quickly as Kay had driven her Polo into the collapsing barricade" (*MP* 234).

Besides such forms of recuperation, power is shown to rely as well on more immediate kinds of control. The most important of these in the text are the forces of the 'repressive state apparatuses' (Althusser 1971) – chiefly the London riot police – and panoptic surveillance. In fact, the more one reads, the more one is gripped by the chilling impression of a hermetically sealed, claustrophobic social space in which dissident acts are virtually impossible because the agents of repression are always waiting just around the corner and because all the cracks and fissures in the system have been tightly closed, all its dark corners brightly lit up, so that no action goes unnoticed. Ballard's novel draws the image of a London whose skies are constantly filled with police helicopters and where security cameras record one's every move. In such a society, in which power, to repeat Kay's words quoted earlier, "has its eyes and ears everywhere" (*MP* 49), Gould's paranoiac-obsessive fear of surveillance cameras – "[t]he world has too many cameras", he states, "[s]tay away from cameras" (*MP* 202, 207), he advises Markham – practically becomes a general condition.

The textual embodiment of this panopticism, and of the inescapable grip of power more generally, is the elusive figure of Major Tulloch, one that has up to now been almost completely ignored by critics. All through the novel, this character remains only a vague and mysterious presence in the background of events, often present but never interfering or even speaking. Tellingly, the only time he does step forth, at the very end of the text, it is to restore order and initiate the narrative of Markham as Gould's killer, thus fashioning a coherent, uncomplicated picture of all that has been happening, one that accords with hegemonic explanations of the events and in which the threat to the social order (represented by Gould's subversive philosophy) is consequently eliminated (see below). It is the very intangibleness of this figure that makes it such a compelling representation of contemporary power, that is, of a power that is only rarely openly repressive or even visible *as power*, but that is nevertheless present all the time and effectively always in control. This is why Tulloch is constantly presented as "scanning" the environment, "keeping an eye on" the revolution, as "ever-watchful" and "all-seeing" (*MP* 30, 203, 237, 266), but also as continuously bored, "unimpressed and detached" (*MP* 287): since there is nothing that escapes the gaze of power, nothing that can really threaten it, it can afford to stand back and allow events to run their course. It is only fitting that, early on in the plot, Tulloch asks Markham's fellow psychologist Henry Kendall to work for him, to "[j]oin demos, *stand back and observe*, map the emerging psychology" (*MP* 32, emphasis added). We may read this as a sign of the system's desire to expand its "micro-physics of power" ever further, to widen its field of visibility, to extend its supervision right down to the depths of society and its most elementary particles, and thus to transform "the whole social body into a field of perception: thousands of eyes posted everywhere, mobile attentions ever on the alert" (Foucault 1979: 26, 214). For the residents of Chelsea Marina, subjected as they are to such a permanent and omnipresent surveillance, visibility is indeed "a trap" (Foucault 1979: 200).

The novel suggests that this trap might be even more cunning than it appears at first sight. It repeatedly implies that power, represented principally by Major Tulloch, not only monitors the revolution's development very closely and prevents it from ever turning into a serious threat, but, more than that, even *welcomes* the insurrection and *thrives* on it, effectively using it as an experiment to test possible directions and dimensions of social resistance as well as ways of managing and containing it. Thus, Stephen Dexter at one point surmises that the authorities are "letting [the rebels] run with the ball. They want to see where this leads." (*MP* 107) Markham later comes to a similar conclusion when, after the revolutionaries' seeming victory over the police, he realizes that "[a]t any time during the riot [the police] [were] free to enter Chelsea Marina in force and attack the residents from the rear" and that therefore "[t]he entire confrontation might well have ended within minutes rather than hours" (*MP* 236). Markham concludes:

> A combined air, sea and land assault on Chelsea Marina might easily have been mounted, but the police, or whoever controlled them, had held back [...].
> Had the entire confrontation, which so lifted our spirits, been staged to test the resolve of the Chelsea Marina residents? By confining their action to a single street the police had kept the revolution within acceptable limits and tested its temper. I thought of the ever-watchful Major Tulloch with his tweed sports jackets[7] and 'links' to the Home Office, clearly bored by the petrol bombs and hysteria. For Scotland Yard the confrontation across the burning Fiats and Volvos had been a ploy to tease out the residents and their possible access to more dangerous weapons than croquet mallets and moral indignation. (*MP* 236 f)

In the end, Markham's suspicion proves correct: not much later, a large police force enters Chelsea Marina and quickly seizes control of the estate, making it clear that the rebels indeed "fell into a trap" (*MP* 245). The fate of the middle-class revolution thus affirms the New Historicist hypothesis that most of the time, a "subversiveness that is genuine and radical [...] is at the same time contained by the power it would appear to threaten", and more than that, that "the subversiveness is the very product of that power and furthers its ends" (Greenblatt 1988: 30). To allude to the title of a much-quoted essay by Stephen Greenblatt, the bullets that are being fired in this battle are largely 'invisible', that is, the subjects involved are often unwitting participants in the larger processes of subversion and containment of which they are nevertheless the vehicles. In this way, Ballard's protagonist ultimately has to realize that all the time he was an active participant in the Chelsea Marina rebellion he was being closely monitored and in fact working 'undercover' for the Home Office: "So, all along I've

---

7 It is perhaps no coincidence that Tulloch is presented as always wearing tweed jackets; after all, this cloth has a long tradition in the performance of political identities in England. There is what might be called a 'cultural politics of tweed' in Britain that links it closely with the Conservative Party and with notions of tradition and continuity as well as stability and order (Baldwin et al. 2004: 235–237).

been a police spy? Without realizing it?" (*MP* 268) In Ballard's novel, as in the early-modern plays so skilfully analyzed by Greenblatt and numerous others, power "not only produces its own subversion but is actively built upon it" (Greenblatt 1988: 30). At the end of the text, the system the revolutionaries set out to attack is not undermined or even weakened but, on the contrary, consolidated. It modifies its hegemonic constructions of reality in order to accommodate and incorporate the voices of dissent and refines its mechanisms of social control. The fact that Chelsea Marina's former manager's office is quickly turned into a "residents' advice bureau" (*MP* 293) after the end of the revolt is emblematic of this refinement: this is the Deleuzian society of control, which successfully projects an image of ever increasing freedom and permissiveness while really, the circuits of command merely change shape, becoming ever more 'horizontal', preemptive, flexible and adaptable. Through this transformation, control seems to disappear, but in truth becomes only more effective.

Perhaps, the abandoned mental asylum of Bedfont Hospital, at which Gould used to work and to which he occasionally returns, can be read as a symbol of an earlier disciplinary society that has now evolved into the society of control. Like a good semiotician, Markham 'reads' the building's impressive architecture, remarking that there are "moral judgements enshrined in every forbidding corbel" and observing that "[t]his [is] the architecture of prisons, cotton mills and steel foundries, monuments to the endurance of brick and the Victorian certainties" (*MP* 127, 129). Hospitals, prisons, factories – these are the characteristic disciplinary institutions analyzed by Foucault, whose walls have today broken down and whose function has spread throughout the social field (Hardt and Negri 2001: 22–27, 329–332). In this contemporary society of control, a rebellion such as the one in Chelsea Marina is no real threat to power. It is rather like a case study, an exercise in 'conflict management', which ultimately allows the system to pull its web of control ever tighter by developing its circuits of subjection in such a way that the recourse to repressive apparatuses like the police will possibly not be necessary any more in the future. It is telling that the 'participant-observer' in this study, Major Tulloch, appears only at the beginning and again towards the end of the novel; he is entirely absent from the events of the plot for over 150 pages. This limited textual presence can be seen as corresponding to his role as the secret conductor of the social experiment of the Chelsea Marina revolution, withdrawing and observing once things have begun to run their course. Tulloch's parenthesis-like presence in the narrative mirrors the all-embracing, controlling and containing grasp of power, which permits no escape and for which even resistance is no true challenge, but only furthers its own ends. One therefore has to disagree with Jeannette Baxter, who, pointing out that the unsuccessful middle-class revolution was being monitored all along, concludes that "[t]he only genuine aspect of the Chelsea Marina rebellion [...] is its lack of authenticity" (2009: 213). As has been shown, the insurrection fails not because of the protesters' "dissimulation" (Baxter 2009: 213), but because of the system's virtually endless power of reterritorialization.

Another reason for this failure is that the subject-positions into which the rebels have been interpellated by their culture, the identities through which they have been subjectivated, cannot easily be dismantled. When, even in the midst of a social revolution, the middle-class dissenters to a certain degree still follow "their instinct for order and good housekeeping" – sweeping the streets, straightening protest banners – so that, in the end, the rebellion remains somewhat "modest and well behaved" (*MP* 233, 3), this could be construed as yet another indication of the revolutionaries' lack of integrity, yet I propose to read this "reversion to type" (*MP* 233) as a sign of the ultimately unshakeable entrenchedness of socially conditioned forms of behavior. Kay and her fellow insurgents' undiscardable "middle-class reflex[es]" (*MP* 158) suggest not their hypocrisy, but the power of the Bourdieuian habitus. At the end of the novel, Markham realizes as much and reasons: "the revolution was doomed from the start. Nature had bred the middle class to be docile, virtuous and civic-minded. Self-denial was coded into its genes." (*MP* 292) Even though he falsely naturalizes what is clearly of social origins, Markham nevertheless correctly recognizes that the failure of the rebellion is also due to the protesters' unsuccessful attempt at desubjectivation.

Most importantly, however, the revolution stands no chance of overthrowing the system because it attacks power on a level at which, as Jean Baudrillard has shown, power continues to exist only as its own simulation. The rebels attack the system with weapons that consequently can have no real effect – even more so since they are tied to a logic derived from the system itself. One of the revolutionaries' main strategies to effect a subversion of the existing order can be said to consist in *appropriation*, a strategy that, of course, has a long history in all kinds of resistance movements. As one protester at one point explains: "people have to work with the conventions they're used to" (*MP* 78). Thus, for instance, when Kay, under the guise of conducting a survey into social habits, goes from house to house in Twickenham trying to unsettle the residents' self-perception and to make them question the status quo, she takes over the device of the test, normally a "fundamental social form of control" (Baudrillard 1993b: 62), and attempts to turn it into a vehicle for subversion. Similarly, by endeavoring to enter the BBC's Broadcasting House and occupy the *World Today* studio in order to "broadcast a true account of the rebellion" and to transmit "the manifesto of middle-class rebellion to the listening nation" (*MP* 149, 155), the rebels aim to seize control of the dominant social "signifying institutions" (Hall 1982:

86) in the way leftist thinkers such as Hans Magnus Enzensberger (1970) have long been calling for. I would argue that the numerous rather inappropriate references and comparisons that are part of the dissenters' self-conception, which were already mentioned at the beginning of this chapter (Boadicea, Kropotkin, Lenin, the French Revolution, the Tolpuddle Martyrs, the miners' strike, etc.), may be read in this context as well. Baxter argues that through these juxtapositions, "complex and ideologically charged narratives [...] are hijacked for aesthetic purposes" (2009: 210). While she correctly identifies these speech acts as acts of appropriation, she is, I think, wrong in considering them as serving aesthetic purposes. For as we have seen, the middle-class revolution is a profoundly political one. According to Baxter, "historical depth and specificity are lost amongst a semantic surface of indistinct signs" (2009: 211) in Chelsea Marina. But in today's mass-mediatized societies of postmodern "depthlessness" and the concomitant "weakening of historicity" (Jameson 1991: 6), historical profundity and specificity are *always already* lost or at least highly precarious. Commenting on Kay's comparison of the toppling of Michelangelo's *David* in the V&A to the fall of the statues of Lenin and Stalin, Baxter remarks:

> The irony inherent in Kay's brand of insurrectionism is that her actions articulate a distorted historical perspective which is itself a media-construct. Her ethically-detached and ahistorical form of historiography is born out of witnessing major historical events (such as the fall of the Iron Curtain) in the comfort of her own lounge. (2009: 211)

Yet, how many of us have *not* witnessed such events in that comfort? History has indeed turned into "a constantly available stream of images" (Baxter 2009: 211), yet not just for Kay but for virtually every one of us in the West, so that, today, *all* our historical perspectives are media-constructs (a fact, it has to be said, of which Baxter's study is generally well aware). Perhaps, as Baudrillard (1995) once provocatively suggested, the Gulf War did not take place; who can tell (cf. Ballard 1996l: 11)?

Somewhat following the Derridean logic of 'iterability' (Derrida 1984b; cf. also Butler 1993, 1999), that is, the possibility to insert signs into ever new contexts – without respect for an original presence, which is always deferred – the revolutionaries cite and appropriate various historical narratives and discourses and in this way position and orient their own struggle and endow it with significance by connecting it with earlier forms of resistance. It is an attempt to create a new map of meaning on which their critique and rebellion can be located, an attempt that should be understood as a response to an age in which all ideological alternatives to capitalism have been exhausted and to a society which therefore continuously repeats the supposed inevitability and, in fact, desirability of the status quo and which hence no longer offers any significant map or discourse through which resistance can be thought and conceptualized. The inappropriate nature of the protesters' comparisons is thus not so much an indication of the skewed historical awareness of a few insincere and media-manipulated individuals, but rather a symptom of the precarious state of revolutionary discourse under late capitalism.

Similarly, the final futility of the dissenters' attack against the system does not result from the fact that their critique fails to meet certain – largely outdated – conceptions or standards of integrity, authenticity and truthfulness, but instead from their misrecognition of the nature of power. Kay and her followers adhere to an obsolete, modernist notion of the political, whose strategies for social change have become ineffective. As Gould and, later, Markham point out, the Chelsea Marina rebels are "still locked into honesty and good manners", "[t]oo reliant [...] on argument and social stance", their targets "too predictable, too sensible" (*MP* 176, 202, 175). Underlying their tactics of appropriation of the test, the media and historical discourses of resistance are the goals, respectively, of creating awareness of the subtle and insidious workings of power, of communicating an accurate image of the character and aims of the revolution, and of articulating a sense of group identity. This means that the revolutionaries' form of resistance remains firmly tied to the idea of opposition and difference, the autonomous subject, of signification, and of truth and reality. Their political practice is securely located on the level of the 'real', where it follows a logic prescribed by the very system it goes up against, a system that, for its part, has shifted to the order of simulation. Nevertheless, as Baudrillard suggests, power unflaggingly continues to conjure up the 'real' and its figures of the political as simulacra, "'hyper-realiz[ing]' them through interminable simulation" (1993c: 4). According to the French philosopher, "[s]imulation is precisely this irresistible unfolding, this sequencing of things as though they had a meaning, when they are governed only by artificial *montage* and non-meaning" (1994f: 15). This preservation of history and the political beyond their death in the form of the 'trans-historical' and the 'trans-political', that is, as spectacle, is a clever ruse of power: keeping reality, the subject, meaning, and the event alive as zombies allows the system to confine resistance to it to the order of this simulacral 'real', which it tightly controls and in which, having long since abandoned it, it can never truly be challenged. It is this snare of power that the Chelsea Marina revolutionaries fall victim to. As many of Ballard's other works, *Millennium People* implies that received forms of political critique and resistance have utterly lost their force in the simulative late-capitalist societies of the late 20th and early 21st century. Arguably more distinctly than any other of the author's texts, the novel portrays a postmodern world ruled everywhere by Baudrillardian simulacra, uncertainty and indeterminacy.

For one thing, this rule is manifest in the by now familiar depiction of the omnipresence and determining influence of medial 'fictions' as well as of the transformation of space, and in the text's imagery. Once again, Ballard's writing confronts us with a world given over entirely to 'hyperreality', which has abolished the distinction between fact and fiction. This is evident, for instance, when patients at a hospital which is testing out a new automated diagnostic system prefer the computerized image of a doctor to a real physician, and when, upon meeting the model for this image, they consider him "not completely real" (*MP* 24). It also becomes apparent in the memorable scene in which the protesters, about to invade Broadcasting House, are listening to a live commentary on their demonstration on their portable radios, which makes Markham muse: "we were taking our orders from the organization against which we were demonstrating" (*MP* 149). As Baudrillard has pointed out, this medial 'real time' "dematerializes historical time, pulverizes the real event" (2005: 132). Beyond this, the hyperreal precedence of the code and the model over the real can also be perceived in a number of passages which describe the characters' change of behavior as soon as they notice the presence of TV cameras (e.g. *MP* 34, 226, 281). More than that, to the insurgents as well as to their enemies, these cameras are of vital importance: when, for example, the police, "[c]onfident of success", alert several television crews before their first attempt to seize control of Chelsea Marina, or when Markham, after the violent confrontation on the estate, spots a TV team relaxing by their van with their entire equipment still unpacked and infers that "[b]y this reliable measure, the revolution at Chelsea Marina [is] over" (*MP* 225, 233), it transpires that the media are in fact attributed a most fundamental, an *ontological* task, that of revealing or even guaranteeing the reality of events. What is not filmed, it seems, does not exist.

This profound transformation in the perception and nature of reality is underscored by the imagery of the text. The characters are constantly compared to actors and actresses or feel themselves like actors, and their lives and environments are likewise repeatedly described as "film set[s]", a "musical" or "productions" (*MP* 3, 34, 169) filled with "stage prop[s]" and "scenery" (*MP* 62, 110). At one point, the protagonist's process of remembering is depicted in terms of "[a] rush of images scann[ing] themselves across [his] mind like a cassette at fast forward" (*MP* 126). Countless similes and metaphors such as these delineate a society given over entirely to simulation, penetrated down to the most intimate realm of people's experience of themselves and the world by simulacra and the logic of mediation.

The novel portrays space, too, as having been affected by this process. In his late work, Ballard once again points to the increasing displacement of 'anthropological places' by 'non-places' (Augé 2008), a development that is evident, for instance, in Heathrow airport and its surrounding area, a realm "hover[ing] between waking and the dream", or in the spread of "[t]he same hotels, the same marinas, car-rental firms" (*MP* 25, 90) across the globe – as Kay contends, "[t]oday's tourist goes nowhere" and therefore "might as well stay home and watch it on television" (*MP* 54, 90).[8] Talking about such typical non-places as "airports, shopping malls, motorways, car parks", Richard Gould, a discerning analyst of our postmodern condition, describes them as realms of "alienation" with "no past and no future", as "zones without meaning", which prove that people are "in flight from the real" (*MP* 133). This, of course, is classical Augéian territory. With the accelerating spread of these non-places, the novel suggests, we are more and more caught in the sphere of simulation. This extends to the architecture of Central London as well. Markham states:

> The dealing rooms [of the City's financial services industry] were a con, and only the river [the Thames] was real. The money was all on tick, a stream of coded voltages sluicing through concealed conduits under the foreign exchange floors. Facing them across the river were two more fakes, the replica of Shakespeare's Globe, and an old power station made over into a middle-class disco, Tate Modern. (*MP* 180)

As Sebastian Groes observes, "Ballard makes a direct connection between the ephemeral nature of money in the late capitalist era and its effect on the physical metropolis. As money has now become immaterial and stripped of its capacity to signify in a simple manner, this dislocated signification expresses itself in simulacral architectural structures" (2008: 92). Restructured and reshaped by the forces of global capitalism, London itself turns into a simulacrum.

Through its depiction of the changing nature of social space and of the determining influence exerted on our lives by medial and other fictions, by models and codes, *Millennium People* powerfully evokes the contemporary age of hyperreality. It is only appropriate that Markham at one point refers to Heathrow as "a huge illusion, the centre of a world of signs that poin[t] to nothing" (*MP* 251) –

---

[8] Kay's critique of tourism echoes that of Guy Debord. The French Situationist writes: "Capitalist production has unified space, breaking down the boundaries between one society and the next. This unification is at the same time an extensive and intensive process of *banalization*. [...] The *free space of commodities* is constantly being altered and redesigned in order to become ever more identical to itself, to get as close as possible to motionless monotony. [...] Tourism [...] is the opportunity to go and see what has been banalized. The economic organization of travel to different places already guarantees their *equivalence*." (2009: 114)

what better image for a world swallowed by simulation, a world of floating signifiers in which the real is irretrievably lost?

In addition to this rather explicit concern with the media and post- or 'supermodern' non-places, there is in the novel a less overt but pervasive sense of profound uncertainty and ambiguity that suggests a hyperreal universe of indeterminacy, in which all received social, cultural and political coordinates are fully relativized. This uncertainty is most marked at the level of identity and threads itself through the entire narrative. It is evident, for example, in Markham's comment that the suit he is wearing for the visit of the Home Secretary is a "disguise" and his remarks only a little later that, nevertheless, "a disguise [can] go too far" and that he is "still unsure what role [he is] playing" (*MP* 4, 5), as well as in the following exchange between Markham and Gould:

> 'I get it now – you're with the Home Office tour. That's why you're wearing your best suit. Camouflage... and I thought you'd changed.'
> 'I have changed.' Deciding to be honest with him, I said: 'You changed me.' (*MP* 273)

Incongruous and puzzling passages like these, in which the characters' identity becomes an object of doubt and ambiguity not only for the reader but for the characters themselves, suggest a postmodern liquefaction and fragmentation of identity and subjectivity, signaling the end of the 'unity', 'coherence' and 'continuity' of the person. The novel depicts a simulative world in which, as Markham puts it, "[a]ppearances prov[e] nothing and everything" (*MP* 4) – they are not derived from and expressive of any 'essence' or personal 'core', yet they are all there is. In the post-essentialist, media-saturated and commodity-driven postmodern universe, manufactured images of the self provide the only means for the construction of identities. This transformation of identity itself into a simulacrum has been hailed by contemporary thinkers such as Gianni Vattimo (1992), Douglas Kellner (1995) or Judith Butler as heralding a new emancipation and "a new configuration of politics" (Butler 1999: 189). Yet, like the works of Baudrillard, Ballard's novel – indeed, as we saw in chapter 4, his entire oeuvre – is less optimistic: instead of being able to perpetually "change [their] self and identity, to move from one identity to another, to revel in the play of multiple and plural identities" (1995: 247), as Kellner has it, his characters frequently find themselves placed in roles and social scripts not of their own making and discover the process of identity-construction as ultimately determined by powers beyond their control. This is most evident in the interpellation and instrumentalization of Markham by the Home Office (see above) as well as in the different name tags pinned on him (*MP* 87, 120, 171), which presents such imposition of identity on a metaphorical level. The simulacral, indeterminate nature of identities finds further expression in the following: the use of a Metropolitan Police bag by the terrorist Richard Gould; the fact that Chelsea Marina revolutionary Joan Chang works for the Royal Academy; the portrayal of Stephen Dexter as a priest who has no faith and is "worldly in the extreme" (*MP* 64); Vera Blackburn's career trajectory from childhood bomb maker and murderer to senior scientific officer at the Ministry of Defence ("[a]ny child that dangerous is going to be very useful to society" [*MP* 96], Kay remarks) and back to terroristic bomb builder; Markham's conjecture that Gould may have been at Bedfont asylum not as doctor but as patient; the fact that Angela, the demonstrator Markham meets at a protest against a cat show, later turns out to be a police sergeant who was working undercover; Markham's own development; as well as his numerous moments of doubt concerning the role or identity of some other character or indeed of himself: actor or true self, foe or friend, impostor or authentic?[9] As all of these examples make clear, Markham's observation that by joining the middle-class revolution, he has "stepped out of [his] own character" (*MP* 102, cf. also 196) can not only be extended to most of the other characters as well, but may in fact beyond that be read as a self-reflexive reference alerting us to the fact that since 'character' or 'identity' today has an entirely different meaning than it did in the 18th or 19th century, the literary 'character' in the novel – traditionally the equivalent of bourgeois individualism – must change its shape, too.

It is no coincidence that, like *Super-Cannes*, *Millennium People* twice alludes to Lewis Carroll's *Alice*-books (*MP* 43, 192). Surrealism has given way to hyperrealism here, but in both works we are confronted with worlds in which the laws and logics of modernity are abolished and where nothing is as it seems. In Ballard's case, this is due not to a 'carnivalesque' inversion but to the universal reign of the "principle of simulation" (Baudrillard 1993b: 2), which has supplanted the 'reality principle'. *Millennium People* draws the image of a society in which this principle dominates all areas of experience and thus blurs or erases the boundary lines between numerous oppositions that have traditionally characterized modern Western thought: real vs. fictitious, true vs. false, authentic vs. fake, natural vs. artificial, depth vs. surface, original vs. imitation, and so forth.

Interestingly, the resulting indeterminacy is mirrored on the formal level of the text. In several passages, the narrative (Chatman's 'discourse') creates an uncertainty that can be considered a reinforcing reflection of the undecidability experienced by the reader at the level of the plot (Chatman's 'story'; 1991). It is striking, for instance, that Ballard's narrator at one point calls attention to

---

9 This last distinction is at one point further undermined by Markham's statement that looking like an impostor is "the fate of anyone who's too sincere" (*MP* 166).

Gould's "chipped nails" and compares his movements to those of "a Philippine faith-healer" (*MP* 59). Here, the attentive reader will pause and remember that only a few pages earlier, in the previous chapter, mention was made of Kay's "deeply bitten nails" and of the fact that Stephen Dexter once worked as "a flying vicar in the Philippines" (*MP* 51, 57). Such an odd, unmotivated concurrence only adds to the general impression of profoundly unanchored identities. Another example of this production of disorientation can be found in Kay and Markham's brief conversation about Dexter. Note the peculiar, ambiguous oscillation between, indeed, amalgamation of, a literal (flying) and a metaphoric (spirituality) level of meaning:

> 'I'm not sure Stephen would pronounce them [the last rites]. He's grounded himself.'
> 'Grounded? He's a pilot?'
> 'As it happens, he was. Though that isn't what I meant. He was a flying vicar in the Philippines, island-hopping with the word of God. Then he crash-landed on the wrong island.'
> 'He can't fly?'
> 'Spiritually. Like you, he's unsure about everything.' (*MP* 57)

Yet another relevant section is to be found at the beginning of chapter 8: "Women moved gently around me, easing off my shoes and loosening my belt. The Chinese girl leaned over the settee and unbuttoned my shirt. A faint but expensive scent floated between us, the tang of an unusual toothpaste, hints of the first-class lavatories on long-haul Cathay Pacific flights" (*MP* 59). Once again, appearances turn out to be deceiving here, for the initial impression of a sexual encounter is immediately deconstructed through the mention of the somewhat incongruous elements of the toothpaste and the airplane lavatories and is shortly after proven wrong when it becomes apparent that the scene really depicts the women's attempt to bring Markham back to his senses after he has passed out. The chapter's title, "The Sleepwalkers", likewise presents a source of ambivalence: while its most obvious connection is with Dexter's remark that half the world today is "sleepwalking through its own brain-death" (*MP* 63), it also seems to refer to the opening scene just discussed and, possibly – as a reference to the idiom 'to sleepwalk into something' – to Markham's reluctant initiation into the Chelsea Marina rebellion (cf. his assertion that he is "[u]nsure what [he is] committing [himself] to" [*MP* 62]).

Obviously, not every one of the examples discussed here is directly related to simulation. Nevertheless, they all contribute to a general sense of uncertainty, which the novel's explicit concern with hyperreality allows us to connect with simulation. It seems that as simulacra increasingly penetrate every area of human experience, the world more and more sinks into a state of radical indeterminacy. In such a condition, the text implies, conventional forms of political practice are no longer effective, so that a new kind of resistance is required to undermine the system. Such resistance is represented in the novel by the meaningless violence of Richard Gould, which challenges power according to its own trans-political logic, and to which we must now turn.

6.3 The Will to Spectacle

Of all the critics who have to this day commented on Ballard's *Millennium People* it is, to my knowledge, only Laura Colombino who, in her brief discussion of the novel, provides a 'positive' reading of the character of Richard Gould and his actions. Whereas Jeannette Baxter and Andrzej Gasiorek condemn his terrorist acts for their cruelty, their spectacularization of violence and for their lack of any concrete political goal, and thus ultimately denounce them as nothing but an "experiment in psychopathic imperialism" (Baxter 2009: 215), Colombino considers Gould, rightly I think, as "the only character who can still create a plot (an unsettling movement) in the otherwise pervasive immobility of the capitalist system as well as the only one capable of freely traversing its scene rather than being entrapped in its net" (2006: 631). Of course, to arrive at such a judgment about a murderer may be taken as a provocation. Yet, it is a provocation inherent in the novel itself. As in the case of Ballard's other texts discussed in this study, I think it is necessary to meet the challenge that this provocation poses. In the vein advocated throughout this book, *Millennium People* should be regarded as advancing another "extreme hypothesis", as one more "extreme metaphor to deal with an extreme situation" (Ballard in Revell 1984b: 42), and not as a 'manual' for the real world. The a-moral space of such a hypothesis requires an equally a-moral criticism, a Nietzschean or Foucauldian 'dangerous' or 'other' thought beyond the confines of political correctness.

To approach the novel from such a point of view means becoming aware of the polyvalence of Gould's brand of terrorism. Once again, diverse discourses overlap here, allowing for different readings of his meaningless violence. Perhaps, the one that suggests itself most immediately is to construe Gould's rebellion, as Gasiorek has done, as a metaphysical one, an expression of "millenarian despair" (Gasiorek 2005: 195) in the face of a universe entirely deprived of meaning. There is a strong current of nihilism in the novel, which portrays the contemporary world as one where "[t]here's nothing we believe in", in which god can only be thought of as "a huge imaginary void" and where people's "lives are empty" (*MP* 115, 136, 176), so that "[a]fter all the theorizing, all the chains of cause and effect, there's [just] a hard core of pointlessness" (*MP* 173). This basic meaninglessness of existence is further underscored by the random accident of Markham's wife – a theme that, subplot-like, runs through the whole novel – and the character of Stephen Dexter. As an "agnostic priest" (*MP* 64), a clergyman who has lost his faith, he can be considered as the epitome of the 'death of god' (Nietzsche 2001: 119 f).[10] The fact that, strangely, he is "camping in his own house", sleeping in a camp bed under a canvas tent in his living room, that he has "trouble with the roof" of his church, and that he is once described by Markham as returning to "the shelter of his unsheltering roof" (*MP* 101, 106, 107) must be read in this context as well, recalling as it does Georg Lukács' description of modernity as an era of "transcendental homelessness", in which "the extensive totality of life is no longer directly given, in which the immanence of meaning in life has become a problem" (1971: 41, 56). Read along these lines, the novel seems to suggest that the late 20th and early 21st century have only aggravated this crisis of meaning, so that in effect, postmodernity is still characterized by the insoluble "confrontation of [the] irrational [of the world] and the wild longing for clarity whose call echoes in the human heart" (1991: 21) that Albert Camus has identified as the essence of the 'absurd'.[11] Gould's determination to defy the universe, to "refus[e] to bow before the arrogance of existence and the tyranny of space-time", and to "find meaning in the most meaningless times" (*MP* 292) might then be related to Camus' conception of the existential 'revolt': "The absurd has meaning only in so far as it is not agreed to." (1991: 31; cf. also 1973) Especially Gould's committed work with disabled children could be read in this context:[12] as a Camusian attempt to rebel against the absurdity of existence through the conscious creation of meaning or at least the obstinate upholding of the demand for it in the face of its essential absence in the world.

While such an existentialist discourse is undoubtedly present in Ballard's text, there are, as Baxter rightly points out, on the whole too many "tensions and inconsistencies" (2009: 215) in Gould's actions and vision to unambiguously identify him with Camus' figure of the metaphysical rebel as Gasiorek (2005: 196) does. Not only does Gould's terrorist violence run counter to Camus' humanism and his emphasis on limit and measure, he also, on closer inspection, does not "attac[k] a shattered world to make it whole" nor "confron[t] the injustice at large in the world with his own principles of justice" (Camus 1973: 29; Gasiorek 2005:

---

10 Cf. Gould's statement that "[t]he gods have died" (*MP* 261).
11 The parallels between Ballard's novel and the work of Camus extend beyond this. Cf. also, for example, Camus' metaphor of the collapsing "stage sets" (1991: 12), which recurs throughout *Millennium People*.
12 It should be noted, however, that Gould's commitment to the children is presented in an ambivalent light since the novel implies that he may be masturbating them.

196) – after all, his brand of terrorism is a decidedly meaningless one.¹³ This pointlessness has to be stressed. It is precisely this, the absence of any motive, justification, principle or goal, that – in light of the failure of the middle-class revolution, Gould's repeated comments on its outdated and ineffective methods, and the simulative nature of the system – suggests an alternative reading of Gould's violent acts, one that construes them not as metaphysical but as *political* – as another catastrophic strategy.

It is only in such a reading that the full meaning of Markham's comment that Gould "lost interest in Chelsea Marina and moved on to a far more radical revolution", which is "closer to [Markham's] heart" (*MP* 3f),¹⁴ becomes apparent. As this remark makes clear, the middle-class insurrection and Gould's terrorism are closely connected, the latter being a reaction to the fate of the former. Both must be seen as political interventions, as forms of opposition to the system.¹⁵ Gould's new radicality of which Markham speaks is emblematically expressed in the fact that among the 'absurd' targets attacked by Gould's action groups – "the Penguin pool at London Zoo, Liberty's, the Soane Museum" (*MP* 204f), and so forth – is also the Karl Marx tomb. This unmistakably signals Gould's departure from the

---

13 As others have already pointed out, the novel's concern with the significance of meaningless violence recalls André Breton's declaration that "[t]he simplest Surrealist act consists of dashing down into the street, pistol in hand, and firing blindly, as fast as you can pull the trigger, into the crowd" (1972: 125). In this context, cf. Markham's mention of the act of "shooting at random into a crowd" (*MP* 194) as an example of a truly pointless act.

14 While lying beyond the scope of this study, a close analysis of the relationship between Markham and Gould would surely yield interesting results. There are numerous ambiguous passages in the text which suggest that their "unusual partnership" (*MP* 178) is fueled by a strong 'homosocial desire' (Sedgwick 1985), an impression that is underpinned by the existence of the mediating female presence of Kay, their "shared lover" (*MP* 3). It seems to me, for example, that Markham's entire rendition of the two men's first face-to-face meeting could be read in terms of a displacement of a (fantasized) homoerotic encounter (cf. the talk about "moving on the fringes of a twilight world", Gould's "stepp[ing] behind" Markham and the latter's imagining Gould holding a [phallic] syringe, Gould's "quick and decisive" movements, his seizing the other man with a "firm grip" and a "hard hand", informing him that "[t]here's so much [Gould] need[s] to show [him]", Markham's impression that a "darker fire [draws] closer" [*MP* 125], as well as the fact that he wakes up the next day with his "thighs jump[ing]" [*MP* 126]). Such homosocial desire seems to exist in other Ballardian texts as well, in many of which we find similar triangular relationships (Gasiorek 2005: 172). It appears that a 'queering' of Ballard's fiction could yield fascinating readings.

15 However, it should be noted that, as in many of Ballard's other texts, the characters' actions are often overdetermined. The novel suggests, for example, that aside from their political motivation, all the main characters are, to some extent, also driven by some kind of personal trauma. This, of course, is another instance of what we have identified as the Ballardian clash of discourses.

logics underlying the Chelsea Marina rebellion and from the revolutionary imagination in its traditional form.[16] In the face of the system's virtually limitless capacity for the reterritorialization of subversive energies, the unshakeable force of subjectivation, and the hyperreality of the whole political field and of power itself – that is, of all the factors that are jointly responsible for the failure of Kay and the other dissenters' protest – Gould and his followers combat the system according to an entirely new (anti-)logic. Their violent acts, as, according to Baudrillard, all contemporary forms of terrorism and other 'extreme phenomena', are a product of the system itself, a kind of 'abreaction' against a social order approaching total integration. Across all of his works, Baudrillard has insistently argued that "logically, and inexorably, the increase in the power of power heightens the will to destroy it" and has concluded that in the age of late capitalism, there consequently exists an "(unwittingly) terroristic imagination which dwells in all of us" (2003: 45, 5). This is what the French philosopher has also referred to as 'the transparency of evil': the 'showing through' or re-emergence of negativity and resistance in 'hyperintegrated' systems reaching their "saturation point": "Viral attack [e.g. in the form of terrorism[17]] is the pathology of the closed circuit, of the integrated circuit" (Baudrillard 1993c: 69, 72). Ballard's novel hence depicts a case of "terror against terror": it is the system's very "orgy of power" (Baudrillard 2003: 9, 59), as manifest in its neutralization of the Chelsea Marina rebellion, that creates its terroristic subversion.

Thus, if Gould's violence originates in nihilism, as Gasiorek avers, it seems that this is no longer primarily the metaphysical nihilism of earlier generations of philosophers. In a short essay on nihilism, Baudrillard has distinguished its contemporary form from its earlier, aesthetic, political, historical and metaphysical manifestations and has argued that "[t]oday's nihilism is one of transparency, and [that] it is in some sense more radical, more crucial than in its prior and historical forms, because this transparency, this irresolution is indissolubly that of the system" (1994c: 159). Postmodern nihilism, Baudrillard contends, is immediately tied to the "destruction of meaning through simulation" (1994c: 161) and to the concomitant disappearance of the real, of history, the political and the social. It is a nihilism that is deprived of its original pathos and mythical energy of denial and anticipation, born out of the vanishing of the "hope of a relation of forces and a stake" and the realization that "[e]verywhere, always, the system is too strong" (Baudrillard 1994c: 163). Gould's terrorism, devoid as it is of any political rationale

---

16 Cf. also that while Kay wants to rechristen the streets of Chelsea Marina (*MP* 231), Gould, according to Markham, dreams of "a city without street signs" (*MP* 294).
17 Interestingly, like Baudrillard, Laura Colombino (2006: 631) in her discussion of the novel compares Gould's terrorism to a virus.

and program, might then be described in similar terms as those which Slavoj Žižek employs in his analysis of the French suburban riots of the fall of 2005. Like these, Gould's revolt appears to be a "zero-level protest" or Lacanian *passage à l'acte* which illustrates our contemporary ideologico-political predicament: "although [capitalism] is global and encompasses the whole world, it sustains a *stricto sensu* 'worldless' [Alain Badiou's term] ideological constellation, depriving the large majority of people of any meaningful cognitive mapping" (Žižek 2009: 64, 67f). While this diagnosis of the present is certainly accurate with regards to Ballard's portrayal of postmodernity, it seems to me that Gould's actions nevertheless differ from the riots (besides the obvious differences of social background) in that the former do not represent an insistence on recognition and, most importantly, in that they are not a sign of impotence (this being Žižek's reading of the unrest). Whereas Žižek – in this respect in line with traditional Marxist thought – ultimately emphasizes the need for a "radical-emancipatory politics" consisting in "authentic political gesture[s]" which, unlike the fundamentally *reactive* outbursts of impotent violence, would be essentially *active*, "enforc[ing] a vision" (2009: 179), the resistance of Richard Gould, for whom, as we have seen, such a politics is no longer an option, is of another kind.

Here, too, the Ballardian clash of discourses allows for different readings. After having, in the passage quoted above, commented on the simulative nature of the contemporary monetary system – what Baudrillard has described as the historical shift from the market and commodity law of value (exchange value) to its structural law (sign value; 1993b: 2f, 6–49)[18] – and on the simulacral cityscape of contemporary London (the Globe, Tate Modern), Markham listens "for an echo of the bomb that ha[s] killed Joan Chang, *the only meaningful event in the entire landscape*" (*MP* 180, emphasis added). The terrorist bomb is here depicted as a means to disrupt hyperreality. As this statement makes clear, Gould's mode of resistance, unlike that of the middle-class rebels, no longer attempts to fight the system on the level of the real, where one is inevitably defeated, but instead represents an attack against the order of simulation itself. In this, Gould appears to be a disciple of Baudrillard:

> We will never defeat the system on the plane of the *real*: the worst error of all our revolutionary strategies is to believe that we will put an end to the system on the plane of the *real*: this is their imaginary, imposed on them by the system itself, living or surviving only by

---

18 Baudrillard later added a fourth stage to his earlier tripartite account of value, arguing that "after the natural, commodity, and structural stages of value comes the fractal stage", at which "there is no point of reference at all, and value radiates in all directions, occupying all interstices, without reference to anything whatsoever, by virtue of pure contiguity" (1993c: 5, 6).

always leading those who attack the system to fight amongst each other on the terrain of reality, *which is always the reality of the system*. This is where they throw all their energies, their imaginary violence, where an implacable logic constantly turns back into the system. (Baudrillard 1993b: 36)

Baudrillard himself has repeatedly suggested that after this end of politics, terrorism must be understood as one of the ways in which power can still be challenged – a claim he reiterated, to much controversy, after the attack on the World Trade Center in September 2001. First published in 2003, *Millennium People* is clearly part of the same historical moment. Indeed, the novel at one point explicitly alludes to the attack, when Gould praises it as "a brave attempt to free America from the 20th century" (*MP* 139).

One possible reading of Gould's terrorism is to see it as an expression of the same "passion for the Real" (2002: 10) that Žižek – adopting a term of Badiou's – has identified in connection with 9/11. Ballard's text repeatedly indicates that Gould's meaningless murders represent a way out of the illusory world of simulacra, a "direct experience of the Real as opposed to everyday social reality – the Real in its extreme violence as the price to be paid for peeling off the deceptive layers of reality" (Žižek 2002: 5f).[19] Gould, for example, states that the random violent acts "carry [people] to a more real world, a richer sense of who [they] are" and Markham similarly speaks of them as permitting him "a glimpse of a more real world" and as "unlock[ing] the door of [his] cell" (*MP* 248, 145, 146). We are already familiar with these ideas; this discourse, which locates authenticity of being along the line of violent transgression and excess, was already analyzed in detail in our discussion of *Crash*. Yet, possibly more than in that earlier novel, this discourse is here significantly weakened by others, which ultimately reveal such aspiration for a recovery of the real in the 'event' to be in vain.

At one point, Gould, talking about the possibility of a plane crash, renders this recovery in the following terms: "That would mean something. An empty space we could stare into with real awe. Senseless, inexplicable, as mysterious as the Grand Canyon. We can't see the road for all the signposts. Let's clear them away, so we can gaze at the mystery of an empty road." (*MP* 249f) This rhetoric clearly recalls the Burkean notion of the 'sublime' (Burke 2008; Gasiorek 2005: 198), a fact that might be said to point us to the essentially Romantic foundation of such thinking. Gould's imagery once again refers us back to the context

---

[19] In an interview, Ballard himself has referred to 9/11 as a "real revolution" that, unlike "pseudo-revolutions" and "media events", "has not yet been repackaged into something with more consumer appeal" (in Baxter 2004: 30) – a distinction that clearly echoes Baudrillard's discrimination between 'absolute' and 'pseudo-events'.

of 9/11, since the arresting images of the collapsing Twin Towers have repeatedly been linked to the experience of the sublime, for instance by Baudrillard (2005: 130f) himself and by Miles Orvell (2006), who speaks of a 'destructive sublime'.

However, the sublime Gould talks about is always caught up in representation; no matter how many 'signposts' he believes to be taking away, all he can ever do is create new signs. The 'road' he is looking for will thus never be truly 'empty'. This becomes immediately clear when one considers his reliance on the media. Gould needs them, indeed depends on them, to disseminate the images of his crimes. But for sure, they are precisely that, *images*, not, as he believes, transparent deliveries of presence. This, of course, is something Gould shares with all terrorists. Both Žižek and Baudrillard have called attention to the inextricable connection between terrorism and the media and ultimately refuted the idea that events like the 2001 attacks in New York City represent a return to the 'desert of the real' (Žižek 2002). Thus, Žižek, in his psychoanalytical approach to 9/11, speaks of an irreducible "dialectic of semblance and Real", in which "[t]he Real which returns has the status of a(nother) semblance" (2002: 19), and Baudrillard similarly argues that "[a]n excess of violence is not enough to open on to reality" (2003: 28). The terrorist act might be said to bring about "an excess of reality", but this reality "is everywhere infiltrated by images, virtuality and fiction" and only seems to outstrip fiction "because it has absorbed fiction's energy, and has itself become fiction" (Baudrillard 2003: 18, 28). Referring to Ballard, Baudrillard explains: "Rather than the violence of the real being there first, and the *frisson* of the image being added to it, the image is there first, and the *frisson* of the real is added. Something like an additional fiction, a fiction surpassing fiction." (2003: 29) To a certain extent, this is already evident in Markham's comment that terrorist attacks mark the emergence into reality of "the unconscious fears projected by a thousand Hollywood films" (*MP* 141), a statement that echoes very similar remarks by Žižek (2002: 15f) and Baudrillard (2003: 7) (although they would speak of fantasies or wishes rather than fears).

Following Baudrillard, I would argue that this inextricability of reality and fiction, in other words, the fact that Gould's terrorism does finally *not* create a path to authenticity and the real but only another spectacle, nevertheless does not weaken its power but, on the contrary, is the source of its true energy. Here, it is necessary to somewhat 'read Gould against himself' by emphasizing the meaninglessness of his violence and neglecting his claims concerning the production of presence, which, it seems to me, the novel itself deconstructs through its insistence on the 'spectacular' nature of his terrorist attacks. I would contend that the essence of Gould's resistance lies in his belief "that the most pointless acts [can] challenge the universe at its own game" (*MP* 292). This is precisely the way in which Baudrillard has always conceptualized

6.3 The Will to Spectacle — 225

resistance. According to the French philosopher, with the transition from the second to the third order of simulacra, from the real to the hyperreal, the revolutionary imagination has lost its force: dialectics, relations of force, use value, the unconscious – "[t]he deployment of third-order simulacra sweeps all this away, and to attempt to reinstate dialectics, 'objective' contradictions, and so on, against them would be a futile political regression" (1993b: 3). This, as we have seen, is why the revolution at Chelsea Marina fails. Its whole logic is based on the prior state of the system, whose forms are integrated into its current state as mere "phantom" or "puppet reference[s]" (Baudrillard 1993b: 3), and in this way, the protest allows itself to be drawn into fighting on the ground of reality, which is always the system's own. Effective subversion must thus be derived from a different order than that described by political economy. It must reproduce the system's transition to a higher order and "mak[e] the system's own logic the ultimate weapon", pushing things "to the limit, where quite naturally they collapse" (Baudrillard 1993b: 4). In brief: "Simulation must go further than the system." (Baudrillard 1993b: 4)

Time and again, Baudrillard has suggested that terrorism is one way of doing this. A crucial aspect of his interpretation of terrorism, and one that is of particular importance in the context of my reading of Richard Gould, is his assertion that despite the terrorists' claims to the contrary, it is basically without meaning. Baudrillard explains:

> there is no longer any ideology behind it. We are far beyond ideology and politics now. No ideology, no cause [...] can account for the energy which fuels terror. The aim is no longer even to transform the world, but [...] to radicalize the world by sacrifice. Whereas the system aims to realize it by force. (2003: 9f)

Gould's insistence on the absolute pointlessness of his violence, on the absence of any rational motivation and goal, thus reveals him to be a perfect embodiment of what Baudrillard considers the true 'spirit of terrorism': "terrorism ultimately has no meaning, no objective, and cannot be measured by its 'real' political and historical consequences. And it is, paradoxically, because it has no meaning that it constitutes an event in a world increasingly saturated with meaning and efficacy." (2003: 57) This striking correspondence between Ballard's terrorist and Baudrillard extends even to rhetoric and imagery. When, for instance, the former declares,

> [w]e need to pick targets that don't make sense. If your target is the global money system, you don't attack a bank. You attack the Oxfam shop next door. Deface the cenotaph, spray Agent Orange on Chelsea Physic Garden, burn down London Zoo. We're in the business of creating unease. [...] A pointless act has a special meaning of its own. Calmly carried out,

untouched by any emotions, a meaningless act is an empty space larger than the universe around it (*MP* 175 f),

his words clearly echo the French philosopher's description of terrorism as not emerging "from passion" and as "*par excellence* an act that punches [...] a hole in a universe (ours) that is both artificial and artificially protected", "puncturing this system with a single act or utterance, so that all our values are suddenly engulfed by the void" (1993c: 85, 95).[20] Richard Gould's violence is an ideal example of what Baudrillard has called 'the mirror of terrorism' (1993c: 85), reflecting, as it does, "the non-meaning and indifference which are at the heart of the system": "Terrorism invents nothing, inaugurates nothing. It simply carries things to the extreme, to the point of paroxysm. It exacerbates a certain state of things, a certain logic of violence and uncertainty." (Baudrillard 2003: 73, 58) Here, the terms 'meaning' and 'non-meaning' constantly fold into each other: on the one hand, the system, especially through the electronic mass media, is incessantly engaged in the production of meaning, yet on the other hand, this (over-)signification turns into an entropic process, in which meaning disappears through its spectacularization, the saturation of images and information, and the speed of communication (e. g. Baudrillard 2007b: 100, passim), while continuing to be produced as simulacrum. Meaning is thus buried beneath its own simulation. In turn, the inexplicability of terrorism, its essential non-meaning, challenges this – effectively meaning-less – "tyranny of meaning" (Baudrillard 2005: 134) of the system and in this way, paradoxically, gains or creates meaning.[21]

I would argue that it is in this – pataphysical – vein that Gould's search for meaning should be (re-)read. His revolt must hence be understood as not primarily a metaphysical but a (trans-)political one, battling a power that can no longer be fought with traditional means. It is, in other words, a catastrophic strategy – something that Gould himself acknowledges when he refers to it as "the last throw of the dice", "a wild card" and "an impossible bet" (*MP* 139).[22] By repro-

---

[20] Similarly, cf. also Baudrillard's use of the metaphor of the 'black hole' throughout *In the Shadow of the Silent Majorities*.

[21] Even though Baudrillard asserts that "[t]he denial of meaning has no meaning" (2007b: 61), in the strict sense, *this itself* and the very fact of the concomitant challenge to power are, of course, *meaningful*. This is an inevitable consequence of (Baudrillard's) discourse. His assertion should therefore rather be taken as an indication of what he sees as the impossibility to reconnect the meaninglessness of terrorism with political reason and to assign it the status of a political negativity.

[22] In the context of a metaphysical reading of Gould's revolt, these phrases, particularly the last one, might also be taken as a reference to Blaise Pascal's (1999: 152–158) notion of the 'wager' of faith.

ducing and, indeed, intensifying and pushing to the limit the meaninglessness of the system, Gould's pointless terrorism represents an attempt to outbid the simulative system at its own reference-less game. His random violence, from the bomb at Heathrow airport to the one at Tate Modern and the assassination of the television presenter, is "a violence in the nature of the image", driven not by political conviction, but by a "will to spectacle" (Baudrillard 1993c: 85, 2007b: 41). All of his terrorist acts replicate already existent medial models and depend for their efficacy on the dissemination of their images through the media. Again and again, the novel has its characters sitting in front of their television sets, following the coverage of Gould's crimes in a state of utter shock and awe, in which the world appears to stand still. Particularly in the case of the news report on the Heathrow bomb – which, with its incorporation of an amateur video, whose film-maker was "evidently too shocked by the violence [...] to put down his camera and offer help to the victims" (*MP* 18), clearly recalls the TV coverage of 9/11 – the text dwells on the spectacular and spellbinding nature of the images of catastrophe (*MP* 16–18). Likewise, when Markham listens to a radio report about the bomb at Tate Modern, he has the impression that all sound withdraws from the streets around him and, "despite [him]self", feels "a surge of excitement and complicity" (*MP* 159). All of this confirms Baudrillard's observation that when it comes to terrorist violence, "the media are made the vehicle of the moral condemnation of terrorism and of the exploitation of fear for political ends, but, simultaneously, in the most total ambiguity, they propagate the brutal fascination of the terrorist act" (2007b: 106). This spectacular nature of mediatized violence becomes evident once again in Gould's assassination of the television presenter. Not only does "[e]very newsreel unit and press photographer in the capital converg[e]" on the scene of the crime after the murder, but, as Markham remarks, the killing itself is of a special kind, one "made all the more meaningless by her celebrity" (*MP* 209, 211): "The cruel murder of the young television performer pressed hard on one of the nation's exposed nerves"; "her death on her own doorstep prompted an outpouring of grief that reminded me of Princess Diana" (*MP* 209).[23]

Underlying Gould's revolt is thus no ideology or political program, only "the radicality of the spectacle, which alone is original and irreducible. The spectacle of terrorism forces the terrorism of spectacle upon us. And, against this immoral fascination (even if it unleashes a universal moral reaction), the political order

---

[23] Appropriately, her funeral service is later described as "a solemn ritual that play[s] to the worst needs of television" (*MP* 213).

can do nothing."²⁴ (Baudrillard 2003: 30) Shifting the struggle from the grounds of 'reality', to which Kay's revolution remained tied and where it was therefore defeated, into the realm of simulation, Gould attacks the system with its own weapons, creating a pure counter-spectacle that is able to subvert the dominant order of simulacra. No longer caught up in the 'traps' of the binary logic of opposition, of meaning, truth, value, and the real, he instead produces a "hypersimulation reduplicating simulation and exterminating it according to its own logic" (Baudrillard 2007b: 66). It is therefore only appropriate that Gould's eyes are described by Markham as "depthless" and his voice as "faint and metallic, the recording of a recording" (*MP* 214, 201). For one thing, these images point us towards the text's posthumanist image of identity: where the eyes are depthless and no longer a window to or mirror of the soul, and where the voice is a recording and no longer – as in the phono- and logocentric philosophical tradition – guarantees presence (Derrida 1997: 12), subjectivity is revealed as a fragmentary social construct without any essence.²⁵ Beyond that, Markham's descriptions can also be read as metaphors for the nature of Gould's resistance: one that does away with foundational 'grand narratives', no longer relying on 'content' or 'message' (nor on a transformation of the 'form' or 'medium'; cf. Baudrillard 2007b: 102–104) but – like a recording of something that was *already recorded* and not the 'real thing' – redoubling the logic of simulation, fighting the spectacle through (an even more spectacular) spectacle.

At the end of the text, this pataphysical (anti-)logic seems to catch hold of the revolution, too. Pondering why the residents of Chelsea Marina all of a sudden, and for no apparent reason, returned to the estate from the exile which they had chosen after the defeat of their revolution, Markham wonders whether, perhaps, "even Chelsea Marina help[s] to prove Gould's point":

---

24 Herein lies a crucial difference between Baudrillard and Gould on the one hand and Guy Debord on the other. For, unlike the former, the latter ultimately still sets his hope on a coming-into-consciousness of the workers and a proletarian revolution (conceived in somewhat Trotskyian terms as "*a revolution that cannot leave anything outside itself*" [2009: 85f]), with particular importance ascribed to the workers' councils (cf. Baudrillard 2002: 27).

25 In contrast to Gasiorek, who sees Gould's violence as an expression of an underlying belief in the primacy and authenticity of the self – indeed, he speaks of a "monadic view of subjectivity" (2005: 197) – it seems to me that, similar to other Ballardian protagonists, Gould actually undoes this socially constituted subjectivity through his actions. I would suggest that the peculiar trance-like state he is in before and after the assassination of the television presenter (*MP* 201f, 206–208) may be understood as the novel's attempt to imagine this erasure of subjecthood and its replacement with a new, rather non-intentional consciousness (cf. chapter 4 of this study).

> Did they [the residents] realize from the start that the Chelsea Marina protest was doomed to failure, and that its pointlessness was its greatest justification? They knew that the revolt in many ways was a meaningless terrorist act [...]. Only by cutting short their exile and returning to the estate could they make it clear that their revolution was indeed meaningless, that the sacrifices were absurd and the gains negligible. A heroic failure redefined itself as a success. Chelsea Marina was the blueprint for the social protests of the future, for pointless armed uprisings and doomed revolutions, for unmotivated violence and senseless demonstrations. Violence, as Richard Gould once said, should always be gratuitous, and no serious revolution should ever achieve its aims. (*MP* 292 f)

In light of the residents' inexplicable – even to themselves – return, and looked at from this Gouldian point of view, the Chelsea Marina revolution can thus be reinterpreted, so that its spectacular nature, criticized by Baxter and Gasiorek, would not be, as these critics maintain, a sign of the protesters' lack of integrity, nor would it be an indication of the inevitable recuperation of the rebellion into the system of simulation, but, instead, a "strategy of turning around and overturning power" (Baudrillard 2003: 73) in the vein of Gould's revolt. In this way, yet another discourse emerges: one that allows us to read the Chelsea Marina rebellion as a deliberate spectacle of revolution, as a simulacrum of political activism that, through its very spectacularity – "[t]he television news showed families arm in arm, surrounded by overturned cars, their faces proudly lit by the flames"; "toddlers were lifted into the air to [...] expose them to the breakfast TV audiences" (*MP* 6, 226) – and through its meaninglessness, challenges the society of the spectacle at its own game.[26] Both Gould's murders and the middle-class insurrection would then be forms of Baudrillardian terrorism, responding to a hyperreal system

> by an *equally hyperreal* act, caught up from the outset in concentric waves of media and of fascination, dedicated from the outset not to any representation and consciousness, but to a mental downgrading by contiguity, fascination and panic, not to reflection or to the logic

---

26 This discourse is already evident at the very beginning of the novel, when Markham states: "[The revolutionaries] rejected all offers of help, refusing to air their real grievances or to say whether any grievances existed at all. [...] For reasons no one understood, the inhabitants of Chelsea Marina had set about dismantling their middle-class world. [...] Curiously, the residents who destroyed Chelsea Marina had shown no anger at all. They had quietly discarded their world as if putting out their rubbish for collection." (*MP* 6) While this account does not really correspond to the events as Markham narrates them hereafter – after all, the rebels do repeatedly articulate their critique and show their anger – it might nevertheless be taken as an indication of how he *remembers* them; what seems to remain with him above all is the revolution's profound inexplicability and meaninglessness.

of cause and effect, but to a chain reaction by contagion – senseless and indeterminate like the system it combats, [...] a non-explosive, non-historical, non-political terrorism [...].
  Terrorism does not aim at making anything speak, at resuscitating or mobilizing anything; it has no revolutionary consequences [...]; it aims at that white magic of the social encircling us, that of information, of simulation, of deterrence, of anonymous and random control, in order to precipitate its death by accentuating it. (Baudrillard 2007b: 68)

Yet, no matter how subversive such meaningless terrorism may seem, in the end, at least in Ballard's novel, it fails. This failure has less to do with Gould's eventual death than with what happens to his persona and his actions after he has been shot. Baudrillard has called attention to the fact that the "active nihilism of radicality" of the terrorist is countered by the system's own nihilism, the "nihilism of neutralization", which consists in the system's power "to pour everything, including what denies it, into indifference" (1994c: 163). It is this "nihilism of meaning" (Baudrillard 1994c: 164) that Gould's revolt ultimately falls victim to. Based as it is on the production of (simulacra of) meaning and of the demand for it, the system must at all costs contain the threat posed to it by Gould's spectacular violence by displacing its essential pointlessness and integrating it into the order of meaning. Again and again, the novel alerts its reader to this "imperative of *meaning*" (Baudrillard 2007b: 39) underlying power; the questionnaire-based efforts of the investigators from the Department of Health to "isolate the underlying grievances" of the Chelsea Marina rebellion and to "find a common psychology at work" (*MP* 153) as well as the various interpretations of Gould's terrorism as protests by "renegade IRA" fighters, by "some demented Muslim group" (*MP* 194), "unknown al-Qaeda extremists" or "an Islamic group protesting against the vilification of Arab peoples in Hollywood films" (*MP* 290, 143) – the (re-)'orientalized' other always serving as a good scapegoat, it seems[27] – or as nothing but "misguided pranks" (*MP* 205) must all be understood in this context. They are attempts at a 'hermeneutic capture', at the attribution of meaning to that which has none. As Baudrillard explains, "[a]ny means will do to impose meaning, to disregard how far terrorism is without legitimacy, without political consequences, without any historical continuity" (2007b: 70). The simulation of meaning here emerges as the system's most powerful means of divesting Gould's violence of its (counter-)spectacular nature and in this way anchoring it on the ground of the real, where it ceases to be a threat. After Gould's death, this strategy becomes fully effective: with the Heathrow bomb being

---

27 The repetitiveness of these references to Islam are clearly an allusion to the highly problematic demonization of Arab peoples by the Bush administration, the mass media and others in the wake of the attacks on the Twin Towers and the American wars in Afghanistan and Iraq (cf. Said 1979, esp. xv – xxx).

blamed on militant Islamism, the other attacks "quietly forgotten", and with Gould identified as a simple "demented paediatrician" (*MP* 290),²⁸ the "hegemony of meaning" (Baudrillard 2007b: 41) and the social order are ultimately restored. Likewise, the events that led to Gould's death are finally signified in a socially acceptable way, consistent with the 'dominant' or 'preferred' social meanings (Hall 1993: 98): according to this account, Gould "kidnapped" Markham's wife and then "lured [him] to Chelsea Marina, intending to kill [them] both", a plan that was thwarted by Markham, who killed Gould and "saved" (*MP* 291, 290) his wife. In this representation, whose representational and ideological codes (Fiske 1989: 4f) are clearly derived from the conventions of Hollywood action cinema – the psychopathic terrorist taking hostage a beautiful but helpless woman (the contemporary version of the classical 'damsel in distress'), who is in the end rescued by the fearless hero – the subversive impetus of Gould's revolt is altogether erased. Thus, the mass media, the main agents in the contemporary "disinformation age" (*MP* 29), finally situate resistance within the dominant framework of meanings, recuperate its threat, and consequently stabilize the simulative system. The function of the entire last chapter of the novel is to tell this disheartening tale of the eventual containment of all radical energies. There is, it seems, ultimately no escape from power.

Here, however, at the very end of the text, the narrative 'performs' a curious 'loop'. For what is striking about the conclusion of the plot is its utterly clichéd character. After all the conflicts, the struggle and strife that marked the story, the last chapter at one stroke resolves all tension and reestablishes total harmony. Thus, the Chelsea Marina rebels all peacefully return to the estate and resume their middle-class lives while the management company, the council and the Home Office in turn acknowledge the residents' complaints and resolve to improve their living conditions. Similarly, no charges are brought against the protesters and most of the attacks are simply forgotten. Kay becomes a successful media presence, the reverend Stephen Dexter recovers his faith and starts to fly again, Markham returns to his job at the Adler Institute and is told that he may well be its next director, Markham and his wife are reconciled, and the latter finally throws away her walking sticks, buys a new car – supposedly one no longer adapted to the needs of the disabled – becomes "a devoted and strong-willed wife", and, as she and her husband "play bridge with Henry Kendall", "finds it inconceivable that she ever decided to be his lover" (*MP* 291). It seems to me that, quite literally, this ending is too good to be true. For that reason, it is not to be trusted. It resembles too much those American (action) movies that, after having

---

28 Cf. also the fact that Markham all of a sudden thinks about Gould as his patient (*MP* 290).

given room to some form or the other of a disturbance of the social order, in the end always anxiously – and often rather unconvincingly – contain the disruptive element and restore the status quo. Thus, at its end, Markham's narrative *itself* repeats the Hollywoodesque logic of the spectacle through which the subversiveness of Gould's meaningless violence was kept in check. The clichéd ending of the novel must therefore be read in terms of a *doubling*, in which the narrative folds back upon itself like a Möbius strip, mirroring or adopting the stabilizing simulation of meaning carried out by the system. We are faced, so to speak, with a spectacle of a second order, an extension or reflection of the first. Yet, at the same time, the novel invites a corresponding observation or reading-position of another order (Luhmann 2000: 54–101), from which this final simulacrum is easily recognized as such. For not only do the events that are recounted in the last chapter read like a contrived and artificial happy ending, the logic of the "everything [will] be well" (*MP* 288) underlying the unexpected abruptness with which every problem without exception is eventually resolved being completely unconvincing. More than that, the events are also presented in a film-like manner: when the chapter, in a quick, staccato fashion, tells the subsequent fate of all the main characters, each one neatly summarized in a few sentences making up a separate paragraph, every paragraph beginning in exactly the same way – with the name of the respective character (the Minister, Kay Churchill, Stephen Dexter, 'I', and Sally, Markham's wife) – this creates the impression that one is witnessing the closing credits of a movie detailing how the characters' lives go on in the future rather than reading the denouement of a novel (*MP* 290 f). In this way, Ballard's novel draws attention to the clichéd, spectacular nature of its ending and thus deconstructs[29] itself.[30] At the moment of closure, then, the text 'gets behind itself' and displaces the system's power of containment through the simulation of meaning by exposing this meaning as a simulacrum. The "millennial charm" (*MP* 293) that everywhere dominates the end of the novel – the 'story' as well as the 'discourse' (Chatman 1991) – is thus forcefully undermined and Gould's radical vision of a different millennium ultimately upheld.

Finally, the ending of Ballard's work appears to have a metafictional relevance as well, especially in light of the repeated self-reflexive references to art

---

29 On the affinities between Luhmann's systems theory and Derridean deconstruction, cf. Wolfe 2010: xvii–xxii, 3–29; cf. also Luhmann 1993.
30 In this, the ending of the novel is somewhat reminiscent of the final scenes of Martin Scorsese's brilliant film *Taxi Driver*. Furthermore, in both 'texts', an inexplicable outbreak of violence is rationalized and contained through the mobilization of received narrative patterns and structures of meaning, patterns and structures which are largely derived from the media.

embedded in the text. Not only are the senseless terrorist attacks of Gould and his followers linked to Futurism and Dadaism and their vehement rejection of the bourgeois notion, recuperation and commodification of art (*MP* 153, 205), it is surely also significant that the simulacral landscape in which one of Gould's bombs is identified by Markham as "the only meaningful event" (*MP* 180) consists of the Globe and Tate Modern, and that the bomb that explodes in the Tate was hidden in a large art book from the museum's book store (*MP* 162). The novel is clearly concerned with the role of art in society, and more specifically, with its possibilities of becoming a vehicle for subversion and critique. As Markham muses: "Not one of the works of art in the gallery [the Tate] remotely matched the limitless potency of a terrorist bomb."[31] (*MP* 188) Read against this background, the ending's doubling of the spectacle and its simultaneous deconstruction could perhaps be seen as an allegory of the realist novel's inevitable participation in the construction and affirmation of the order of meaning and communication, and consequently also in the "freezing over of meaning" and the "precession of simulacra" (Baudrillard 1994c: 161). The self-consciously clichéd conclusion of the story might then be said to retroactively put the entire narrative 'under erasure' (Derrida 1997; Spivak 1997) by drawing attention to its ultimate complicity with the spectacular order of the real, which only senseless acts of terrorism can shatter. By *representing* such terrorism, the novel inescapably drags it into the realm of signification and thus, despite itself, cannot but deprive it of some of its subversive power. I would argue that it is the function of the novel's ending to expose and hence, to some extent, undermine this unavoidable form of recuperation.

Subversion and containment thus continually cross and re-cross each other in *Millennium People*. Indeed, the novel presents a veritable testing ground for the possibilities of emancipatory practice in the 21st century, turning London into a political arena in which the text stages multiple confrontations between the system and its opponents. As in Ballard's other works, power here appears so pervasive and total that received forms of political action and critique, as represented by the Chelsea Marina rebellion, are shown to be no longer effective. Only a catastrophic strategy such as Gould's meaningless violence, which chal-

---

[31] Here and elsewhere, *Millennium People* echoes in interesting ways with American writer Don DeLillo's fascinating novel *Mao II*, in which one character states: "There's a curious knot that binds novelists and terrorists. [...] Years ago I used to think it was possible for a novelist to alter the inner life of the culture. Now bomb-makers and gunmen have taken that territory", while another asserts: "Everything else is absorbed. The artist is absorbed, the madman in the street is absorbed and processed and incorporated. [...] Only the terrorist stands outside. The culture hasn't figured out how to assimilate him." (1992: 41, 157)

lenges power at its own reference-less game, seems to be able to subvert the system today. Yet, as the conclusion of the novel makes clear, even such radical practices may in the end not measure up to the society of simulation and control. Ballard's late novel shows very clearly that the political struggle goes on and that there is a continued need for critical thought and dissident action – but it also makes clear that open spaces are continuously shrinking and that the prospects for change under late capitalism are highly uncertain.

7 Conclusion: New Weapons

> There is no need to fear or hope, but
> only to look for new weapons.
> *Gilles Deleuze*

It seems to me that the fact that Ballard not only once again addresses the question of resistance in a late work such as *Millennium People*, but even makes it its central thematic concern must be seen as evidence of his continued preoccupation with this topic and of the enduring, if not increasing, relevance it had for him. Through the readings of the preceding chapters, this study has attempted to investigate this preoccupation and reveal this relevance.

J.G. Ballard is a political writer, or better: a writer of the 'trans-political' – this has been the underlying thesis of all the analyses carried out here. For one thing, I have investigated this as yet largely neglected political dimension of his oeuvre through a detailed exploration of his critical portrayal of the late-capitalist realities. His fiction dissects postmodernity in various dimensions; it tackles – to name only some of the most important aspects – its new spatialities (non-places, hyperspace, the metro area, Disneyfied space, etc.), depthlessness and simulation, the waning or death of affect, the contemporary forms of subjectivation, that is, of the social construction of subjectivity as well as of the body, dromology, the end of history, the new, global Empire, integral reality, the society of control, biopower, and post-democracy. In Ballard's work, these new realities on the one hand entail a profound transformation of the 'lifeworld' that is frequently depicted as deeply alienating, and on the other involve an unprecedented degree of subjection.

In my reading, the extreme behavior of Ballard's protagonists represents a novel form of resistance against this situation. This study has argued that, somewhat similar to the philosophy of Jean Baudrillard, Ballard's fiction in fact constitutes a sustained pataphysical exploration of the possibilities of resistance under late capitalism. The counterintuitive, non-commonsensical and radical nature of this exploration results, in Ballard as in Baudrillard, from the realization of the exhaustion of virtually all received modes of politically emancipatory action. As particularly *Millennium People* illustrates, these modes are utterly incapable of disrupting the contemporary networks of power, which have proved to be absolutely pervasive and infinitely malleable, able not only of containing any disorder but of productively using it for their own consolidation. Against the background of this cancellation of all established forms of resistance, Ballard's work appears – to take up Deleuze's words from the epigraph of this conclusion –

as a veritable search for 'new weapons'. The only response to a near-all-powerful system, his texts suggest, are catastrophic strategies – strategies that, though highly destructive in their repercussions, at least temporarily produce cracks in the webs of power and open up alternative horizons of meaning and being. Following Ballard's own characterization of himself as a scientist, my study has read his fiction as a pataphysical laboratory in which various experiments regarding catastrophic modes of resistance are conducted and various 'extreme hypotheses', as Ballard says, formulated.

Thus, *Crash*, the first of the texts discussed here, stages the violence of the protagonists' intentional crashing of cars and the concomitant wounding of the body as manifestly emancipatory events. Differently coded by separate discourses, the crash appears at once as a radical limit-experience shattering the experiential structures constructed by the dominant order, as a way to fashion a new corporeality and new configurations of pleasure and desire distinct from those produced and sanctioned by normalizing power, and as a form of Baudrillardian 'symbolic exchange'.

Similarly, my analysis of Ballard's *Concrete Island* has revealed the main character's precarious existence on the eponymous traffic island as an escape from the controlling grip of the system. The 'heterotopic' island space emerges, as it were, as a kind of blank spot in the grid of power. The adoption of a Deleuzoguattarian theoretical perspective has made it possible for us to identify and examine the various liberatory 'deterritorializations' and 'becomings' taking place in this counter-space. Yet, it has also allowed us to see that the social scripts and discourses that have produced Ballard's protagonist time and again reassert themselves, so that he is, in the end, never entirely able to free himself from the codes and strata that bind him.

Another catastrophic strategy identified in my study – one, in fact, that recurs throughout Ballard's oeuvre – is that of abdication. This 'siding with the object', as Baudrillard has it, has been traced in various of Ballard's works and analyzed in detail in the short story "News from the Sun". Just like the other texts, this story performs the thought-experiment, not of a remaking of subjectivity and identity, but of their complete dissolution – the erasure of the subject as a response to its 'death' or 'decentering'.

My discussion of *Cocaine Nights* and *Super-Cannes*, too, has addressed a means of resistance that preoccupied Ballard throughout his career: transgressive madness. Here, once again, Ballard's avant-garde legacy became evident. As we have seen, his novels place themselves in a tradition of radical thought ranging from Blake to Foucault, a tradition that considers transgressive, 'psychopathic' behavior as a potent resource to defy power and that Ballard's works appropriate and update for the age of postmodernity. Yet, my study has also shown that in both texts, this catastrophic strategy is ultimately unable to effectively resist the powers of late capitalism, by which it is in the end always contained, indeed, harnessed, and, in the case of *Super-Cannes*, even produced. The two novels thus emerge as among the most pessimistic in the Ballardian oeuvre, with particularly *Super-Cannes* appearing as perhaps Ballard's most thoroughly dystopian work.

A similar ambivalence as regards the ultimate success of catastrophic strategies is also evident in *Millennium People*, the last of the texts discussed in this study. As has been shown, Ballard's late novel represents his most explicit and systematic investigation of the exhaustion of received forms of political action. Through the failure of the text's middle-class rebellion, whose critique, methods and goals evince the 'classical' revolutionary imagination, Ballard illuminates the various trappings of power to which, I have argued, the terrorism carried out by the character of Richard Gould constitutes a trans-political response. His violent terrorist attacks have been read as assaults against power that follow a radically new logic, attempting to outdo a system that is presented here as a distinctly simulative one at its own reference-less game. However, as we have seen, the ending of the novel implies that even such radical practices may ultimately not match up to the ever more adaptable contemporary circuits of control.

As this ambiguity regarding the effectiveness of the different catastrophic strategies makes clear – an ambiguity particularly the discussions of *Concrete Island*, *Cocaine Nights*, *Super-Cannes* and *Millennium People* have brought out – there is in Ballard's work a profound uncertainty in how far the contemporary structures of power can still be broken up *at all*. On the whole, the outlook of the Ballardian oeuvre, similar to the one which transpires in the work of Foucault or Baudrillard, is thus still quite gloomy. If there is, to quote Foucault, a "light of hope" (1994: 397, trans. in Ransom 1997: 201n6) here, it is a rather faint and flickering one.

Nevertheless, the analyses carried out in this study have made it clear that critics of Ballard's work who construe it as a-political or quietist are certainly mistaken. For just as bleak man-made landscapes (abandoned buildings, deserted runways, empty swimming pools, etc.) and technological, social and environmental change (*Collins English Dictionary*), Surrealist aesthetics (Jeannette Baxter), transcendence (Gregory Stephenson), 'in-betweenness' (Roger Luckhurst), etc. are defining elements of the 'Ballardian', so is the political. My study has demonstrated that Ballard's oeuvre effectively constitutes a sustained critical mapping of the postmodern world of late capitalism and, more than that, in fact continuously raises the question of resistance, time and again probing the possibilities of dissident and emancipatory action in the present. The themes of Ballard's writing should hence not be taken as signaling a renunciation of the political – merely of 'politics' – but as an acknowledgement of the changed nature of the system and of the necessary transformation of the modes of resistance this entails. As the work of Baudrillard and others does in the realm of theory, so does Ballard's work in the realm of literature mark the shift from the political to the trans-political and from revolutionary to catastrophic strategies.

Of course, my investigation of this shift in Ballard's fiction is far from exhaustive. Many other texts which I have not had the space to discuss, for example the novels *High-Rise* or *Kingdom Come*, are interesting objects of study in the context of an exploration of Ballard's politics. In how far, for instance, does the apartment block in which the former novel is set constitute another 'heterotopic' counter-site? Can the transformations taking place inside of it be read in terms of another catastrophic strategy making possible a 'carnivalesque' deconstruction of established values, hierarchies and identities and permitting a reconstitution of the collective along the lines of Michel Maffesoli's notions of the 'orgiastic' and of 'neo-tribalism'? What does the peculiar convergence of 'elective insanity', consumerism and fascism in *Kingdom Come* suggest about the latest rearrangements of the social force field, the mutations of the late-capitalist system and the (im-)possibility of resistance?

Beyond this, it would be worthwhile to investigate to what extent the work of other writers of the late 20th and 21st century can likewise be read as articulating and exploring the shift to the trans-political. Is the concept of the 'catastrophic strategy' transferable to other writings? Is there, perhaps, something like a 'canon of the catastrophic'? And further, does the notion of the 'clash of discourses' constitute a useful tool for the analysis of texts written by different authors? What other writers occupy the interstitial zone of 'theory-fiction'/'fiction-theory' as Baudrillard and Ballard do?

As we move further into the 21st century, Ballard's work not only continues to fascinate, provoke and challenge us, but also proves its enduring relevance. It is a writing that is wholly of the present moment, in numerous ways exploring, as the title of a recent volume on contemporary literature has it, 'what happens now' (Adiseshiah and Hildyard 2013). Specifically, as this study has attempted to show, it articulates the ongoing crisis of the political. In a time in which many feel the need for radical political change but at the same time see no way in which such a change could be effected, Ballard's oeuvre may be taken to recast the questions asked by Paul Gauguin's 1897 painting *Where Do We Come From? What Are We? Where Are We Going?* in a political light: it maintains that we *are* in a state of profound subjection to power, in which many of the concepts and strategies anchored in the critical traditions we are *coming from* are no longer viable or effective, and from which the possibilities for emancipatory practice in the future we are *going to* look very uncertain at best.

Works Cited

Abrams, M.H. 1971. *The Mirror and the Lamp: Romantic Theory and the Critical Tradition*. Oxford: Oxford University Press.
Adams, Parveen. 1999. "Cars and Scars". *New Formations* 35: 60–72.
Adiseshiah, Siân and Rupert Hildyard (eds.). 2013. *Twenty-First Century Fiction: What Happens Now*. Basingstoke: Palgrave Macmillan.
Agamben, Giorgio. 1998. *Homo Sacer: Sovereign Power and Bare Life*. Stanford, CA: Stanford University Press.
Agamben, Giorgio. 2007. *Profanations*. New York: Zone Books.
Althusser, Louis. 1971. "Ideology and Ideological State Apparatuses (Notes towards an Investigation)". *Lenin and Philosophy and Other Essays*. New York: Monthly Review Press. 127–186.
Amis, Martin. 2001. *The War against Cliché: Essays and Reviews, 1971–2000*. London: Jonathan Cape.
Anderson, Perry. 1998. *The Origins of Postmodernity*. London: Verso.
Anderson, Perry. 2000. "Renewals". *New Left Review* 1: 1–20.
Appadurai, Arjun. 1996. *Modernity at Large: Cultural Dimensions of Globalization*. Minneapolis, MN: University of Minnesota Press.
Armitage, John. 2000. "From Modernism to Hypermodernism and Beyond: An Interview with Paul Virilio". In: John Armitage (ed.). *Paul Virilio: From Modernism to Hypermodernism and Beyond*. London: Sage. 25–55.
Ashcroft, Bill, Gareth Griffiths and Helen Tiffin. 2005. *The Empire Writes Back: Theory and Practice in Post-Colonial Literatures*. London: Routledge.
Augé, Marc. 2008. *Non-Places: An Introduction to Supermodernity*. London: Verso.
Avanessian, Armen (ed.). 2013. *#Akzeleration*. Berlin: Merve.
Avanessian, Armen and Robin Mackay (eds.). 2014. *#Akzeleration#2*. Berlin: Merve.
Badiou, Alain. 2007. *Being and Event*. London: Continuum.
Baker, Brian. 2008. "The Geometry of the Space Age: J. G. Ballard's Short Fiction and Science Fiction of the 1960s". In: Jeannette Baxter (ed.). *J. G. Ballard*. London: Continuum. 11–22.
Bakhtin, Mikhail. 1984. *Rabelais and His World*. Bloomington, IN: Indiana University Press.
Baldwin, Elaine, Brian Longhurst, Scott McCracken, Miles Ogborn and Greg Smith. 2004. *Introducing Cultural Studies*. Harlow: Pearson Education.
Balibar, Etienne. 1991. "Is There a 'Neo-Racism'?" In: Etienne Balibar and Immanuel Wallerstein. *Race, Nation, Class: Ambiguous Identities*. London: Verso. 17–28.
Ballard, J.G. 1991. "A Response to the Invitation to Respond". *Science Fiction Studies* 18.3: 329.
Ballard, J.G. 1996a. "A User's Guide to the Millennium". *A User's Guide to the Millennium: Essays and Reviews*. New York: Picador. 17–22.
Ballard, J.G. 1996b. "Back to the Heady Future". *A User's Guide to the Millennium: Essays and Reviews*. New York: Picador. 192–194.
Ballard, J.G. 1996c. "Cataclysms and Dooms". *A User's Guide to the Millennium: Essays and Reviews*. New York: Picador. 208–209.
Ballard, J.G. 1996d. "Fictions of Every Kind". *A User's Guide to the Millennium: Essays and Reviews*. New York: Picador. 205–207.

Ballard, J.G. 1996e. "Hitman for the Apocalypse". *A User's Guide to the Millennium: Essays and Reviews*. New York: Picador. 131–133.
Ballard, J.G. 1996f. "Hobbits in Space?" *A User's Guide to the Millennium: Essays and Reviews*. New York: Picador. 14–16.
Ballard, J.G. 1996g. "In the Voyeur's Gaze". *A User's Guide to the Millennium: Essays and Reviews*. New York: Picador. 65–69.
Ballard, J.G. 1996h. "Kafka in the Present Day". *A User's Guide to the Millennium: Essays and Reviews*. New York: Picador. 146.
Ballard, J.G. 1996i. "Memories of Greeneland". *A User's Guide to the Millennium: Essays and Reviews*. New York: Picador. 137–139.
Ballard, J.G. 1996k. "Myth Maker of the Twentieth Century". *A User's Guide to the Millennium: Essays and Reviews*. New York: Picador. 126–130.
Ballard, J.G. 1996l. "Push-Button Death". *A User's Guide to the Millennium: Essays and Reviews*. New York: Picador. 11–13.
Ballard, J.G. 1996m. "Sticking to His Guns". *A User's Guide to the Millennium: Essays and Reviews*. New York: Picador. 134–136.
Ballard, J.G. 1996n. "The Car, the Future". *A User's Guide to the Millennium: Essays and Reviews*. New York: Picador. 262–267.
Ballard, J.G. 1996o. "The Cosmic Cabaret". *A User's Guide to the Millennium: Essays and Reviews*. New York: Picador. 202–204.
Ballard, J.G. 1996p. "The Innocent as Paranoid". *A User's Guide to the Millennium: Essays and Reviews*. New York: Picador. 91–98.
Ballard, J.G. 1996q. "The Lure of the Madding Crowd". *A User's Guide to the Millennium: Essays and Reviews*. New York: Picador. 237–239.
Ballard, J.G. 1996r. "The Sweet Smell of Excess". *A User's Guide to the Millennium: Essays and Reviews*. New York: Picador. 3–5.
Ballard, J.G. 1996s. "Time, Memory and Inner Space". *A User's Guide to the Millennium: Essays and Reviews*. New York: Picador. 199–201.
Ballard, J.G. 1996t. "Which Way to Inner Space?" *A User's Guide to the Millennium: Essays and Reviews*. New York: Picador. 195–198.
Barthes, Roland. 1975. *The Pleasure of the Text*. New York: Hill and Wang.
Barthes, Roland. 1977. "The Death of the Author". *Image, Music, Text: Essays*. New York: Hill and Wang. 142–148.
Barthes, Roland. 1981. *Camera Lucida: Reflections on Photography*. New York: Hill and Wang.
Barthes, Roland. 1982. *Empire of Signs*. New York: Hill and Wang.
Barthes, Roland. 1994. *Roland Barthes*. Berkeley, CA: University of California Press.
Barthes, Roland. 1995. "Vocabulary". In: François Peraldi (ed.). *Polysexuality*. New York: Semiotext(e). 205–207.
Bataille, Georges. 1985a. "Formless". *Visions of Excess: Selected Writings, 1927–1939*. Ed. Allan Stoekl. Minneapolis, MN: University of Minnesota Press. 31.
Bataille, Georges. 1985b. "Sacrificial Mutilation and the Severed Ear of Vincent Van Gogh". *Visions of Excess: Selected Writings, 1927–1939*. Ed. Allan Stoekl. Minneapolis, MN: University of Minnesota Press. 61–72.
Bataille, Georges. 1985c. "The Notion of Expenditure". *Visions of Excess: Selected Writings, 1927–1939*. Ed. Allan Stoekl. Minneapolis, MN: University of Minnesota Press. 116–129.

Bataille, Georges. 1985d. "The Psychological Structure of Fascism". *Visions of Excess: Selected Writings, 1927–1939*. Ed. Allan Stoekl. Minneapolis, MN: University of Minnesota Press. 137–160.
Bataille, Georges. 1985e. "The Use Value of D. A. F. de Sade (An Open Letter to My Current Comrades)". *Visions of Excess: Selected Writings, 1927–1939*. Ed. Allan Stoekl. Minneapolis, MN: University of Minnesota Press. 91–102.
Bataille, Georges. 1986. *Erotism: Death and Sensuality*. San Francisco: City Lights Books.
Bataille, Georges. 1987. "L'abjection et les formes misérables". *Oeuvres complètes*. Volume 2. Paris: Gallimard. 217–221.
Bataille, Georges. 1988. *Inner Experience*. Albany, NY: State University of New York Press.
Bataille, Georges. 1991. *The Accursed Share: An Essay on General Economy*. Volume 2: *The History of Eroticism* & Volume 3: *Sovereignty*. New York: Zone Books.
Bataille, Georges. 2006. *Literature and Evil*. London: Marion Boyars.
Bataille, Georges. 2007. *The Accursed Share: An Essay on General Economy*. Volume 1: *Consumption*. New York: Zone Books.
Baudrillard, Jean. 1990. *Seduction*. New York: St. Martin's Press.
Baudrillard, Jean. 1993a. "Game with Vestiges: Interview with Salvatore Mele and Mark Titmarsh". *Baudrillard Live: Selected Interviews*. Ed. Mike Gane. London: Routledge. 81–95.
Baudrillard, Jean. 1993b. *Symbolic Exchange and Death*. London: Sage.
Baudrillard, Jean. 1993c. *The Transparency of Evil: Essays on Extreme Phenomena*. London: Verso.
Baudrillard, Jean. 1994a. "Crash". *Simulacra and Simulation*. Ann Arbor, MI: The University of Michigan Press. 111–119.
Baudrillard, Jean. 1994b. "Hypermarket and Hypercommodity". *Simulacra and Simulation*. Ann Arbor, MI: The University of Michigan Press. 75–78.
Baudrillard, Jean. 1994c. "On Nihilism". *Simulacra and Simulation*. Ann Arbor, MI: The University of Michigan Press. 159–164.
Baudrillard, Jean. 1994d. "Simulacra and Science Fiction". *Simulacra and Simulation*. Ann Arbor, MI: The University of Michigan Press. 121–127.
Baudrillard, Jean. 1994e. "The Beaubourg Effect: Implosion and Deterrence". *Simulacra and Simulation*. Ann Arbor, MI: The University of Michigan Press. 61–73.
Baudrillard, Jean. 1994f. *The Illusion of the End*. Stanford, CA: Stanford University Press.
Baudrillard, Jean. 1994g. "The Precession of Simulacra". *Simulacra and Simulation*. Ann Arbor, MI: The University of Michigan Press. 1–42.
Baudrillard, Jean. 1995. *The Gulf War Did Not Take Place*. Bloomington, IN: Indiana University Press.
Baudrillard, Jean. 1998a. *Paroxysm: Interviews with Philippe Petit*. London: Verso.
Baudrillard, Jean. 1998b. *The Consumer Society: Myths and Structures*. London: Sage.
Baudrillard, Jean. 1999. *America*. London: Verso.
Baudrillard, Jean. 2002. *The Perfect Crime*. London: Verso.
Baudrillard, Jean. 2003. *The Spirit of Terrorism and Other Essays*. London: Verso.
Baudrillard, Jean. 2005. *The Intelligence of Evil or the Lucidity Pact*. Oxford: Berg.
Baudrillard, Jean. 2007a. *Forget Foucault*. Los Angeles: Semiotext(e).
Baudrillard, Jean. 2007b. *In the Shadow of the Silent Majorities or the End of the Social*. Los Angeles: Semiotext(e).
Baudrillard, Jean. 2008. *Fatal Strategies*. Los Angeles: Semiotext(e).

Bauman, Zygmunt. 2003. *Liquid Love: On the Frailty of Human Bonds*. Cambridge: Polity Press.
Baxter, Jeannette. 2004. "Reading the Signs: An Interview with J.G. Ballard". *Pretext* 9: 27–35.
Baxter, Jeannette (ed.). 2008. *J. G. Ballard*. London: Continuum.
Baxter, Jeannette. 2008. "Visions of Europe in *Cocaine Nights* and *Super-Cannes*". In: Jeannette Baxter (ed.). *J. G. Ballard*. London: Continuum. 94–106.
Baxter, Jeannette. 2009. *J. G. Ballard's Surrealist Imagination: Spectacular Authorship*. Surrey: Ashgate.
Baxter, Jeannette and Rowland Wymer. 2012. "Introduction". In: Jeannette Baxter and Rowland Wymer (eds.). *J. G. Ballard: Visions and Revisions*. Basingstoke: Palgrave Macmillan, 1–15.
Baxter, Jeannette and Rowland Wymer (eds.). 2012. *J. G. Ballard: Visions and Revisions*. Basingstoke: Palgrave Macmillan.
Baxter, John. 2011. *The Inner Man: The Life of J.G. Ballard*. London: Weidenfeld & Nicolson.
Beckman, Karen. 2010. *Crash: Cinema and the Politics of Speed and Stasis*. Durham, NC: Duke University Press.
Bell, Daniel. 2001. *The End of Ideology: On the Exhaustion of Political Ideas in the Fifties*. Cambridge, MA: Harvard University Press.
Benjamin, Walter. 1969a. "The Work of Art in the Age of Mechanical Reproduction". *Illuminations: Essays and Reflections*. Ed. Hannah Arendt. New York: Schocken, 217–251.
Benjamin, Walter. 1969b. "Theses on the Philosophy of History". *Illuminations: Essays and Reflections*. Ed. Hannah Arendt. New York: Schocken, 253–264.
Benjamin, Walter. 2005. "Capitalism as Religion". In: Eduardo Mendieta (ed.). *The Frankfurt School on Religion: Key Writings by the Major Thinkers*. New York: Routledge. 259–262.
Berardi, Franco. 2009. *Precarious Rhapsody: Semiocapitalism and the Pathologies of the Post-Alpha Generation*. London: Minor Compositions.
Bergson, Henri. 2001. *Time and Free Will: An Essay on the Immediate Data of Consciousness*. Mineola, NY: Dover.
Berman, Marshall. 1983. *All That Is Solid Melts into Air: The Experience of Modernity*. London: Verso.
Bhabha, Homi K. 2006. *The Location of Culture*. London: Routledge.
Blake, William. 1973. *The Marriage of Heaven and Hell*. In: Harold Bloom and Lionel Trilling (eds.). *Romantic Poetry and Prose*. New York: Oxford University Press. 34–44.
Blanchot, Maurice. 1988. *The Unavowable Community*. Barrytown, NY: Station Hill Press.
Bloch, Ernst. 1988. "A Philosophical View of the Detective Novel". *The Utopian Function of Art and Literature: Selected Essays*. Cambridge, MA: The MIT Press. 245–264.
Bök, Christian. 2002. *'Pataphysics: The Poetics of an Imaginary Science*. Evanston, IL: Northwestern University Press.
Bois, Yve-Alain and Rosalind E. Krauss. 1999. *Formless: A User's Guide*. New York: Zone Books.
Boorstin, Daniel J. 1975. *The Image: A Guide to Pseudo-Events in America*. New York: Atheneum.
Bordo, Susan. 1995. *Unbearable Weight: Feminism, Western Culture, and the Body*. Berkeley, CA: University of California Press.

Botting, Fred and Scott Wilson. 2003. "Sexcrash". In: Jane Arthurs and Iain Grant (eds.). *Crash Cultures: Modernity, Mediation and the Material*. Bristol: Intellect. 79–89.
Bourdieu, Pierre. 1977. *Outline of a Theory of Practice*. Cambridge: Cambridge University Press.
Bourdieu, Pierre. 1986. "The Forms of Capital". In: John G. Richardson (ed.). *Handbook of Theory and Research for the Sociology of Education*. New York: Greenwood Press. 46–58.
Bourdieu, Pierre. 1989. *Distinction: A Social Critique of the Judgement of Taste*. London: Routledge.
Bourdieu, Pierre. 1992. *The Logic of Practice*. Cambridge: Polity Press.
Bradshaw, Peter, Deyan Sudjic, Dave Simpson, Iain Sinclair and Mark Lawson. 2009. "How JG Ballard Cast His Shadow right across the Arts". *The Guardian* April 20: <http://www.theguardian.com/books/2009/apr/20/jg-ballard-film-music-architecture-tv> [accessed 27 July 2016].
Bresson, Catherine. 1982. "J. G. Ballard at Home". *Métaphores* 7: 5–29.
Breton, André. 1972. *Manifestoes of Surrealism*. Ann Arbor, MI: The University of Michigan Press.
Brigg, Peter. 1985. *J. G. Ballard*. Mercer Island, WA: Starmont House.
Broderick, Damien. 2000. *Transrealist Fiction: Writing in the Slipstream of Science*. Westport, CT: Greenwood Press.
Bröckling, Ulrich. 2013. *Das unternehmerische Selbst: Soziologie einer Subjektivierungsform*. Frankfurt am Main: Suhrkamp.
Brooks, Peter. 1992. *Reading for the Plot: Design and Intention in Narrative*. Cambridge, MA: Harvard University Press.
Brown, Norman O. 1985. *Life against Death: The Psychoanalytical Meaning of History*. Middletown, CT: Wesleyan University Press.
Bryman, Alan. 2004. *The Disneyization of Society*. London: Sage.
Bukatman, Scott. 2005. *Terminal Identity: The Virtual Subject in Postmodern Science Fiction*. Durham, NC: Duke University Press.
Burke, Edmund. 2008. *A Philosophical Enquiry into the Origin of Our Ideas of the Sublime and Beautiful*. Oxford: Oxford University Press.
Burns, Alan and Charles Sugnet. 1981. *The Imagination on Trial: British and American Writers Discuss Their Working Methods*. London: Allison and Busby.
Burroughs, William. 2010. *Naked Lunch: The Restored Text*. London: Fourth Estate.
Butler, Judith. 1993. *Bodies That Matter: On the Discursive Limits of "Sex"*. New York: Routledge.
Butler, Judith. 1997. *The Psychic Life of Power: Theories in Subjection*. Stanford, CA: Stanford University Press.
Butler, Judith. 1999. *Gender Trouble: Feminism and the Subversion of Identity*. New York: Routledge.
Butterfield, Bradley. 1999. "Ethical Value and Negative Aesthetics: Reconsidering the Baudrillard-Ballard Connection". *PMLA* 114.1: 64–77.
Caillois, Roger. 2001. *Man and the Sacred*. Urbana, IL: University of Illinois Press.
Callinicos, Alex. 1989. *Against Postmodernism: A Marxist Critique*. Cambridge: Polity Press.
Camus, Albert. 1973. *The Rebel*. Harmondsworth: Penguin.
Camus, Albert. 1991. *The Myth of Sisyphus and Other Essays*. New York: Vintage.

Castells, Manuel. 1989. *The Informational City: Information Technology, Economic Restructuring, and the Urban-Regional Process*. Oxford: Basil Blackwell.
Castells, Manuel. 1996. *The Information Age: Economy, Society, and Culture*. Volume 1: *The Rise of the Network Society*. Oxford: Basil Blackwell.
Castells, Manuel. 1998. *The Information Age: Economy, Society, and Culture*. Volume 3: *End of Millennium*. Oxford: Basil Blackwell.
Certeau, Michel de. 1988. *The Practice of Everyday Life*. Berkeley, CA: University of California Press.
Chatman, Seymour. 1991. *Story and Discourse: Narrative Structure in Fiction and Film*. Ithaca, NY: Cornell University Press.
Chernin, Kim. 1981. *The Obsession: Reflections on the Tyranny of Slenderness*. New York: Harper & Row.
Colebrook, Claire. 2005. *Philosophy and Post-Structuralist Theory: From Kant to Deleuze*. Edinburgh: Edinburgh University Press.
Colombino, Laura. 2006. "Negotiations with the System: J.G. Ballard and Geoff Ryman Writing London's Architecture". *Textual Practice* 20.4: 615–635.
Connor, Steven. 2000. "Destitution". In: Steven Connor (ed.). *StevenConnor.Com*. <http://www.stevenconnor.com/destitution> [accessed 27 July 2016].
Cormack, Alistair. 2012. "J. G. Ballard and William Blake: Historicizing the Reprobate Imagination". In: Jeannette Baxter and Rowland Wymer (eds.). *J. G. Ballard: Visions and Revisions*. Basingstoke: Palgrave Macmillan. 142–159.
Coverley, Merlin. 2006. *Psychogeography*. Harpenden: Pocket Essentials.
Coward, Harold G. 1990. *Derrida and Indian Philosophy*. Albany, NY: State University of New York Press.
Creed, Barbara. 1993. *The Monstrous-Feminine: Film, Feminism, Psychoanalysis*. London: Routledge.
Crouch, Colin. 2005. *Post-Democracy*. Cambridge: Polity Press.
Davies, Bronwyn. 2011. "Intersections between Zen Buddhism and Deleuzian Philosophy". *Psyke & Logos* 32: 28–45.
Davis, Lennard J. 1997. "Nude Venuses, Medusa's Body, and Phantom Limbs: Disability and Visuality". In: David T. Mitchell and Sharon L. Snyder (eds.). *The Body and Physical Difference: Discourses of Disability*. Ann Arbor, MI: The University of Michigan Press. 51–70.
Davis, Mike. 2000. *Ecology of Fear: Los Angeles and the Imagination of Disaster*. London: Picador.
Davis, Mike. 2006. *City of Quartz: Excavating the Future in Los Angeles*. London: Verso.
Day, Aidan. 2000. "Ballard and Baudrillard: Close Reading *Crash*". *English* 49.195: 277–293.
Debord, Guy. 2009. *Society of the Spectacle*. Eastbourne: Soul Bay Press.
Deleuze, Gilles. 1989. "Coldness and Cruelty". In: n.ed. *Masochism*. New York: Zone Books. 7–138.
Deleuze, Gilles. 2004a. *The Logic of Sense*. London: Continuum.
Deleuze, Gilles. 2004b. "The Philosophy of Crime Novels". *Desert Islands and Other Texts 1953–1974*. Los Angeles: Semiotext(e). 81–85.
Deleuze, Gilles. 2011. "Postscript on the Societies of Control". In: Imre Szeman and Timothy Kaposy (eds.). *Cultural Theory: An Anthology*. Malden, MA: Wiley-Blackwell. 139–142.
Deleuze, Gilles and Félix Guattari. 1983. *Anti-Oedipus. Capitalism and Schizophrenia*. Minneapolis, MN: University of Minnesota Press.

Deleuze, Gilles and Félix Guattari. 1987. *A Thousand Plateaus. Capitalism and Schizophrenia*. Minneapolis, MN: University of Minnesota Press.
DeLillo, Don. 1992. *Mao II*. London: Vintage.
Delville, Michel. 1998. *J. G. Ballard*. Plymouth: Northcote House.
Derrida, Jacques. 1984a. "Différance". *Margins of Philosophy*. Chicago: The University of Chicago Press. 1–27.
Derrida, Jacques. 1984b. "Signature Event Context". *Margins of Philosophy*. Chicago: The University of Chicago Press. 307–330.
Derrida, Jacques. 1988. *Dissemination*. Chicago: The University of Chicago Press.
Derrida, Jacques. 1997. *Of Grammatology*. Baltimore, MD: The Johns Hopkins University Press.
Derrida, Jacques. 2001a. "From Restricted to General Economy: A Hegelianism without Reserve". *Writing and Difference*. London: Routledge. 317–350.
Derrida, Jacques. 2001b. "Structure, Sign and Play in the Discourse of the Human Sciences". *Writing and Difference*. London: Routledge. 351–370.
Derrida, Jacques. 2006. *Specters of Marx: The State of the Debt, the Work of Mourning and the New International*. New York: Routledge.
Dollimore, Jonathan. 1991. *Sexual Dissidence: Augustine to Wilde, Freud to Foucault*. Oxford: Oxford University Press.
Douglas, Mary. 2002. *Purity and Danger*. London: Routledge.
Douglas, Mary. 2003. *Natural Symbols: Explorations in Cosmology*. Abingdon: Routledge.
Dowling, Stephen. 2009. "What Pop Music Tells Us about JG Ballard". *BBC News Magazine* April 20: <http://news.bbc.co.uk/2/hi/8008277.stm> [accessed 27 July 2016].
Durham, Scott. 1993. "The Technology of Death and Its Limits: The Problem of the Simulation Model". In: Verena Andermatt Conley, on behalf of the Miami Theory Collective (ed.). *Rethinking Technologies*. Minneapolis, MN: University of Minnesota Press. 156–170.
Durkheim, Émile. 2001. *The Elementary Forms of Religious Life*. Oxford: Oxford University Press.
Eagleton, Terry. 1991. *Ideology: An Introduction*. London: Verso.
Eagleton, Terry. 1992. *Marxism and Literary Criticism*. London: Routledge.
Eagleton, Terry. 2004. *After Theory*. London: Penguin.
Eco, Umberto. 1979. *The Role of the Reader: Explorations in the Semiotics of Texts*. Bloomington, IN: Indiana University Press.
Ehrenberg, Alain. 2010. *The Weariness of the Self: Diagnosing the History of Depression in the Contemporary Age*. Montreal: McGill-Queen's University Press.
Elias, Norbert. 1978. *The Civilizing Process*. Volume 1: *The History of Manners*. New York: Pantheon.
Enzensberger, Hans Magnus. 1970. "Constituents of a Theory of the Media". *New Left Review* 64: 13–36.
Evans, Eric J. 1997. *Thatcher and Thatcherism*. London: Routledge.
Filippo, Paul Di. 1991. "Ballard's Anatomy: An Interview with J. G. Ballard". *Science Fiction Eye* 8: 66–75.
Finkelstein, Haim. 1987. "'Deserts of Vast Eternity': J. G. Ballard and Robert Smithson". *Foundation* 39: 50–62.
Fiske, John. 1989. *Television Culture*. London: Routledge.
Fitting, Peter. 1979. "The Modern Anglo-American SF Novel: Utopian Longing and Capitalist Cooptation". *Science Fiction Studies* 17.6: 59–76.
Foucault, Michel. 1972a. *The Archaeology of Knowledge*. New York: Vintage.

Foucault, Michel. 1972b. "The Discourse on Language". Appendix. *The Archaeology of Knowledge*. New York: Vintage. 215–237.
Foucault, Michel. 1976. *Mental Illness and Psychology*. New York: Harper & Row.
Foucault, Michel. 1978. *The History of Sexuality*. Volume 1: *An Introduction*. New York: Pantheon.
Foucault, Michel. 1979. *Discipline and Punish: The Birth of the Prison*. New York: Vintage.
Foucault, Michel. 1980. "Two Lectures". *Power/Knowledge: Selected Interviews and Other Writings 1972–1977*. Ed. Colin Gordon. Brighton: The Harvester Press. 78–108.
Foucault, Michel. 1982. "The Subject and Power". Afterword. In: Hubert L. Dreyfus and Paul Rabinow. *Michel Foucault: Beyond Structuralism and Hermeneutics*. Brighton: The Harvester Press. 208–226.
Foucault, Michel. 1985. *The History of Sexuality*. Volume 2: *The Use of Pleasure*. New York: Pantheon.
Foucault, Michel. 1986a. "Of Other Spaces". *Diacritics* 16.1: 22–27.
Foucault, Michel. 1986b. *The History of Sexuality*. Volume 3: *The Care of the Self*. New York: Pantheon.
Foucault, Michel. 1987. "Gespräch zwischen Michel Foucault und Studenten: Jenseits von Gut und Böse". *Von der Subversion des Wissens*. Ed. Walter Seitter. Frankfurt am Main: Fischer. 91–105.
Foucault, Michel. 1994. "La torture, c'est la raison". *Dits et écrits 1954–1988*. Volume 3. Ed. Daniel Defert and François Ewald. Paris: Gallimard. 390–398.
Foucault, Michel. 1996a. "An Ethics of Pleasure". *Foucault Live: Collected Interviews, 1961–1984*. Ed. Sylvère Lotringer. New York: Semiotext(e). 371–381.
Foucault, Michel. 1996b. "Clarifications on the Question of Power". *Foucault Live: Collected Interviews, 1961–1984*. Ed. Sylvère Lotringer. New York: Semiotext(e). 255–263.
Foucault, Michel. 1996c. "Intellectuals and Power". *Foucault Live: Collected Interviews, 1961–1984*. Ed. Sylvère Lotringer. New York: Semiotext(e). 74–82.
Foucault, Michel. 1996d. "Passion according to Werner Schroeter". *Foucault Live: Collected Interviews, 1961–1984*. Ed. Sylvère Lotringer. New York: Semiotext(e). 313–321.
Foucault, Michel. 1996e. "Power Affects the Body". *Foucault Live: Collected Interviews, 1961–1984*. Ed. Sylvère Lotringer. New York: Semiotext(e). 207–213.
Foucault, Michel. 1996f. "Sade: Sargeant of Sex". *Foucault Live: Collected Interviews, 1961–1984*. Ed. Sylvère Lotringer. New York: Semiotext(e). 186–189.
Foucault, Michel. 1996g. "Sex, Power and the Politics of Identity". *Foucault Live: Collected Interviews, 1961–1984*. Ed. Sylvère Lotringer. New York: Semiotext(e). 382–390.
Foucault, Michel. 1996h. "Sexual Choice, Sexual Act". *Foucault Live: Collected Interviews, 1961–1984*. Ed. Sylvère Lotringer. New York: Semiotext(e). 322–334.
Foucault, Michel. 1996i. "The End of the Monarchy of Sex". *Foucault Live: Collected Interviews, 1961–1984*. Ed. Sylvère Lotringer. New York: Semiotext(e). 214–225.
Foucault, Michel. 2002. *The Order of Things: An Archaeology of the Human Sciences*. London: Routledge.
Foucault, Michel. 2006. *History of Madness*. London: Routledge.
Francis, Sam. 2008. "'Moral Pornography' and 'Total Imagination': The Pornographic in J. G. Ballard's *Crash*". *English* 57.218: 146–168.
Francis, Samuel. 2011. *The Psychological Fictions of J. G. Ballard*. London: Continuum.
Franklin, Benjamin. 2003a. "Advice to a Young Tradesman". In: Ralph Ketcham (ed.). *The Political Thought of Benjamin Franklin*. Indianapolis, IN: Hackett. 51–54.

Franklin, Benjamin. 2003b. *The Autobiography*. In: Nina Baym et al. (eds.). *The Norton Anthology of American Literature*. 6th ed. Volume A: *Literature to 1820*. New York: Norton. 538–610.

Franklin, Benjamin. 2003c. "The Way to Wealth". In: Nina Baym et al. (eds.). *The Norton Anthology of American Literature*. 6th ed. Volume A: *Literature to 1820*. New York: Norton. 516–522.

Franklin, H. Bruce. 1979. "What Are We to Make of J. G. Ballard's Apocalypse?" In: Thomas D. Clareson (ed.). *Voices for the Future: Essays on Major Science Fiction Writers*. Volume 2. Bowling Green, OH: Bowling Green University Popular Press. 82–105.

Freud, Sigmund. 1999. *Totem and Taboo*. London: Routledge.

Frick, Thomas. 2012. "The Art of Fiction". In: Simon Sellars and Dan O'Hara (eds.). *Extreme Metaphors: Selected Interviews with J.G. Ballard, 1967–2008*. London: Fourth Estate. 181–198.

Fukuyama, Francis. 1989. "The End of History?" *The National Interest* 16: 3–18.

Fukuyama, Francis. 1992. *The End of History and the Last Man*. New York: The Free Press.

Gasiorek, Andrzej. 2005. *J. G. Ballard*. Manchester: Manchester University Press.

Geier, Manfred. 2004. *Kants Welt: Eine Biographie*. Reinbek bei Hamburg: Rowohlt.

Gelernter, Mark. 1999. *A History of American Architecture: Buildings in Their Cultural and Technological Context*. Manchester: Manchester University Press.

Giddens, Anthony. 1994. *Beyond Left and Right: The Future of Radical Politics*. Cambridge: Polity Press.

Giddens, Anthony. 1998. *The Third Way: The Renewal of Social Democracy*. Cambridge: Polity Press.

Girard, René. 1989. *The Scapegoat*. Baltimore, MD: The Johns Hopkins University Press.

Girard, René. 2005. *Violence and the Sacred*. London: Continuum.

Graham, Elaine L. 2002. *Representations of the Post/Human: Monsters, Aliens and Others in Popular Culture*. Manchester: Manchester University Press.

Gramsci, Antonio. 1971. *Selections from the Prison Notebooks of Antonio Gramsci*. Ed. Quintin Hoare and Geoffrey Nowell Smith. London: Lawrence and Wishart.

Gray, John. 2003. *Straw Dogs: Thoughts on Humans and Other Animals*. London: Granta.

Gray, John. 2012. "'Technology Is Always a Facilitator': J.G. Ballard on *Super-Cannes*". In: Simon Sellars and Dan O'Hara (eds.). *Extreme Metaphors: Selected Interviews with J.G. Ballard, 1967–2008*. London: Fourth Estate. 374–382.

Greenblatt, Stephen. 1988. *Shakespearean Negotiations: The Circulation of Social Energy in Renaissance England*. Oxford: Clarendon Press.

Groes, Sebastian. 2008. "From Shanghai to Shepperton: Crises of Representation in J. G. Ballard's Londons". In: Jeannette Baxter (ed.). *J. G. Ballard*. London: Continuum. 78–93.

Groes, Sebastian. 2012. "The Texture of Modernity in J. G. Ballard's *Crash*, *Concrete Island* and *High-Rise*". In: Jeannette Baxter and Rowland Wymer (eds.). *J. G. Ballard: Visions and Revisions*. Basingstoke: Palgrave Macmillan. 123–141.

Grosz, Elizabeth. 1994. *Volatile Bodies: Toward a Corporeal Feminism*. Bloomington, IN: Indiana University Press.

Habermas, Jürgen. 1990. *The Philosophical Discourse of Modernity: Twelve Lectures*. Cambridge, MA: The MIT Press.

Habermas, Jürgen. 1993. "Modernity versus Postmodernity". In: Joseph Natoli and Linda Hutcheon (eds.). *A Postmodern Reader*. Albany, NY: State University of New York Press. 91–104.

Habermas, Jürgen. 1997. "Modernity: An Unfinished Project". In: Maurizio Passerin d'Entrèves and Seyla Benhabib (eds.). *Habermas and the Unfinished Project of Modernity: Critical Essays on* The Philosophical Discourse of Modernity. Cambridge, MA: The MIT Press. 38–55.

Habermas, Jürgen. 2004a. *The Theory of Communicative Action.* Volume 1: *Reason and the Rationalization of Society.* Cambridge: Polity Press.

Habermas, Jürgen. 2004b. *The Theory of Communicative Action.* Volume 2: *The Critique of Functionalist Reason.* Cambridge: Polity Press.

Halberstam, Judith and Ira Livingston. 1995. "Introduction: Posthuman Bodies". In: Judith Halberstam and Ira Livingston (eds.). *Posthuman Bodies.* Bloomington, IN: Indiana University Press. 1–19.

Hall, Stuart. 1982. "The Rediscovery of 'Ideology': Return of the Repressed in Media Studies". In: Michael Gurevitch, Tony Bennett, James Curran and Janet Woollacott (eds.). *Culture, Society and the Media.* London: Methuen. 56–90.

Hall, Stuart. 1988. *The Hard Road to Renewal: Thatcherism and the Crisis of the Left.* London: Verso.

Hall, Stuart. 1993. "Encoding, Decoding". In: Simon During (ed.). *The Cultural Studies Reader.* London: Routledge. 90–103.

Hall, Stuart. 1996. "The West and the Rest: Discourse and Power". In: Stuart Hall, David Held, Don Hubert and Kenneth Thompson (eds.). *Modernity: An Introduction to Modern Societies.* Cambridge, MA: Blackwell. 184–227.

Hall, Stuart. 2003. "New Labour's Double-Shuffle". *Soundings* 24: 10–24.

Han, Byung-Chul. 2010. *Müdigkeitsgesellschaft.* Berlin: Matthes & Seitz.

Han, Byung-Chul. 2011. *Topologie der Gewalt.* Berlin: Matthes & Seitz.

Haraway, Donna. 2010. "A Manifesto for Cyborgs: Science, Technology, and Socialist Feminism in the 1980s". In: Vincent B. Leitch et al. (eds.). *The Norton Anthology of Theory and Criticism.* 2nd ed. New York: Norton. 2190–2220.

Hardt, Michael and Antonio Negri. 2001. *Empire.* Cambridge, MA: Harvard University Press.

Hardt, Michael and Antonio Negri. 2005. *Multitude: War and Democracy in the Age of Empire.* New York: Penguin.

Hardt, Michael and Antonio Negri. 2012. *Declaration.* New York: Melanie Jackson Agency.

Harvey, David. 1990. *The Condition of Postmodernity: An Enquiry into the Origins of Cultural Change.* Malden, MA: Blackwell.

Hayles, N. Katherine. 1991. "The Borders of Madness". *Science Fiction Studies* 18.3: 321–323.

Hayles, N. Katherine. 1999. *How We Became Posthuman: Virtual Bodies in Cybernetics, Literature, and Informatics.* Chicago: The University of Chicago Press.

Hebdige, Dick. 1979. *Subculture: The Meaning of Style.* London: Routledge.

Hegel, G.W.F. 1978. *Phenomenology of Spirit.* Oxford: Clarendon Press.

Hobbes, Thomas. 2008. *Leviathan.* Oxford: Oxford University Press.

Hobsbawm, Eric. 1996. *The Age of Extremes: A History of the World, 1914–1991.* New York: Vintage.

Hocquenghem, Guy. 1995. "To Destroy Sexuality". In: François Peraldi (ed.). *Polysexuality.* New York: Semiotext(e). 260–264.

Homer. 2006. *The Odyssey.* London: Penguin.

Horkheimer, Max and Theodor W. Adorno. 2002. *Dialectic of Enlightenment: Philosophical Fragments.* Stanford, CA: Stanford University Press.

Huntley, Jake. 2012. "The Madness of Crowds: Ballard's Experimental Communities". In: Jeannette Baxter and Rowland Wymer (eds.). *J. G. Ballard: Visions and Revisions*. Basingstoke: Palgrave Macmillan. 215–229.
Jacoby, Russell. 1999. *The End of Utopia: Politics and Culture in an Age of Apathy*. New York: Basic Books.
Jameson, Fredric. 1974. *The Prison-House of Language: A Critical Account of Structuralism and Russian Formalism*. Princeton: Princeton University Press.
Jameson, Fredric. 1991. *Postmodernism, or, The Cultural Logic of Late Capitalism*. Durham, NC: Duke University Press.
Jameson, Fredric. 1992. *Signatures of the Visible*. New York: Routledge.
Jarry, Alfred. 1996. *Exploits & Opinions of Dr. Faustroll, Pataphysician*. Cambridge, MA: Exact Change.
Jenks, Chris. 2003. *Transgression*. London: Routledge.
Kaomea, Julie. 2003. "Reading Erasures and Making the Familiar Strange: Defamiliarizing Methods for Research in Formerly Colonized and Historically Oppressed Communities". *Educational Researcher* 32.2: 14–25.
Kellner, Douglas. 1995. *Media Culture: Cultural Studies, Identity and Politics between the Modern and the Postmodern*. London: Routledge.
Klesse, Christian. 2000. "'Modern Primitivism': Non-Mainstream Body Modification and Racialized Representation". In: Mike Featherstone (ed.). *Body Modification*. London: Sage. 15–38.
Kojève, Alexandre. 1980. *Introduction to the Reading of Hegel: Lectures on the Phenomenology of Spirit*. Ed. Allan Bloom. Ithaca, NY: Cornell University Press.
Kristeva, Julia. 1982. *Powers of Horror: An Essay on Abjection*. New York: Columbia University Press.
Kristeva, Julia. 1984. *Revolution in Poetic Language*. New York: Columbia University Press.
Kristeva, Julia. 1986. "Word, Dialogue and Novel". In: Toril Moi (ed.). *The Kristeva Reader*. New York: Columbia University Press. 34–61.
Kroker, Arthur and Marilouise Kroker. 1993. "Scenes from the Last Sex: Feminism and Outlaw Bodies". In: Arthur Kroker and Marilouise Kroker (eds.). *The Last Sex: Feminism and Outlaw Bodies*. New York: St. Martin's Press. 1–19.
Kutzbach, Konstanze. 2007. "The Two-…, One-…, None-Sex Model: The Flesh(-)Made Machine in Herman Melville's 'The Paradise of Bachelors and the Tartarus of Maids' and J. G. Ballard's *Crash*". In: Konstanze Kutzbach and Monika Mueller (eds.). *The Abject of Desire: The Aestheticization of the Unaesthetic in Contemporary Literature and Culture*. Amsterdam: Rodopi. 181–196.
Labour Party. 1996. *New Labour, New Life for Britain*. London: Labour Party.
Lacan, Jacques. 2004. "The Mirror Stage as Formative of the Function of the I as Revealed in Psychoanalytic Experience". In: Julie Rivkin and Michael Ryan (eds.). *Literary Theory: An Anthology*. 2nd ed. Malden, MA: Blackwell. 441–446.
Lacan, Jacques. 2008. *The Seminar of Jacques Lacan. Book 7: The Ethics of Psychoanalysis*. Ed. Jacques-Alain Miller. London: Routledge.
Laclau, Ernesto. 1990. "The Impossibility of Society". *New Reflections on the Revolution of Our Time*. London: Verso. 89–92.
Laclau, Ernesto and Chantal Mouffe. 2001. *Hegemony and Socialist Strategy: Towards a Radical Democratic Politics*. London: Verso.
Lafargue, Paul. 1999. *The Right to Be Lazy*. Ardmore, PA: Fifth Season Press.

Laing, Ronald D. 1967. *The Politics of Experience*. New York: Pantheon.
Landon, Brooks. 1991. "Responding to the Killer B's". *Science Fiction Studies* 18.3: 326–327.
Latour, Bruno. 1993. *We Have Never Been Modern*. Cambridge, MA: Harvard University Press.
Lecercle, Jean-Jacques. 1994. *Philosophy of Nonsense: The Intuitions of Victorian Nonsense Literature*. London: Routledge.
Lefebvre, Henri. 2003. *The Production of Space*. Oxford: Blackwell.
Lemke, Thomas. 2011. *Biopolitics: An Advanced Introduction*. New York: New York University Press.
Letvin, Alice Owen. 1990. *Sacrifice in the Surrealist Novel: The Impact of Early Theories of Primitive Religion on the Depiction of Violence in Modern Fiction*. New York: Garland.
Letwin, Shirley Robin. 1993. *The Anatomy of Thatcherism*. New Brunswick, NJ: Transaction.
Lifton, Robert Jay. 1999. *The Protean Self: Human Resilience in an Age of Fragmentation*. Chicago: The University of Chicago Press.
Lingis, Alphonso. 1983. *Excesses: Eros and Culture*. Albany, NY: State University of New York Press.
Lotringer, Sylvère. 1995. "Defunkt Sex". In: François Peraldi (ed.). *Polysexuality*. New York: Semiotext(e). 271–297.
Lotringer, Sylvère. 2007. "Exterminating Angel". Introduction. In: Jean Baudrillard. *Forget Foucault*. Los Angeles: Semiotext(e). 7–25.
Louit, Robert. 2012. "Crash & Learn". In: Simon Sellars and Dan O'Hara (eds.). *Extreme Metaphors: Selected Interviews with J.G. Ballard, 1967–2008*. London: Fourth Estate. 72–77.
Luckhurst, Roger. 1997. *'The Angle between Two Walls': The Fiction of J. G. Ballard*. Liverpool: Liverpool University Press.
Luhmann, Niklas. 1993. "Deconstruction as Second-Order Observing". *New Literary History* 24.4: 763–782.
Luhmann, Niklas. 2000. *Art as a Social System*. Stanford, CA: Stanford University Press.
Lukács, Georg. 1971. *The Theory of the Novel: A Historico-Philosophical Essay on the Forms of Great Epic Literature*. Cambridge, MA: The MIT Press.
Luttwak, Edward. 2000. *Turbo-Capitalism: Winners and Losers in the Global Economy*. New York: Harper Perennial.
Lyotard, Jean-François. 1984. *The Postmodern Condition: A Report on Knowledge*. Minneapolis, MN: University of Minnesota Press.
Lyotard, Jean-François. 2004. *Libidinal Economy*. London: Continuum.
MacCannell, Dean. 1992. *Empty Meeting Grounds: The Tourist Papers*. London: Routledge.
MacCannell, Dean. 1999. *The Tourist: A New Theory of the Leisure Class*. Berkeley, CA: University of California Press.
Mackay, Robin and Armen Avanessian (eds.). 2014. *#Accelerate#: The Accelerationist Reader*. Falmouth: Urbanomic.
Maffesoli, Michel. 1993. *The Shadow of Dionysus: A Contribution to the Sociology of the Orgy*. Albany, NY: State University of New York Press.
Maffesoli, Michel. 1996. *The Time of the Tribes: The Decline of Individualism in Mass Society*. London: Sage.
Magliola, Robert R. 1984. *Derrida on the Mend*. West Lafayette, IN: Purdue University Press.
Mandel, Ernest. 1984. *Delightful Murder: A Social History of the Crime Story*. London: Pluto Press.
Mandel, Ernest. 1999. *Late Capitalism*. London: Verso.

Marcuse, Herbert. 1998. *Eros and Civilization: A Philosophical Inquiry into Freud*. Abingdon: Routledge.
Margaroni, Maria. 2007. "The Becoming-Woman of the East/West Conflict: The Western Sacralization of Life and the Feminine Politics of Death". In: Griselda Pollock and Victoria Turvey Sauron (eds.). *The Sacred and the Feminine: Imagination and Sexual Difference*. London: Tauris. 111–124.
Marx, Karl. 1977. *Capital: A Critique of Political Economy*. Volume 1. New York: Vintage.
Marx, Karl. 1979. "The Eighteenth Brumaire of Louis Bonaparte". In: Karl Marx and Frederick Engels. *Collected Works*. Volume 11. New York: International Publisher. 99–197.
Marx, Karl. 1982. *Critique of Hegel's 'Philosophy of Right'*. Cambridge: Cambridge University Press.
Marx, Karl. 1994. "Theses on Feuerbach". *Selected Writings*. Ed. Lawrence H. Simon. Indianapolis, IN: Hackett. 98–101.
Massumi, Brian. 1992. *A User's Guide to* Capitalism and Schizophrenia: *Deviations from Deleuze and Guattari*. Cambridge, MA: The MIT Press.
Mauss, Marcel. 1973. "Techniques of the Body". *Economy and Society* 2: 70–88.
Mauss, Marcel. 1990. *The Gift: The Form and Reason for Exchange in Archaic Societies*. London: Routledge.
McLuhan, Marshall. 1994. *Understanding Media: The Extensions of Man*. Cambridge, MA: The MIT Press.
Merleau-Ponty, Maurice. 1986. *Phenomenology of Perception*. London: Routledge.
Mills, Catherine. 2007. "Normative Violence, Vulnerability, and Responsibility". *differences: A Journal of Feminist Cultural Studies* 18.2: 133–156.
Moulier Boutang, Yann. 2011. *Cognitive Capitalism*. Cambridge: Polity Press.
Myers, Ben. 2009. "JG Ballard: The Music He Inspired". *The Guardian* April 20: <http://www.theguardian.com/music/musicblog/2009/apr/20/jg-ballard-music-inspired> [accessed 27 July 2016].
Nancy, Jean-Luc. 2008. *The Inoperative Community*. Minneapolis, MN: University of Minnesota Press.
Newsome, David. 1974. *Two Classes of Men: Platonism and English Romantic Thought*. New York: St. Martin's Press.
Niethammer, Lutz. 1994. *Posthistoire: Has History Come to an End?* London: Verso.
Nietzsche, Friedrich. 1998. *Twilight of the Idols, or, How to Philosophize with a Hammer*. Oxford: Oxford University Press.
Nietzsche, Friedrich. 1999. *The Birth of Tragedy and Other Writings*. Cambridge: Cambridge University Press.
Nietzsche, Friedrich. 2001. *The Gay Science*. Cambridge: Cambridge University Press.
Nietzsche, Friedrich. 2006. *Thus Spoke Zarathustra*. Cambridge: Cambridge University Press.
Norris, Christopher. 1990. *What's Wrong with Postmodernism: Critical Theory and the Ends of Philosophy*. New York: Harvester Wheatsheaf.
Noys, Benjamin. 2007. "Crimes of the Near Future: Baudrillard / Ballard". In: Simon Sellars (ed.). *Ballardian*. <http://www.ballardian.com/crimes-of-the-near-future-baudrillard-ballard> [accessed 27 July 2016].
Noys, Benjamin. 2014. *Malign Velocities: Accelerationism and Capitalism*. Alresford: Zero Books.

Orvell, Miles. 2006. "After 9/11: Photography, the Destructive Sublime, and the Postmodern Archive". *Michigan Quarterly Review* XLV.2: <http://hdl.handle.net/2027/spo.act2080.0045.201> [accessed 27 July 2016].

Orwell, George. 1968. "The Limit to Pessimism". *The Collected Essays, Journalism and Letters of George Orwell*. Volume 1: *An Age Like This 1920–1940*. Ed. Sonia Orwell and Ian Angus. New York: Harcourt, Brace & World. 533–535.

Paddy, David Ian. 2012. "Empires of the Mind: Autobiography and Anti-Imperialism in the Work of J. G. Ballard". In: Jeannette Baxter and Rowland Wymer (eds.). *J. G. Ballard: Visions and Revisions*. Basingstoke: Palgrave Macmillan. 179–197.

Paddy, David Ian. 2015. *The Empires of J. G. Ballard: An Imagined Geography*. Canterbury: Gylphi.

Park, Jin Y. 2006. *Buddhisms and Deconstructions*. Lanham, MD: Rowman & Littlefield.

Parry, Benita. 2004. *Postcolonial Studies: A Materialist Critique*. London: Routledge.

Pascal, Blaise. 1999. *Pensées and Other Writings*. Oxford: Oxford University Press.

Pasquinelli, Matteo. 2011. "Animal Spirits: A Ballardian Bestiary". In: Simon Sellars (ed.). *Ballardian*. <http://www.ballardian.com/animal-spirits-a-ballardian-bestiary> [accessed 27 July 2016].

Pêcheux, Michel. 1982. *Language, Semantics and Ideology: Stating the Obvious*. London: Macmillan.

Peraldi, François (ed.). 1995a. *Polysexuality*. New York: Semiotext(e).

Peraldi, François. 1995b. "Postface: Masochism and Polysexuality". In: François Peraldi (ed.). *Polysexuality*. New York: Semiotext(e). 167–170.

Pettman, Dominic. 2002. *After the Orgy: Toward a Politics of Exhaustion*. Albany, NY: State University of New York Press.

Platzner, Robert. 1983. "The Metamorphic Vision of J. G. Ballard". *Essays in Literature* 10.2: 209–217.

Popcorn, Faith. 1992. *The Popcorn Report: Faith Popcorn on the Future of Your Company, Your World, Your Life*. New York: Harper Business.

Pordzik, Ralph. 1999. "James G. Ballard's *Crash* and the Postmodernization of the Dystopian Novel". *Arbeiten aus Anglistik und Amerikanistik* 24.1: 77–94.

Pordzik, Ralph. 2006. "Die Zukunft als Neurose. Ein struktural-psychoanalytischer Versuch zu George Orwells *Nineteen Eighty-Four*". *Anglistik. Mitteilungen des Deutschen Anglistenverbandes* 17.2: 151–164.

Pordzik, Ralph. 2009. "Persistence of Obedience: Theological Space and Ritual Conversion in George Orwell's *Nineteen Eighty-Four*". In: Ralph Pordzik (ed.). *Futurescapes: Space in Utopian and Science Fiction Discourses*. Amsterdam: Rodopi. 111–127.

Porter, Roy. 1987. *A Social History of Madness: Stories of the Insane*. London: Weidenfeld and Nicolson.

Porter, Roy. 2003. *Madness: A Brief History*. Oxford: Oxford University Press.

Prakash, Gyan. 2000. "Subaltern Studies as Postcolonial Criticism". In: Catherine Hall (ed.). *Cultures of Empire: Colonizers in Britain and the Empire in the Nineteenth and Twentieth Centuries. A Reader*. Manchester: Manchester University Press. 120–136.

Pringle, David. 1979. *Earth Is the Alien Planet: J. G. Ballard's Four-Dimensional Nightmare*. San Bernardino, CA: The Borgo Press.

Punter, David. 1985. *The Hidden Script: Writing and the Unconscious*. London: Routledge.

Radiohead. 1997. "Fitter Happier". *OK Computer*. Parlophone.

Rancière, Jacques. 1999. *Disagreement: Politics and Philosophy*. Minneapolis, MN: University of Minnesota Press.
Ransom, John S. 1997. *Foucault's Discipline: The Politics of Subjectivity*. Durham, NC: Duke University Press.
Reich, Wilhelm. 1972. *The Sexual Revolution: Toward a Self-Governing Character Structure*. New York: Farrar, Straus and Giroux.
Revell, Graeme. 1984a. "Critique". In: V. Vale and Andrea Juno (eds.). *RE/Search 8/9: J. G. Ballard*. San Francisco: RE/Search Publications. 144–145.
Revell, Graeme. 1984b. "Interview with J. G. Ballard". In: V. Vale and Andrea Juno (eds.). *RE/Search 8/9: J. G. Ballard*. San Francisco: RE/Search Publications. 42–52.
Reynolds, Simon. 2006. *Rip It Up and Start Again: Post-Punk 1978–1984*. London: Faber and Faber.
Richardson, Michael. 1994. *Georges Bataille*. London: Routledge.
Richardson, Michael. 1998. Introduction. In: Georges Bataille. *Essential Writings*. Ed. Michael Richardson. London: Sage. 1–4.
Rimmon-Kenan, Shlomith. 2008. *Narrative Fiction: Contemporary Poetics*. London: Routledge.
Roden, David. 2003. "Cyborgian Subjects and the Auto-Destruction Metaphor". In: Jane Arthurs and Iain Grant (eds.). *Crash Cultures: Modernity, Mediation and the Material*. Bristol: Intellect. 91–102.
Roes, Michael. 2007. *Perversion und Glück*. Berlin: Matthes & Seitz.
Rosa, Hartmut. 2005. *Beschleunigung: Die Veränderung der Zeitstrukturen in der Moderne*. Frankfurt am Main: Suhrkamp.
Ruddick, Nicholas. 1992. "Ballard/*Crash*/Baudrillard". *Science Fiction Studies* 19.3: 354–360.
Russell, Bertrand. 2004. *In Praise of Idleness and Other Essays*. London: Routledge.
Said, Edward W. 1979. *Orientalism*. New York: Vintage.
Sandison, Alan. 1986. *George Orwell: After 1984*. Basingstoke: Macmillan.
Sargent, Lyman Tower. 1994. "The Three Faces of Utopianism Revisited". *Utopian Studies* 5.1: 1–37.
Sartre, Jean-Paul. 1947. "Un nouveau mystique". *Situations*. Volume 1. Paris: Gallimard. 143–188.
Scarry, Elaine. 1985. *The Body in Pain: The Making and Unmaking of the World*. New York: Oxford University Press.
Scholes, Robert and Eric S. Rabkin. 1977. *Science Fiction: History, Science, Vision*. New York: Oxford University Press.
Schopenhauer, Arthur. 1966a. *The World as Will and Representation*. Volume 1. Mineola, NY: Dover.
Schopenhauer, Arthur. 1966b. *The World as Will and Representation*. Volume 2. Mineola, NY: Dover.
Sedgwick, Eve Kosofsky. 1985. *Between Men: English Literature and Male Homosocial Desire*. New York: Columbia University Press.
Seeber, Hans Ulrich (ed.). 2012. *Englische Literaturgeschichte*. 5th ed. Stuttgart: Metzler.
Self, Will. 2006. *Junk Mail*. London: Bloomsbury.
Sellars, Simon. 2000. "Freefall in Inner Space: From *Crash* to Crash Technology". In: Andy Sawyer and David Seed (eds.). *Speaking Science Fiction: Dialogues and Interpretations*. Liverpool: Liverpool University Press. 214–231.
Sellars, Simon. 2007. "'Magisterial, Precise, Unsettling': Simon Reynolds on the Ballard Connection". In: Simon Sellars (ed.). *Ballardian*.

<http://www.ballardian.com/simon-reynolds-on-the-ballard-connection> [accessed 27 July 2016].
Sellars, Simon and Dan O'Hara (eds.). 2012. *Extreme Metaphors: Selected Interviews with J.G. Ballard, 1967–2008*. London: Fourth Estate.
Seltzer, Mark. 1998. *Serial Killers: Death and Life in America's Wound Culture*. New York: Routledge.
Sennett, Richard. 1998. *The Corrosion of Character: The Personal Consequences of Work in the New Capitalism*. New York: Norton.
Shaviro, Steven. 1990. *Passion & Excess: Blanchot, Bataille, and Literary Theory*. Tallahassee, FL: The Florida State University Press.
Shaviro, Steven. 2003. *Connected, or What It Means to Live in the Network Society*. Minneapolis, MN: University of Minnesota Press.
Shaviro, Steven. 2009. "Belatedly, Ballard". In: Steven Shaviro (ed.). *The Pinocchio Theory*. <http://www.shaviro.com/Blog/?p=749> [accessed 27 July 2016].
Shildrick, Margrit. 2009. "Prosthetic Performativity: Deleuzian Connections and Queer Corporealities". In: Chrysanthi Nigianni and Merl Storr (eds.). *Deleuze and Queer Theory*. Edinburgh: Edinburgh University Press. 115–133.
Shusterman, Richard. 1997. *Practicing Philosophy: Pragmatism and the Philosophical Life*. New York: Routledge.
Shusterman, Richard. 2008. *Body Consciousness: A Philosophy of Mindfulness and Somaesthetics*. Cambridge: Cambridge University Press.
Sloterdijk, Peter. 2010. *Rage and Time: A Psychopolitical Investigation*. New York: Columbia University Press.
Sobchack, Vivian. 1991. "Baudrillard's Obscenity". *Science Fiction Studies* 18.3: 327–329.
Soja, Edward W. 1989. *Postmodern Geographies: The Reassertion of Space in Critical Social Theory*. London: Verso.
Soja, Edward W. 1998. *Thirdspace: Journeys to Los Angeles and Other Real-and-Imagined Places*. Malden, MA: Blackwell.
Sontag, Susan. 1983. "The Pornographic Imagination". *A Susan Sontag Reader*. Harmondsworth: Penguin. 205–233.
Spivak, Gayatri Chakravorty. 1988. "Can the Subaltern Speak?" In: Cary Nelson and Lawrence Grossberg (eds.). *Marxism and the Interpretation of Culture*. Urbana, IL: University of Illinois Press. 271–313.
Spivak, Gayatri Chakravorty. 1997. Translator's Preface. In: Jacques Derrida. *Of Grammatology*. Baltimore, MD: The Johns Hopkins University Press. ix–lxxxvii.
Spivak, Gayatri Chakravorty. 2003. *A Critique of Postcolonial Reason: Toward a History of the Vanishing Present*. Cambridge, MA: Harvard University Press.
Stallybrass, Peter and Allon White. 1986. *The Politics and Poetics of Transgression*. Ithaca, NY: Cornell University Press.
Standop, Ewald and Edgar Mertner. 1992. *Englische Literaturgeschichte*. Heidelberg: Quelle & Meyer.
Starr, Peter. 1995. *Logics of Failed Revolt: French Theory after May '68*. Stanford, CA: Stanford University Press.
Stephenson, Gregory. 1991. *Out of the Night and into the Dream: A Thematic Study of the Fiction of J. G. Ballard*. Westport, CT: Greenwood Press.
Sweetman, Paul. 2000. "Anchoring the (Postmodern) Self? Body Modification, Fashion and Identity". In: Mike Featherstone (ed.). *Body Modification*. London: Sage. 51–76.

Szasz, Thomas. 1991. "The Myth of Mental Illness". *Ideology and Insanity: Essays on the Psychiatric Dehumanization of Man*. Syracuse, NY: Syracuse University Press. 12–24.
Tew, Philip. 2008. "Situating the Violence of J. G. Ballard's Postmillennial Fiction: The Possibilities of Sacrifice, the Certainties of Trauma". In: Jeannette Baxter (ed.). *J. G. Ballard*. London: Continuum. 107–119.
Thatcher, Margaret. n.d. Interview for *Woman's Own*. In: n.ed. *Margaret Thatcher Foundation*. <http://www.margaretthatcher.org/document/106689> [accessed 27 July 2016].
Travers, Martin (ed.). 2001. *European Literature from Romanticism to Postmodernism: A Reader in Aesthetic Practice*. London: Continuum.
Tschumi, Bernard. 1994. *Event-Cities*. Cambridge, MA: The MIT Press.
Turner, Bryan S. 2000. "The Possibility of Primitiveness: Towards a Sociology of Body Marks in Cool Societies". In: Mike Featherstone (ed.). *Body Modification*. London: Sage. 39–50.
Turner, Victor. 1995. *The Ritual Process: Structure and Anti-Structure*. Hawthorne, NY: Aldine de Gruyter.
Vale, V. 2012. "Interview with JGB". In: Simon Sellars and Dan O'Hara (eds.). *Extreme Metaphors: Selected Interviews with J.G. Ballard, 1967–2008*. London: Fourth Estate. 146–169.
Vale, V. n.d. Frequently Asked Questions. In: V. Vale (ed.). *RE/Search Publications*. <http://www.researchpubs.com/about/faq/> [accessed 27 July 2016].
Vattimo, Gianni. 1992. *The Transparent Society*. Cambridge: Polity Press.
Viney, William. 2007. "'A Fierce and Wayward Beauty': Waste in the Fiction of J.G. Ballard". In: Simon Sellars (ed.). *Ballardian*. <http://www.ballardian.com/a-fierce-and-wayward-beauty-parts-1–2>, <http://www.ballardian.com/a-fierce-and-wayward-beauty-part-3> [accessed 27 July 2016].
Virilio, Paul. 1994. *The Vision Machine*. London: British Film Institute.
Virilio, Paul. 1997. *Open Sky*. London: Verso.
Virilio, Paul. 1999. *Polar Inertia*. London: Sage.
Virilio, Paul. 2006. *Speed and Politics: An Essay on Dromology*. Los Angeles: Semiotext(e).
Virilio, Paul. 2007. *The Original Accident*. Cambridge: Polity Press.
Virilio, Paul. 2008. *Negative Horizon: An Essay in Dromoscopy*. London: Continuum.
Virilio, Paul. 2009. *The Aesthetics of Disappearance*. Los Angeles: Semiotext(e).
Virilio, Paul. 2012. *Lost Dimension*. Los Angeles: Semiotext(e).
Virilio, Paul and Sylvère Lotringer. 2008. *Pure War*. Los Angeles: Semiotext(e).
Wagar, W. Warren. 1982. *Terminal Visions: The Literature of Last Things*. Bloomington, IN: Indiana University Press.
Wagar, W. Warren. 1991. "J.G. Ballard and the Transvaluation of Utopia". *Science Fiction Studies* 18.1: 53–70.
Wallerstein, Immanuel. 1979. *The Capitalist World Economy*. Cambridge: Cambridge University Press.
Wang, Youxuan. 2001. *Buddhism and Deconstruction: Towards a Comparative Semiotics*. Richmond: Curzon Press.
Watt, Ian. 1987. *The Rise of the Novel: Studies in Defoe, Richardson and Fielding*. London: Hogarth Press.
Watt, Ian. 1996. *Myths of Modern Individualism: Faust, Don Quixote, Don Juan, Robinson Crusoe*. Cambridge: Cambridge University Press.

Weber, Max. 1958. *The Protestant Ethic and the Spirit of Capitalism*. New York: Charles Scribner's Sons.
Weber, Max. 2004. "The Vocation of Science". In: Sam Whimster (ed.). *The Essential Weber: A Reader*. London: Routledge. 270–287.
Weiss, Richard. 1988. *The American Myth of Success: From Horatio Alger to Norman Vincent Peale*. Urbana, IL: University of Illinois Press.
Whiting, Emma. 2012. "Disaffection and Abjection in J. G. Ballard's *The Atrocity Exhibition* and *Crash*". In: Jeannette Baxter and Rowland Wymer (eds.). *J. G. Ballard: Visions and Revisions*. Basingstoke: Palgrave Macmillan. 88–104.
Williams, Raymond. 1958. *Culture and Society 1780–1950*. London: Chatto & Windus.
Williams, Raymond. 1977. *Marxism and Literature*. Oxford: Oxford University Press.
Winthrop, John. 2003. "A Model of Christian Charity". In: Nina Baym et al. (eds.). *The Norton Anthology of American Literature*. 6th ed. Volume A: *Literature to 1820*. New York: Norton. 206–217.
Wolfe, Cary. 2010. *What Is Posthumanism?* Minneapolis, MN: University of Minnesota Press.
Wordsworth, William. 1973a. "Ode: Intimations of Immortality from Recollections of Early Childhood". In: Harold Bloom and Lionel Trilling (eds.). *Romantic Poetry and Prose*. New York: Oxford University Press. 176–181.
Wordsworth, William. 1973b. "Tintern Abbey". In: Harold Bloom and Lionel Trilling (eds.). *Romantic Poetry and Prose*. New York: Oxford University Press. 146–150.
Wymer, Rowland. 2012. "Ballard's Story of O: 'The Voices of Time' and the Quest for (Non)Identity". In: Jeannette Baxter and Rowland Wymer (eds.). *J. G. Ballard: Visions and Revisions*. Basingstoke: Palgrave Macmillan. 19–34.
Zinik, Zinovy. 2012. "Russia on My Mind". In: Simon Sellars and Dan O'Hara (eds.). *Extreme Metaphors: Selected Interviews with J.G. Ballard, 1967–2008*. London: Fourth Estate. 356–363.
Žižek, Slavoj. 2002. *Welcome to the Desert of the Real! Five Essays on September 11 and Related Dates*. London: Verso.
Žižek, Slavoj. 2004. *Organs without Bodies: On Deleuze and Consequences*. New York: Routledge.
Žižek, Slavoj. 2009. *Violence: Six Sideways Reflections*. London: Profile Books.
Žižek, Slavoj. 2011. *Living in the End Times*. London: Verso.
Zukin, Sharon. 2000. *The Cultures of Cities*. Malden, MA: Blackwell.

Index

abdication   16, 100, 108–111, 113–122, 124–128, 131, 133, 236
abject (Kristeva)   43–46, 48–50, 61–63, 75, 86, 98 f, 117, 156, 165, 189
Abrams, M.H.   129
acceleration   22, 28 f, 134, 170, 174–176, 186
Adams, Parveen   50, 65
Adorno, Theodor W.   12, 137, 167, 196 f
Agamben, Giorgio   162, 183–185, 190
alienation   15, 19, 28, 34, 49, 83 f, 113, 135, 143, 151, 165, 176, 179, 186, 214, 235
Althusser, Louis   98, 109, 119, 198 f, 201, 206
Amis, Kingsley   1
Amis, Martin   1, 39
Anderson, Brad   1
Anderson, Perry   147–149
anti-psychiatry   96, 153–155
Appadurai, Arjun   164
Aristotle   24, 183
Arnell, Vaughan   77
Aron, Raymond   147
Ashcroft, Bill   106
Atrocity Exhibition, The (Ballard)   1, 9, 13, 24, 38, 76, 127, 135, 142, 154
Augé, Marc   26 f, 83, 139–142, 174 f, 214
Avanessian, Armen   174

Bacon, Francis   134
Badiou, Alain   19, 40, 222 f
Baker, Brian   122
Bakhtin, Mikhail   46 f, 157
Balibar, Etienne   189
Ballantyne, R.M.   120
bare life (Agamben)   183–185, 190
Barthes, Roland   11, 14, 49 f, 55, 72, 80, 122
Bataille, Georges   4, 19, 33–38, 40 f, 43, 56, 65, 69, 74, 80, 86, 98 f, 144, 153, 156–159, 161, 165 f, 187–189
Baudelaire, Charles   156
Baudrillard, Jean   1, 4 f, 7–10, 12 f, 15 f, 18–21, 24 f, 29–33, 42, 48 f, 65–80, 97, 105, 108, 111–114, 116 f, 119, 123 f, 126–128, 131, 133, 136, 141, 146, 150 f, 168–170, 172–179, 186, 188, 210–213, 215 f, 221–231, 233, 235–238
Bauman, Zygmunt   12, 140
Baxter, Jeannette   1–4, 6, 13, 18, 33, 44, 60, 70, 77–79, 115, 135, 137, 157–160, 165, 171, 188, 190 f, 193 f, 203, 209–211, 218 f, 223, 229, 237
Baxter, John   2
Beck, Ulrich   12
Beckett, Samuel   103
Beckman, Karen   55
Bell, Daniel   146 f
Benjamin, Walter   30, 162, 167 f, 179
Berardi, Franco   33
Bergson, Henri   94
Berman, Marshall   150
Bhabha, Homi K.   103 f
biopolitics   17, 180 f, 183–185, 187 f
biopower   22 f, 136, 180–182, 184, 199, 235
Blair, Tony   148 f
Blake, William   33, 35, 128 f, 156, 236
Blanchot, Maurice   161
Bloch, Ernst   138
Boadicea   211
body without organs (Deleuze/Guattari)   54, 59, 65, 96 f, 100–102
Bök, Christian   8
Bois, Yve-Alain   86
Bonnard, Pierre   171
Boorstin, Daniel   140
Bordo, Susan   48
Botting, Fred   67
Bourdieu, Pierre   42, 45, 200 f, 210
Boyd, William   1
Breton, André   128, 144, 220
Brigg, Peter   2
Bröckling, Ulrich   178
Brooks, Peter   55
Brown, Norman O.   64

Bryman, Alan 140
Buddhism 16, 100, 126, 131, 133
Bukatman, Scott 12, 33, 100
Burgess, Anthony 1
Burial 1
Burke, Edmund 223
Burnside, John 113
Burroughs, William 1, 3, 53
Bush, George W. 230
Butler, Judith 43f, 45, 48f, 55, 62, 76, 109f, 117f, 156, 211, 215
Butterfield, Bradley 7, 69

Cabaret Voltaire 1
Caillois, Roger 36
Callinicos, Alex 4
Campanella, Tommaso 134
Camus, Albert 219
carnivalesque (Bakhtin) 46, 157, 216, 238
Carroll, Lewis 137, 216
Carter, Angela 1
Castells, Manuel 12, 82, 134, 163
catastrophic strategy 1, 8–11, 15, 17, 19, 33, 42, 45, 49, 63, 80f, 111, 136, 151f, 157, 159, 161, 186, 190, 192, 194, 220, 226, 233, 236–238
Certeau, Michel de 83
Chatman, Seymour 216, 232
Chernin, Kim 48
clash of discourses 13–15, 18, 65, 128, 143, 220, 222, 238
Clear, Nic 1
Clinton, Bill 149
Coates, Nigel 1
Cocaine Nights (Ballard) 16, 134–162, 167f, 171, 173f, 186f, 189, 236f
Coetzee, J.M. 113
cognitive mapping (Jameson) 6, 13, 222
Colebrook, Claire 117, 124
Coleridge, Samuel Taylor 129
Colombino, Laura 81, 84, 87, 98, 107, 218, 221
colonialism 102–104, 164
commodification 44, 71, 112, 140f, 149, 172, 188, 205f, 233
communism 6, 146f, 149
Comsat Angels, The 1

Concrete Island (Ballard) 1, 16, 20, 81–107, 109–111, 189, 196, 236f
Connor, Steven 99f
Cooper, David 154
Cormack, Alistair 35
counter-culture 64, 125f, 151
Crash (Ballard) 1f, 4, 12–15, 18–83, 91, 96, 142, 145, 152, 187, 223, 236
Creed, Barbara 45
Cronenberg, David 1, 50, 65
Crouch, Colin 148, 173
Crouch, Tim 113
Crystal World, The (Ballard) 36, 108, 150
culture industry (Horkheimer/Adorno) 196f, 201
cyberpunk 12f
cyborg (Haraway) 58–60, 62f

Dadaism 156, 233
Dalí, Salvador 127, 130, 154
Davis, Lennard J. 60, 63
Davis, Mike 85, 142
Day, Aidan 31f, 78, 123
Dean, Tacita 1
death of affect (Ballard) 135, 142, 176, 235
Debord, Guy 141, 195, 205, 214, 228
Debray, Régis 6
deconstruction 37, 77, 117, 120, 122, 126, 154, 195, 201, 217, 224, 232f, 238
"Deep End" (Ballard) 119
Defoe, Daniel 101–103, 119–121
Deleuze, Gilles 15f, 18, 39, 54–56, 59f, 64f, 74, 80–102, 107, 114, 136–138, 143, 154, 156f, 160, 173, 179f, 187f, 201, 209, 235f
DeLillo, Don 233
Delville, Michel 3, 7, 12, 137
Derrida, Jacques 2, 4, 14, 37, 39, 106, 109, 122, 147, 211, 228, 232f
Descartes, René 47, 102, 111, 154
destitution (Connor) 97–100
desubjectivation (Foucault) 15, 19, 56, 63, 80, 201, 203, 210
Dick, Philip K. 77
différance (Derrida) 122, 132
disability 53, 59f, 63, 219, 231

Index

disciplinary power (Foucault)   43, 52, 88f, 101, 111, 119, 171, 177–181, 183, 190, 199, 209
Disneyfication   140, 235
Django Django   1
Dollimore, Jonathan   51
Domínguez, Oscar   127
Douglas, Mary   43, 64
dromology (Virilio)   15, 22–24, 28f, 235
Drought, The (Ballard)   118f
Drowned World, The (Ballard)   16, 115–119, 122, 133
Durham, Scott   69
Durkheim, Émile   35
dystopia   2, 15, 17–20, 110, 135, 166, 180, 190, 192, 237

Eagleton, Terry   4, 133
Eco, Umberto   122
Ehrenberg, Alain   176–178
Eisenhower, Dwight D.   145
Elias, Norbert   45
Empire of the Sun (Ballard)   1, 134
end of history   16f, 134–136, 144–151, 153, 173f, 176f, 235
Enlightenment   7, 103, 119, 122, 150, 153f, 173, 182, 196f
"Enormous Space, The" (Ballard)   108, 119–121, 126, 128, 131, 133
Enzensberger, Hans Magnus   211
Ernst, Max   127f
Escher, M.C.   137
excess   13, 18, 33–35, 37f, 41, 47, 50, 60, 65, 76f, 95, 99, 155, 158, 161, 171, 174, 176f, 223f
existentialism   219
expenditure (Bataille)   19, 33–37, 80, 158, 165, 187

fascism   61, 146, 161, 166, 168, 185f, 188f, 191, 238
Fincher, David   40, 191
Finkelstein, Haim   3
Fiske, John   231
Fitting, Peter   3, 6
Fitzgerald, F Scott   8, 171

Foucault, Michel   4, 6, 14f, 19f, 22f, 25, 40–43, 49, 51–54, 56, 60, 63–66, 75, 80, 86, 88f, 95, 109–112, 114, 118–120, 133, 153–157, 179, 181, 183f, 199–201, 207, 209, 218, 236f
Francis, Samuel   2, 38
Franklin, Benjamin   122–125
Franklin, H. Bruce   3, 6
Freud, Sigmund   3, 43, 50f, 64, 91, 159
Fukuyama, Francis   146f
Futurism   233

Gasiorek, Andrzej   3, 5, 13, 18, 27, 44, 78, 81, 83, 89f, 96, 102, 108, 115–119, 135, 137, 143, 150f, 154, 167, 180, 191–194, 197, 218–221, 223, 228f
Gates, Bill   164
Gauguin, Paul   238
Gehlen, Arnold   145
Gehry, Frank   170
gender   55, 59–63, 156
Genette, Gérard   95
Gennep, Arnold van   152
Giddens, Anthony   12, 148
Girard, René   159
Golding, William   120
Gonzalez-Foerster, Dominique   1
Graham, Elaine L.   61
Gramsci, Antonio   197f, 201
Gray, John   182, 188
Greenblatt, Stephen   124, 208f
Greene, Graham   1, 171
Griffiths, Gareth   106
Groes, Sebastian   12, 27, 84f, 214
Grosz, Elizabeth   54
Guattari, Félix   16, 18, 51, 54–56, 59f, 64f, 74, 80–102, 107, 114, 143, 154, 157, 160, 173, 188, 236

Habermas, Jürgen   4, 41, 150f, 173
habitus (Bourdieu)   42, 176, 200, 210
Halberstam, Judith   61f
Hall, Stuart   125, 147, 149, 191, 204, 210, 231
Han, Byung-Chul   177–179, 185f
Haneke, Michael   1
Haraway, Donna   58–60, 62, 64

Hardt, Michael   7, 16, 25, 61, 85, 112, 135, 163–165, 168, 171, 173, 180 f, 183, 186 f, 189, 192, 195 f, 202, 209
Harvey, David   5, 20, 83, 85
"Having a Wonderful Time" (Ballard)   135
Hayles, N. Katherine   18, 61
Hebdige, Dick   128, 203, 206
Hegel, Georg Wilhelm Friedrich   103, 144, 146, 150
hegemony   14, 16, 21, 48, 63, 85, 87, 91, 107, 124 f, 133, 149, 155, 186, 197, 200, 205–207, 209, 231
Heidegger, Martin   28
heterotopia (Foucault)   16, 86, 106, 134, 157, 236, 238
High-Rise (Ballard)   1, 13, 20, 157, 166, 238
Hirst, Damien   1
Hitchcock, Alfred   137
Hitler, Adolf   190
Hobbes, Thomas   65
Hobsbawm, Eric   5
Hocquenghem, Guy   54, 63, 93
Homer   166
homo sacer (Agamben)   184 f, 190
Horkheimer, Max   137, 167, 196 f
Howard, Ebenezer   134
humanism   61 f, 109–111, 118, 123 f, 133, 147, 153, 219
Huntley, Jake   189
Husserl, Edmund   28
Huxley, Aldous   190
hybridity   13, 48, 58, 60–62, 64, 104, 168, 180
hyperreality (Baudrillard)   5, 7 f, 12, 30–33, 65 f, 70, 73, 76 f, 80, 169, 213–217, 221 f, 225, 229
hyperspace (Jameson)   8, 27, 169 f, 235

ideological state apparatus (Althusser)   119, 198
imperialism   2, 16, 62, 85, 101, 112, 119, 135 f, 144, 147, 157–159, 162–169, 172 f, 180 f, 183, 186, 189, 192, 194, 218, 235

integral reality (Baudrillard)   67, 128, 172, 186, 235
interpellation (Althusser)   103, 198, 210, 215

Jameson, Fredric   1, 5 f, 135 f, 20 f, 27–29, 42, 109, 137, 140–142, 145, 168–170, 211
Jarry, Alfred   8 f
Joy Division   1
Joyce, James   14
Jung, C.G.   117

Kafka, Franz   137
Kant, Immanuel   111, 118, 129, 132
Keats, John   132
Kellner, Douglas   112, 215
Khrushchev, Nikita   6, 145
Kindness of Women, The (Ballard)   24
Kingdom Come (Ballard)   25, 153, 166, 238
Klaxons   1
Klossowski, Pierre   144
Kode9   1
Kojève, Alexandre   144–147
Koolhaas, Rem   1, 85
Krauss, Rosalind E.   86
Kristeva, Julia   13, 43–45, 50, 72, 105 f, 117
Kroker, Arthur   61
Kroker, Marilouise   61
Kropotkin, Peter   193, 211
Kutzbach, Konstanze   55

Lacan, Jacques   40, 43, 45, 47, 50, 54, 91, 109, 117, 128, 132, 144, 222
Laclau, Ernesto   14, 124 f
Lafargue, Paul   139
Laing, R.D.   90, 154, 156 f
Landon, Brooks   13
Laqueur, Thomas   55
"Largest Theme Park in the World, The" (Ballard)   135
Latour, Bruno   61
Leavis, F.R.   11
Lecercle, Jean-Jacques   137
Lefebvre, Henri   20, 101, 142
Lemke, Thomas   185
Lenin, Vladimir   149, 193, 211

liberalism 8, 25, 52, 61, 109, 118, 123, 133, 146–148, 166, 171, 173, 179f, 182f, 197, 204
Lifton, Robert Jay 112
Lingis, Alphonso 54
Lipset, Seymour Martin 147
Livingston, Ira 61f
Lotringer, Sylvère 7, 24, 64, 160
Luckhurst, Roger 2–4, 13, 18, 26, 55, 66, 81, 127, 154, 237
Luhmann, Niklas 232
Lukács, Georg 219
Luttwak, Edward 176
Lynch, David 1, 137
Lyotard, Jean-François 5, 65, 145

MacCannell, Dean 121, 140f, 147
Mackay, Robin 174
madness 3, 8, 20f, 26, 30, 33–35, 39, 42, 44, 47, 50f, 53, 59, 64, 67, 86, 90, 98, 125, 128, 130, 137, 144, 153–160, 162, 181, 183, 185–187, 190f, 193, 200, 214, 217, 227, 236f
Maffesoli, Michel 74, 238
Major, John 169
Mandel, Ernest 4, 138
Manic Street Preachers 1
Mao 6, 233
Marcuse, Herbert 64
Marey, Etienne-Jules 127
Marx, Karl 144, 163, 191, 196, 220
Marxism 3f, 7, 64, 83, 133, 196, 198, 200f, 222
Massumi, Brian 88–92, 112, 114, 163
Matisse, Henri 171
Mauss, Marcel 33, 42, 68
May 1968 6f, 64
McLuhan, Marshall 57
Melville, Herman 113
"Memories of the Space Age" (Ballard) 121
Merleau-Ponty, Maurice 28, 144
Michelangelo 193, 211
micro-physics of power (Foucault) 5, 88, 207
Miéville, China 1
Millennium People (Ballard) 11, 17, 131, 145, 153, 155, 163, 193–235, 237

Miller, Henry 87
mimicry (Bhabha) 103
Miracles of Life (Ballard) 23f
mirror-stage (Lacan) 43, 45, 91, 117, 128
modernism/modernity 4f, 20, 22, 47, 61, 83, 150f, 161, 171, 173–175, 187, 212, 216, 219
More, Thomas 139
"Motel Architecture" (Ballard) 166
Mouffe, Chantal 14, 124f
Moulier Boutang, Yann 163
Muybridge, Eadweard 127
"Myths of the Near Future" (Ballard) 121

Nancy, Jean-Luc 161
Negri, Antonio 7, 16, 25, 61, 85, 112, 135f, 162–165, 168, 171, 173, 180f, 183, 186f, 189, 192, 195f, 202, 209
neo-liberalism 125, 147–149, 162, 173, 178, 190
Neutra, Richard 170
New Historicism 124f, 208
New Labour 148
New Wave (music) 1
New Wave (science fiction) 115
"News from the Sun" (Ballard) 16, 108, 114, 121–133, 236
Nietzsche, Friedrich 8, 11, 37, 129, 143, 156, 159, 186, 218f
nihilism 194, 218, 221, 230
non-place (Augé) 26, 83, 89, 139, 142, 214f, 235
Normal, The 1
Norris, Christopher 4
Noys, Benjamin 172, 174, 188
Numan, Gary 1

O'Hara, Dan 2
Orwell, George 110, 180, 190
"Overloaded Man, The" (Ballard) 108, 153

Paddy, David Ian 2, 134f, 160
Palahniuk, Chuck 40
panopticism (Foucault) 88, 95, 101f, 160, 199, 206f
paragram (Kristeva) 105
Parry, Benita 104

Pascal, Blaise   226
Pasquinelli, Matteo   12
pataphysics (Jarry)   7–10, 12f, 15f, 80, 113, 194, 226, 228, 235f
Pêcheux, Michel   201
Peraldi, François   56
permissiveness   64, 124f, 178, 209
Pettman, Dominic   177
Picasso, Pablo   171f
Piranesi, Giovanni Battista   137
Plato   29, 129–131, 134, 143, 146
Platzner, Robert   2
Plotinus   130f
Poe, Edgar Allan   136, 156
Pop Art   114f
Popcorn, Faith   142
Pordzik, Ralph   2, 18, 110
pornography   33, 38f, 76f
Porter, Roy   154, 156
Portman, John   169
post-politics   136, 148
Post-Punk   1
postcolonialism   102, 112
posthumanism   16, 19, 60–64, 94, 114, 118, 126, 131, 133, 228
postmodernism/postmodernity   4–8, 11f, 14–20, 25–29, 32f, 37, 40, 48, 60, 69, 74, 85f, 88, 109, 112, 114, 126, 133, 135, 140, 142, 145f, 161f, 165, 168–170, 174, 177, 189, 191, 194, 201, 203, 211, 213–215, 219, 221f, 235–237
poststructuralism   4–6, 13, 72, 109, 126, 131
Pot, Pol   190
Prakash, Gyan   15
Pringle, David   21, 169
psychoanalysis   3, 40, 43, 50–52, 91f, 104, 153, 224
psychogeography   172
psychopathy   14, 17, 134, 136, 153f, 156f, 161, 186f, 189, 194, 218, 231, 236
Punter, David   26, 81, 109–111

Radiohead   1, 183
Rancière, Jacques   173, 204
Reagan, Ronald   149
Réage, Pauline   38

realism   21, 55, 76f, 133, 233
Reich, Wilhelm   64
Reith, John   197
repressive state apparatus (Althusser)   98, 206, 209
Revell, Graeme   6, 9, 11f, 18, 20, 38, 40, 154, 186, 218
reversibility (Baudrillard)   67f, 70, 73f, 76f
revolution   5–7, 17, 22, 29, 55, 63f, 90, 112f, 151, 163, 186, 188, 193–197, 199, 201–213, 216, 220–223, 225, 228–230, 237f
revolutions of 1989   135, 145, 147–149
Reynolds, Simon   1, 12, 33
rhizome (Deleuze/Guattari)   54, 60, 63, 74, 87, 90f, 96f, 101, 106
Riefenstahl, Leni   189
Riesman, David   179
Rimmon-Kenan, Shlomith   103
Roden, David   58
Roes, Michael   11
Romanticism   4, 11, 16, 37, 128–133, 155f, 194, 223
Rosa, Hartmut   134, 174–176
Ruddick, Nicholas   18
Running Wild (Ballard)   166, 186
Russell, Bertrand   139
Ryman, Geoff   81

Sacher-Masoch, Leopold   39
sacrifice   20, 34, 36, 69–71, 73, 77, 158f, 179, 184, 225, 229
Sade, Marquis de   33, 38f, 50
sadomasochism   41, 56, 187
Said, Edward W.   230
Sargent, Lyman Tower   135
Sartre, Jean-Paul   37, 144
Saussure, Ferdinand de   105
Scarry, Elaine   40, 42
Schérer, René   93
Schopenhauer, Arthur   129
Schroeter, Werner   56
science fiction   2f, 12, 18, 33, 114f, 121, 124, 131, 137
Scorsese, Martin   232
Scotus, John Duns   94
Sedgwick, Eve Kosofsky   220

seduction (Baudrillard)   20, 59, 74–77, 79, 128
Self, Will   1, 11, 14, 18, 156f, 186
Sellars, Simon   1f, 12f, 33
Seltzer, Mark   40
Sennett, Richard   176
September 11, 2001   223f, 227
sexuality   15, 19, 31–33, 35, 37–39, 41f, 44, 47–67, 71, 73–80, 114, 127, 154, 177, 183, 187, 200, 217
Shakespeare, William   101, 103, 106, 119, 214
Shaviro, Steven   12, 37, 163, 169
Shelley, Percy Bysshe   132
Shildrick, Margrit   59f
Shusterman, Richard   41f, 63
simulacrum (Baudrillard)   5, 7, 19, 21, 29f, 32f, 42, 65f, 70, 73, 76–78, 140f, 169, 171f, 212–215, 217, 222f, 225f, 228–230, 232f
simulation (Baudrillard)   5, 7f, 19, 30–33, 42, 65–68, 70, 73–76, 80, 141, 169–171, 203, 210, 212–217, 220–222, 225–232, 234f, 237
Sinclair, Iain   1
Situationist International   81, 172, 214
Sloterdijk, Peter   11, 147, 165
smooth space (Deleuze/Guattari)   83–89, 91, 93f, 97f, 101, 173
Sobchack, Vivian   18
socialism   6f, 133, 148f
society of control (Deleuze)   136, 171, 180f, 183, 190, 201, 209, 235
socio-spatial dialectic (Soja)   20, 142, 170
Soja, Edward W.   20, 85f, 142, 170
Soleri, Paolo   125, 149
Sontag, Susan   1, 38
Spielberg, Steven   1
Spivak, Gayatri Chakravorty   15, 104, 156, 233
Stalin, Joseph   144f, 193, 211
Stallybrass, Peter   48, 50, 202
Starr, Peter   6
Stephenson, Gregory   2f, 37, 81, 89–91, 93, 237
striated space (Deleuze/Guattari)   83–86, 89, 91, 94, 101f

subjectivation   5, 16, 96f, 101, 109, 111, 117, 119, 177f, 210, 221, 235
Super-Cannes (Ballard)   16f, 23, 134–136, 148–150, 153, 160–192, 216, 236f
Surrealism   2f, 8, 11, 16, 37, 78, 114f, 119, 127f, 131, 133, 154, 156, 216, 220, 237
symbolic exchange (Baudrillard)   15, 18–20, 67–74, 77, 80, 236
Symbolism   156
Szasz, Thomas   154f

Tanguy, Yves   119
Taylor, Elizabeth   31, 35, 70, 76, 78
terrorism   17, 69, 179, 193f, 216, 218–227, 229–231, 233, 237
Tew, Philip   36, 159
Thatcher, Margaret   125f, 149, 169, 202
Third Way (Giddens)   148f
Tiffin, Helen   106
trans-politics (Baudrillard)   4, 10, 15, 17, 87, 89, 113, 133, 161, 194, 212, 218, 226, 235, 237f
transcendence   2f, 37–39, 41, 131–133, 180, 237
transgression   17, 19, 33, 35, 38, 41, 44, 47, 50, 52, 56, 61f, 64, 66, 75, 81f, 93, 101, 121, 134, 136, 151–153, 156–161, 171, 187f, 202, 223, 236
Trotsky, Leon   228
Tschumi, Bernard   86
Turner, Victor   152

Unlimited Dream Company, The (Ballard)   35
utopia   2, 41, 46, 60, 110, 134–136, 138f, 141, 143, 146, 150f, 157, 170, 175, 178, 186

Vale, V.   6, 10
Vattimo, Gianni   215
Viney, William   45, 48, 86f, 97
Virilio, Paul   4, 22–25, 28f, 143, 147, 176
"Voices of Time, The" (Ballard)   121, 126

Wagar, W. Warren   2
Wallerstein, Immanuel   135
War Fever (Ballard)   13

Watt, Ian   119, 133
Weber, Max   122f, 129, 159, 162
Weiss, Jonathan   1
Wheatley, Ben   1
White, Allon   48, 50, 202
Whiting, Emma   44
Whyte, William H.   179
Williams, Raymond   201, 204
Williams, Robbie   77
Wilson, Scott   67

Wind from Nowhere, The (Ballard)   115
Winthrop, John   167
Wolfe, Cary   232
Wordsworth, William   128–130
Wymer, Rowland   1f, 126, 133

Žižek, Slavoj   40, 84, 133, 164f, 185, 191, 222–224
Zukin, Sharon   140

www.ingramcontent.com/pod-product-compliance
Lightning Source LLC
Chambersburg PA
CBHW030614230426
43661CB00053B/1985